Looking for God in Brazil

Looking for God in Brazil

The Progressive Catholic Church in Urban Brazil's Religious Arena

John Burdick

UNIVERSITY OF CALIFORNIA PRESS

Berkeley / Los Angeles / London

University of California Press
Berkeley and Los Angeles, California

University of California Press, Ltd.
London, England

Copyright © 1993 by The Regents of the University of California

First Paperback Printing 1996

Library of Congress Cataloging-in-Publication Data
Burdick, John, 1959–
     Looking for God in Brazil : the progressive Catholic Church in
urban Brazil's religious arena / by John Burdick.
          p.   cm.
     Includes bibliographical references and index.
     ISBN   978-0-520-20503-1 (alk. paper)
     1. Catholic Church—Brazil—History—20th century.
2. Liberation theology.   3. Basic Christian communities—Brazil.
4. Sociology, Christian (Catholic).   5. Urban anthropology—
Brazil.   6. Brazil—Church history.   I. Title.
BX1466.2.B87   1993
261.8′0981—dc20   92-32556
                                                                                      CIP

Printed in the United States of America

11   10   09   08   07
12   11   10   9   8   7   6   5

The paper used in this publication meets the minimum requirements
of ANSI/NISO Z39.48-1992 (R 1997) (Permanence of Paper). ∞

Contents

PREFACE   vii

Introduction: Paradoxes in a Religious Arena   1

1
Getting Bread at Rodrigo's   17

2
The Religious Arena   33

3
"The Church is Open!": Class Fractions in the
Religious Arena   68

4
"I Struggle at Home Every Day": Women and
Domestic Conflict in the Religious Arena   87

5
Escape from the Snake's Nest: Unmarried
Youth in the Religious Arena   117

6
Slaves and Wanderers: *Negros* in the Religious Arena   146

7
Catholics, *Crentes*, and Politics   182

Conclusion: Looking for Liberation   221

    NOTES   231

    GLOSSARY   257

    BIBLIOGRAPHY   259

    INDEX   275

Preface

I heard of liberation theology for the first time during the heady weeks surrounding the Sandinistas' triumphant march into Managua. Fresh out of college, where I had learned that religion and revolution did not mix, I marveled at reports of Nicaraguan priests carrying guns. A few months later, Oscar Romero, the Archbishop of San Salvador, was assassinated by death squads. This was how I learned, along with many students of my generation, about the politically progressive wing of the Latin American Catholic Church. I started reading liberation theology, which argued that Christian Base Communities (CEBs),[1] congregations that had begun to read the Bible as a progressive political manifesto, were the best hope in the struggle for social justice in Latin America. The logic was irresistible: the Latin American masses were deeply religious; they were Catholic; they respected the word of the priest; priests were calling on them to struggle for social justice; therefore, they would respond.[2] The proof of how menacing this doctrine was to the established Catholic hierarchy came in 1984, when the Vatican denounced liberation theology and silenced the Brazilian theologian Leonardo Boff.[3]

I did not doubt that many people were having their political consciousness raised by the Church. Yet I found myself puzzling over the implications of Brazilian field reports sent by parish priests to the Church's Commission on CEBs, which made clear that in any given town those who participated actively in the Catholic Church comprised only a very small minority. They made it clear, too, that the Church was rarely the only available religious option: report after report mentioned "other churches," the "*crentes,*" ("believers," meaning adepts of pentecostal churches), the "spiritists," as well as the mass of nonparticipants. It became increasingly clear to me that in most towns the pentecostals were far more numerous than active members in the CEB. Why, I wondered, hadn't the CEB swept all these other people off their feet?

The question is a politically ticklish one. Many Catholic leaders resent suggestions that the progressive Catholic project may not be working the way they wish or expect. They tend to brand people who make such suggestions as lacking idealism, harping on the negative, or, worse yet, playing into the hands of reaction. It may indeed seem to some that I have harped on the negative in this book. Nonetheless, I am hoping that readers will bear in mind that this work is meant to provide counterpoint to the tenor of much of the existing literature, which, some would say, harps on the positive.

There is, however, a rather more important reason for the critical tone I have adopted throughout this book. I have adopted a particular stance, one shared by a growing segment of the progressive clergy itself.[4] Simply put, I presume that any worthwhile idealism ought to be informed and disciplined by sensitivity to the layers and contradictions of reality. Far from playing into the hands of reaction, we thus strengthen our own hand and reduce the chances of being duped.

Debates about the role of the academic in contributing to social movements, long on the agenda of sociology, have only recently penetrated anthropology, where they have remained largely at the level of general exhortation, such as Gordon's plea that "we [anthropologists] must participate in breaking down the web of hegemonic ideas which is blocking the acceptance of liberating knowledge."[5] How are such exhortations to be implemented? Touraine's call for direct involvement by academic observers in social movements' evaluation meetings, though certainly the most direct way anthropologists might contribute to the deepening of a movement's self-critique, will no doubt strike many anthropologists as mechanical.[6]

Less formally, anthropologists might engage movement leaders in dialogues about their theory and praxis while continuing to write for multiple audiences. I regard my own work as partly an effort to assist Catholic pastoral agents and clergy by identifying the external and internal obstacles to their project. While in the field, both in private conversations and in public evaluation meetings, I tried to bring to the attention of movement leaders the multiple, often contradictory understandings of the movement's official discourse by different follow-erships.[7] This, I believed, might nurture a greater appreciation of both diversity and common ground, possibly improving internal communi-cation and building consensus around core issues and themes. I tried as well to make available to movement leaders (and followers) an insider's view of at least some of the people outside the movement, to help erode the facile view that the main obstacles to their mobilization were laziness, apathy, or lack of consciousness.[8] In particular, I tried to act as a channel for communicating to CEB members outsiders' reactions to specific ritual or discursive innovations in the Church.

From time to time I felt vindicated. One CEB leader, for instance, had been used to making proclamations in meetings and then calling for unanimous assent. After several conversations with her, in which I brought to her attention the various views of CEB members, I had the opportunity of witnessing her replace her call for unanimity with a call for a vote during a meeting. "We have to vote," she said. "This con-sensus stuff is a little artificial."

Of course I had to be careful. In addition to preserving informants' anonymity, I took care in individual and group meetings to present my observations not as fact but as points of departure in dialogues about objectives, tactics, and obstacles. These conversations were among the richest I had in the field. Here I was no longer simply asking questions, but re-presenting both the voices of those present and of others not present, problematized and refracted through my own voice, submitted to my interlocutors for further problematization. They, in turn, would seek to refine my understanding with counterexamples and counter-quotations, while at the same time acknowledging I was pushing them to look at their project in a new light.

Of course, what I had to say was not always credited or well-received, most commonly by young, university-trained pastoral agents. Though my introduction into the parish through a major Brazilian progressive organization must have set at least some of their suspicions to rest, they continued to be troubled by the contrast between their project—to raise people's consciousness by presenting them with a utopian vision—and what appeared to be my penchant for harping on the negative. But while I may have convinced some of them that a deeper self-critique might help improve the movement's appeal, many of them remained skeptical about my work.

Perhaps they were just more candid than most. After all, their skep-ticism was but one variant of a more general concern on the part of all my informants—the awareness that I would eventually leave. The enterprise of ethnography is premised on this tension: between, on the one hand, the drive to obtain the kind of intimate knowledge of people and places that normally is possible only for longstanding neighbors, friends, or relatives; and, on the other, the need eventually to return "home," to the place one intends to build one's life and career. Despite all the rationales offered both to ourselves and our informants (we must serve as "bridges," we must seek to raise the awareness of our fellow citizens, etc.), the tension remains. Surely part of what being an anthropologist means is feeling forever dissatisfied with one's efforts to resolve this tension.

Some efforts, however, are made in better faith than others. The anthropologist studying social movements can develop long-term relationships with the movements, through repeated visits and letters to members and leaders, and by making his or her work—whether lectures, papers, articles, documentaries or books—accessible to movement leaders and followers through translation and distribution.[9] Yet it is important to avoid self-importance, the temptation to overestimate the influence of anthropological knowledge—or any other kind of specialized knowledge—to social movement work. For every time the academic observer helps make an issue clearer, there are as many instances of such observers obscuring issues, denying or avoiding them, or being entirely irrelevant to them. Aspiring "organic intellectuals" must scrape for evidence that their interventions have had any effect. Connections between anthropological knowledge and action are in any case indirect, manifesting themselves only in the long run. Thus, much of the knowledge I accumulated in the field was either obvious to locals or largely irrelevant to the development of social movements, and made its way into this book primarily for the benefit of my non-local (and academic) audiences. Thus, for all my enthusiasm about "mutual dialogues," this exchange remained asymmetric: I get the surplus value of appealing to multiple audiences, while members of the social movements I studied must perforce rest content with a few perspectival insights and the hope that a few of my questions and hypotheses may someday come in handy.

My greatest debt will always be to the people of São Jorge, who opened their homes and lives to me, an odd foreigner on a bicycle, and answered with heroic patience my endless, embarrassing, and often silly questions. Not only because they number more than two hundred, but because of the socially delicate nature of much of what they told me, I cannot name all of my informants here; so I will refrain from naming any.

Several local people, however, contributed to this project in ways not related to talking about themselves or local matters. I would not have been able to begin my research in São Jorge without the support of Alcino. Zé-Aparecida, Baixinho, Jair, and Eduardo were crucial in helping me coordinate my census through the neighborhood association, and Zé helped directly to analyze data from the 1979 census. Jorge, Alcino, and Carlinhos put me in touch with vital regional contacts. Beyond São Jorge, many people provided advice, guidance, contacts, and friendship. In the parish of the fourth district of Duque de Caxias, I received a wide range of assistance from Domingos, Armando, Mario, Agnaldo, Rafael, Frei Davi, Paula, Oneize, Maria, Claudio, and Solange.

In Rio de Janeiro I benefited from conversations at the Instituto de Estudos de Religião (ISER) and the Centro de Documentação e Informação (CEDI) with the following people: Caetana Damaceno, Rubem Cesar Fernandes, Micênio Santos, Sônia Giacomini, Lygia Dabul, Regina Novaes, Zêlia Seiblitz, Henry Decoster, Flávio Lenz, Pierre Sanchis, and Zwinglio Dias. In São Paulo, Paulo Krischke provided support and advice. At Fulbright, Lolita Anísio was a source of both technical support and good humor. Also in Rio, I became part of the Dória family for several months in 1985, for which I am grateful to Flávio, Renato, Laise, Tininha, Janete, Sílvia, and Marianinha.

In the United States, the following people have provided comments on the project at various stages: Thomas Bruneau, Johnetta Cole, Jean Comaroff, Margaret Crahan, Arturo Escobar, Robert Levine, Scott Mainwaring, Cecilia Mariz, Roberto Motta, and David Stoll. At the City University of New York, I owe an enormous debt to Eric Wolf, Jane Schneider, Vincent Crapanzano, and Ralph Della Cava for their careful work in helping to shepherd this project from proposal to thesis to book. Also at City University I have been stimulated by conversations with Carmen Ferradas, John Finch, Christine Grabowski, Aisha Khan, David (Chris) Leonard, Rodrigo Munoz-Reyes, Jonathan Poor, Robin Sheriff, Alessandro Scassellati, and Lygia Simonsen. Terri Vulcano and Judith Attride smoothed my path through the bureaucratic tangles of the Graduate Center, as they have done for so many other students over the years.

In 1985, preliminary research was supported by a U.S. Department of Education Title VI Language Study Grant, and in 1986 by a Sigma Pi Research Grant and a summer grant from the Graduate Center of the City University of New York. Fieldwork from 1987 to 1988 was funded by Grant BNS-8709863 of the National Science Foundation, and by a

Fulbright-Hayes Dissertation Research grant. The first year (1988–1989) of writing was funded by the Leonard Silk Dissertation Writing Fellowship. I extend my gratitude to all these institutions.

A postdoctoral fellowship at Rutgers University's Center for Historical Analysis in 1990–1991 gave me the opportunity to revise the thesis for publication. At the Center I was delighted to have the chance to discuss my ideas with John Gillis, Marjorie Beale, Mara Miller, Rhys Isaac, Robert Thornton, Michael Moffatt, Sharla Fett, and Jermaine Jackson.

My parents, Harvey and Dolores Burdick, have sustained my faith in intellectual endeavor for as long as I can remember. Judith Malkin took a leap of faith and went into the field with me very soon after we had met and married, creating a bond that we are still, years later, continuing to discover. For having had the wild idea of agreeing to marry an anthropologist, I dedicate this book to her, and to our son Ben.

Introduction

Paradoxes in a Religious Arena

For over two decades, in what some have called the most revolutionary Catholic movement since the Reformation, priests throughout Latin America, inspired by liberation theology, have preached the Gospel as a call for social justice and the democratization of religious authority.[1] Their message springs from the same founts that have watered Christian radicalism for nearly two millennia. Liberation theologians argue that the prophesies of both the Old and New Testaments promise a Kingdom in which humanity will live in peace, equality, and justice, and, as foretold by the Apocalypse, that this Kingdom will be realized, not in Heaven, but on earth. Moreover, just as God used Moses to free His people, so too will He establish His Kingdom with the assistance of human agency. This is why, liberationists declare, it is up to humanity to struggle for the coming of the Kingdom.[2]

While liberation theology has familiar roots, its branches are new. One of those branches is the belief that in the struggle for the Kingdom, the poor are pivotal actors. It is "the poor, the little people, the anonymous ones," who are faithful "to the contract with God of equality and brotherhood"; it is they who are "the natural bearers of the utopia of God's Kingdom."[3] In place of the traditional Catholic vision of charity, in which the better-off receive religious merit by giving to the poor, liberation theologians substitute a new vision of social rights, in which the poor struggle to bring about the Kingdom by demanding their just deserts. In this struggle the poor confront institutionalized violence and

1

social injustice, which threaten to beat them into passivity, fatalism, and apathy. It is, therefore, up to the Church to help the poor overcome their fear, rediscover their spirit of community, and develop a critical under-standing of the social nature of the violence they face. Such conscious Catholics will then fulfil their role in the battle for the Kingdom, by entering political and social movements for progressive societal change.[4]

The burden of realizing this vision falls to the Christian Base Com-munities, known throughout Latin America as "CEBs," the acronym for *comunidad(e) eclesial de base*. CEBs are Catholic congregations in which clergy and pastoral agents are engaged, in one way or another, in efforts to raise political and social awareness. The most distinctive aspect of the CEBs is the presence of small reflection groups, in which, with the help of liberationist study guides and pastoral agents, members read the Bible together, discuss its implications for their everyday lives, and are inspired by it to struggle for social justice.[5] "After centuries of silence," writes Leonardo Boff,

the People of God are taking over the word; they are no longer simply a client of the parish, but are reinventing the Church in a concrete historical sense . . . the people, motivated by a faith illuminated in the Bible circles and lived in the CEBs, are organizing themselves, no longer accept to die before their time, and are struggling for better alternatives.[6]

Nowhere in Latin America have CEBs become as numerous or re-ceived more official support from the hierarchy of the Church than in Brazil.[7] In the 1950s, many Brazilian bishops began turning away from the urban, elitist model of the Church toward a vision of themselves as the "voice of the voiceless." With the repression of the late 1960s, many bishops became outspoken in their denunciation of human rights' abuses and in their calls for social justice. The bishops shielded priests who had come to see powerful connections between the material and spiritual lots of their flocks, and whose practice of establishing CEBs accelerated after receiving the stamp of approval, in 1968, of the episcopal conference at Medellín. By the early 1980s, the number of CEBs in Brazil was esti-mated at around 80,000.[8]

The Numerical Paradox

Brazil's *comunidades de base*, like those of Latin America in general, have often been represented in political, journalistic, and scholarly discourse as a rapidly growing mass movement with the power to transform Brazilian politics and society.[9] The view that the People are naturally disposed to embrace the message of liberation as purveyed by the Church underlies both the argument that the Popular Church is a strategy engineered from above and that it is a response to demands from below.[10] In either case, many observers of the Brazilian progressive Church assume, with Della Cava, that "the receptivity of ordinary and long-suffering believers to this 'revolution within the church' [is] itself extraordinary."[11]

While there can be no doubt that Brazil's CEBs are a politically important movement, the extent of their penetration among "ordinary and long-suffering believers" may be questioned. Estimates of the number of CEB participants are notoriously difficult to pin down, partly because of the lack of definitional consensus about CEBs themselves.[12] For the purposes of this book, I am less concerned with the true number of CEB participants, than with what can be roughly known about their relative proportion to other major national religious movements.

If we take "participant" to mean anyone who participates in one or more CEB activities (especially Bible circles) other than Mass, the limited available evidence suggests that, whether calculated nationally or locally, the number of CEB participants is rather less impressive than the number of pentecostals and practitioners of the Afro-Brazilian religion of *umbanda,* even in areas where the CEBs are highly active. Several studies suggest that at the regional and local levels, pentecostals may outnumber CEB participants on the order of three to one. In the strongly progressive archdiocese of Vitória, no more than 3 to 4 percent of local adults actively participated in the CEBs, percentages that paralleled those discovered in surveys of progressive parishes in Goiás, as well as in ethnographic studies in Pernambuco and São Paulo. In these same studies, pentecostals were found to make up between 8 and 10 percent of local populations.[13]

Although national figures are less reliable, they do tend to corroborate these relative percentages. Initially, the problem here is to estimate the number of participants in an "average" CEB. *Comunidades* obviously vary in size depending on the population of the neighborhood or town in which they are situated. This variation, however, tends to be limited by the Church's policy of founding new *comunidades* whenever established ones "grow too large," as one progressive priest put it. Thus, in a survey of CEBs in and near São Paulo, Hewitt found that "membership ranged from 5 to 50, with an average of 22."[14] Comblin has observed: "In practice, the CEBs include only some of the baptized: groups of twenty to a hundred people, generally closer to twenty than to a hundred, in the middle of a population of 500, 1,000, even 10,000 baptized Catholics who do not belong to the CEB."[15] Frei Betto arrived at similar numbers.[16] If we generously assume a national average at the high end of this range, and if we increase the estimate of CEBs to a hundred thousand, this translates into five million participants, or a little more than 5 percent of Brazil's current population aged fifteen and over.[17]

Meanwhile, in the mid-1980s, the Assembly of God, Brazil's largest pentecostal church, claimed alone to have thirteen million baptized members in good standing.[18] Although this number is undoubtedly inflated, it is consistent with the best estimates that place Brazil's overall pentecostal population in the mid-1980s at between twelve and fifteen million.[19] The numbers are less clear for *umbanda,* but Diana Brown has mentioned the figure of twenty million regular participants, while other observers have claimed that over half of all Brazilians have consulted in an *umbanda* center at one time or another.[20] Thus, even if we accept the most conservative national figures, and hold them constant for the early 1990s, they still indicate that pentecostals and *umbandistas* outnumber active CEB participants on the order of at least two, and possibly as much as three or four to one.

This, then, is one of the main paradoxes of Brazil's People's Church. While that Church was conceived, in part, as a way to increase clerical influence among the masses, the masses continue to be more enthusiastic about the Church's major religious rivals. A growing number of observers in and outside of the Church have begun to recognize this. Daniel Levine has commented that, whatever the reasons for the scholarly interest in CEBs, "[s]urely it is not for the numbers they attract."[21] Comblin, one of the earliest theoreticians of the CEB movement, has recently acknowledged that "frequently the *comunidades* do not want to expand but even exclude expansion . . . The laity of the CEBs avoid contact with the mass of people," allowing them to be snapped up by other religions.[22] Or, as Brandão has observed in a report of findings from a survey of over thirteen thousand respondents in Goiás,

It is quite evident that an intensive pastoral project of the progressive Catholic church, realized without any interruption of "line" or of its agents for more than fifteen years, has not resulted in a statistical advantage in its favor. . . . We are faced with a paradox. The Church that theologians and pastoral agents call "a church that is being born of the people" is struggling with great difficulty to be accepted by the people itself.[23]

In this book, I will explore this paradox. Why is the People's Church less popular than its rivals? Why are the CEBs losing the battle for souls? What do pentecostalism and *umbanda* signify and offer to Brazil's masses that the People's Church does not?

The Political Paradox

Despite being demographically weaker than other religious movements, CEBs have made themselves felt in Brazil at the level of collective movements for social change. Indeed, some writers have claimed that liberationist discourse is inherently persuasive to *comunidade* participants and is therefore sweeping them all into political struggle. "The people," writes Macêdo,

come to find in the discourse that emanates from the pulpit a representation of reality compatible with the one it already has. . . . There is a verisimilitude in the discourse of the priests, which produces identification of the people with that being presented. The poor of today are like the poor of yesterday. For them, Christ came. And they must respond to his call. They must struggle for the Kingdom . . .[24]

Although this is certainly an overstatement, there can be no doubt that over the last generation, CEBs have supplied an umbrella for a variety of struggles for social justice, encouraged the development of progressive political leaders, and, by instilling in at least some of their members the values of struggle and this-worldly liberation, helped motivate numerous poor Brazilians to become involved in neighborhood organizations, land reform movements, labor unions, and political parties.[25]

At the same time, a growing number of observers have noted that other, less socially activist tendencies are often present in the *comunidades,* even in those with long histories of influence by progressive clergy and pastoral agents. In Vitória, for example, a diocese that has benefited from over twenty years of progressive pastoral work, a survey of 70,000 active CEB members revealed that a majority remained uninterested in social movements or other political matters. Instead, they emphasized "the liturgy and the sacraments, the greater participation of the laity in the Church, and the rapprochement with the Bible."[26] Even among *comunidades* in São Paulo, usually celebrated for their high level of politicization, Hewitt has reported that "given the choice between initiating bible study or charity circles, or reflection and political discussion groups, the former has won out."[27] Ireland's report of a nun's complaint about a CEB in the Northeast is suggestive: "the fishing folk had not, over the years of her work, been formed into a grassroots community of the kind that fulfilled her ideals and the ideals of her church."[28] Most generally, Comblin has suggested that "frequently there is an unconscious and more or less latent antagonism between what the pastoral agents expect from their CEBs and their concrete accomplishments. The CEBs adopt the language of the pastoral agents, but passively resist their calls to action."[29] In a more polemical tone, Dom Angélico, longtime progressive in São Paulo, recently complained that the CEBs had "betrayed" the progressive clergy.[30]

This, then, is our second paradox: While theologians conceive of the CEBs as a means to instill in the People a politically activist message of liberation, it has become increasingly clear that many, if not most, CEB participants understand and respond to the message in other ways. What are some of these understandings? Who understands what and why? How and why do some CEB participants come to connect the discourse of liberation with the practice of social movements while others do not?

In contrast to the CEBs, pentecostalism has been portrayed in both the scholarly literature and the popular press as an inherently conservative force that teaches acceptance of the existing class order, inculcates submission to authority, erodes collective identity, and undercuts justifications for social action. In this view, the *crentes'* occasional forays into collective movements for social justice can only be regarded as temporary ruptures from their usual resignation to the status quo.[31] These observers, not surprisingly, conclude that CEBs present a "better means to collaborate in the acceleration of the processes of social change" than do the *crentes*.[32] One writer has argued that Brazil's political fate hinges on which side triumphs in the struggle between the CEBs and the "sects."[33]

Yet here, too, recent observers have begun to complicate the conventional picture, by pointing out that the self-valorization brought about by evangelical conversion often paves the way for a strong sense of natural rights and citizenship.[34] Regina Novaes, for instance, has argued that pentecostals who participated in a rural union in the Brazilian Northeast tended "to have greater conviction about their rights" than did non-pentecostals.[35] Clearly, the image of pentecostals as being hopelessly apathetic fails to do justice to such complexity. What then are the linkages between pentecostal identity and a range of political tendencies, and what are the conditions under which any given tendency prevails?

Elucidating the Paradoxes: Theorizing Religious Arenas

Because the questions I have raised with regard to "the two paradoxes" are all implicitly comparative, traditional single-religion ethnography is not an appropriate model to follow.[36] In the context of Brazil's urban periphery, where religious migration is the norm, not the exception, where people adhere to different religious groups in succession and at the same time, the traditional model is especially ill-suited. The following case is not atypical: Maria was born a Catholic, and remained exclusively loyal to the Church for the first decades of her life; in her thirties she began to frequent an *umbanda* center, eventually becoming a medium; later she converted to pentecostalism; and by her fifties had grown so disillusioned with the latter that she returned once again to the Catholic fold, now in the form of a CEB. If our aim is to explore the patterns at work in such experiences, the single-religion model clearly will not do.

The single-group focus also too easily slips into the assumption that a religion's social composition reveals the extent and nature of its appeal. In the polyreligious field of Brazil's urban periphery, people with similar social characteristics attend or adhere to different religious groups. One cannot simply report that because a certain percentage of a given group's members are black, or female, or old, or poor, that the group in question has a special attraction for this cluster of people. One must, rather, consider how the percentages of such clusters, as well as their absolute numbers, vary from religion to religion. Single-religion studies of CEBs, for example, often point out that they are made up predominantly of women, concluding that the People's Church has a special affinity for women.[37] If, however, such studies were to compare CEBs with pentecostal churches in the same towns, they would most likely find anywhere from three to five times as many local female *crentes* as *comunidade* participants. Focusing on this discrepancy would force into the open the need to investigate what the pentecostal church offered local women that the CEB did not.

Rather than examine a single CEB in isolation, then, I will explore the field of religious options of which the CEB is a part. The models for studying polyreligious arenas are scarce.[38] To find a model sufficiently fluid to analyze religion in the Brazilian urban periphery, we must turn to the field of medical anthropology. Building on Kleinman's model of a field of healing options,[39] we may regard competitive, polyreligious arenas as contexts in which people do not simply belong to one of several neat theologico-organizational wholes, but rather encounter a complex set of partly overlapping discourses and practices. In such encounters, people may move over time through the entire religious gamut, circulating through the field as loyal members and affiliates, frequenters, or simply as religious-service users.

Although an improvement, the medical model still has limitations: above all, it runs the risk of slipping into a facile market view of choice and identity. In this view, the presenting complaint remains unanalyzed, and the main criteria of choice between healing alternatives are reduced to such matters as availability, cost, and location.[40] The model thus runs the risk of allowing us to come to the most unenlightening of conclusions: that trajectories through the religious arena are purely opportunistic efforts to solve concrete problems. Indeed, some sociologists of Brazil conclude by depicting religious mobility in precisely this way, as purely idiosyncratic and unpatterned.[41] Macêdo puts the position clearly:

The potential adepts believe they have the right to go from agency to agency, and choose to "consume" the "products" that best meet their necessities. . . . Belief moves from one place to another, from one object to another, from one ideology to another. There is no necessary connection between belief and its object. People believe in their momentary ideas, in what they have heard most recently, without any further concern.[42]

Teixeira adds:

For the people . . . there are no dramas of conscience, but rather anxieties and necessities. But these anxieties are not about meaning, theodicy or anthropodicy. There is only the search for solutions to concrete problems, of partial explanations and answers to partial questions.[43]

There are several problems with this view. First, it fails to account for the widespread phenomenon that Brazilians, regardless of their "concrete problems," often refuse to consult with certain religious specialists, or resist affiliating with specific religious groups; second, it fails to pose the question of whether some religious options work more often for some kinds of people than for others, and if so, why?

A partial corrective to the free market view is suggested by those medical anthropologists who insist that coping with problems, however concrete, is constrained by prior belief, identity, and social networks.[44] I would add that "concrete problems" tend to be symptomatic of bundles of social experience. The intense headache a woman brings to be prayed over in an *umbanda* center is often the result of domestic strife; a young person's fainting spells may point to intergenerational conflict; a *negro*'s spirit possession may be connected to ambivalence about race identity. We would, therefore, be well-advised to seek different religions' abilities to solve surface problems by looking at how they address them at a deeper level. We will soon discover that not all religious options deal as effectively with domestic strife, or intergenerational conflict, or race ambivalence—it becomes clear that not any religion will "do." Indeed, at this level religious choice begins to look less like opportunism and precisely more like ongoing "dramas of conscience," "searches for theodicy," and the complex construction of religious identity—and identity in general.

For our model of the religious arena to do justice to both fluidity and constraint, I suggest that our analytic point of departure should be clusters of people as they enter into and interact with the whole panoply of religious discourses, practices, and specialists. By "clusters," I mean people who share constructed identities, such as being a *negro*, or important experiential commonalities discoverable through ethnography, such as domestic conflict. The empirical task then becomes to explore how these clusters of people cope, through available religious acts and language, with their experiential predicaments. By examining how people in such clusters understand and move between the options in the religious arena, we may begin to grasp the reasons for the rise or fall of a particular religion within it. Furthermore, by investigating how different clusters of people within a religion understand and appropriate its discourse and practice, we can better grasp the religion's internal political tendencies and contradictions.

THE SIGNIFICANCE OF VARIATION

Central to this model is the view that religious discourses and practices are seized upon and understood in different ways by different audiences. This view may be distinguished from recent work in the anthropology of religion, inspired by Turner and Bourdieu, that insists on the power of religious ritual to produce relatively uniform subjectivities, habits of thought, and ideological commitments.[45] Even granting Bourdieu's point that many practices are not accessible to conscious reflection, it remains possible that the same practice may generate in different audiences different habits of thought. The principal way to test this possibility, however, is to pay attention to the voices of the people exposed to the practices.[46]

Yet in ethnographies of religion, all too often the verbal exegesis of informants is employed to illustrate uniformity, not difference. Comaroff's brilliant analysis of the Tshidi Zionists, for example, points out that adepts wear yarn cords "evocative" of nineteenth-century initiation rites.[47] No doubt the cords evoke these rites for some adepts; but is it possible that for some Zionists the cords evoke something else, perhaps nothing at all? Comaroff also reports that male Zionists bearing ritual staffs signify a superiority to which "women serve, by and large, as submissive foils."[48] But how do Zionist women perceive the staffs? Is it possible that some of them reject or reinterpret the masculine version? We do not know, because we do not hear the Zionists, as an internally differentiated group, speaking their minds and telling their personal stories. Rooting multivoicedness in specific clusters of people would, in contrast, reveal a political economy of polyphony.[49]

Life stories are a crucial resource for building this kind of polyphony, for exploring the different meanings religion has for different clusters of adepts. It is difficult in the course of fieldwork to witness many key events in informants' lives, episodes in which the connection between religious discourse and lived experience comes dramatically into relief. It is through life stories that a conceptual-historical bridge may be built "between the private and the public, the individual and the communal."[50] By eliciting both exegeses and life stories, then, we reveal the range of meanings a given signifying practice can have on subjectivity, and come closer to understanding the degree to which participants in religious groups place into their own foregrounds those meanings that resonate with their particular life experiences.

São Jorge: A Town in Rio's Urban Periphery

São Jorge is a settlement of about eight thousand people, wedged in a valley in the foothills of the Serra dos Marcondes, at the northern rim of the great, flat drainage basin known as the Baixada Fluminense, twenty miles north of metropolitan Rio de Janeiro. It is classified as a *bairro*, a town, within the semirural fourth district of the municipality of Duque de Caxias. At about a million inhabitants, Duque de Caxias is currently the largest suburb of Rio de Janeiro.

For centuries the São Jorge valley was home only to thick mangrove forest. It was not until the 1930s, when Rio de Janeiro's industrial expansion was already well underway, that land-hungry migrants began cutting down the mangrove to supply the city's demand for fuel and construction materials.[51] Then in 1941, in an effort to coax Brazil away from a wartime alliance with Italy, the United States financed the construction of the National Motor Factory (FNM), the first airplane engine plant in Latin America, located a kilometer southwest of the São Jorge valley.[52] In the late 1940s, a private company partitioned the valley among speculators who, in turn, drove the first wave of squatters into the hills and sold parcels to newly-arriving workers.[53] Most of these were men from Minas Gerais.

By the late 1950s, the initial stream of migrants to the valley had slowed, and the local population had stabilized at about three hundred families. Then, between 1958 and 1968, in response to the demand for labor to build and run the massive Petrobrás refinery, located almost twelve kilometers south of São Jorge, the average yearly arrival of people tripled.[54] Before and after the military coup of 1964, FNM and Petrobrás (the state-run petrochemical industry) sought to lower labor costs by farming out production to subcontractors that could avoid labor legislation, pay a lower wage than the state, and undermine labor unity by hiring fresh rounds of workers for each contract. Since wages paid by a subcontractor were not sufficient to support a family, workers had to supplement their income by odd-jobbing in the informal sector.

Between 1968 and 1973, during the Brazilian "miracle," the military government turned Duque de Caxias into an industrial pole, doubling the number of its textile, glass, chemical, pharmaceutical, food processing, and metallurgical plants, and mercilessly cutting the wage bill.[55] This explosive growth started yet another flood of workers to the São Jorge valley, this time from the Northeast, Espirito Santo, and the *favelas* of Rio.[56] The touted miracle began to slow and its true price to be felt after 1973, the first year of tangible inflation. Low wages, limited advancement, and rampant price increases forced an ever-growing proportion of São Jorge's men in the 1970s to supplement their wages by *biscate* (odd-jobbing), and of women to enter the wage labor market in manufacturing.[57]

In 1981, after several years of decline, the FNM plant shut down. Some assembly-line workers entered other capital-intensive industries in the region at comparable wages, but most were forced to turn to lower-paid menial work, stevedoring, and subcontracted labor. Hundreds of men were forced to work further away from town, the informal construction market grew rapidly, and a growing percentage of wives had to become part-time domestic servants. For a very few the plant closing proved a blessing: the company paid three months advance wages as indemnity, a major windfall for workers with little or no savings; a few of the best-paid workers parlayed this money into small mercantile enterprises such as grocery bars.

Today, fully a third of local men work in the civil construction trades, one quarter combine social security and odd jobs, about a fifth work in factories in the industrial pole, one tenth work in supervisory and white collar jobs, and smaller percentages are truckers and merchants. Among the women, two-thirds work only at home, 14 percent work as domestic servants, 5 percent labor in factories, and smaller percentages work in commerce, service, and white collar jobs.[58]

The Religious Arena in São Jorge

What makes São Jorge's active Catholics a *"comunidade"* is the fact that since 1982, when the progressive priest arrived in the parish, they have had an elected council and several small, neighbor-hood-based Bible reflection circles; that through the circles and periodic *cursinhos* ("little courses") they have been continuously exposed to a rights-oriented reading of the Bible; and that they have learned clearly to identify themselves as a *"comunidade."* Among São Jorge's almost thirty-five hundred people aged fifteen and over, ninety or so regularly participate in the activities of the *comunidade* (Bible circles, pastorals of baptism, *cursinhos,* and so forth). Of these, forty or so take an active role in coordinating these activities, and another fifty participate, with less fervor, in them.

These are the people who regard themselves, and each other, as "members" of the *comunidade.* Those who show up in church simply to take Communion, whether once a week or once a month, are outsiders, and ineligible to vote at the monthly general assembly of the *comunidade* for directors, ministers, or on proposals. *Comunidade* members refer to such people by the belittling terms of *misseiros* or *papa–hostias* ("host-eaters").

Hewitt has suggested a political continuum along which six types of *comunidade de base* may be located, ranging from purely apolitical devotional groups, to those that limit their nondevotional activity to consciousness-raising, to those engaged in joint-labor initiatives, to groups involved in extra-*comunidade* social action.[59] São Jorge's *comunidade* appears to be of the second type: for although its members are having their consciousnesses "raised," they are not generally engaged in non-Church social movements.

The relative political quiescence of São Jorge's *comunidade* should not be taken as representing the CEB phenomenon as a whole. In São Jorge's own diocese, several *comunidades* have successfully mobilized members to enter social movements. The reasons for this kind of variation are complex, but may in part be related to the fact that São Jorge had an infrastructure of traditional pre-Conciliar and Conciliar lay organizations already firmly in place when the progressive priest arrived in the parish, while the few towns with politically more activist *comunidades* tended not to. It is thus possible that *comunidades* like São Jorge's include more members whose politico-religious visions were formed institutionally before the arrival of the progressive Church, thus making them generally less amenable to direct political activism. Yet this does not tell the whole story. São Jorge's political inactivity is typical of other *comunidades* in the region, even those without a traditional lay infrastructure; and, if the literature cited earlier is any indication, CEB members' preference for church over non-church activities represents an important national trend as well.

The Protestants are numerically more important in São Jorge than *comunidade* members. Two nonpentecostal churches, the Baptists and the Adventists, claim almost one hundred and twenty members between them, and two small pentecostal churches, the House of Blessing (*Casa da Benção*) and God is Love (*Deus é Amor*) each have about fifty baptized congregants. But these numbers are modest in comparison to São Jorge's largest church: by 1987, the Assembly of God could boast about two hundred and seventy full-fledged, card-carrying members, and a house of worship more imposing than the Catholic chapel. Thus, while *comunidade* Catholics represented about 2½ percent of the town's population over fifteen, the pentecostals represented over 10 percent. All told, São Jorge's pentecostals outnumbered *comunidade* members by about four to one.[60]

More telling than simple arithmetical sums is the fact that the level of participation in the local institutional Catholic Church has declined over the past ten years, while that of the Assembly of God has increased. Every leading and nonleading Catholic I interviewed voiced concern about what they perceived as the pronounced decline in participation of both members and *misseiros* since the early 1980s. The following complaint, from a current leader, is typical: "This Church used to be filled, filled to capacity! Look at how many people come now. There isn't that participation there used to be."

My best information confirmed these reports. As best I could determine, in the late 1970s about twenty leaders coordinated São Jorge's *capela*'s activities, about two hundred and fifty adults engaged in one or more Church activities other than Mass, and another hundred attended Mass and nothing else. That is, over the course of a decade, while the number of leaders of São Jorge's central Catholic congregation has probably doubled, the number of its nonleading participants has fallen off dramatically. In contrast, the Assembly of God church has continued in the 1980s to grow at a rate of about fourteen new converts per year.

The numbers of locals who regularly frequented an *umbanda* center were harder to determine. In my census of 350 households, only a small number of household heads acknowledged being active practitioners or frequenters of *umbanda*. Other evidence, however, pointed to widespread involvement in the religion. Among over one hundred informants, at least half admitted to having consulted with a medium at some time or another, and a fifth were either regular participants or mediums. Although there were only two *umbanda* centers in São Jorge, located in the hilly rural section of town, most locals frequented centers in neighboring towns, some of which had upwards of a dozen centers.

The *comunidade* in São Jorge, like *comunidades* throughout Brazil, is thus on the defensive, struggling to remain an active force in an arena in which it seems to be losing ground on a daily basis. *Comunidade* members observe the ranks of their Church declining and those of other religions growing, and they are troubled by the contrast. They complain about the difficulty of getting people to participate, with a bitterness born of their awareness of how easily others snap them up. "So few people come to Church any more," a participating Catholic complained. "They're going to other religions," commented another.

The Argument of the Book

Why, in São Jorge, are pentecostalism and *umbanda* expanding, while the *comunidade* is not? What do the people of São Jorge find in other religions that they do not find in the *comunidade*? My answer to this question comes in four parts. First, I argue that the CEB model has reinforced the association between the institutional Catholic church and relatively more stable, literate, and better-off segments of the local working class, while pentecostalism tends to accommodate a broader sociomaterial range of workers. Second, I suggest that married women find it difficult to resolve domestic problems through progressive Catholicism, because the Church nurtures an atmosphere of gossip; they turn instead to pentecostalism and *umbanda*, where they encounter the supportive atmosphere of groups which recruit members on the basis of suffering. Third, I contend that unmarried youths, squeezed between the urban pressures of unemployment and heightened expectations for consumption and sexuality, find that pentecostalism permits a clear break with the past (which the CEB does not) and the forging of alternative, less-pressured social networks. Finally, one reason so few *negros* are to be found in the CEB, and so many in *umbanda* and *crença*, is that the CEB has failed to forge an effective counterdiscourse to racism. *Umbanda* and pentecostalism, in contrast, through the inversions made possible by their peculiar kind of spirit possession, have created compelling—though tensely contested—counterdiscourses to racism.

I then turn to the political paradoxes of both CEB Catholicism and pentecostalism. While the traditional subjects of CEB studies have been those participants who speak and act according to the ideal, I have broadened my focus to include not only those CEB participants who articulate liberationist discourse fluently, but those who do not. I argue that, far from being an ideological monolith, the people in São Jorge's *comunidade,* and elsewhere, have heard, interpreted, and applied the Church's message in various ways; and that, in fact, only a small, identifiable minority have responded to the message in the way the progressive clergy had hoped. Furthermore, I suggest that *comunidade* members' religio-political visions tend to be fragile, leading them to be easily demobilized when their leaders drift or move away. Meanwhile, through an examination of the patterns of *crente* political discourse and practice, I argue that the *crentes* hold a good deal more promise for Brazilian progressive politics than they are usually given credit for. I thus hope to disclose the Brazilian religious arena as full of rich, though often hidden, possibilities.

1

Getting Bread at Rodrigo's

On a cold early morning, I looked out across the valley from the balcony of our house to the mountains of the Serra dos Marcondes, silent and black against the dark blue sky. I watched as their peaks slowly turned blue and their parched brown foothills emerged from the shadows while further down emerald-green sugar cane and banana leaves shimmered in the morning sun. From its station on the tallest promontory in sight, the gleaming white facade of the Catholic chapel, a simple rectangular building of brick and corrugated metal, looked down on the valley with a gently scolding air, as if impatient for it to awake.

The São Jorge valley is named after the little stream that rushes through it, which, in its more glorious days, helped to carve this once richly-forested valley. Now, reduced to a gurgle, it rinses the laundry of women without access to freshwater wells, gives up its spare yield to men and boys with fishlines, and receives sewage through long white plastic pipes. The waters of the São Jorge empty into the Saracuruna river ten kilometers to the west, then flow south thirty kilometers across the wide flat drainage basin known as the Baixada Fluminense, before finally disappearing into Rio de Janeiro's Guanabara Bay.

From the vantage of my balcony, one would hardly have guessed the valley was home to a town of more than eight thousand souls, one of hundreds of *bairros* in the great suburban sprawl of Rio de Janeiro. Although I could see São Jorge's main road clearly, the majority of the

The view from our balcony

town's inhabitants lived on its small branch paths, hidden under a deep-green cloak of sugar cane and acacia, banana, and mangueira trees. It was only the water reservoirs, power lines, and television antennae jutting above the leaves that betrayed the presence of habitation. In those reservoirs good clean water was stored, pumped from excellent underground sources, mountain springs, or caught during rainfalls. Those power lines had been carrying electricity into the central part of town for nearly twenty years.

As I watched the stars fade above the mountains, I savored the stillness, soon broken by roosters and dogs, then by the laughter of men making their way duckfooted to the bottom of our steep dirt street to wait for the bus. There, about thirty men and women, some smoking, some already warmed by a shot of *cachaça*, were waiting. At six o'clock I heard the bus's diesel engine a kilometer away as it turned the corner from the Washington Luiz highway onto São Jorge's main thoroughfare, then thundered along the asphalt artery that snaked through the heart of town. The vehicle rattled past the butchershop, Mario's tile-bedecked house, the Snake Nest bar, and Astolfo's grocery store, until at last, crossing the bridge over the river, it shifted into low gear, and climbed with a roar the last hundred meters to the asphalt's end.

After filling with passengers, the bus clattered back to the highway and hurtled southward, past sweeps of forest and clay-earth hillock, flat expanses of one- and two-story brick and asbestos dwellings beneath chaotic electric lines, and rain-stained pedestrian overpasses speckled with grafitti and scraps of political posters, until it arrived and unloaded workers at the foundries, textile mills, food-processing factories, and petro-chemical plants that comprised Duque de Caxias's industrial pole. Some would stay on the bus as it slowed to a crawl and the highway became an avenue choked with compact cars, until it made its final stop at Duque de Caxias's gray central square. There the remaining passengers would disembark and make their way to jobs as janitors, domestics, and clerks.

It was already seven o'clock. The hills were bathed in sunlight, the morning mist was dissipating, and hot bread from Joel's bakery would soon be arriving at Rodrigo's bar. I gathered up my notebook and walked down our street, muddy from the rain of the previous night, past two-story plastered brick houses with wood doors and windows, and roofs of tile, asbestos, and concrete. I inhaled the stench of smoking garbage, of sewage emptied through surface pipes into shallow dirt gutters where chickens pecked at the debris. The air was already vibrating with the electronic blare of soap-opera theme songs, love tunes from Minas Gerais, Rio pop-rock, and pentecostal hymns. Uniformed children with knapsacks ran giggling on their way to early classes at the two elementary schools in town. Little boys splashed a soccer ball in the mud. The skeletal remains of kites looked down from the power lines in which they had been ensnared, and where they accumulated whenever children were not in class, which was much of the time.[1]

Near the bus stop, men and women were already lining up at the health clinic where once a week they received free medicine in the shadow of a huge sign that read, "Another Achievement of the Mayor, Juberlain de Oliveira."[2] Next to the sign stood the Assembly of God church, an impressive cream-colored, four-story structure. Already at this hour, the Assembly's loudspeakers were busy bellowing hymns and the message of salvation for the benefit of the town's lost souls.

The four bars located near the bus stop enjoyed a brisk business. They were incipient grocery stores, stocked not only with liquor and beer, but sausages, spices, wine, candy, cookies, chewing gum, toilet paper, and soap. Here, beneath raftered pork rib and hemmed in by skillfully stacked bags of rice, corn meal, and black beans, the bar-owners held court, purveying not only dry and wet goods, but news, banter and gossip.

Morning in São Jorge

Competition between them was fierce. During my first months in town, I mistook their mutual joviality for the milk of human kindness, until each began to tell me how the others were trying to steal his customers. "Denirio charges ten cruzados for a shot of *cachaça*," one of them said. "Here, it's fifteen. Here bread is twenty-two, there it's nineteen. So competition starts between us, and, unfortunately, that brings the evil eye." Lest one contribute to this unfortunate process, it was only prudent to buy bread and beer at the same place.

My place was Rodrigo's. Shirtless men in shorts and thongs were already congregating there amid an enveloping aroma of fresh-baked

The São Jorge river

bread, drinking *cachaça* and Coke, talking about work, soccer, and the price of bricks. Women, dressed in brightly-colored T-shirts, skirts, blue jeans, and light sleeveless dresses, paused to chat with Rodrigo's wife Katia before leaving with their warm loaves. One man snacked on an egg-and-coconut *quindim,* another on a manioc cake and pig's ear stewed in black beans. In the afternoon, men would play snooker here, sharing the contents of ice-cold bottles of beer, four to the bottle.

Rodrigo had done well for himself. A light-skinned man in his fifties, he had worked for twenty-five years as a machine operator at the National Motor Factory, collected his indemnity after the shutdown in 1981, and started selling liquor out of his house. In the past few years he had finally started to regard himself as "*melhor de vida*" ("better-off"), a phrase that referred in local usage to families who owned the best-quality houses, including, in addition to the town's merchants, local civil ser-

A bar in São Jorge

vants, white-collar workers, political appointees, and police. Those who were *melhor de vida* were rather less prosperous than those who were "*bom de vida*" ("well-off"), a phrase that applied only to the few wealthy *carioca* doctors, lawyers, and businessmen who had built fancy weekend homes in the hills.

As befitted a family that was *melhor de vida,* Rodrigo's consumed (in addition to the basic fare of black beans and rice) superior cuts of meat three or four times a week, a variety of vegetables, and soft drinks. On occasion Rodrigo even hosted a *churrasco,* barbecuing beef and pork sausages over a brick brazier, accompanied by large quantities of beer. His house could be distinguished from those of his less fortunate neighbors by its façade of sparkling white and blue tiles, decorative iron grills, and costly concrete roof. Inside, the floors were fully-tiled, and the *sala* displayed all-wood furniture, a color television, and a state-of-the-art stereo system. A new refrigerator and blender graced the kitchen, and the bathroom boasted a toilet seat and electric shower head. Rodrigo had even been able to buy an old Volkswagen, which he used to pick up supplies and give rides (for a fee) to the municipal hospital.

Rodrigo and Katia, who had been charter members of the town's Marian Congregation and Apostolate of Prayer back in the 1950s and 1960s, considered themselves "good Catholics." In the early 1980s, however, when the new priest began implementing strange innovations, they had drifted away from the Church. They disliked, in particular, what they called the Church's new "mixture of religion and politics." When the Church returned to sanity, Rodrigo told me, they would return as well.

As soon as Rodrigo saw me enter, he started to rummage through his basket of loaves, looking for one with a darkly toasted crust. I was the only one in town who liked my crusts dark. He had a running joke with me: "You must have the blood of *pretos* [blacks]!" This made him laugh heartily.

Chico was leaning negligently against the counter. He forced a smile, then turned to me and offered a warm hand and a profusion of saints' blessings. "Oh, Sr. Jonas, *que Deus abençõe o Senhor* ("God bless you"). May Saint George protect you."

A *negro* (black) in his seventies, fiery eyes set in a wrinkled face, Chico was one of the first settlers in the region, having come from Minas Gerais as a young man to cut wood in the hills on the southern flank of the valley. At that time he lived near the bottom land, but had been pushed out by speculators later, in the 1940s. He now lived in what locals called "*miseria*." After a prolonged sickness, Chico had remained chronically unemployed, and lacking a supportive extended family survived on a meager pension and odd-jobbing. He lived with his wife in the hills, at the end of a rocky path, in a cramped, rented wattle and thatch box with a dirt floor, rag-covered openings for windows, no indoor plumbing, and a few wooden tables and chairs. He relied on neighbors for water, had no refrigerator, and ate a monotonous diet of rice, beans, and noodles cooked over a wood-burning stove. Often he was unsure about how he was going to get his next meal.

Though Chico considered himself a Catholic, he had little to do with the institutional Church, and rarely took Communion. Every so often he would ask a *benzedeira* to say prayers over his left leg, which had given him chronic pain for years.

"Has the professor been making many visits?"

"And how. Any news?"

"Everything the same, everything old. Next week Angela will come to visit *Se Deus quiser* ("God willing")."

Angela was Chico's eldest daughter, who worked as a maid in Rio. Like other hill people, Chico had been unable to keep any of his children in school past the elementary grades; his sons had moved away to work as menial laborers in Rio, his daughters as domestic servants and then to marry. In the valley, sons build houses on their father's plots, bringing their wives to live with them. "In the hills," Chico said, "all young people want to do is leave."

As Rodrigo was slicing me a piece of Minas cheese, Mario and Rosana entered the bar, accompanied by Geraldo. A boisterous round of greetings ensued.

"Good morning to all!" cried Rosana, a large, humorous, gray-haired, white woman in her late fifties. "How is everyone this morning? I can't stay, I'm just making sure Mario gets his coffee."

Rodrigo dispensed the coffee from a tall thermos. Though already sweetened, Mario thickened it with yet more sugar. "We *mineiros*," Mario professed, throwing me a look of mock seriousness, "must have a little coffee with our sugar."

A balding, literate, light-skinned man in his sixties, Mario had lived in São Jorge for over forty years. The son of a shoemaker in a mid-sized town in Minas Gerais, he had migrated to São Jorge in the 1940s, when the National Motor Factory had sent recruiting trucks to his town. The recruiters had specifically sought out the sons of shopkeepers, who (they assumed) would be better equipped for skilled labor. At the factory, Mario had acquired specialized skills and early promotion, and by the 1950s had become a section leader. Since the factory shut down in 1981 he had worked as an electrician for a big film processing plant, for which he earned a better than average wage. Like other literate, skilled machinists, electricians, and carpenters working for capital-intensive firms, Mario's income was so reliable that he did not have to work second jobs, overtime, or Sunday shifts, and could resist any suggestion that Rosana work for wages.

Mario referred to his family's condition as *"razoável"* ("getting along reasonably"). They usually ate meat once or twice a week, though only lesser flank cuts, smoked pork, sausage, and chicken. Their house, though comfortable, was not as well-appointed as Rodrigo's. Its facade displayed tiles only from the ground to the bottom of its windows, and the remaining exposed plaster was cracked, stained and faded from heat, humidity, and rain. Inside, the floor was of red-waxed cement rather than tile. The best living-room furniture was of wood, but most of it was particle-board, and the TV and stereo were older than in Rodrigo's home. Mario and Rosana had, however, been able to keep their children in school until the eighth grade, giving them the chance to attend vocational school and become skilled workers and technicians.

Mario and Rosana had long been mainstays of São Jorge's Catholic Church. Mario's father had led the Marian Congregation back in Minas, and in the late 1950s he continued his father's tradition by founding the Congregation's first local chapter. Later he spearheaded the construction of the local Catholic chapel and served as its director for over twenty years. In 1982, however, the new priest insisted Mario prove his leadership in a free election. After his defeat by a slate supported by the priest, he had ceased to participate in the local Church.

"I can't stay," Rosana repeated, smiling broadly, "I have to run an errand."

Rosana was always running errands, mainly for the Church, in which she had remained active. Like her husband, she had grown up in Minas Gerais, where her father, a shopowner in a mid-sized town, was a leader of the Catholic League, and her mother belonged to the Apostolate of Prayer. In the late 1940s, soon after migrating with Mario to the São Jorge valley, Rosana had helped establish the local Apostolate of Prayer. A superlative conciliator, she kept her counsel while outwardly accepting most everything her interlocutors said. I had witnessed a spiritist lecturing her on the doctrine of reincarnation, while she nodded politely and said, "well, that's interesting. In the Catholic Church we have something just like that." She read well, and kept abreast of the printed matter that constantly issued from the parish seat; and though she did not agree with many of the young priest's innovations, and especially resented what she regarded as his plot to replace her husband's group "with unprepared people," she had accepted it all with considerable grace, and continued to serve as Minister of the Eucharist and coordinator of catechism and the pastoral of baptism.

Errand or no, she waited a while longer to hear her husband expatiate on bricks, gravel, and asbestos roofing. Like most other men in town, Mario had built his house with his own hands, from digging the foundations to mixing the mortar. His house, also like most homes in town, seemed perpetually under construction. "I am going to add a room," he announced, "for my daughter-in-law, who will be coming soon. And then I've got to put tiles into the kitchen. There's always something to do."

Geraldo nodded knowingly and took a swig of coffee. "Yes, Sr. Mario, that is true. I don't know how long I've had bricks out back, waiting for the mortar. When I can afford it, up they'll go."

A *mulato* in his sixties, with enormous calloused hands, Geraldo always spoke softly and seemed to move under a heavy invisible weight. He was unhappy, I thought, about never having had the chance to develop his reading facility and (as a construction worker for contractors) about never having advanced beyond the status of *servente*. Like other semiskilled workers in the informal and subcontracting sectors, Geraldo was obliged to work double-shifts, overtime, night-shifts, and weekends. His household, he had told me, was not *razoável;* it was just *comendo* ("eating" or "getting by"). When his family ate meat, the meat tended not to be beef but rather pork stomach, fried chicken tails, and the gelatinous interior of beef bones. In contrast to Mario's house, his family's sported no tiles, and the floors were of bare cement. The roof was not concrete, but serrated clay on a wood frame that rotted easily from rain and termites. All the furniture was particle-board, except for a frayed hand-me-down upholstered chair. The television was second-hand and black-and-white, and they owned no stereo. To make ends meet, Geraldo's wife and grown children contributed to the family budget; consequently, his children had not reached the eighth grade, and had been unable to go to vocational school.

Back in Minas Gerais, Geraldo had participated in the Marian Congregation. Since arriving in São Jorge, however, his work as a contract laborer simply left him no time for such pursuits. Although he had gone to Mass for years, with the "new way of being a Church" he had ceased doing even that. Because he could not keep up a high level of participation, he "didn't feel accepted there."

"Oh, Sr. John," he said, "Dona Sebastiana would like the pleasure of a visit today." I assured him I would come by in the afternoon. I knew his wife's housework would be done by then, and we could sit quietly with the doors and windows open as she cut bamboo into sticks for a toy manufacturer.

Mario was beginning to shadowbox with Chico, who was not amused. "Come, Sr. Chico, come show us what a mean *preto* can do!" Chico was edgy, and called for another shot of *cachaça*. As Rodrigo poured, the din from the Assembly of God sent little tremors through the glasses lined up to dry on the counter. Mario could not suppress his irritation.

"Do you know something?" he asked, addressing no one in particular. "Those people aren't interested in God, they're interested in only one thing." He slid his thumb across the pad of his index finger, a sign for filthy lucre. "I heard the other day they were asking for money, like this: 'Who can give five hundred for Jesus?' 'Who can give a thousand for Jesus?'" He imitated the *crentes'* rolling intonation, and Rosana burst into laughter.

"No, Mario," she chided, "They're just praising God in their own way." She was trying hard to stop laughing. "They do it their way, we do it ours."

"No, Dona Rosana," said Geraldo, emboldened by Mario's remark. "With all respect, Dona Rosana, in the Bible it is written, you know, there Jesus says, 'Go into your room, and shut the door, and pray in secret.' No need for all that yelling! God isn't deaf."

Rodrigo nodded. "See how they strut? They want to be seen, so we'll think they're holy, so they can say only they are saved. They say 'Lord, Lord, Lord!' They can say it as much as they want, it's what's inside that counts."

Geraldo chimed in. "That is for people without faith. They used to be Catholics, every one. But they didn't have faith in their church. Something happened to them, a sickness, or whatever, a *crente* comes along and says, 'Jesus will cure you!' But He will cure me in my church as well as there!"

Chico had been waiting to down his shot, which he finally did, cocking his head back flamboyantly. He wiped his mouth, then let his opinion be known. "*Macumba,* that's what it is." The others looked at each other and smiled, and Rosana giggled. "It's the same thing. No difference at all. I've seen it in *macumba* and I've seen it there. Evil spirits come and take you over, those people in there shaking like that, it's the same noise they make in *macumba*."

Mario warmed to the subject. "I've heard that the ones who go there, they all were once in *macumba*. That's how they . . ."

He did not finish the sentence, for Manuel had just walked in. "The peace of the Lord be with you all," he said, grinning broadly, his enormous cheeks rising so high they creased his lower eyelids. This squat *negro* in his sixties, clad as usual in a frayed checked flannel shirt and worn-out dark woolen trousers, might not at first glance strike one as remarkable. True, he wore an old hat and shoes (rather than thongs), showing he was a *crente* of long standing; but there were other old *crentes* who dressed the same way. Perhaps it was the way he moved: rather than walk, he seemed to glide. But no: it was something about his eyes. The left iris was chipped, and always seemed to be looking not only at you, but at someplace else inside of you.

Manuel was the greatest prayer-healer in the region. It was well-known that people came to him from as far away as Rio. Never in a hurry, he refrained from proselytizing, was always ready with a story, and (though entirely illiterate) could open the Bible and read it miraculously. Before devoting himself full time to prayer-healing, he had wielded a pick in a quarry, and had since survived on his pension, contributions from his sons-in-law, and the gifts of his well-to-do recipients of prayer. His family, he said, was only *comendo*. He now lived in a compound with his wife and seven daughters, three of whom lived there with their husbands. The more typical local pattern of patrilocal residence had thus been reversed in his case, for Manuel's sons-in-law had been eager to live close to his charismatic power.

"Oh, Sr. Rodrigo, a loaf of bread, if you please. Light. Good day, Sr. Chico. How are you?" Chico made a nervous, ingratiating gesture. The chanting from next door had not let up. Manuel turned to Mario. "I would beg to differ with you, Sr. Mario. It is not *macumba*."

Mario was embarrassed.

"Sr. Manuel, I didn't mean . . ."

"No, no, that is what many say." His voice was soothing. "But I see the face of the Devil every day, Sr. Mario. Yes, Sr. Chico, you know I do, too. Sr. John here, he has visited these places too, to do his *pesquisa* [research]. I was in that myself, I was a slave to Satan for many years in *macumba*, before Jesus saved me." Rosana jutted out her lower lip and nodded intently. "That noise you hear is a glorious sound, Dona Rosana, it is praise of God."

Mario had been put at ease. "But Sr. Manuel, why do *crentes* yell like that? Is God deaf?"

Manuel chuckled. "No, of course not. God hears everything, and He especially hears the sincere prayers made to Him in our church. And this isn't what it used to be! The Lord does not work in our church the way He used to! A few years back, well, Sr. Mario, you remember how it was! Back then you could hear the Lord working there as far away as the highway! Isn't that so?" Mario nodded. "Now it's in these places, in God is Love and the other one, that House of Blessing, that is where people open themselves to the Lord. But our pastor is good, our church is a good one, and the Lord is working His plan."

Rosana smiled. "Yes, Sr. Manuel, that's true."

Just then the eight o'clock bus to Duque de Caxias arrived, whipping up clouds of dust, and cutting off further theological reflection. Mario left to catch it, and everyone took their leave. I promised Manuel I would drop by later in the day.

I started the walk back to my house. The sun was ablaze, its fire dancing so brightly on television antennae that I could hardly look at them. I was still thinking about the differing opinions of the Assembly of God.

I looked up and saw Gilberto.

"Good morning, Sr. Gilberto!" Gilberto was a literate, fortyish, light-skinned *moreno* who sported a bushy black moustache and a general air of restlessness.

"Good morning, Sr. John!"

As custom required, I offered him some bread, which, also following custom, he declined.

A well-paid crane operator for Petrobrás, Gilberto had attained what he regarded as a *razoável* degree of economic comfort. He was also an active member of the Catholic *comunidade*. Ever since the victory of his slate for the directorate in 1982, he had served the *comunidade* in various capacities: as treasurer, on the construction team, on the pastoral of baptism, on the council, and as head of his neighborhood's Bible circle. He spoke the language of the new Church with fluency. He had never, however, participated in any political or social movement outside the Church itself.

"There is a meeting tomorrow night in the Church," he said. "You should come."

"What about?"

"Oh, this thing, this year, for the Brotherhood Campaign, about how the *negro* is mistreated in Brazil, about slavery and all that. It will be interesting."

"What do you think of the Campaign this year?"

"It is good, it is good . . ." He paused. "Some don't like it. Well, it will be over soon. But it is a project of the Church, and everyone in the *comunidade* should participate, it is good to participate and be *conscientizado*."

Though I was eager to get back quickly and prepare my morning coffee, I knew that it would be considered rude to end a conversation unless obliged by forces beyond my control. To pass the time, I asked Gilberto about the hypnotic prayers emanating from the Assembly of God.

He wrinkled his nose.

"Exploitation. Exploitation, that's what it is. Of ignorant people. These poor people, they will believe anything, they want to be cured of their suffering, so these pastors, they say 'liberation,' but it's really enslavement. Those who are *conscientizado* don't fall for that stuff."

As he spoke, we heard the distant diesel engine of the eight-fifteen bus to the Petrobrás refinery. He took his leave and I began the ascent of the dirt street to my house.

There Dona Luana was, washing clothes in her worn concrete basin. A prodigious *negra* in her sixties, Luana always wore flowing, dark wrap-around skirts, brightly-colored T-shirts and, when at home, armloads of bracelets. The bracelets were a favorite of her *preta velha* (the spirit of an old black slave), who regularly possessed her. Though she had long practiced her mediumship in a *centro* in Rio, Luana now offered consultations only at home. She had worked as a domestic servant for a wealthy Rio family until she married, in her early twenties, a fare-collector for municipal buses. Since his death while she was in her mid-thirties, Luana had worked as a cook in a Rio factory, never re-married, and retired ten years ago due, she said, to high blood pressure. Her only daughter married a man from São Jorge; so Luana had, after retiring, moved to town in order to be closer to her daughter and five grandchildren. She collected a small monthly social security check, received support from her son-in-law, and spent most of her time cooking, washing, and mending for her grandchildren.

It was always difficult simply to say hello or goodbye to Dona Luana. Her talk was filled with litanies of ritual greetings and blessings, and I feared if I grew impatient she would see me as under the influence of bad winds or the evil eye.

"Good morning, Dona Luana."

"Oh, my love, your servant Dona Luana do Carmo blesses you, asks God to open all your ways."

She made a conspiratorial gesture for me to enter her house. She often called me in so her *preta velha* could advise me; such consultations she distinguished from our "interviews," when I would enter with my tape recorder to ask her questions.

Inside, on a shelf above the gas stove, Luana, like other women in town, had arranged her pots from largest to smallest, handles pointed in the same direction. Already at this hour, two covered pots were whistling steam the flavor of onions and carrots. She motioned me into her *sala*. A dagger-shaped plant known as *espada* (sword), set on a side table, protected her home from the evil eye. The radio was tuned to a program that dispensed Catholic prayer-formulae and marital advice. On the cracking plaster walls hung prints of the Last Supper, of Moses parting the Red Sea, and of a castle in a European forest identical to those in dozens of other houses in town. Incense wafted into the *sala* from the adjoining room, where it burned before a table piled with plaster statuettes of saints.

She wanted, she said, to warn me against receiving visits from Delson, a young man who, I believed, suffered from a nervous disorder and came over every so often to drink coffee and chat with me.

"But why, Dona Luana? He's harmless, he's a good person."

She shook her head, smiling at my innocence. "Of course he is. But what he has with him . . . You see all the candy he eats? It is a *criança* [spirit of a child]. And there in your house it will make trouble, it will leave bad influences."

"But Dona Luana, what is the danger?"

She sighed. "It has already started. If you are not careful it will get worse. When the child goes into the house, it brings bad influences, and all sorts of fights can result." Then I understood. My relationship with my wife had been under some strain, and Luana sensed this, especially when Judy arrived in the evening after a two-hour bus ride, and I was still rapt in interviews with Luana herself. I told her I would keep her advice in mind. She nodded knowingly, approving of what she said was my "goodness," and promised to say protective prayers for our house. Then, as I was leaving, I turned again to her.

"Oh, Dona Luana, you hear those prayers from the Assembly of God?"

"Naturally."

"What do you think of them?"

Her eyes narrowed. "Ah, Jonas, they are a problem. They deny what they are. But they know what the truth is."

I asked her to explain.

"They want to be pure," she said. "They want to be white as snow, so they say it is not what it is. They want to look down on us, and say we *negros* are the servants of the Devil! They just want to pretend they are not one of us. But those are the same spirits we receive. No one is pure enough to receive the spirit of God Himself."

"But," I ventured, "the Catholic Church, why does the Church denounce the spirits, either there in the Assembly or in your *umbanda*?"

She paused, and studied me carefully. "You are right, Jonas, they criticize it because they are afraid. If they didn't criticize it, all their churches would close. The priests know the spiritual power of the *negro*. The priests doubt things because they have education. But when I receive a spirit, it's something direct, there's no way for me to doubt. The priests are afraid of a spiritual force that's so powerful."

I was writing furiously in my notebook. When I looked up, Luana's eyes were closed, and she was swaying her head gently. She was on the verge of receiving her *preta velha*, the spirit of an old slave woman. "Come and see the *velha* later," she said.

2

The Religious Arena

São Jorge's religious arena comprises numerous ritual specialists and collectivities deploying a broad variety of discourses. In this chapter, I will explore only the official discourses of a limited part of this arena, that is, the ritual practices and theological claims articulated and enacted by specialists endowed with charismatic or institutional authority by the Catholic church, one of several *umbanda* centers, and the pentecostal Assembly of God church. My remarks are not exhaustive, but are intended to give the reader a general feel for the chief alternatives present in São Jorge's religious arena.

Noninstitutional Catholicism

Catholicism in São Jorge is a palimpsest involving four distinctive constellations of discourse associated with four different kinds of ritual specialist and collectivity, introduced into the area in four successive historical waves. The first men and women to arrive in the São Jorge valley brought with them the noninstitutional Catholicism of Minas Gerais's hinterlands. Having lived distantly from towns, these migrants grew up rarely attending Mass or catechism, and had little experience of organizing collective Catholic rituals such as saint's-day festivals, Christmas *novenas,* and pilgrimages to saints' shrines.[1] "As a

33

child," recalled an early settler, now in his seventies, "where we lived, everything was very far away, the church was far. We'd go to church to baptize children but nothing else. We had a lot of faith, but it was all at home, not in the church."

While these *mineiros'* Catholic identity rested upon their having been baptized in the Catholic church, their religious practice centered on consulting *benzedeiras* ("blessers"), *rezadeiros* ("prayers"), or *curandeiros* ("curers"), men or women who offered individualized cures for sickness and defenses against evil eye.[2] These specialists generally possessed a store of arcane knowledge, had mastered a few Latin prayers, and sometimes were clairvoyant.[3] A supplicant would visit the *benzedeira* in her home, and use the opportunity to discuss the afflictions, from arthritis to abusive husbands, that were distressing her. Then the *benzedeira* would tell her caller to have faith in God, make a sign of the cross on her forehead, recite a prayer, and burn incense to chase away evil influences. These gestures were *free*, because "what God has given freely, so must man." Still, satisfied petitioners would often reward *benzedeiras* with small gifts.

To this day, the *benzedeira* is unique among Catholic ritual specialists in her willingness to deal with evil eye, and her unwillingness to pass judgment on the sufferers who come to her. This is in contrast to institutional Catholic ritual specialists such as lay ministers, who believe that those who suffer from evil eye are either deluded or bring the misfortune upon themselves. "If you are modest and humble," declared an elderly scion of the Church, "a good Christian, no one is going to attack you [with evil eye]." *Benzedeiras,* in contrast, not only refrain from placing moral opprobrium on victims of evil eye, but on its perpetrators as well. "They can't help it," they say. These religious specialists counsel their supplicants to respond to evil eye not through countermeasures, but by protective prayers and by following the Golden Rule. *Benzedeiras* have thus long served a critical function among Catholics: while facilitating the articulation of inter-household tensions, they present no threat to their institutional Catholic petitioners' effort to maintain the nonretributive stance required by Christian ethics.

Benzedeiras are, however, disappearing in São Jorge. They are now beset on all sides, receiving attacks not only from pre-Conciliar Catholics, but also from *crentes* and Catholics steeped in post-Conciliar discourse—all of whom accuse *benzedeiras* of being practitioners of the dreaded Afro-Brazilian religion of *macumba*. Fear of such accusations makes *benzedeiras* maintain a low profile, and prompts potential ones either to seek other avenues of spiritual expression, such as charity, or, in some cases, to renounce religious specialization altogether.

The Apostolate of Prayer:
The Pre-Conciliar Church

Starting in the 1940s, the migrants from small-town Minas Gerais who arrived in São Jorge brought with them the tradition of lay associations closely affiliated with the pre-Vatican II Church. Organizations such as the Daughters of Maria, the Catholic League, the Marian Congregation, and the Apostolate of Prayer coordinated festivals for patron saints, constructed chapels, prepared hymns for Mass, kept the chapel clean and candles lit, organized visits to the sick, and collected charity.[4] In São Jorge, for example, Mario carried on his father's tradition by founding a local chapter of the Marian Congregation, the group that in the 1960s led the effort, through the painstaking collection of donations of material and labor, to build the town's chapel—as many leaders still say proudly—"brick by brick."

The chapel is certainly something to be proud of. The visitor must pass through a metal gate at street level, climb a steep incline, and negotiate forty cement steps before facing the plastered-brick building with corrugated tin roof and white-peaked façade. The chapel is breezy and spacious. Its chalky blue walls are lined by paneless windows, through which birds and moths fly in the evenings to circle bare, dangling lightbulbs. When filled to capacity, about two hundred and fifty people can fit into sixteen pews. A life-size cross is bolted to the back wall, directly behind a simple table set on a dais. To the left is a lectern equipped with a microphone that rarely works; to the right are the small wooden sacristy and a statuette of Our Lady of Aparecida on a pedestal; and in the left-hand corner, a statue of the town's patron saint, nearly life-size, raises a hand in silent benediction.

The Marian Congregation lapsed into desuetude in the 1970s (partly as a result of the Vatican-II Church's abandonment of such associations), but the Apostolate of Prayer is still going strong. This small group of ten to fifteen married, older Catholic women periodically meet to pray, upon invitation, in the homes of afflicted members of the *comunidade*. Women become involved through kinship or friendship ties to established mem-

The Catholic *capela* of São Jorge

bers; some simply inherit the role from their mothers. The Apostolate is thus a way simultaneously to associate with other Catholic women and fulfill one's Christian duty to perform charity.

The elderly women of the Apostolate were socialized into pre-Conciliar Catholicism and to this day continue to articulate its vision. At the heart of this vision is a conception of human agency as driftwood on a sea of divine design. "You lay all your plans," one of the women of the Apostolate said to me, "that you are going to build a fence, say. But if God doesn't want you to build that fence, you'll never build it." These women regard it as their duty to demonstrate resignation in the face of affliction. "Suffering," one of them said, "is God's way of testing our faith." The highest pre-Conciliar praise goes to the person who, like Mary, embraces the *via crucis,* the shouldering of the cross, and endures suffering unflinchingly. "Faith," one elderly Catholic woman insisted, "will sustain you through suffering and tears. God gives patience to the faithful."

The women of the Apostolate rely extensively on intermediaries to God. Beyond asking for prayer from the Apostolate, it has long been customary for pre-Conciliar Catholics to ask for special prayers from the congregation during Mass at the moment of *intenções,* or from those present at collective prayers in neighbors' homes for high holidays, saints' days, births, weddings, and funerals. In devotions to saints, the women of the Apostolate commit themselves to pray to particular saints for protection and support. Such prayers are usually simple requests (*pedidos*), but sometimes take the form of a *promessa*.[5] *Promessas* are often interpreted as based in the belief that one can "trade with God." Actually, *promessa*-makers believe saints grant miracles not in exchange for the promised deed, but as a reward for the good will, suffering, and patience that preceded it. One woman in the midst of excruciating labor pains made a *promessa* to Our Lady of Aparecida that if she would grant her a successful childbirth at home, she would baptize the infant in white and blue clothing, the colors associated with Our Lady. Her wish fulfilled, she dutifully carried out the *promessa*. I asked her whether she would have done so had her request gone unsatisfied. "Of course not," she replied. "That would mean that Our Lady had seen me as unworthy."

The women of the Apostolate strongly denounce *benzedeiras*. In part, they are moved to this by what they regard as *benzedeiras*' short-term promises to relieve suffering. These promises, in their view, subvert the *via crucis*. "They go there," one woman lamented, "thinking everything is going to be solved quickly, but nothing is solved quickly." The women of the Apostolate are committed to institutional Catholicism's effort to wrench the Golden Rule out of the goal-oriented contexts of neighborhood relations and interpersonal politics, and to freeze it instead into the status of an absolute, universal duty to be followed irrespective of consequences. In contrast, the *benzedeira*'s advice to follow the Golden Rule is little more than a tactical matter to avoid evil eye. "If you treat your neighbor well," said a *benzedeira*, "you will have nothing to fear from him." While the *benzedeira* sees fighting the evil eye as a way of restoring social peace, pre-Conciliar Catholics see it as a moral crusade. The women of the Apostolate simply cannot forgive *benzedeiras* for what they regard as the *benzedeiras*'s distortion of brotherly love.

The Post-Conciliar Church

In the late 1960s, a young priest named Aniceto began giving sermons in São Jorge imbued with a new vision, and a new institution arrived on the scene. The *cursilho de cristandade* ("little course on Christianity"), introduced into São Jorge in the late 1960s,[6] revolved around a weekend-long retreat with an encounter-group atmosphere, whose initiates formed Bible circles to disseminate *cursilho* songs and the *cursilhista* reading of the Bible. That reading, and the new vision of the priests, embraced the conclusions reached by the bishops assembled at the Vatican Council between 1962 and 1965. The Council embraced the Enlightenment view that human freedom was at the center of both earthly and divine history. In Conciliar orthodoxy, God is an entirely benevolent father content to let His children discover Christ and commit themselves to following His example of their own free will. In contrast to the pre-Conciliar Church, post-Vatican II orthodoxy declares that God feels no need to test His children's love, nor to require them to prove themselves through the *via crucis*. Post-Conciliar Catholics thus take a step beyond the pre-Conciliar reluctance to speak of evil eye, and question its reality altogether. In the pre-Conciliar view, wicked people manipulate evil forces and weak people succumb to them; for the post-Conciliar Catholic, God permits no such forces to test His children.[7]

It would be a mistake, however, to conclude that by turning away from the *via crucis* and theologizing external evil forces out of existence, Conciliar doctrine aimed to lighten the moral burden of the faithful. Father Aniceto feared that belief in evil eye failed to place the entirety of moral blame squarely where it belonged: on the shoulders of the individual believer. He declared the Devil identical to selfishness, deceit, hypocrisy, and greed. Or, as one initiate of the *cursilho* explained, "If I always said I did wrong because the Devil made me, that's just running away from responsibility." It was in the fertile soil of this commitment to human responsibility that the progressive Catholic vision would later grow.

If the Devil is simply the equivalent of bad will, then rather than seeking protection against mystical social danger, one should pray for one's own and one's neighbor's release from un-Christian sentiments. While the pre-Conciliar Catholic turns to God in an attitude of submission and self-renunciation, the post-Conciliar Catholic learns to see God as working through human freedom. Timidity thus ceases to be a virtue. Rather than turn in fear to spiritual or human intermediaries, proclaimed Aniceto and the *cursilho,* one should pray self-reliantly and directly to God, Christ, and to Mary if necessary. Aniceto reminded his parishioners of Jesus' summons to "enter your room, and with the door shut and in secret, pray to God" (Matthew 6:6). These prayers, he urged, should above all involve requests for the strength and courage to accomplish goals designed by humans themselves.

A logical corollary of this view was the decentering of the saints.[8] While the *cursilhistas* acknowledged the ability of saints to intercede for the living, they stressed the primacy of devotion to Christ. They were especially critical of the *promessa*, which they saw as reinforcing a vision of ritual efficacy, fear, and obligation rather than one of sincerity, conscience, and freedom. What saints desired rather than *promessas*, they said, was imitation. Aniceto gained a reputation in São Jorge for opposing saint-worship, by encouraging churchgoers who intended to make pilgrimages to saints' shrines to make local donations to charity instead. "This way," he had said, "you really please the saint. The saint wants you to imitate her."

Aniceto and the *cursilhistas* reserved their bitterest criticism for pre-Conciliar Catholics' belief that saints could become physically present in their images. One member of the Apostolate of Prayer held that figurines had to be blessed by the priest in order to "be open to the saint," while another compared saints' statues to "channels" or "lenses" of the saint's spirit. In contrast, the *cursilhistas* proclaimed all gestures, images, and words to be mere signs of an inner commitment to follow Christ, not objective conductors of spiritual power. Saints' images, therefore, were of no greater significance than photographs of loved ones: the good Catholic should regard such images as nothing more than mnemonic devices and aids to faith. Aniceto therefore refused to bless images and removed many of them from the *capela*.

The *Comunidade de Base*: The Liberationist Church

In 1981, the CNBB (Conferência Nacional dos Bispos do Brasil) created the diocese of Duque de Caxias, and appointed as its caretaker the well-known progressive bishop, Dom Mauro Morelli.[9] Morelli promptly installed throughout the diocese priests trained in liberation theology. In particular, he removed the old priest from Duque de Caxias's fourth district, and in 1982 replaced him with Father Cosme, a stripling not yet thirty years old, fresh from his training at the Pontifical Catholic University in Rio de Janeiro.

From the moment of his arrival, Father Cosme worked to instill in his parishioners what he called "*consciência*," a key component of which was "self-valorization," the self-esteem that allows people to act on their own behalf. The first step toward teaching self-valorization was the replacement of the authoritarian parish by democratic, self-governing communities of believers.[10] On the theory that smaller local groups were more democratic, he divided the old *capela* into four *comunidades,* and insisted that local people attend church in the one closest to their homes. Cosme went on to replace the old appointive church directorate with elected councils. All decisions of the council were henceforth subject to ratification by the *assembléia,* that is, by all participating, baptized Catholics in good standing. Finally, Cosme decentralized tasks to a whole host of subgroups within the *comunidades,* including pastorals of baptism, marriage, and liturgy; the mother's club and youth group; committees of the tithe, construction works, and festivities; and various *ad hoc* groups formed around the preparation for and participation in ritual events.

By holding an election for the Church directorate, Cosme displaced entrenched leaders with people who had never before acted in this capacity. By multiplying the number of subgroups that comprised the *comunidade* and insisting that each subgroup have its own coordinator, he took an important stride toward putting an end to the concentration of tasks and authority. By at least one measure, São Jorge's democratizers could be proud of their accomplishment: whereas in 1980 the Church had been run at the local level by a cabal of no more than a dozen people, by 1987 the affairs of the *comunidade* were seen to by a company of no fewer than forty.

Cosme sought to democratize both administrative and spiritual authority. It is true that Aniceto had already devolved some authority to the laity in the form of ministries of the Eucharist.[11] Cosme, however, went much further in his democratizing project. Before his arrival, lay ministers had been appointed by the priest; now, he insisted, they should be elected by the *comunidade* assembly. Before, they had been obliged to attend a difficult preparatory course that lasted for months; now they needed only a brief, weekend-long orientation. Before, they only distributed pre-consecrated communion wafers; now they offered homilies and could, *in loco clerensis,* perform baptisms, marriage ceremonies, and last rites.

Spiritual self-valorization was not limited to the lay ministry. At baptisms and weddings, Cosme sought to communicate *comunidade*

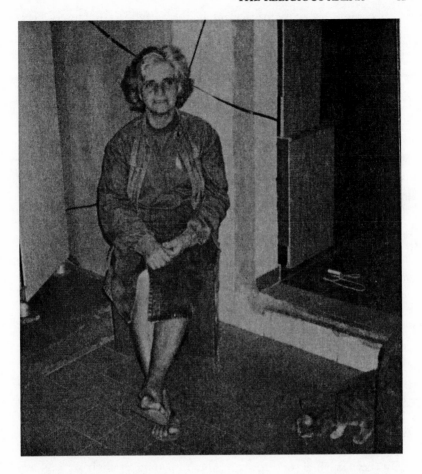

A leader of the *comunidade*

members' spiritual sovereignty by calling upon the whole congregation to extend hands with him in blessing new-born infants or newly-married couples. This is also why, like post-Conciliar clergy in general, he did not encourage devotion to saints. "The more you rely on the saint," he said, "the more you devalue your own power." The phrase "we are all saints" began to appear in *comunidade* songs, sermons, and guidesheets; and on the day in May when children in catechism classes traditionally crowned the statue of the Virgin Mary, Cosme insisted on substituting an old, living woman in its place.

But the self-esteem nurtured in these ways was not an end in itself; rather, it was a means by which the "conscious" Catholic could commit to becoming an active participant in the Catholic community. This meant maintaining a high level of participation in one or more of the *comunidade*'s subgroups. In practice, this criterion became the most visible means by which the *comunidade* marked its boundaries. Though there were thousands of people in São Jorge who called themselves "Catholic," those who failed to participate according to the new standards found their very identity as Catholics placed into doubt. As one *comunidade* member remarked,

You see someone and you ask his religion, he'll tell you he's Catholic. But if you ask him how many times a year he goes to Mass, how many groups in the church he goes to, whether he participates in a reflection group . . . if he frequents the youth group, if he goes to meetings of the council of the *comunidade* . . . I mean, he'll never have consciousness of all that, because he isn't really anything, he's nothing!

The importance of participation in defining *comunidade* membership (in contrast to the days when anyone who had been baptized could consider him- or herself a full member of the Catholic church) is well-illustrated by how it came to influence access to the sacraments. If an infant's parents and godparents were not already reputable participants in the Church, for them to baptize the child they had now to participate for three months in the *comunidade*'s subgroups and a series of preparatory courses.[12] One woman who had grown up in São Jorge but had moved away recently to get married, wanted to baptize her daughter in São Jorge's *capela*, but the local pastoral of baptism refused, "because she no longer participated in the *comunidade*."

The new standard of participation has transformed what used to be a universalist, all-absorbing institution into an increasingly sectoral, exclusivist one. "They are just like the *crentes*," one man who had drifted away from the Church told me. "The Catholic [church] is for everyone. But they want to have it a closed group, like the *crentes* . . . Next thing they'll want people to carry cards." Church leaders allow little latitude to those who wish to attend services of *crente* prayer-healers or *umbanda* mediums. If word gets out that a member of the *comunidade* has frequented either of these, he or she must either move quickly to quash the rumor, or suffer the consequences in gossip and lower standing in church. "It is one thing or the other," said Rosana. "It used to be that someone could call themselves a 'Catholic' but still go to these other things. That has to stop."

Beyond self-valorization and participation, *consciência* means thinking about evil and misfortune in new ways. According to Cosme, the conscious Catholic should come to the conclusion that sins like adultery, prostitution, murder, and robbery must no longer be regarded merely at the individual level, but must be placed in the context of the larger social sins of inequality, injustice, and class oppression. Furthermore, conscious Catholics cannot rest content with seeing misery as an individual matter, but have to recognize society's responsibility both for creating and relieving it. To help instill these views, Cosme called upon his flock to cease asking forgiveness for individual sins, and to do penance instead, in weekly public confessionals during Mass, for sins such as failure to help abandoned youths, forgetting those without land or bread, selfishness, and lack of fraternity.

If the most important sins are selfishness and individualism, their best antidote is the nurturance of fraternity. Thus Cosme sought to introduce, both in Masses and distributions of the host by lay ministers (known as *celebrações*), ritual elements that would encourage the efflorescence of social sentiments. During the intonation of "Our Father," for example, congregants would henceforth hold each other's hands; during the offering, everyone would greet each other with a handshake. In special *celebrações*, Cosme called for loaves of bread to be passed around church, and for each congregant to tear off a crumb.

Truly conscious Catholics, however, could not rest content with ritual gestures: they had to translate the value of fraternity into everyday practice. They could no longer take comfort in occasional almsgiving or pious prayers, but should join with their *comunidade* to struggle against social evil. Ideally, conscious Catholics would participate in struggles for social change, such as neighborhood organizations, labor and rural unions, and political parties. Cosme encouraged the formation of a regional land pastoral, to provide financial, technical, and advisory support to the oppositional faction of a union representing smallholders and agricultural day laborers. He also urged *comunidade* members to participate in neighborhood improvement associations. While the *comunidade* of São Jorge was typical of the region by not coming to dominate the local neighborhood association, since Cosme's arrival four neighborhood associations elsewhere in the fourth district have been led by *comunidade* Catholics.

These, then, were the elements of *consciência*. I have already mentioned several of the ritual gestures through which Cosme tried to instill these elements in his parishioners. For much of the time I knew him, however, Cosme believed, along with most other progressive priests in the mid-1980s, that the best way to teach *consciência* was through rational reflection upon selected Biblical passages, under the careful guidance of the Church. This reflection involved the "connection of faith and life": that is, reading the Bible in the light of worldly experience, and vice versa. According to liberation theology such reflection is most effective when carried out in small, intimate groups. Theologians like Carlos Mesters and Leonardo Boff insist that Bible circles are the ideal places for connecting faith with life, for discussing personal experiences in the light of the Bible.[13] Cosme, like other progressive clergy, regarded the neighborhood-based Bible circles as the most important vehicles for raising consciousness.

When Cosme came on the scene, there were already four Bible groups in São Jorge, but these were very different from the Bible circles he hoped to create. In Cosme's view, the circles established by the *cursilhistas* were too large and unwieldy to serve as cells of consciousness-raising. He divided each group (of between fifty and eighty affiliators) into smaller ones of about twenty members, and restricted membership to immediate neighbors. Since the early 1980s, three circles have stopped meeting. Now, each of São Jorge's remaining five Bible circles enjoys a core membership of about ten people, with another ten or so coming and going as a function of the dynamism of leadership.

The format of Bible-circle meetings is straightforward. The groups assemble once a week in rotation among members' houses. After some chit-chat, hymn-singing, and prayers for the sick, the group's coordinator reads the week's Biblical passage (assigned by the parish), then comments, following the parish guidesheet's interpretation. The coordinator asks all present to comment. Commentary either repeats what the coordinator has already said or articulates general lessons such as the importance of thanking God, having greater faith, loving each other, helping the needy, being charitable, accepting suffering, and avoiding slipping from Church.

Although Cosme's vision of the *comunidade,* with all of its discursive, ritual, and institutional innovations, represents an important break with the past, it remains the site of equally important continuities with deeply-rooted traditions of Catholic discourse and practice. Despite the progressive Church's commitment to democratization, for example, the power of the liberationist priest remains extensive. Thus Cosme retains control over consecration of the host, and influences every detail of liturgy, scheduling, and short- and long-term goals of the *comunidade.* When, for instance, Cosme ruled against members attending more than one reflection group, they generally went along, though few understood the decree's rationale. In another case, when Cosme substituted an old woman for the figure of Mary, though many members of the *comunidade* took offense, none raised open objections. Furthermore, it is Cosme who decides whether new *comunidades* should be formed; it is he, not members, who recruit leaders and call organizing meetings. And when he calls "consultative" meetings, all too often (as he readily admitted to me) he is simply presenting for confirmation positions already formed at the diocesan level.

A further continuity between liberationists and the rest of the Catholic fold is the rejection of the notion that a gap exists between the secular world and the Church. To be a Catholic of any kind means believing that God does not apply a test of absolute virtue but uses rather a sliding scale, as Weber has observed, "compatible with average human qualifications."[14] For Catholics, salvation does not depend on the total eradication of sin from life, but on recognizing one's sins and engaging in a sincere effort to eradicate them. Salvation is thus a gradual, life-long maturation. As one Catholic woman put it, "It takes your whole life to be saved."[15]

The Catholic Church has thus never required of its adepts a rupture with their worldly identities. Rather, it has always implicitly accepted that its communicants carry much of their worldly identities with them into church. "I am a sinful creature," a Catholic woman proclaimed, "and I am sinful in Church too!" This is why Catholics are always suspicious of the claims to radical change inherent in conversion and spirit possession. Cosme sermonized that

the *crentes* think of everything as day or night. You're in nighttime, then you just say "Hallelujah, Jesus!" and suddenly you're in the day. We don't think of things that way. For us, we are always in the half-darkened hours just before sunrise: not all light, not all dark, but full of the promise of day.

"No one is transformed," concluded another Catholic, "we all continue the same way as before. The *crentes,* they think that if you have been a murderer, all you have to do is say 'I accept Jesus' and all that is gone forever. No! People don't change overnight."

Liberation theology places the most recent spin on this deeply-rooted Catholic notion that the world and church stand in a continuous relation with each other. The call to "connect faith and life" teaches the adept, whether in church or Bible circle, to avoid regarding him- or herself as entering what Victor Turner called a liminal state in which social relations are suspended, but rather to *remember* one's worldly status, role, and position. It is precisely in one's status as neighbor, worker, or family member that one is expected to "connect faith and life."

The belief in continuity between secular and religious identities shaped patterns of recruitment to the Church both before and after Cosme's arrival in 1982. The Apostolate of Prayer, for example, recruited its members and petitioners through established Catholic identity, friendship, and kinship ties, and a shared aspiration to the respectability that accompanies being identified with a long-standing Catholic lay organization. Indeed, for some, membership is largely symbolic: they store their initiatory ribbons at home and call themselves members of the Apostolate, but remain otherwise inactive in the organization. Similarly, participants in the *comunidade*'s Bible circles are recruited not according to the logic of inverting secular identities, but of continuing them; not by the leveling experience of affliction, but through preexisting social criteria such as growing up in a Catholic family, being respectable members of the community, and residing near a *capela*. Only regular churchgoers and their friends and kin are normally invited to participate in the circles, while alcoholics and ne'er-do-wells, known frequenters of *umbanda*, or those with bad blood with core members, can expect *de facto* exclusion.

The Catholic notion of a life-long, and potentially always unfinished, salvific project has been transmitted to one of the most versatile terms in the liberationist lexicon: "*caminhada*." Literally, the term means a march or path. The *caminhada* carries the connotation of pilgrimage: a hardship carried out in the spirit of self-sacrifice and love. Thus the image of walking the path applies simultaneously to individual spiritual growth, the *comunidade*'s collective development toward greater love and solidarity, and the physical displacement of either in efforts to make the world accord more closely to brotherly love. This multivocalic metaphor is invoked to respond to any and all efforts to point out contradictions and ambiguities in progressive practice: for the Church, it is said, is "still *caminhando*."

Finally, standards for being a conscious Catholic perpetuate, in disguised form, the perennial Catholic allocation of responsibility to people for either causing, being insufficiently resigned to, or prolonging their own suffering. Progressive Catholics, though valuing resistance over resignation, carry on the pre-Conciliar tradition of judging the victim: for although they regard the ultimate cause of affliction as sociostructural, they see its immediate cause in the sufferer's lack of *consciência*. Is someone mentally troubled, disturbed, depressed? Is she having trouble with her husband? Does she feel tired and unable to participate? Is she or her children chronically ill? Is she afraid of evil eye or that she may be subject to demons? In all such cases, members of the *comunidade* say the problem lies in the failure of the person to "participate" and thereby to become "more *consciente*." As one woman said when another became angry because her mentally disturbed child was not receiving visits from the *comunidade*: "What can we do? That's not a matter for us. He should be more *consciente*." The pattern is summed up, albeit in an uncharacteristically harsh manner, by the remark of a woman speaking about people massacred in Guatemala: "What can they expect? They are so passive, they are not struggling to defend themselves."

Becoming an *Umbanda* Medium

Because of *umbanda*'s stigma in and around São Jorge, it is difficult to reconstruct its local history. It is possible to infer, however, that the first local mediums appeared in São Jorge during the 1960s with the first families from Rio de Janeiro, a state with a long and deep experience of *umbanda*. In the early 1960s, a *negro* named Tiago arrived from Rio's hinterland to work for a contractor, and started an *umbanda* center in the hills with the help of his wife and six children. Shortly thereafter, a *mãe de santo* ("mother of the saint") moved from a Rio shantytown to São Jorge's hills with her children and husband, and started an *umbanda* center there as well. Now, locals attend these centers, but more commonly they travel by bus to other towns, where they can frequent centers in greater anonymity.

Umbanda is a religion based on a karmic model of spiritual purification, the details of which are known mainly to *chefes* and *ogãs*,[16] that combines elements of Kardecist spiritualism, Catholicism, and *candomblé*.[17] Central to *umbanda*'s theology is the image of the world as lying beneath an astral plane, stratified into numerous levels of increasing spiritual purity. One's place after death in the astral plane is determined by one's deeds during life: the more good one does, the purer and less indebted one is after death, and the more quickly one becomes a "spirit of light."[18] Those still burdened after death with social debts continue to wander on earth as spirits "without light." All such spirits are given the chance, through reincarnation and the performance of charity, to increase their purity and rise in the astral plane.

Like *candomblé*, *umbanda* calls down possessing spirits characterized by human-like emotions and appetites. Unlike *candomblé*, the spirits that descend have all lived on earth and return to fulfil "missions." Whereas in *candomblé* the great African *orixás* such as Oxossí, Ogun, and Shango descend, in *umbanda* such deities, having no need to purify themselves, have no reason to descend. If one of them did try to descend, according to one informant, "it would kill the medium," because, as a human, the medium "isn't pure enough to receive it."[19]

Guias, meanwhile, are spirits that are less pure than the *orixás*, for they were all once alive. It is common to see petitioners chat with possessed mediums in an informal way, while mediums speak of their *guias* in an intimate, familiar manner. To purify themselves, the *guias* descend to perform charity, in the form of advice, divination, purification, protection, cure, and justice. They are, therefore, entirely dependent on the living: on mediums to serve as their vehicles, and on petitioners to allow them to practice charity.[20]

As an ethical system, *umbanda* conceives of the cosmos in shades of gray. Because *guias* are forever trying to purify themselves, they fall not into neat boxes of good or evil, but along a moral continuum. As one medium put it, "All [of the spirits] can do either good or bad. There are spirits of light that work alongside the spirits of the shadows." The priority of *guias* is to help people in the short run; absolute standards of good and evil are best left to God. The *guia* expects no more than the simple respect due to the elder, the wiser, or the more powerful, and will thus attend even an unrepentant murderer who shows respect.

The three main categories of *guias* are *caboclos*, *pretos velhos*, and *exús*. The *caboclos*, often conceived of as the purest of the *guias*, are spirits of romanticized Indians.[21] When a medium is possessed by a *caboclo*, he or she remains standing, makes loud whooping noises, clasps and unclasps her forehead, gestures expansively, and smokes cigars. Mediums and frequenters associate the *caboclos* with raw power and the forces of nature: the hunt, warfare, courage, vanity, creatures of the forest, waterfalls and rivers, the sun, moon, and stars. These spirits are highly intelligent and especially gifted in concocting natural cures and medicines. Yet because *caboclos* are "uncivilized," they must be tamed and taught their duty to perform charity.

The *pretos velhos* ("old blacks") are the spirits of deceased slaves. These spirits occupy the lowest ranked line, or spiritual category: that of "dead souls," sometimes referred to as the "African" line. *Pretos* are often said to be less spiritually evolved than the *caboclos,* in part because of the supposed racial inferiority of Africa. The respect due their age and the lack of parental tension in their role are signaled by the fact that one addresses them as aunts, uncles, or grandparents. *Velhos* are humble, loving, kind, gentle, and patient. They walk slowly and hunch-backed, sit down in order to consult with their petitioners, speak in soft, stereotyped slave Portuguese, and puff on pipes. Diana Brown has suggested that "the *preto* has a white soul, has been acculturated. He represents the selection of servitude over freedom, humility over pride, the transformation of African into Brazilian."[22]

The *exú* has usually been interpreted as the embodiment of the marginal *negro,* the petty thief, the trickster, the flim-flam man, what Brazilians call the *malandro.*[23] Before the start of every *umbanda* session, these spirits are placated with offerings and exhorted to leave the *terreiro.* Yet the *exú*'s identity is more complex than this, as is hinted at by the fact that they are addressed, as are patrons, by the term "*compadre.*" Like patrons, *exús* work on the basis of negative reciprocity dressed in generalized garb, having little patience for those who fail to live up to their end of patron-client bargains. "The only spirit you really get indebted to," one frequenter of *umbanda* explained, "are the *exús.* If you promise him something, you have to give it. If you don't, he'll take it anyway. Let's say the *exú* asked for a glass of rum; if you don't give it to him, he'll do everything for you to satisfy him." The *exú* thus personifies both potential and actual negative reciprocity, the social relation that undergirds both patronage and extortion. That is why the *exú* is so subversive. As keeper of crossroads, the *exú* reveals the basic forked hypocrisy of Brazilian society, its efforts to deny the *sub rosa* equivalence of patronage and theft.[24]

All spirits depend upon human mediums. These, in turn, as suggested by the double meaning of *medium* in Portuguese, serve as "halves" or "half-way points" between the human and spiritual realms. The medium has less to say in the matter than does the spirit: it is the *guia* that decides whom it will use as its "horse." Whoever resists the *guia* suffers violent collisions between their own spirit and the *guia,* which may result in sickness and even death. The spirits can be jealous, possessive, quick to punish those who fail to meet obligations, and capable of treachery. Some mediums have been known to reject their *guias'* authority altogether and seek to escape them. The human spirit thus always remains wary of the *guia,* and must absent itself during the *guia*'s descent, for

An *umbanda* medium

were there to be a side-by-side meeting the tension would be too great. This is one of the reasons mediums cannot remember what transpires during possession episodes.

Mediums distinguish between having mediumship "by birth" and "by vocation." An *umbandista* parent says a child has mediumship "by birth" when he or she receives spiritual dreams or displays clairvoyance, such as warning that a pot is about to fall from the stove. In families with traditions of mediumship, children, especially female children, begin at eight or nine years of age to accompany women of ascendant generations to a *centro*. The youths may not, however, don the white garments of the *terreiro* until they reach thirteen or fourteen. Fully developing mediumship can take years, as one learns basic cosmology, the *pontos*, how to control possession behavior, and how to fulfil obligations to the spirit.

Terreiros are ritual places that generally include the *mãe de santo*'s residence, smaller edifices that house shrines and ritual paraphernalia (*pegis*), and a large, central building for the cult. The membership can include anywhere from a handful to several hundred mediums, depending on location, leadership, and history. Stress is laid among mediums on vertical social relations. Thus, while mediums do not address each other with sibling terms, they are called "sons" and "daughters of the saint," and the *chefe* "father" or "mother of the saint." In a given *centro*, the visitor encounters mediums at various stages of development: some novices, some still developing, some seasoned and fully developed. The most recent mediums jerk uncontrollably at the onset of possession; more mature mediums receive their *guias* so easily it is sometimes impossible to tell when the spirit has entered them. The most developed medium tends to be the *chefe* of the *terreiro*, the one who receives the highest-ranked and most powerful *guias*. The *guia* gains entry into the medium's body through the head; indeed, the process of developing mediumship is often referred to as "breaking the head." The medium thus regards her head as sacred, and remains forever vigilant as to who touches it. This is one reason mediums steer clear of *crente* healers, for they know these adversaries seek to lay hands upon their heads.

The obligations mediums carry out to maintain good relations with their *guia* range from wearing the *guia*'s favorite colors, to eating its favorite foods and avoiding those it dislikes, to saying special daily prayers. Believing the body to be the locus of the flow of good and bad fluids, mediums abstain from sex before sessions, doff their shoes to allow the positive fluids of the earth to enter from below, and dress in clothing purified by censers. All such ritual observances fortify mediumship by keeping at bay negative influences and vibrations that might weigh one down with bad burdens, or close one's path to the *guia*. Mediums must also avoid wrongdoing, not because God forbids it, but because it may create enemies and resentments, which in turn produce the bad vibrations that render mediumship difficult. A *guia* concerned by its medium's conduct sends warnings in the form of stomach aches, minor accidents, or more serious afflictions. "The *guias* want you to be obedient," explained a medium, "so you can be a strong horse."

Most mediums regard themselves as Catholics, and see no inconsistency between their beliefs and practices and those of the Roman Church. "Jesus Christ was a great spirit," one medium told me. "He incorporated on earth, he became flesh, just like the *guias*. There is no difference." Many mediums say that Catholic saints are spirits of light who now occupy the astral realm and are too pure to descend into mediums. Instead, they receive messages from the *guias* and transmit them to God. Where saints fit in the spiritual hierarchy varies according to informant, but generally they exist more or less as equals to the great African *orixás*. Some mediums have syncretized *orixás* and saints altogether, claiming that they are the same beings. "Saint George," one medium told me, "is just the white man's name for Ogun."

Mediums are, however, aware that many Catholics do not wish to regard them as their coreligionists. This they attribute to snobbery, fear, and ignorance. The object of their greatest irritation are the priests who denounce them. "They are just jealous," said one medium, "because they have all their learning, and that has killed the spiritual part. They want to get it back, and have it like us. They know we are Catholics; they just are afraid people will listen to us and not them." Even worse are the *crentes*, who themselves receive *guias* but claim they are receiving the Holy Spirit. "That is nonsense," a medium told me.

They know it is not the Holy Spirit. If it were, do you know what that would do? That would kill them. Ogun, the saints, not even they can descend without threatening the life of a medium, so how can it be the Holy Spirit? [But why do the *crentes* say that what you do is the work of the Devil?] Hah! I know they say that. They say that all the time. The Enemy! The Dog! [laughs] They know they are the same as us. Like Manuel, he used to be a medium. All those *crentes*, they used to be in *umbanda*. So they know what it is. [Then why are they rejecting you now?] Don't you see? They want to be better than us. They are going up in the world. It is better to be a *crente,* people accept you more. So they can keep receiving the spirit, but now they can be accepted. That's all.

CONSULTING WITH THE SPIRITS

Once the medium has started to develop, she receives her spirits during sessions and assists all those seeking aid. It is common for people to develop loyalties to a single medium or *terreiro.* Before sessions, on the compounds' clearings, regulars are easily identifiable by their exchange of hugs and kisses. Mediums refuse to call these people "clients"; they speak of them instead as "visitors," "onlookers," "guests," or "people who come to consult." Anyone is welcome, as long as they come in good faith. Those who come out of mere curiosity, or to ridicule or proselytize, bring negative vibrations and interfere with the *centro's* work.

Despite much variation among *umbanda* centers in size, constellations of spirits, and degree of syncretism with Catholicism, the ritual structure of sessions remains fairly constant. They begin in the early evening, or, on weekends, in mid-afternoon. After socializing in the compound's clearing (some *terreiros* sell soft drinks), visitors approach the main building, cross themselves, and enter the section designated for them. In one *centro,* this meant passing into a room with dark blue walls, then sitting on long pews facing a lacy light-blue curtain. Women and men sat on opposite sides of a central aisle. Statuettes of saints and *caboclos* leaned against the walls, while a faded announcement that "Your concentration helps us" watched from behind.

A low rumbling from the other side of the curtain began to still visitors' small talk, the aroma of incense wafted through the room, and the *ogã,* barefoot and in white, emerged to cense the visitors. The rumbling gradually, imperceptibly became the *a capella* hymn, "I purify, I purify my *umbanda/*so that they, so that they may arrive." The curtain opened, revealing three male and ten female mediums swaying in front of a diorama of saints' figures festooned with streamers and holiday lights. As the drummers beat the *umbanda* samba, the *mãe de santo* appeared, her skirts bustling, waving a white-gloved hand.[25]

Soon after her appearance, the pulsating drums drove the mediums into a circle, where they started to chant and move in a slow-stepping clockwise march toward possession. Each soon broke from the circle, throwing her or his head and upper body back, then settled into possession. The *preto velhos* sat and smoked pipes; the *caboclos* stood, whooped, and lit cigars; and *pombagiras* (*exuas* that are the spirits of prostitutes) posed seductively.

Now the session realized its *raison d'être*. Crossing the curtained threshold, guests took off their shoes, jewelry, watches, and glasses, all obstacles to the flow of good fluids. They then approached the mediums in search of help with unemployment, sickness, bureaucratic trouble, or interpersonal ills, or seeking generic protective prayers or purification. Regular frequenters sought out favorite mediums; some mediums were so popular that lines formed in front of them. First-time visitors chose at random or followed companions' advice.

When a visitor had settled on their spiritual interlocutor, she knelt before her. The *preto*, in particular, would then ask, "Now, what does my child want to tell her *Vóvó* [grandmother]?" Petitioners made their requests unhurriedly, some in loud, bantering tones, others in whispers, still others in sobs, until the sacred blue room echoed with chatter, laughter, and the occasional whooping of a *caboclo*. Spirits recited prayers, passing hands over their petitioners, snapping fingers at their sides to chase away evil influences, purifying them with incense, anointing them with puffs of smoke, and prescribing herbal baths and prayers. Two full hours passed before everyone wanting to consult had done so. The session ended when the mediums danced and sang once again, sending the spirits back to the astral realm.

In such sessions, the petitioner-spirit relationship is relaxed. Consultations are an opportunity to discuss troubles at length and in unhurried one-on-one encounters with sympathetic listeners. *Pretos velhos* and *caboclos* follow the rule of generalized reciprocity, offering advice and blessings not in exchange for the gifts they sometimes receive, but in order to fulfill their missions. One petitioner explained that a *guia* who helped her find work had requested a doll as a gift. "If I hadn't given the doll," she said, "the *guia* would have been sad, but she wouldn't have taken away what she gave."

The spirit's mission is to do everything it can to relieve suffering. While successive Catholic orthodoxies look with a critical eye upon those who wish to free themselves rapidly from suffering, *umbanda* spirits adopt a nonjudgmental attitude toward sufferers, insisting that the real culprits are human and spiritual agents outside of them. The *guias* are not interested in moralizing, but in solving the problem at hand.[26] Consider those problems, such as emotional distress, malaise, and interpersonal conflict, that the *guias* sometimes interpret as due to the petitioner's own negative influences and thoughts. Once, when I told a *preta velha* that my marriage was under stress, she announced that my negative thoughts were contributing to the situation, since I wanted "an excuse for when [my] work isn't going well." She interpreted my "bad thoughts," however, as due to "bad influences" I had received from bad people near me. Thus, no sooner had blame touched me than it was swiftly hurried away. In some cases, the identity of the ultimate source of bad vibrations remains obscure: it could be anyone who happened to pass one by in the street. While relieving individual guilt, this diagnosis refrains from assigning blame to specific others. Once, for instance, a medium told me she had received a bad influence from me (it is possible I was short with her), yet she hastened to assure me I was not the ultimate cause, for, she said, "it must have latched on," unbeknownst to me, as I went on my daily rounds.

Still, the spirits are able to allocate responsibility quite precisely when they have a mind to do so. A variety of problems, such as unemployment and trouble with the bureaucracy, are usually diagnosed as due to the overt bad will of someone with power over the victim. I once complained that the Brazilian government would not grant me an extension on my visa. The *preta* told me that a certain person in a high office wished me ill because he "doesn't like Americans." In such a case, the ill will of the other must be softened through the appropriate prayers and, if necessary, recourse to *exús*.

Evil eye may also be implicated, above all if the problem appears to reside in intra- or inter-household tension (evil eye generally can be perpetrated only by those who live physically close, or who have visited the victim in her home). The basic *umbandista* assumption is that no matter how much faith and love one has in one's heart, one may still be afflicted by envious or unscrupulous neighbors. One medium warned me to avoid a certain man who, she said, was envious of my marriage. She knew our relationship was tense, for she lived close by, and had concluded that the fault lay in the evil eye of the other man. In such cases the spirit will hint at the suspect's identity, and will prescribe avoidance of him. "If you avoid the person," explained a medium, "they won't know as much about what you're doing."

If one falls seriously ill, or starts to break things, yell violently or swear for no apparent reason, the spirit is likely to diagnose, not evil eye, but *coisa feita* ("something done"). While evil eye involves only minor disturbances created involuntarily by jealous or greedy neighbors, *coisa feita* is a deliberate, vindictive effort to destroy the victim by calling upon the active assistance of an *exú*. *Exús* are not inherently evil; in their role as go-betweens and messengers, they are an amoral force. It is humans who harness *exús* for antisocial purposes. This is why the *guia* blames not the *exú*, but the ill-intentioned person who calls upon it. "Evil comes from our hearts," said one medium, "not from the *exús*."[27]

Self-defense against *coisas feitas* requires, as with evil eye, identifying the human perpetrator, usually someone known to be holding a grudge against the victim. In serious cases, one may have to call upon an *exú* in self-defense, paying for elaborate *despachos* ("dispatches," or marching orders). In one case, a man's father-in-law was trying to steal his property. "He went to a *centro* to hurt me," he reported, "but I defended myself. He called the spirits, but I just sent them packing back. So he got sick, not me! He even asked me if I'm sending *exús* at him, but I just say I'm returning what he's sending to me!"

If all this sounds a bit complicated, that is precisely the point. *Umbanda*'s diagnoses of misfortune shift responsibility away from petitioners and allocates it instead to a network of multiple, sometimes simultaneous, interrelated human and spiritual causes. *Umbanda* offers the supplicant a world full of gradations of agency, not, as Jean Comaroff has suggested, "the 'zero-sum' and moral absolutes of Christian orthodoxies."[28]

It is not, however, just the complexity and gradations of moral responsibility that characterize *umbanda*; it is its impulse to explain misfortune as due to the evil that lurks in *other* people's hearts. The primary response of *umbanda* to such evil is not, in contrast to Christianity, the stimulation of a set of inner emotional states on the part of the petitioner, but rather the orchestration of harmony among external forces.

Salvation and Liberation

In the early 1960s, the first pentecostals of the Assembly of God arrived in the São Jorge valley and began to carry out open-air and in-house prayer meetings. In less than two years they had claimed thirty souls, the minimum number required to gain congregational status. Their petition to the head-church in Duque de Caxias to grant their small but growing flock this status was successful, and the head-church soon allocated funds to build São Jorge's temple.[29]

This little group thus joined the other half-dozen congregations that depended on Duque de Caxias' head-church. By the late 1960s, when São Jorge's congregation had grown to sixty souls, it obtained the status of head-church. The head-church's pastors and presbyters resisted for a time, but it was eventually in their interest to grant autonomy, for they did not wish to run the risk of having their orders disregarded, always a dangerous precedent in a church which publicly values the authority of the Spirit. Thereafter, São Jorge's Assembly of God continued to grow at a rate of about ten converts per year. By 1975, the church boasted over one hundred members, and ten years later it could claim nearly three times that number, with five congregations under its jurisdiction.

PRAYER-HEALING

What does the Assembly of God offer converts? Foremost, it offers them liberation from earthly affliction. Each day, from dawn till dusk, a steady stream of women and men arrives in the compound of Manuel, São Jorge's most famous prayer-healer. To get to Manuel's one must walk a path lined by tall brick walls, augmented by ivies, tropical plants, and shrubs. At night the path can be hazardous, for it is littered with rocks, potholes, and tile-shards, and when it rains the path becomes a river of mud. The gate to Manuel's compound opens onto a private enclosure, graced by several fruit and banana trees, sugar cane, dogs, a few chickens, a pigsty, a small vegetable garden, and laundry hung up on lines stretched across the yard.

Greeted and guided by Manuel's wife Julinha, the visitor passes through the smoky kitchen, down a short corridor, and through an open door into Manuel's small, pink-plastered prayer room. As few as two or as many as fifteen people will be sitting there on wooden benches, poor locals alongside an occasional *doutor* from Rio, all eyes on the short, pudgy, bespectacled *negro* clad in old clothing and sandals, holding forth on some weighty Biblical theme. The atmosphere is warm, filled with jokes and good-natured ribbing. Manuel enchants his callers with his mellifluous voice and gentle unblinking gaze, exhorting, telling stories, chatting, and "reading" from the Bible.[30]

Though he reminds visitors that accepting Jesus will liberate them permanently from affliction, he also insists that the power of his prayers does not depend on petitioners' own spiritual condition. After all, as another *crente* once pointed out to me, if relief depended on the supplicant, "it would be impossible to pray for a madman, an unconscious person, someone who was deathly ill." Most importantly, Manuel never pressures anyone to convert. The *crentes* I met accepted with equanimity the fact that most non-*crentes* who received cures through their prayers would remain "in the world." The crucial religious aspect of prayer-cure is that news of it may convert someone, if not its direct beneficiary and, further, that it deprives the unconverted, on Judgment Day, of the ability to plead ignorance of God's miraculous power.

Manuel proceeds to the next phase of his enterprise when the mood hits him. Beaming a smile toward each caller, he asks "Do you want to talk about something?" Everyone does: about ailments, unemployment, interpersonal distress, domestic conflict, economic hardship. On one occasion, a woman complained about the disobedience of her daughter, another of her husband's violence, another of her mate's inability to work. Once everyone has explained their plight, Manuel embarks upon the third phase of his work. Beckoning each petitioner to kneel before him, he gently lays hands upon her head, and prays aloud, eyes shut tightly and building vocal speed, mixing prayer with tongue-speaking, as he publicly defines the cause of the sufferer's affliction.

It is essential that when he does this, Manuel blames no human agent, casting rather all affliction as the work of God or the Devil. Serious illnesses like lung cancer or heart disease are, he says, part of divine plans to test the sufferer's faith or to bring her closer to God. Lesser ailments such as high blood pressure, toothache, stomachache, headache, fevers, and colds are also "from God," but are the result not of a divine test but of "material things" such as pollution, weather, overwork, and exposure to toxins—all, ultimately, wages of original sin. In such cases, prayer is still the most effective cure, but Manuel acknowledges the power of medicines and doctors, both of which, he says, work by the will of God.

Manuel refers to "spiritual problems" as those due not to God but to the Devil, including evil eye, *coisas feitas,* and evil spirits. Unlike *umbanda* mediums, Manuel shifts blame for all such misfortune away from the sufferer; but whereas *umbanda* mediums believe evil emanates from human, not spiritual will, Manuel sees all evil as emanating from the Devil, for whom human will is but a plaything. Because it is the Devil, not humans, who is responsible for evil eye, for example, Manuel prays for it in defused, benign language. "I never say who is doing it," he explained. "If I said that a neighbor is there doing something against his neighbor, then I'd be turning neighbor against neigbor. The important thing is for God to resolve things. Who it is, is not for us."

As for *coisas feitas,* the use by humans of evil spirits to visit affliction upon others, again Manuel adopts a nonjudgmental stance. He once interpreted the paralysis of a man's leg as due to *macumba,* because he knew the man had wanted to name his newborn child after an enemy of his *umbandista* grandparents. Yet he studiously avoided assigning blame to the grandparents, speaking of them instead as victims. "The Devil has stolen them, poor things," he said. He thus reformulates possible feelings of anger into pity and compassion. Similarly, he does not blame the victims of demonic possession. When a woman came to him trembling and shrieking, he prayed for her, and later told me that she was "very weak, very vulnerable. She lost a child a week ago, and the Devil took advantage of her weakness to possess her."

BECOMING A *CRENTE*

The liberation Manuel helps to effect is, by its nature, temporary. As long as one remains "in the world," one is bound to relapse into affliction. Only conversion to *crenca* can bring permanent liberation, extracting the sufferer from the world, sending him or her into an alternative world in which suffering does not reoccur, and promising that the sufferer will sit at the right hand of God.

Salvation is inherently difficult. It cannot be achieved through good works, for the human heart, according to *crentes,* cannot be trusted, even when practicing charity. "From the heart," preached the pastor, "comes not only life, but death." One never *deserves* salvation; thus the Catholics' call to imitate Jesus is impossible at best and the sin of pride at worst. To be saved, for *crentes,* requires transcending human ethics altogether. If it is human to do good only in exchange for good, then salvation involves renouncing the instrumental good deed; if it is human to get away with following rules minimally, then salvation must involve making God's Word so strict that every day is a sacrifice. There is little room for play, there is no "sliding scale": either one accepts Jesus and follows His Word or one does not. As such, salvation for *crentes* is not universal; only a few will obtain it. In contrast to Catholic orthodoxy's democratic phrase "we are all saints," for *crentes* we are most assuredly not.

To be saved requires two things: faith in Jesus and obedience to the Word. *Crentes* are fond of saying that faith and obedience may seem simple enough, but that man's pride interferes with genuine faith, and his rebelliousness undermines the duty to obey the Word. True faith occurs only when a man humiliates himself, recognizes his utter powerlessness, and surrenders to the total salvific power of Jesus. Indeed, so powerful is human pride that the act of accepting Jesus is often presented as requiring divine intervention. "I didn't want to have anything to do with the things of the Lord," went one woman's story, "but the Lord worked in me, and held me, I didn't know what hit me. I tell you, the day that I raised my hand for the Lord, I had no intention at all. I was on my way somewhere else, but I felt myself being dragged there, like you drag a little puppy."

Though the acceptance of Jesus may occur anywhere and at any time, to become a church member one must make a public profession of faith inside the temple. The labor required to enter the temple symbolizes its removal from the world. One starts the journey by crossing through a heavy gate to an inner enclosure, where members congregate to chat before services. Then one must pass through the imposing front door, where a deacon stands watch, turning back anyone who is not properly dressed. Finally, one must climb two flights of stairs to the main temple, a cavernous hall that can accommodate three hundred people. There, ten bare lightbulbs hang from the ceiling, and five rotating fans fight the humidity of hot summer evenings. Unadorned, block-lettered posters advertise the choral groups "Heroes of Faith" and "Conquerors for Christ," while behind the pulpit of bright yellow wood falls a massive beige curtain. Here, at the end of every Sunday-night service, a presbyter invites those who wish to accept Jesus to come forward, amidst thunderous prayer and song. If someone approaches the pulpit, the presbyter asks those who know her whether she has accepted Jesus before. If she has not, he has her kneel, raise her right hand, and say "I accept Jesus," then writes her name into a large leatherbound ledger, while announcing she is being inscribed into the Book of Life.

Raising one's hand for Jesus is, however, only the first step on the path to becoming a full member of the Assembly of God. *Crentes* interpret the Apostle Paul's declaration that "faith without works is dead" to mean that faith saves only when accompanied by obedience to the church's doctrine of conduct. This is why, once one has accepted Jesus, one must still spend anywhere from three months to a year being indoctrinated before being baptized. During this period, God tests the convert's faith, and the congregation gauges the conversion's seriousness.

Crentes believe that the church's regulations of conduct and appearance embody God's will for His people. They are tests of obedience, ways of discouraging vanity, of keeping the mind focused on God, and of

The Assembly of God

establishing a public parting of the ways with one's prior identity. As one young deacon insisted, "A *crente* must show the world that he no longer is in it, he now is in the world of God." Much of pentecostal doctrine operates by challenging modes of dress and conduct associated with the male prestige sphere. It includes prohibitions against drinking, smoking, swearing, gambling, adultery, dancing, fighting, and carrying firearms. Women, meanwhile, are forbidden to enhance their physical allure: they may not wear jewelry or makeup, cut or style their hair, or wear clothing that reveals the leg above the knee or the arm above the elbow. A host of other prohibitions have muddier rationales.[31] During services, a deacon peers up and down the rows, satisfying himself that everyone is dressed correctly; repeated infractions can lead to temporary exclusion from the church. For both men and women, violations of doctrine require rites of purification: a fast, extended prayer, and public services in which one begs forgiveness in the sight of others and God.

Only after new converts have demonstrated their willingness fully to obey doctrine are they ready for baptism. Baptisms are major festive occasions. At least twice a year the entire congregation marches to the beat of trumpets, horns, drums, and two hundred upraised voices, to the spot in the hills where the São Jorge river rushes clean and pure around a great granite outcropping. There, dressed in white, the pastor immerses converts in the waters, from which they emerge soaked and ready to live a full life in Jesus. Only now will the convert be allowed to address other *crentes* with the greeting "Paz do Senhor" (Peace of God); only now will he be able to call them "brother" or "sister"; only now will he have the right to attend Tuesday-night members'-only services.

The seating arrangement in church communicates the contrast between those who have passed through the watery divide and those who have not, and between those who know doctrine, and those who have only begun to be exposed to it. The longer one has been a baptized, card-carrying member, the closer one sits to the pulpit. Nearest the pulpit, in three rows perpendicular to the rest of the congregation, sit the deacons, while the presbyters and pastor sit on a raised dais behind it. Newly baptized members are seated in the middle rows; recent, unbaptized converts sit further back; and unconverted visitors remain closest to the door. No explicit rules govern the seating arrangement; rather, it occurs because the pulpit is regarded as the most sacred spot in church. Proximity to the pulpit requires purity of mind and spirit, qualities presumed to be enhanced by long-term adherence to doctrine. There is thus frequently a subtle jockeying to sit closer in church to those known for their sanctity, and to maximize distance from the less sanctified. *Crentes* sometimes avoided sitting next to me because I was known to be "worldly."

Once one has been baptized, membership becomes strictly exclusive. Even the hint that one might have been seen at an *umbanda* center or worshiping in the Catholic church is enough to force a meeting with the pastor and possible exclusion. After all, these other religions are the Devil's playgrounds. Historical Protestant churches such as the Baptists or Methodists are also off limits, for these condone the use of make-up, short pants, and coiffed hair for women. A *crente* of the Assembly may, however, occasionally frequent with impunity other pentecostal churches of the same or stricter doctrines, such as the Wesleyan. If such frequentation becomes too regular, however, this may be interpreted as a sign of dissatisfaction with the Assembly, and a first step toward changing to another church.

Being a *Crente*

For the baptized convert, everything is part of a great divine story, the playing out of God's plan. Every moment is charged with cosmic meaning, in which Biblical events, prophecies, and injunctions are as relevant to the quietest moment of housework as to major life-changing decisions. If a neighbor comes by with a gift of fruit from her tree, it is a sign from God that "by their fruit shall thee know them," or an augury that God has a special plan for the neighbor. If there is no corn flour today, it is because God wants me to seek out my sister-in-law, ask for flour and thereby mend fences with her. If I must take a long walk to visit someone, it is because "Jesus walked far and near." The *crente* life is lived in constant allusion to divinity, an allusiveness filled with extraordinary intensity and excitement: upon arising, the *crente* knows his or her day will not be ordinary, but will be filled with innumerable signs of God's carefully guiding hand. Whereas the leaders of the Catholic church feel compelled to call for a "connection between faith with life," the Assembly of God's pastor does not need to put out such a call to those who are truly converted; after all, they do it all the time. For the true *crente*, divinity is immanent in every aspect of life.

Among the commonest modalities through which God makes His will known to *crentes* are visions: metaphorically coded moral and spiritual lessons. One woman told me that during a prayer session she had a vision that a man was sitting next to me, crying. She said the man must have been the Devil, frustrated at not being able to steal my soul. During another prayer session, a *crente* had a vision of an open window and a waterfall. The window, he explained, was a soul open to Christ, and the waterfall was the grace of Christ pouring into the soul. The vision's message was that "we must open our souls as we open windows on a beautiful day." Such divine messages also come in dreams. One woman dreamed she was standing on a bridge, the sea on one side, a sparkling crown on the other. The sea, she said, was her worldliness, the crown was the promise of a pastorate for her husband, and the bridge was her own indecision. God, she said, was "revealing that I must go to Minas with my husband and there rediscover my spiritual life."

More dramatic still than such signs is the second kind of baptism, one that not all *crentes* are blessed to experience: the baptism of the Holy Spirit. Those who receive this baptism—often described as feeling like fire, in contrast to the cool wateriness of the first—are able to speak in tongues, prophesy, or cure with prayer. Receiving the gifts of the Holy Spirit, like developing *umbanda* mediumship, has a strong involuntary dimension. *Crentes* say the Holy Spirit "uses" its "vessels." Manuel, the prayer healer, told the pastor he had no choice but to carry out his *obra*.[32] "God has called me," he said. "I have little choice but to follow." Yet while "God uses whom He chooses," a *crente* inhibits the entry of the Spirit if he or she backslides into worldliness. Conversely, whoever increases their own sanctity, by observing doctrine to the letter, fasting, or praying late into the night, thereby makes him or herself more receptive to the Spirit. This is why, many say, some receive the Spirit frequently, others less often, and some not at all. At the same time, someone filled with the Spirit can transmit it to others simply through touch. One young man became filled with the Holy Spirit while sitting next to a friend who had received it. "I touched his hand," he recalled, "and it transmitted to me. I felt that warmth enter, moving inside of me."

The physicalness with which the Spirit is often conceived encourages a certain mechanistic logic. Many *crentes* conceive of prayer as the vehicle for an impersonal substance that can be transmitted through verbal and physical contact. Thus prayers are believed to become stronger through repetition: if one prayer is good, two must be better, and seven must be really very good—a logic similar to that associated with the accumulation of material things. Similarly, many *crentes* believe that objects and substances can be infused, through prayer, with the Holy Spirit, and thereby assume apotropaic and thaumaturgical properties. Some *crentes* apply anointed oil to swollen fingers, minor wounds, gastric pain, headache, and fever. One prayer-healer administered spoonfuls of oil internally to expel the evil within the bodies of his petitioners. Glasses of water and articles of clothing can accumulate Holy Spirit as well, and may be drunk or worn to alleviate physical problems.

The most spectacular gift of the Holy Spirit is prophecy. Prophecy gives the Assembly's prayer vigils and services a dramatic, addictive quality, as members wait suspensefully to hear the voice of God amongst them. It happens without warning: a man or woman begins to shout, and everyone falls silent. The prophet, sitting or standing, alternates between tongue-speaking and repetitive, staccato Portuguese, rolling like a wave and crashing, not always intelligibly, into the public ear. Prophecy is highly formulaic, following the format of Old Testament prophecies or of the Sermon on the Mount's "You have heard . . . but I say unto you," warning of the dangers of neglecting doctrine or of the presence of a sinner in the church's midst.

In contrast to the unconsciousness of *umbanda* mediums, *crentes* say they remain conscious during episodes of prophecy. "It felt like a ball of fire, throwing me to the floor," recounted one woman. "Then it raised me up, my mind left. I didn't feel any more who was at my side, I didn't feel it was me. And then came these words into my head, in my mouth, without me wanting it. Those beautiful words left my mouth like a ray of fire. Afterwards, I felt exhausted." This consciousness is partly due to the fact the Holy Spirit, unlike the spirits of *umbanda,* is incapable of betrayal. No tension troubles the relation between the *crente*'s spirit and that of God, and the two may coexist peacefully when the prophet is inspired.

In recent years, however, the pastor of São Jorge's congregation has started to worry that prophecy may have gotten out of hand, and has tried to control it. He now insists that episodes of prophecy conform strictly to the Apostle Paul's dictum that the spirit be "subject to the prophet." A host of doctrinal rules governing bodily movement and voice during prophecy have been enforced by reprimand and exclusion. The true prophet, for example, is supposed to remain seated or stand in place: those who run about and roll on the floor are now said either to be shamming, deluded by their flesh, or, worst of all, possessed by the Devil. Such pressures against prophecy have created strains in the church. "I don't know what they're after now," one man reported. "They're trying to silence the prophets, they don't trust them."

This offensive is understandable as part of the classic process of institutionalization. By the mid-1980s, São Jorge's rapidly growing church had developed a four-rung hierarchy of offices for men, two tiers for women, a Sunday school, numerous singing groups, weekend re-treats, collective trips to other churches, charity collections, and weekly members'-only meetings. It was no longer the church it had been in the

1960s, open to all, relieving torment on demand; it had become a hierarchical organization in which presbyters valued Biblical knowledge as much as the Holy Spirit, and self-control as much as the spontaneous expression of religious ecstasy. "It used to be," lamented Manuel, "you could hear us praising God and prophesying all the way to the highway. But now the pastor is closing his fist. The presbyters are thinking too much about the Word these days, not enough about the Spirit."

Conclusion

The key differences between the main contenders for souls in São Jorge lie in their respective stances toward the possibility of personal transformation, on the one hand, and toward the allocation of responsibility for and proper response to misfortune, on the other. Catholics in the *comunidade,* like all Catholics, regard themselves as neither entirely "of the world" nor "of the spirit," but as a mix of both, and consequently as forever unfinished and imperfect in the sight of God. Catholics mistrust experiences such as conversion or spirit possession, which assume that people may undergo a sudden, total spiritual transformation. Liberation theology itself embraces this theme, declaring that, to the extent that Catholics are inevitably "of the world," they have a duty to try throughout their lives to reshape that world. In this way, rather than suspend secular identities, even temporarily, the *comunidade* tends to reinforce them.

The Assembly of God, meanwhile, portrays the soul as the site of a battle between good and evil, a battle in which good actually has a chance of triumphing totally, in the here and now. This dichotomous, totalizing vision nurtures a conception of the person as susceptible to discontinuities with the world, with the person's past and, when invaded by the Holy Spirit, with the person's self. As for *umbanda,* although like Catholicism conceiving of humans as irremediably filled with the world's impurities, it remains thoroughly a cult of spirit possession, and thus requires accepting the fundamental discontinuity between the self as possessed and the self as unpossessed. The transformative discourse inherent in both *umbanda* and pentecostalism, in contrast to Catholicism, forges new possibilities for suspending, questioning, inverting, and re-creating secular identities.

Catholicism's stance toward misfortune has long been imbued with a deep, abiding judgmentalism toward sufferers, tending toward the position that people bring suffering upon themselves by their own weakness of faith or un-Christian sentiments. Liberation theology's phrase "lack of consciousness" is but the most recent version of this judgmentalism. In contrast, both pentecostalism and *umbanda* may be regarded, at least in part, as cults of affliction,[33] religions that recruit frequenters and members primarily not through preexisting social identities, but through the anti-structural experience of suffering. Because they are cults of affliction, pentecostalism and *umbanda* do not call for patience and perseverance in the face of suffering, but rather promise prompt relief. Most importantly, they do not stigmatize sufferers, but blame instead powerful outside humanlike forces, whether the generalized power of the Devil, or a variety of human and spiritual agents.[34]

These contrasts between world-continuity and judgment on one side, and transformation, the focus on affliction, and the suspension of moral judgment, on the other, are at the heart of how these three religions articulate and respond to the existential predicaments of various clusters of people in São Jorge. As we discover the extent to which these clusters find a focus on transformation and affliction more effective than a focus on world continuity as a response to their predicaments, we will move closer to understanding the differential growth of religions in contemporary urban Brazil.

3

"The Church is Open!"

Class Fractions in the Religious Arena

In the fall of 1987, in a pastoral letter distributed to nearly two hundred *comunidades de base* in the diocese of Duque de Caxias, Bishop Dom Mauro Morelli produced a diagram that purported to represent the Catholic church before and after its transformation by the spirit of the *comunidades*. On the left-hand side of the page was a figure of an inwardly-turning spiral above the caption "closed"; to the right, the word "open" was emblazoned inside a circle radiating a dozen arrows. In meetings throughout the diocese, pastoral agents explained that the figures symbolized the Church's opening up to the poor. "Before," one nun announced, "the Church was closed to the poor. Now, the Church is open and includes everyone. Now we have an open Church, where everyone participates." A young man studying to be a priest sermonized that "we are really becoming a missionary church. We welcome everybody, no exceptions. The Church is trying to reach out and welcome people into it, like it never did before. Before the Church was just for the great ones, now it is for the little people."

These exegeses are rooted in one of the chief goals of the progressive Catholic project: to expand the institutional Catholic church beyond its traditional social base in the middle sectors, to reach a broader constituency among the poor. The poor, the argument runs, despite their frequently ardent religiosity, have long remained at the margins of institutional Catholic life. "The Church in Brazil," a young liberationist priest told me,

was dominated throughout its history by the well-heeled, the merchants, the big landowners. They were the ones who commanded. Outside the cities, in small towns, the parish was run by local bigwigs, people in nice houses. The rest just watched as they ordered things . . . The landless worker, the hungry, the one who earns a minimum salary, he didn't see any place for himself in the Church. He said his prayers at home, occasionally he came for Mass. Most had nothing to do with the Church at all . . .

The new, more egalitarian church, liberationists claim, has a special appeal for the poor. As Brazil's bishops declared in 1982, "the poor are better at living the values of fraternity, mutual aid, and service that are crucial to our way of being Church. . . . They are more open . . . to the things of God, both in terms of time and interest."[1] Consequently, the *comunidades* were places "for integrating into the Church large numbers of simple, uneducated, poor people as active, participating members."[2] An older liberationist priest affirmed, too, that

the poor are now entering back into the Church and taking it over again, returning it to the way it was at the time of Christ. Those are the ones we are trying to reach, to welcome them back in. It is their Church.[3]

In and around São Jorge pastoral agents often claim that the ideal of returning the Church to the poor has been achieved. One nun declared of São Jorge: "In the old days the church here was dominated by merchants. But with the preferential option for the poor, they all left. Now only the poor and oppressed are in the Church. This is a church of the people [*povo*]." Many of the local lay leaders say the *comunidade* is currently led by "*os pobres*" (the poor), in contrast to the past, when the "*grandes*" and "*ricos*" ran things. As Rosana put it, "Before there was inequality. Now we are all equal, and equally poor."

What is striking about such claims is their dichotomization of a social world which locals' own everyday speech typically renders as multileveled. In the official discourse of the *comunidade*, the phrase "the poor" abolishes the more nuanced local distinctions between *melhor de vida, razoável, está comendo,* and *miserável.* In so doing, it fails to do justice to the tendency of São Jorge's *comunidade*, not toward incorporation, but exclusion of the locally least well-off segments of the working class. Translated into the local lexicon, the followership and leadership of the post-1982 Catholic church appear to be converging at the level of the *razoáveis,* while those who are flocking to the pentecostals tend more commonly to be *comendo* and *miseráveis.* From the viewpoint of these segments of the population, it is not the Catholic *comunidade,* but the Assembly of God that welcomes them with the most open embrace.

That active Catholics in São Jorge tend on average to be slightly better off than *crentes* emerged as a pattern from a variety of sources, including a comparative survey of forty active Catholic men and forty active members of the Assembly of God.[4] Of the men active in the *comunidade,* twenty-five identified themselves as *razoável,* eleven as *comendo,* and four as *melhor de vida.* No active Catholic identified himself as *miserável.* In contrast, twenty-two *crente* men said they were *comendo,* thirteen that they were *razoável,* three that they were *miserável,* and only one that he was *melhor de vida.* Despite this small sample, the comparative pattern is suggestive. Most strikingly, male heads of household who were active in the Catholic *comunidade* were about twice as likely as *crente* male heads of household to regard their material condition as *razoável.*

The data on occupation corroborated the pattern. The most suggestive occupational contrast between the active Catholics and *crentes* had to do with their respective representation among the highest-paying industrial jobs, such as skilled machinists, electricians, and pipefitters. While such jobs were overrepresented among members of the *comunidade,* the Assembly of God's sampled members paralleled the proportions of skilled and unskilled workers in the population at large.[5] The contrast was clearest at the level of leadership. *Crente* leaders included *serventes* and unskilled *biscateiros* (odd-jobbers) just as frequently as they occurred in the local population. Among leading Catholics, however, skilled industrial and civil construction workers outnumbered unskilled factory workers by about three to one.

This last point is important, for it suggests that rather than corresponding to an irruption of a new social class, the shift in leadership of the *comunidade* after 1982 reflected, at least in part, the transfer of power from one to another cohort of the same class fraction. Upon his arrival, Cosme encountered in São Jorge a small circle of families that had dominated the top roles in the lay associations and Church directorate for nearly four decades. These men and their wives were the children of shopkeepers in Minas Gerais who had fallen heir to their parents' institutional religious roles as leaders of traditional Catholic associations like the Marian Congregation and the Apostolate of Prayer. The majority of them were skilled workers in stable, relatively well-paying jobs at the National Motor Factory. Cosme held elections for a new council, and threw his weight behind a ticket composed of new men.

What distinguished these new men and their wives from the old was not class, but age and recency of arrival in town. The 1960s and 1970s saw the arrival of skilled, younger workers who could not translate their good economic standing into comparable religious status, because they were excluded from the networks of kinship, friendship, and coparent-hood that knit together the Catholic elite that migrated and settled the town together. The men of the old guard, deprived of their accustomed role, drifted away from the Church, with their wives remaining as their representatives.

That skilled, relatively well-paid and stably employed men and their wives would retain leadership in the Catholic church is perhaps not surprising, given the requirements that Catholic leaders, both before and after 1982, be able to read and have ample discretionary time for meetings. What is surprising is that not just leaders, but most of the membership of São Jorge's *comunidade,* are increasingly limited to relatively better-off sectors of the working class. Why is this the case? In the following pages I will explore some of the main causes and consequences of this trend.

Small-Group Interaction

Central to the *comunidade*'s practice is its commitment to small, intimate groups. Though conceived as a means to foster greater mutuality and fraternity, in practice small Catholic groups render the markers of local intra-class differentiation increasingly visible, while providing little means to transcend them.

We can witness this process at work in several ways, the most striking of which derive from the ability of clothing and houses to serve as metonyms for locally-defined sociomaterial hierarchy. Though the ability to dress "nicely" for Church has always been a marker of socio-material difference, when Church meetings were larger, those unable to afford fine clothes had been less visible. In large religious meetings, especially those that brought together people from a wide geographic range, people in plain attire felt immune to neighborly gossip, less constrained by the critical eye of others, and more able to melt into the anonymous crowd. Listen to Cinira, an elderly woman who lives in what locals call "*miséria*." She had participated in the Catholic Church for years before the arrival of the *comunidade*, during the time it had been a "big church."

In a big church they don't look at you, because they don't know you, they're not thinking, "I saw her wearing that dress yesterday on the street, and here she is wearing it today!"

In contrast, the *comunidade*'s small groups have made it easier for Church members to "look at what you are wearing." Not only is anonymity harder to achieve in a small group, but because Catholic discourse, particularly its liberationist variant, stresses continuity between the church and the world, participants' worldly status tends to be on everyone's minds. This is why, according to Cinira, in the *comunidade*

they look at you funny if you wear the same dress twice. But I only have one dress! . . . Before all this division, no one looked, you just went and prayed, and that was that . . . Now there are fewer there, each looks at the other one, and comments, and wonders what they are wearing. I said, no, I'm not going to stay with that!

As important as clothing as a marker of income level are the quality and furnishings of one's home. Although locals' skittishness about inviting each other to their homes is partly a way of avoiding evil eye, it also conveniently avoids having one's furnishings and hospitality subjected to the judgment of coreligionists. Whenever one pays a visit to a neighbor's house, a whole array of little ritual gestures ensues. The visitor offers to take off his or her sandals, the host insists he or she leave them on; the visitor apologizes for trespassing into the host's home, the host refuses to accept the apology. These are the classic gestures by which the house is demarcated as an intensely private social domain. Perhaps most tellingly, however, is the host's demand that visitors not "look at the house" ("*não repare, não*"). The appropriate response to this is to insist these are the finest surroundings one has ever encountered, and to add that "in any case true wealth lies not in the house but in the heart." The house visit thus becomes a flashpoint for one of the constant underlying tensions in neighborly relations in São Jorge: the invidious comparison of sociomaterial status. This tension is further revealed by the fact that locals who are obliged to move to a new house prefer to do so under cover of darkness: though they say this is to avoid causing their neighbors sorrow, many privately confess that this way "the neighbors won't be able to see our furniture."

Now it becomes easier to grasp why the poorest locals in São Jorge are reluctant to attend the new Bible groups. In the pre-1982 period, Bible circles met in the homes of well-off *cursilhistas*, who served their guests corncake and coffee. Now that the circles not only have shrunk but require each member to host meetings, the poorest locals have kept their distance as a way of avoiding having to invite a dozen better-off neighbors into their homes.

Consider Chico, who has been chronically ill and unemployed for years, and now tries to make ends meet by rustling up odd jobs. He and his wife live, as I mentioned earlier, in a rented wattle and thatch box with dirt floors, rag-covered openings for windows, and no indoor plumbing. All they have is a radio, a wooden table, and chairs. They consider themselves *miseráveis*. Despite identifying themselves as Catholics, they participate in none of the activities of the *comunidade*. I asked Chico if he had ever attended a Bible circle.

There's a bunch that goes from house to house. . . . I went over there, I was invited. And then it was my turn, so I invited them, the women of the Church, for one of these meetings. . . . They came in, looked around, sniffed. I saw how they were looking. Look, I'm poor, what can I do?

He never invited them back.

The Assembly of God naturally has its own intra-class tensions and, as in the *comunidade*, congregants sometimes experience those tensions condensed in the symbols of dress, houses, and furnishings. At the same time, the *crente* church's official position on the uniformity of dress, its explicit call to transcend the material world, and the pastor's frequent denunciations of vanity all place the stigma on those who would proudly display their own wardrobe or possessions, or judge those of others. As one deacon put it, "brothers, don't look next to you, look only to God." Put another way, because *crença* insists on an irrevocable rupture between church and world, *crentes* are able within their small groups temporarily to forget (and have others forget) their sociomaterial selves.

Thus, when Cinira eventually converted to the Assembly of God, her reasons were complex, but at least one of them had to do with the *crente* church's stance on "vanity." She explained:

After they split up the Church the women got haughty. They were looking at me . . . I would go there to shake hands, and they wouldn't. Too much *luxo* [caring about what people wear]! But there at the Assembly, there is none of that, no one is watching that.

Similarly, Chico once received several *crente* women in his house, who had come to pray for him. Though he did not convert to *crença*, he emphasized how much he appreciated the *crentes'* attitude upon arriving in his hovel. Though little more than a shack, he felt that his visitors had paid their material surroundings no heed. "They were there for a Godly thing," he recounted, "not to give the eye, not to look around and say, 'he should live in a finer house'!"[6]

The Problem of Sickness

The stance of *comunidade* leaders and Catholic pastoral agents toward illness is that, while prayers are important, the sick person must, sooner or later, see a physician. "We try to discourage the belief in miraculous cures," said Cosme. "We want to nurture people's confidence in human powers, the ability and knowledge of the doctor to cure. Not to throw up one's hands and simply let God do it all." Thus, before and after prayers for sickness in Bible circles, leaders usually inquire of the sick person or her representative what biomedical steps are being taken. "Prayer is essential," said Rosana. "But you have to go to the doctor."

Nonetheless, this insistence on scientific rationality occurs against the backdrop of the local populace's more general mistrust of biomedical doctors. Medical exams with state-paid doctors are humiliating affairs: after a wait of one to four hours, the exam is generally perfunctory and fraught with tension. "They don't care about poor people," one woman complained. "They look at you like, 'Who cares if you're sick?' They tell you to take something, then they call the next person in." Stories circulate about incompetent, bewildered doctors and failed diagnoses. Medical cures are notorious for dragging on and being inconclusive. Some locals even suspect that doctors prescribe drugs as a way of keeping patients dependent on them.

While such suspicions are widespread, they are especially significant to people of relatively lesser economic means. To see a doctor usually requires giving up a day's work, setting everything aside, and spending busfare to travel an hour or two to Duque de Caxias or Petrópolis. How irritating to those who cannot afford the ride to have a Bible circle leader lecture them on the necessity of submitting themselves to a medical exam! "In the circle," reported one woman, "I wanted a prayer for my coughing. They did it, but they just kept saying: you must go to see Dr. Feijó! . . . I have seen many doctors, and I cannot afford that any more."

From this perspective it is not difficult to understand the appeal of the Assembly of God's stance toward healing. The Assembly does not disdain medical doctors. In fact, one *crente* told me that "doctors are blessed, they have great gifts of knowledge, received from God." For most ailments, however, *crentes* recommend prayer and self-care with home remedies and herbs, advising recourse to doctors only as a last resort. One *crente* explained that consulting a doctor for problems of middle-range seriousness demonstrated a lack of faith in God. "First God. People rush to the doctor for anything, they want him to cure them. No! Only Jesus really cures."

The most dramatic way Jesus cures is through the invocation of His name in prayer-healing. Pentecostal prayer-healers promise rapid, conclusive cures, and deliver them often enough to swell their reputations and followings. Such cures come at no monetary cost, within walking distance, and free of the disdain that characterizes encounters with biomedical practitioners. How soon one gives up on biomedicine and turns to healing by the Holy Spirit depends on a variety of factors, one of which is the sufferer's financial condition. As one woman recounted who identified herself as *comendo,*

I had a pain, a terrible, gnawing pain in my side. I went to Petrópolis, and the doctor gave me some pills, and said to come back . . . I took those pills, nothing, it only got worse. So here, Manuel prays, and I went to him. [Did you go back to the doctor?] No. [Why?] Why should I go back there? And spend another day, and the bus, and all? When his pills didn't work? No, I walk over to Manuel's.

In this woman's case, the healing worked, but she has not converted to *crença.* In other cases, however, being healed of an ailment is often the first step toward conversion.

The New Emphasis on Literacy

Throughout the history of the local Catholic Church, from its *mineiro* origins among such lay associations as the Marian

Congregation, a significant criterion of leadership has been the ability to read passably well. After all, the business of the lay associations' directorates has always revolved around minutes, bulletins, notices from the parish and the central branch of the association, and other written materials. As one old member recalled, "To be in there you had to read, in order to do all that." In the lay organizations, skilled, literate workers and section leaders assumed roles of leadership, while less-literate operatives became simple members. "The Congregation," Mario told me, "was led by the ones with more capacity, who knew how to read."

Still, before 1982 Church leaders in São Jorge had expected neither literacy nor a special degree of articulateness from followers; they had expected them simply to learn prayer litanies and hymns and recite them dutifully during Masses and *novenas*. It was only after 1982 that the clergy deemphasized preset prayers such as *Ave Marias* and began sending instead to each *comunidade* a weekly flood of circulars, pamphlets, discussion guides, handbooks, newsletters, and songsheets—all filled with specialized vocabulary. These written materials are constantly used in ritual contexts, as foci for collective prayer, singing, and reflection. The parish chooses new Biblical passages each week to be read aloud in various contexts, including Bible circles, celebrations of the Eucharist in the homes of the sick, and at wakes. In such contexts, memorization of prayer litanies can no longer serve common Church members, while those who read and speak fluently are quickly endowed with special prominence and authority.

In theory, interpretations of Biblical texts by all full participants in the Church are supposed to enjoy equal status. As Boff has argued, "popular exegesis is very close to the ancient exegesis of the Fathers. It is an exegesis which goes beyond the words and which grasps the living (or spiritual) meaning of the text."[7] Every person is in any case supposed to be valued according to their unique talents, whether or not they can read well.[8] In practice, however, the new Church pounds home the value of literacy. The *cursinhos bíblicos* ("little Bible courses"), for example, encode the values of literacy and articulateness. The *cursinho* is led by young people whose literacy gives them prestige and authority: their fluent readings of Biblical passages are followed by ritual applause, and they commonly adopt the role of professor, asking the assembled congregants to answer questions about the week's Biblical lesson. In such situations, illiterates depend on literates to read or at least explain the lesson to them. The readings are often complex, utilizing specialized vocabulary. For many members this vocabulary resembles, in its unintelligibility, the Latin of pre-Conciliar prayer. One *cursinho* booklet declared that

we suffer many prejudices and all kinds of consequences of a society that marginalizes, but we will not desist, because we know the experience of solidarity. We arrive from the peripheries of the Baixada, from where life is not valorized and the people are treated as an enemy of the state; but we will assume our *caminhada*, for we know what citizenship is, and we have the power to renovate and reconstruct our history.[9]

As one leader observed, "I hardly understand what I'm reading out loud; how in the world are others supposed to understand this stuff?"

The unprecedented value placed on literacy reveals itself in other contexts as well. In Bible circles, the lion's share of time is taken up as leaders establish correct readings, and by articulate members vying to impress each other with how faithfully they can reproduce the orthodoxy. In some meetings, time for commentary disappears entirely, as leaders struggle to stay on schedule by simply reading through the required pamphlet pages. A common complaint on the part of group leaders is that "most people stay silent through the whole thing." Those who read are well aware of the connection between such silences and the valuation of literacy. "In meetings," said one member,

there are people who may even know how to explain things, but they don't know what's there on the paper, so they stay quiet, waiting for the one who can read to speak. They feel ashamed and self-conscious.

In the *comunidade*, then, despite the claim that all members are equal, those who read well or articulate the new orthodoxy clearly in public are more equal than others. If one is illiterate, the chances of becoming a Minister of the Eucharist, a Bible-circle coordinator, or any other sort of leader are slim indeed. One illiterate woman, who was appointed by Father Cosme to the council but could not endure the refusal of other council members to treat her as an equal, eventually resigned.

Nor does one need to look exclusively to the arena of leadership to catch a glimpse of the deep-seated prejudice in the *comunidade* against illiteracy. People who read or speak haltingly, or fail to reproduce accurately the new orthodoxy, are excluded from the lists of those eligible to read during *celebrações*. In Bible circles, I saw leaders publicly point out that so-and-so would not read because he or she did not know how. Some literate Catholics lack even this much delicacy. One leader, while telling me of a dispute between two men, remarked: "Even an illiterate can see they don't like each other!" Another literate man gleefully recounted how a participant in his Bible group had tried to interpret Jesus' summons that Peter build his Church upon a rock. "He thought it meant a real rock! But anyone who knows how to read can see that Jesus meant by the rock the people of God." And a leader confided that "illiterates can't reason, they can't really reflect on the words they hear. All they can do is repeat them like a parrot."

Such superciliousness is not lost on those with scant reading and speaking skills. A less than literate woman who used to participate in the Apostolate of Prayer distanced herself from the Church once reading became a central activity. "There in the groups," she said, "they only like people who can respond prettily, according to what's written there in their books. They no longer value faith, just reading." Another who used to participate in the Bible circles left shortly after Cosme's arrival. "I couldn't understand what they were talking about," she reported. "They used a lot of very strange words. I felt stupid, the readers seemed to understand it all."

How different is the Assembly of God? Common sense suggests that if any religion were to value literacy, it would be pentecostalism with its insistence on the centrality of the Word. Yet a closer look immediately reveals that although *crentes* value the Word, they value the Spirit even more. While *crentes* value knowing the Bible, they regard such learning as neither essential to their identity nor the highest form of religious knowledge. They value close adherence to doctrine, fervor, devotion to prayer and music far more than they do literacy. Above all they confer status on those who receive the Holy Spirit, regardless of their literacy or articulateness. Someone unschooled in the Bible yet visited by the power of the Spirit knows that the voice of God speaking through him or her carries even more weight than when speaking through a vessel learned in the Bible. "The Spirit revives," goes one oft-repeated quotation from the Apostle Paul, "but the letter kills." Manuel remarked that if the *crente* grows too preoccupied with the written word,

he forgets about the Spirit, closes himself off to it. The Bible is fine, but someone can get too loaded with such wisdom, thinking they know a lot about the Bible, and then the spiritual part dies.

A young *crente* happily admitted he was "not much on reading the Bible or studying in general. I don't have any knowledge. I have to pray a lot, ask for illumination from the Holy Spirit. That's what counts." It is thus

not surprising that numerous auxiliaries, deacons, and even some presbyters proclaim themselves to be entirely illiterate.

Some individuals with inferior reading ability who have drifted away
from the Catholic Church have turned to the Assembly of God, and
speak of literacy as figuring prominently in their conversions. One
woman reported that

I have been a Catholic all my life. All my life. But they started getting very snobby.
I saw those young people get up and read and sing the new words from the
sheets, but no one taught me. . . . I felt ashamed. . . . In the *crente* church, they
don't make someone like me, who doesn't know how to read, feel ashamed. You
can go up and testify, you don't have to read anything!

Another man, who had been a participant in his street's Bible circle,
complained that

when they started reading these booklets, all these strange things, they started
showing off, and they wouldn't greet me any more. Just because I can't do that.
They would look at me out of the corner of their eye. They think they're the
only ones. . . . When I was invited to the *crentes*, the first thing I noticed was
how they don't make that separation, everyone is as good as everyone else.

Given these contrasting stances on the written word, the figures I
collected on comparative scolarity, though patchy, are suggestive. Because of the far higher rates of illiteracy among women, the contrast
among them is not very pronounced. While only one-tenth of my overall
sample of 209 women had one year of schooling or less, 14 percent of
57 active Catholic women and 18 percent of 34 *crente* women had this
little. At the higher end of the scale, while around 5 percent of all women
and active Catholics had five years or more of schooling, no *crente*
women had this much. And while the Catholics included a few women
who were continuing their education beyond the eighth grade, no *crente*
woman was doing so.

The contrast among men is clearer. In 1988, only 22 percent of the
crente men I sampled had attended school for four or more years,
compared to 30 percent of the overall male population and active Catholics. Moreover, while four-fifths of the participating Catholic men had
attended school for more than two years, only two-thirds of the sampled
crente men had done so. And while about a tenth of local active male
Catholics had attended school beyond eighth grade, none of the sampled
crentes had gone this far.[10]

Of course, levels of schooling do not invariably correspond to income levels. It is possible for men who know neither how to read nor write to acquire on-the-job skills that command relatively high wages. I knew several machinists, for example, who had learned their skill over the course of a decade's apprenticeship in the motor factory. On the other hand, simply having finished high school does not ensure receiving a high wage. The constraints of the job market and the pressures of family life prevent many high school graduates from attending vocational school or landing a relatively well-paying job. Many remain *biscateiros* and *serventes*.

Still, the level of schooling usually reflects the class standing of one's family, which after all was able to dispense with one's labor for several years and encourage aspirations for education and mobility. Literacy increases access to higher skilled, higher wage jobs, which in turn reduce the need to work overtime or multiple jobs and thus increase the discretionary time needed for church work. Illiterate men with skilled jobs are in fact the exception that proves the rule: for they tend to belong to an older generation that did not depend on vocational training. Nowadays, the best paid, most highly skilled jobs, such as operating cranes and other sophisticated machinery, all require literacy.

The New Standards of Participation

One reason skilled, well-paid workers at the National Car Factory could maintain a monopoly of power in the Church in the decades before Cosme's arrival was that they had considerable discretionary time on their hands. Higher pay meant they could afford to decline overtime and weekend hours, allowing correspondingly more time for Church. As Mario put it, "We were the ones with the best jobs, we had the best schedules, weekends off. We had the time to be at the head of things, go to meetings, keep the reins in our hands." In contrast, those who labored for subcontractors, remembered Geraldo, "earned less, you didn't know when it would end, you didn't have weekends off." Such men were often obliged to work night shifts and overtime, and consequently had less available time to spend on church work. "If you worked for a subcontractor," Geraldo told me, "you could hardly keep up with the meetings of the Marian Congregation."

Yet while pre-CEB leaders in São Jorge were defined by time availability, Catholic membership was not. The right to call oneself a "good Catholic" was governed, rather, by the easily fulfilled criteria of baptism and belief in God. Even taking Communion, though important, was not essential. Those who had not taken Communion in years, or who had never taken it, still called themselves Catholics, despite sporadic challenges.[11] No shame attached to the inability to sustain a high level of participation in Church. "It used to be," said one elderly Catholic, "if you missed Mass, the Church didn't concern itself with that."

In the *comunidade* model, in contrast, standards of participation that had long been confined to the most active laity were generalized to all those who wished to be considered "good Catholics" and members of the *comunidade*. To be a "good Catholic" now meant, at the very least, attending one or two, and preferably more, weekly meetings of the *comunidade*'s various groups, whether Bible circle, youth group, liturgy team, tithing team, catechism, or pastoral of baptism. Those who failed to do so quickly found themselves the target of criticism. "Now," complained one Mass-goer, "a person misses even a little, others start saying you're no longer a Catholic."

The seriousness with which pastoral agents take the new standard is revealed in the following episode. A certain Dona Josefa, a middle-aged woman and longstanding participant in the Church, had been assigned the task of presenting to the assembled *comunidade* the difference between the old and new churches. After reciting a series of conventional generalities, she broke nervously into a commentary at odds with orthodoxy. "Back then," she said, "people in church had more faith. Faith has diminished: now with all these activities in Church, there is less time to pray." She repeated this point several times, was met with nervous laughter and finally was drowned out with applause.

The nun who was present was not pleased, however, and rose to speak.

Dona Josefa has expressed an important insight. She has said that the Church has changed. Before, what did Catholics do? They went to Church once a week, and when they left the Church, that was it. People would go home, and would do nothing else until the following Sunday. There were no meetings in people's homes. Now, thank God, we have meetings during the week, we have the *comunidade*. But Dona Josefa also said that faith had diminished. But can this be true? [awkward pause] She said that faith had declined because people pray less, they have less time to pray. But is faith only prayer? Isn't it also living? [pause again] It isn't that faith has declined. Faith is simply encountering new difficulties. That's the way it is: to be a true Catholic today, you must have courage. It may be easier to attend some other church that does not require commitment, that lets you only pray. Our church is a committed church. It demands work, effort; it isn't easy. So Dona Josefa discovered something important: things used to be easier. Today, praying also means committing yourself.

An important consequence of this new standard of "commitment" is that in order to maintain active membership in the *comunidade,* one must enjoy a flexible work schedule. For example, older housewives without young children, and older, retired men were overrepresented in my sample of active Catholics.[12] Relying on pensions and the support of children, such people enjoy comparatively more time to participate in the Church. I also found that self-employed construction workers were overrepresented among active male Catholics.[13] Such work, usually carried out on small-scale local projects, offers a maximum of scheduling flexibility: labor stops at dusk, leaving evenings free; small projects rarely have strict deadlines, allowing for control of work rhythms; and work-sites in the vicinity of church and home make it possible to leave on short notice. One participant, for example, was at work plastering the walls of a neighbor's house one Saturday when he was told that a major Church meeting had been called in Caxias that afternoon. "I could plaster any day," he said, "but the meeting was right then."

Correlatively, people with heavy and inflexible labor schedules find they have a hard time maintaining membership in the *comunidade.* Women with young children find the heightened demands placed on them by the *comunidade* difficult to meet. As one woman with several small children complained, "I'd like to participate, but I can only make it out of the house from time to time. That's not good enough for them. They say: 'You are not a member of the *comunidade*'!" Another woman in her thirties, with four young children, commented: "To be a good Catholic I have to do all that? I can't! I am struggling enough with my own life at home."

A significant proportion of people with heavy and inflexible labor schedules belong to the category of those who *estão comendo.* Such schedules are not confined to low income households: relatively well-earning people such as merchants, truckdrivers, and tradesmen all have schedules that interfere with church work, and many women whose time is entirely taken up with caring for young children and housework live in households with higher incomes than older women with time on their hands. Yet it is above all those who *estão comendo* who have been obliged, in the context of the economic downturn of the 1980s, to work over-time, weekends, night shifts, or at multiple jobs. Thus, while approxi-mately a third of the local adult men I surveyed had to work overtime, second jobs, or Sundays, I found that only four of forty active male participants in the *comunidade* had to do so. Listen to Daniel, who works as a fare-collector by day and as a janitor at night. "All week long I have struggled," he explained, "gotten up at four in the morning to go to work, arrive home at ten, overtime, money is little, and then they tell me to struggle some more?" Women in poorer households, too, have been obliged to work outside the home for wages. It is thus revealing that housewives who work outside their homes were underrepresented in my survey of participating Catholic women.[14] As one woman explained, "If I worked, I couldn't go to the meetings of the Church!"

Now consider the Assembly of God's participatory standards. São Jorge's Catholics frequently commented on the intensity with which *crentes* participated in their church, on how they were "always there, praying, day in, day out," to the point of holding them up as a model to be emulated. "Look at them," a *comunidade* leader once remarked to me. "If we participated with half their fervor, just where would we be today?"

Certainly the Assembly of God provides its converts with compelling motivations to attend. When conversion and the baptism of the Holy Spirit transform one's life, guarantee eternal salvation, and liberate from earthly affliction, even those who have worked a double shift find time to attend services. The power of the Holy Spirit erodes the distinction, dearly held by Catholics, between "leisure" and "church" time. As one *crente* explained, "my leisure is with the Lord! Why then shouldn't I be in church with Him?" How different this is from the Catholic who told me that attending church meant he "couldn't relax after work."

Yet even the excitement of the Spirit is sometimes not enough to overcome the sheer exhaustion and schedule conflicts created by overtime and double shifts. What Catholics who admire the high level of *crente* participation do not know is that of the Assembly's nearly three hundred card-carrying members, around half fail to attend most week-night services, mostly because they are working or tired. Ernani would arrive home from work at eight o'clock, just when week-night services began. "I want to go," he said, "but by the time I take my shower and have a bite to eat, the praying is halfway done. So I stay home and open a Bible here, and I pray."

Ernani's testimony offers an important clue to the Assembly of God's participatory ethic. While *crentes* value church attendance, they do not base their identity on it. The *crente* is taught to believe that the primary criterion of church membership is an inner transformation carried about wherever he or she goes: that religious identity is based not so much on presence at meetings and collective ritual, as in constant daily prayers and efforts to evangelize others. If circumstances oblige the *crente* to attend church only once a week, he or she will neither lose status nor be gossipped about. "It is good to go to church," declared one believer, "but God does not only work there. The Holy Spirit can work wherever the *crente* is and has faith."

By tolerating a broad range of participatory levels, the Assembly of God allows men and women with heavy and inflexible work loads to remain upstanding members of the church while maintaining a minimal level of participation.[15] While women with small children have trouble maintaining the level of participation required to identify themselves as members of the *comunidade,* as long as they have been baptized and show up from time to time in the Assembly of God, no one questions their *crente* credentials. According to one young *crente* woman,

There are days, my God, I simply cannot make it. The kids are sick, or crying, need to be fed . . . [Does anyone remark on this to you, that you "missed church"?] Oh, no! They understand! What am I supposed to do? I sing my hymns at home, no one bothers me with that, they sing "Hallelujah!" too. [No one says, "You're not a good *crente*"?] [She laughs] The good *crente* follows the law of God, and believes in Christ. Do I not do these? No, no one comments on that!

Significantly, fully one-third of the crente women I surveyed were young mothers in their twenties, compared to only a fifth of the active Catholic women.

The Assembly of God's greater accommodation of men's schedule pressures undoubtedly played a role in the fact that self-employed construction workers were rather less common in the Assembly of God than in the *comunidade*[16] and that *crente* men were more than twice as likely as their counterparts in the *comunidade* to be under fifty years old, thereby not yet having the luxury of relying on pensions and the support of children. Most important, men working overtime, second jobs, or weekend shifts were twice as common among the *crente* men I surveyed than among active Catholic men.[17]

The contrast between the *crentes'* and the *comunidade's* treatment of workers obliged to work a second job is well illustrated by comparing Oswaldo, a Catholic, and Antônio, a *crente*. Oswaldo had been a participating member of the *comunidade* until circumstances forced him to take a second job, making it impossible for him to attend church except on Sundays. His authority in the *comunidade* declined immediately: belittling talk began behind his back, his wife felt obliged to attend meetings and apologize for his absence, and although he had once served on several committees, his name was not even proposed at election time. Antônio, too, worked two jobs, allowing him to attend church only on Sundays. Yet he dutifully fulfilled his role as deacon, received the Holy Spirit during services, and never did I hear an uncomplimentary word spoken of him.

Conclusion

The proposition that the *comunidade* recruits more members from the better-paid, more literate, less overworked segments of the working class than do the *crentes* finds support from studies elsewhere in Brazil. In Recife, Mariz observed that "CEB members are recruited among leaders and people who are better off in their community, rather than the poorest in the area," and often "have a better economic background (some owned cars and telephones) and situation than the majority of Pentecostals."[18] In Itapira, Brandão found the CEB there led by "skilled workers and professionals, small shopowners, and white-collar workers."[19] In São Paulo, William Hewitt noted "the absence of the neediest people" from CEBs, and Rolim remarked upon the significant proportion of *comunidade* members who were white-collar workers and "petit bourgeois."[20] Levine, too, has observed that "With rare exceptions CEB membership is not drawn from the very poorest sectors of the population . . . In the cities, small-scale artisans, vendors, and keepers of tiny shops are the norm, along with public employees like bus drivers or policemen. Few are recent migrants; fewer still are permanently unemployed or in the so-called 'informal sector.' "[21] As Jose Comblin, a theologian of liberation, has recently admitted, "it is not the poorest who are members of the CEB."[22] According to a number of writers, the hardest-pressed sectors of the working class tend to gravitate not toward the *comunidade*, but toward the *crentes*. Brandão has pointed out that in a peripheral settlement in São Paulo "the pentecostals occupy both the unasphalted streets of the periphery of the city, and the lowest occupations in the local labor system,"[23] and Rolim has argued that a large percentage of *crentes* are members of the informal proletariat of *biscateiros.*[24]

The irony is evident. Conceived as a way of broadening the appeal of the Church to neglected social strata, many of Brazil's *comunidades de base* may instead be extending the old pattern of exclusivity from Church leadership to its membership as a whole. In São Jorge, at least, the old and new leaderships alike belong to a working-class elite of skilled, literate, and stably-employed workers with comparatively flexible work rhythms and schedules, while followers tend now to have greater skill, literacy, and access to discretionary time than before 1982. Put another way, the *comunidade* of São Jorge is fast becoming a church of the *razoáveis*.

Although I met a number of converts to the Assembly of God who had been marginalized from the *comunidade* for what they regarded as socioeconomic reasons, it would be a mistake to conclude that the changes in the Catholic Church are directly or automatically linked to the growth of the *crentes* among those who *estão comendo* and are *miseráveis*. Most of those who feel excluded by the *comunidade*'s new practices simply remain inactive Catholics. Still, to the extent that recent Catholic innovations have weakened the affiliation of the poorest of the poor with the Church, they have swelled the pool of people susceptible to affiliation with and conversion to the Assembly of God. In this sense, the *comunidades,* conceived in part as a way to weaken the appeal of the *crentes,* may have in fact inadvertently increased it.

This possibility remains implicit in much of the recent outpouring of revisionism among the ranks of liberation theologians, as they search for ways to stanch the hemorrhage of the faithful to the "sects." The problem is usually phrased as one of recapturing the "masses" who continue to remain outside the *comunidades de base.* "Above all," the theologian Clodovis Boff has recently written,

we are finding people in the autonomous religious movements, in the sects. They are very present there, expressing themselves as the masses, and above all the masses of the excluded, of those who are outside the formal labor market, who live from odd-jobbing, in under- and unemployment. I see here a crucial area for the theology of liberation to develop. It is no longer enough to work only with the *comunidades de base,* which are merely groups. It is essential also to work with the masses.[25]

4

"I Struggle at Home Every Day"

Women and Domestic Conflict in the Religious Arena

Clues to a Pattern

Whether one visits a Bible circle meeting, Mass, pentecostal service, or *umbanda session,* it is evident even to a casual observer that female participants outnumber males. The people of São Jorge frequently point out that "women are more religious than men." There are many reasons for this pattern, including the congruence between norms of female emotionality and religious spirituality, the distinctiveness of the religious domain as one of the few extra-domestic arenas women are allowed to frequent, women's social role of caretaker and minister to the sick, scheduling compatibilities between housework and religious participation, and women's overall experience of greater daily adversity.[1]

None of these reasons, however, takes us very far in understanding the differential appeal of religions. São Jorge's women are about three times more likely to belong to the Assembly of God, than to be active in the Catholic *comunidade.*[2] Most of the people who come to see Manuel (the prayer-healer) or to frequent an *umbanda* center are women, all but a few of whom call themselves Catholics. What do Catholic women find in the Assembly of God and *umbanda* that they do not find in their own church?

A hint of an answer to this question appeared one night as I was sitting with Manuel at an hour when the flow of his supplicants had thinned.

"What kind of problem do women bring to you most often?" I asked. Manuel did not skip a beat.

Discord in the home. Problems of separation, of fighting, between husband and wife, mother and children, the wife is fighting with her husband because he is unemployed, or with another woman, and so on.

Some time later I was with Margarida, the rich-voiced prayer leader of a nearby *crente* congregation. What were the earthly reasons, I asked her, that led women so often to her church? Though I had not mentioned Manuel's response, Margarida answered in virtually identical terms:

Discord in the home, problems at home, husbands wanting to leave wives, husbands unemployed and the wife is all nervous because of that. That's the way the Devil works: he sends discord, the woman gets sick, all headaches, then she comes to the church for relief, and ends up accepting Jesus.

Later I sought out Zélia, a *mãe-de-santo*, and asked her to describe the commonest troubles women brought to mediums. Again, without a moment's hesitation, she answered "problems of marriage, problems at home, with husbands and children." As for why women became mediums, she said, "they see what the spirit can do for them, give them peace at home, make them happy, tame their husbands."

I was clearly on to something. Finally, I approached Armanda, the coordinator of a Catholic Bible group. Had she, I asked, ever observed women speaking of their domestic problems in the group? "I don't hear people telling stories about themselves there," she replied. "Things in the house, that's not for there. . . . If a man is the way he is, what can a woman do? That's the way they are. Women have to struggle in life."

Armanda's answer, along with those of the others, led me to investigate the nexus between Brazilian women's social experience and their religious trajectories. In particular, I was prompted to explore the possibility that the fortunes of the different groups in São Jorge's religious arena could be understood partly in relation to how they addressed the problem of domestic strife.

Domestic Conflict in the Urban Periphery

Subjection to unreliable and abusive men is one of the chief afflictions facing adult women in São Jorge, as it is throughout much of urban Latin America. Though my female informants' accounts no doubt romanticized their small-town pasts in Minas Gerais, it was still with striking unanimity that they pointed to an increase, since their arrival in the urban periphery, in "fights in the home." In the context of unstable employment and inflation, these fights tended to center on the conflict between men's involvement in the male prestige sphere (e.g., gambling, drinking, adultery), on the one hand, and women's desire for decent treatment, a stable household, and their children's education, on the other.[3] A common pattern was illustrated by a *mineiro* sharecropper who brought his family to São Jorge, lost his job after one year, and was eventually obliged to work for a subcontracting firm at half his former salary. He began drinking heavily. "The salary was small," his wife recounted,

nothing was going to be left over to feed the family. He just couldn't spend money on drink and cigarettes, because there wouldn't be enough. So we ended up fighting. I yelled, pleaded, complained, and he didn't like it. I was worried the children wouldn't get to study.

The many nonfamilial entertainments available to men in the city aggravate conjugal tensions. "At night in the countryside," one woman explained, "you just wanted to rest from all the work. In the city, there are bars, and shows [where men go]. . . . In the country, things are further away, you can't stand around in the street." Moreover, women contend, the city has made adultery more common. Rumors of extramarital liaisons are easily spread in the dense urban neighborhood, while city busses make these rumors plausible by offering men access to neighboring towns and the excuse that late arrivals are due to snarled traffic. "In the old days," one woman maintained, "men were more faithful, it was easier to keep one till the end."

Women in São Jorge are also faced with new roles. About a fourth of the women in São Jorge must now work for wages, either to help families and husbands in an increasingly exploitative economy, or to survive separation or abandonment.[4] In addition, with the rise of male alcoholism, unemployment, and adultery, more and more women are avoiding marriage altogether. Now *amigadas* (consensual unions) account for nearly a third of all conjugal pairs in São Jorge. The arrangement ensures women most of the rights of legal marriage, while sparing them its hassles. If an *amigada* turns sour, the woman avoids the sex-biased process of suing for divorce and the stigma of losing a husband.

Most significantly, women in *amigadas* retain greater control over their property and earnings than do married women. "If you marry," one woman explained,

everything you get is earned by your husband. But in an *amigada*, the money was mine, even though he wanted it. I'd give him just a little. With the rest, I'd buy decorations for the house, plates, and so on. . . . Those were my things, not his.

Women who earn wages outside the home or live in *amigadas* tend to be at the cutting-edge of skepticism about marriage and male dominance. For instance, a woman who had supported herself and her daughter for a number of years felt that as a general rule, "a woman should be able to work outside [the home], and the man do some work inside [the home], not just the woman doing everything." Married women working at home are well aware of such attitudes. "Women didn't use to have the active voice they have now," an older married woman said, "we were humbler, dumber. Now you see all these girls working, like my daughter; I could never have done what she's doing."

The existence of such alternatives has unleashed male backlash, which has made at least some women's lives even harder than before. Many local men fear working women will become too independent, or will increase their demands for equality at home. They thus either prohibit their wives from working or, when this is not possible, require them to find jobs close to home. Even husbands of married women who do not work often restrict them to the house and become angry if they wander too far. "He says that if I go out," one woman complained, "that we might as well be living in an *amigada*."

These new strains in the domestic sphere help account for the growing epidemic of "nerves" among women in São Jorge. "In Minas," said one older woman, "no one had nerves. Well, some did, but now you look around and what do you see? Everyone has nerves." A good deal of recent research has suggested that this syndrome, which includes fatigue, irritability, headache, nausea, fainting, and bodily aches, is an idiom through which women somatize and express the psychosocial stresses of kinship and household.[5] In São Jorge one does not have to be a sociologist to realize this. "Women here are sick a lot with nerves," one woman observed. "Why?" I asked. "Because," she replied, "they have many worries, with their husbands and kids. And no one helps them. So they get sick."

Frequenting the Religious Arena

Like other married women who called themselves Catholic, Ivanda was one of those who had found it necessary to turn for spiritual assistance to both an *umbanda* medium and a pentecostal prayer-healer. Ivanda was like many women in town. A semiliterate *morena* in her late thirties, she lived with her husband of twenty years and two of her three children in an unfinished compound. Whenever I spoke with her, usually in the mornings, she would sit me down at a table covered by a flowery plastic tablecloth, pour me a cup of coffee from a tall thermos, and busy herself in the kitchen, which she had prettified with such things as a lace jacket placed carefully over the dishsoap. She was especially proud of her refrigerator. Among the women in São Jorge, the refrigerator is an item with considerable emotional charge: women without refrigerators are obliged to keep food in the corner of a neighbor's cooler, and speak longingly of saving up enough to buy one second-hand. On a shelf above the refrigerator Ivanda kept her pots, which, by their carefully-kept shine and painstaking arrangement from largest to smallest, conveyed her pride in and affection for her family.

Ivanda, the daughter of a sharecropper, grew up in Minas Gerais near the town of Muriaé. At the age of eighteen, she married Aldyr, the son of a neighboring sharecropper, and within a year had given birth to their first child. The family moved to São Jorge, where Aldyr worked on the assembly line of the National Motor Factory for the next ten years. During those years, Ivanda fondly remembered, she and Aldyr had gotten on well. It was the factory layoffs of the late 1970s that changed her family's fortunes. Aldyr turned to low-paying, unpredictable *biscate* in neighboring towns, and Ivanda was obliged to make beds at a cheap motel on the highway. "Aldyr didn't like that at all," she recalled. "He said I should stay home. That really bothered him." He started to drink and stay away from home for extended periods. "I would ask him, he would say he had a job here or there, then snap at me, saying to mind my own business." She had known Aldyr for years as a considerate, gentle man, and felt confused by the change in him. "I was upset. Things had always been so good. I was worried, about us, about the house. . . . I was worried about the children. Without the support of their father, what was going to happen to them?"

THE LIMITS OF THE
CATHOLIC CHURCH

A crucial source of strength for many Catholic women in dealing with pressures like those confronting Ivanda is devotion to the Virgin Mary. A Catholic woman explained: "When he arrives home drunk, you know, swearing, I think of Our Lady, because didn't she also suffer? So there, I can suffer a little." Ivanda, too, asked the Virgin for her support. Yet for her such prayers alone could not suffice. She had come of age after Vatican II, and had learned that God did not want people to suffer passively. "We all have a cross to bear," she said, "but you can't just stay at home, you have to go out and do something."

Ivanda might have sought support from her neighborhood Bible circle, which, since the early 1980s, had supposedly been focused on "life problems." Father Cosme had suggested that Bible circles "should try to focus on all the dimensions of life, on the dimensions of neighborhood, family, community, survival." But when I asked Ivanda whether she had discussed her domestic trouble in the Bible circle, she dismissed the idea as ludicrous. Her dismissal is understandable when we consider the actual practice of the Bible circles. In practice, Catholic churchgoers regard as taboo any discussion in the Bible groups of one's own household conflicts. Participants sometimes intone generic prayers such as "May Jesus unite all divided families," but in my weekly attendance at various Bible circles, I never once heard participants speak openly about their own domestic problems or request prayers to resolve specific domestic conflicts. Why?

The first part of an answer is that Bible circles are social spaces that are heavily encumbered. As I have suggested, the groups recruit members on the basis of friendship, kinship, neighborhood, and prior Catholic identity. I have also suggested that neither the bonds of suffering nor possession by the Holy Spirit are at work to suspend group members' secular roles. Consequently, participants tend to interact with each other as friends, relatives, and neighbors, in much the same way inside the circles as they do outside of them. Such interactions nurture the taking of sides in disputes, and the passing of mutual judgment; in short, what locals call *fofoca* (gossip).

This is an important point. Liberation theology's assumption that the smaller the group the more natural its solidarity and mutual good will quite simply flies in the face of the tension-ridden, gossip-prone reality of neighborhood and kin relations. Consider the so-called "bonds of neighborhood." Certainly there is a strong popular discourse of neighborly mutual aid: locals frequently say that "neighbors must have unity" and that "neighbors must help each other." In practice, neighbors do each other favors, such as putting up TV antennas or helping to lay concrete roofs. When someone has a party, invitations are extended to everyone on the street. When they want to lay asphalt, or install sewage pipes, they mobilize along the street, going from house to house, appealing to the principle that neighbors must lend each other a helping hand.

Yet living in close quarters with neighbors has its price. Neighbors hear each others' raised voices at night, know who drinks and who does not, whether one sings hymns or prays, the frequency of domestic disputes, timing of meals, and so on. Such knowledge, achieved both through simple observation and through gossip in yards, on the street, in bars, and over windowsills, fosters the need to always keep in mind what the neighbors may think. Suspicion of evil eye is common among neighbors. Locals rarely leave their front gate or door open; at night, windows remain shuttered; and visiting takes place among nonrelatives more often over windowsills and walls, in bars and on the street, than inside houses themselves. The gathering of neighbors in one's house for a Bible circle meeting, then, far from being an occasion of unsullied unity and trust, is often fraught with tension and ambivalence.

Such tension is reinforced by the fact that many Bible circle participants are sisters-in-law. Because women in São Jorge have generally moved to their husbands' town, and brothers tend to live close to each other, sisters-in-law tend to be neighbors. Although they often exchange childcare and other help, sisters-in-law are also frequently in competition for the approval of their mother-in-law. It is therefore risky to confide in sisters-in-law, especially about problems with husbands, for, as one woman pointed out, "She'll tell her husband, and then of course he'll talk with his mother. So you just keep your mouth shut."

As a result, the atmosphere of the Bible circles is less than fully conducive to the articulation of domestic trouble. For example, when a visitor to a Bible group dared complain about her husband, women who were loyal to her husband's family glared at her, while those sympathetic to her found it politic to refrain from publicly taking her side. In another instance, the members of a Bible circle wanted to take up a collection for a woman who had been abandoned by her husband. On its face, this was an admirable effort to act upon Christ's call to help the downtrodden. In practice, however, the gesture required taking

sides in a marital dispute. The husband's relatives in the circle denounced the good Samaritans as "a bunch of gossipy women" who had
better tend to their own affairs before meddling in those of others. The
Bible circle abandoned the plan. "Look," one woman remarked, "how
can I talk about private matters there? These are my neighbors. The
circle may be all nice and pretty, but when it's over, I have to live next
door. . . . If I say something in there tonight, by tomorrow, half the
town will know."

Catholic discourse compounds this problem by making women feel
guilty about domestic conflict. For older women, the paradigm of the
via crucis still reigns supreme. "I have gone through so much with
him," an older Catholic told me, "That is my cross." Conciliar theology
offers scarcely more reassurance: calling upon people to take responsibility for affliction, it views marital conflict as the fruit of the spouses' own
wills. As a *cursilhista* member of the Bible group put it, "if a couple isn't
getting along, it's no one's fault but their own."

At first glance, progressive Catholic discourse would, in this regard,
seem to be an improvement. Liberation theology, after all, as ensconced
in the Puebla Conference's final document, declared that "women are
doubly oppressed and marginalized."[6] Father Cosme sermonized that
Saint Paul's insistence that women submit to their husbands did not
apply to twentieth-century Catholics. Women's leadership roles expanded dramatically after the arrival of the *comunidade* in 1982. Prior
to that date, the church directorate was made up exclusively of men; since
then, women have served in it every year. The experience of leadership
has been empowering for many women. "I never thought I could do
these things before," said one new female leader. "Running things, that
was for men. But I can do all that too."

Women's roles in the *comunidade* are still limited in important ways.
It is the *comunidade*'s men who fill the roles that require public speech,
control of finances, and the representation of the group to outsiders:
they dominate the *comunidade*'s council, administer the *comunidade*'s
treasury and construction team, and continue to outnumber women as
coordinators of the town's Bible circles. Women, meanwhile, continue
to predominate in the sex-stereotyped roles of charity, catechism, caring
for the sick, preparing food for Church events, and cleaning up after the
men.

Most significantly, despite its call for gender equality, liberationist
Catholicism generally looks upon domestic issues as less pressing than

the question of class oppression. As Sonia Alvarez has argued, liberation theologians see the solution to women's problems as lying in "increasing their participation in the public world of politics and production," rather than in dealing with the inequality present in the household.[7] One pastoral agent admitted as much. "If there's something wrong at home, it's because the husband is unemployed. But why is he unemployed? That's the question we want people to think about. So we tend to look at these things from the 'macro' perspective."

Indeed, Bible group guidesheets consistently skirt domestic issues. "There," said one group member, "if you talk about that, you're not connecting life with the Bible. Because the connection between life and the Bible doesn't mean things about husbands and wives." On the rare occasion when a guidesheet does touch upon domestic conflict, it lays the "macro" perspective on with a trowel. One guidesheet called for reflection on a story similar to Ivanda's.

Dona Marta's husband lost his job, and he started taking it out on his family. Then Marta learned in her group that it was not just her husband who was unemployed but that unemployment was sweeping through the poor workers in Brazil. She learned that the minimum wage has fallen in value by 150 percent in the last two years. She started joining her *comunidade* when it went to the authorities to demand stability of employment and higher wages for all workers.

It is possible, of course, that some women may overcome their domestic problems by learning wage statistics and throwing themselves into political work. Idealizing such women, however, stigmatizes those who fail to respond in this manner, while subtly shifting responsibility away from husbands and on to wives. This view also places an onus on those women who cannot discharge both domestic and extra-domestic duties. "If you are really *conscientizado*," one lay leader asserted, "you can't just help your own family. Any woman takes care of her family. You have to do something further: that's what's difficult! If you just help your own family you're not Christian. The true Christian helps people outside her home."

Many women resent being criticized for limiting themselves to the domestic struggle. One woman, in response to the guidesheet's question "How are we, today, at the service of life?", replied "By washing, making food, cleaning, sewing." She was met with the haughty retort that "No, the question is about helping people outside your home." Though she said nothing at the time, she later said to me, "How am I supposed to help all these people outside my home? It's hard enough to take care of things at home!" And another ex-member complained,

They say "struggle, struggle, struggle!" But they mean unions, and neighborhood associations, and political parties, things like that. But I struggle here in my own home every day. They don't speak about that.

Let me return to Ivanda. If it was out of the question for her to ask the Bible circle for help in coping with her domestic troubles, there were other spaces in the Catholic Church to which she might have turned. For instance, she might have sought prayers from the Apostolate of Prayer. Here, it seems, it should have been possible to escape the burdens of social roles for a time, and articulate delicate personal problems. Yet here, too, Ivanda was reluctant. Though she had at other times asked the Apostolate to pray for her children's health, "for this problem, no, I didn't ask for a prayer from them. . . . I would be embarrassed."

To understand this embarrassment, we must remember that the Apostolate recruits its members in a way similar to the Bible circle: not through suffering, but through coresidence, Catholic identity, friendship and kinship ties, and a common aspiration to the respectability of being identified with a long-standing Catholic lay organization. Social status, not affliction, is the cement that binds the women of the Apostolate together. In fact, receiving the Apostolate's prayers is, in practice, largely restricted to upstanding Catholics, for supplicants must approach each Apostolate member individually to ask for prayer, a requirement that ensures that petitioners will generally already be familiar with the group. Moreover, since Apostolate members tend to be older, they usually embrace the ethic of the *via crucis,* calling on women to bear their cross. For these reasons, far from creating a socially safe space for the expression of domestic conflict, the Apostolate suffers from the same reputation for judgment and gossip as the Bible circles. As one member of the Apostolate said to me, "if we try to help, they accuse us of gossiping, of mixing into their lives."

My periodic visits to Apostolate prayer meetings suggested that the majority of prayers requested there were for "guiltless" afflictions such as physical illness, rather than for domestic troubles. When, for example, Ana Maria, a woman in her fifties who had been active in the Catholic Church her entire life, found herself faced with a serious family problem, she studiously avoided bringing it to the attention of the Apostolate. The only example I could find of a woman taking a domestic problem to the Apostolate was an exception that proved the rule. Soon after the Apostolate had prayed for a woman's husband to return to her, the story leaked, and the husband's mother publicly accused the Apostolate of spreading the story through the town. The denunciation was especially vehement because the husband's mother assumed that the women of the Apostolate had taken sides against her son.

What about the priest? Isn't he supposed to be confessor, confidant, and counselor? Ivanda seems to have thought so. In the early 1980s, she paid a call on Father Cosme. She knew he had discouraged the practice of private confession. In a conversation with me, he explained this:

It's like someone coming to your house to visit you, and you ask her how she is, and so she tells you about her difficulties: her husband is drinking and fighting at home, her son is unemployed and is making everyone tense at home, comes home late. In most cases, in these confessions, there really isn't any sin; it's rather a life drama, and the difficulties they face in all this. So I began to think that there were major limitations to the individual confession. You don't have a chance to help people grow in their level of consciousness, to have a more communitarian consciousness, to perceive the other faults that are common to the community.

Rather than a confession, Ivanda decided to settle for a face-to-face chat with the priest. She left feeling dissatisfied. "He said," she recalled, "that it was a crisis we were all passing through. . . . I thought he wasn't really interested." She was probably right.

Yet even had Cosme wished to act as marriage counselor, Brazilian men's notorious reluctance to submit to the priest's authority would have made him a weak ally in Ivanda's domestic dispute. Comments like "the priest just meddles, he's not God, he's no saint!" have long been foam on an ocean of jokes and innuendos about the clergy's sexual hypocrisy and ignorance of family life. It is not surprising that priests often appear quite powerless in women's eyes to affect their husbands' behavior. As one woman explained,

it doesn't help to bring a domestic fight (*briga de casa*) to the priest. Let's say a woman has a husband who likes another woman, so that he is betraying her; she goes to the priest: "Oh, father so-and-so, come to my house and say something to my husband." So the priest goes and says, "You have to be faithful to your wife," and so on. He listens to all that. But if he likes the other woman, he's going to see her. [But why? Why doesn't he listen and obey the priest?] Because the priest doesn't know anything about family life. They don't respect his opinion. Believe me, they don't respect it.

Ivanda had reached a point where she could no longer dismiss the possibility of going outside the Church; yet she hesitated to venture entirely beyond her faith. Turning to *crente* prayer-healers was as of yet out of the question. She had in her youth imbibed the opinion that "*crentes* were heretics, we weren't even supposed to look at their churches." Her religious training also inhibited her from consulting, as yet, with an *umbanda* medium; for, like other Catholics who had been taught to equate *umbanda* with witchcraft, Ivanda felt it was "a bad religion. Ever since I was little, I learned that."

FREQUENTING AN *UMBANDA* CENTER

The only specialist to whom Ivanda would consider turning at this point was a *rezadeira*.[8] Because consultations with these noninstitutional Catholic specialists are usually held privately in the *rezadeira*'s home, they reduce the danger of gossip. "With a *rezadeira*," Ivanda observed, "it's just you and her. No one else is listening." One of the few *rezadeiras* left in São Jorge told me that women seemed to come to her more to talk than be prayed over, and that their talk was almost invariably about "home things."

Ivanda had another reason for seeking out a *rezadeira*. Because her husband's conduct stood in stark contrast to his earlier self, she had begun to suspect evil eye. Her years of good fortune, she thought, may have made someone jealous. With a *rezadeira* she might receive protective prayers against the eye. "This is what they do," she said. "They always take care of things like that." She knew that, in contrast, respectable church-bound Catholics impugned those who believed themselves victims of evil eye as weak in faith or, worse, as having given others cause to be envious.

Ivanda knew no *rezadeira* personally, since by the early 1980s very few existed in São Jorge. She thus had to act on the advice of a trusted neighbor, who directed her to a "good *rezadeira*," named Zélia. When she arrived at Zélia's house, she knew she had stumbled into a *centro*. (Such unintentional arrivals at *centros* account for a significant proportion of initial visits to *umbanda* by institutionally-affiliated Catholics.) Trying to make the best of an awkward situation, she bit her lip and spoke to the medium. What she heard not only challenged her stereotype of *umbanda*, but impressed her deeply. "She didn't say anything about *despachos*, she didn't ask for anything, she didn't speak badly about anyone." She soon overcame her initial hesitancy, and came to appreciate the atmosphere of the *centro*, which she found well-suited to her urge to speak of her domestic afflictions. "It was good to talk there," she recalled. There she "could talk about such things, the spirit was interested in that."

Five main factors make the *umbanda* center a good place for female frequenters to articulate domestic issues. First, when one speaks to a medium, one is confiding not in a human but in a spirit. In contrast to human interlocutors, *pretos velhos* and *caboclos* are not gossips. As one woman explained, "I couldn't speak about these things with human beings. With people, they comment to each other; but with an *orixá*, the thing stays with it alone." A Catholic woman recounted that when she suspected her daughter of being pregnant, she had refused to confide in her Bible group "because they would gossip," and turned instead to an *umbanda* medium to whom she "could say what was going on."

Second, in order to escape the disapproval of Catholic and *crente* neighbors, visits to *umbanda* centers tend to be clandestine and, when possible, far from visitors' homes. The supplicants at any given session thus tend to be strangers, for the most part. As one regular frequenter commented, "there are people from one place, and from another. They can't go back home and talk about you, no one there knows you." And because visitors do not wish to draw attention to their own visits, they can be trusted to keep quiet about anything personal they hear. On the rare occasion a frequenter meets a neighbor in a *centro,* the bond of clandestinity puts fears of disclosure to rest. "I went to a *centro* once," confided a leading Catholic, "and I saw a colleague there from my neighborhood. She turned so red! And she said to me, 'Oh, please, this is between you and me! You won't tell anyone, will you?' And I said, 'Of course not. Here everything is secret. . . . If I said you were here, wouldn't I have to explain what I was doing here too?' "

Third, the *centro,* as a cult of affliction, forges a bond of sympathy among supplicants. During the consultation period, though first-time visitors tend to speak to the spirits in low whispers, regular frequenters often talk in loud, chatty voices. They have learned, as one of them put it, that "everyone is there because of their problems. They can't say anything about your problem, because they're there for the same reason." In one *centro,* I witnessed the *chefe,* while possessed, sing publicly about the troubles each visitor had brought to him. When I asked a woman whether the singing had embarrassed her, she replied, "Oh, no! That is the spirit singing there, that is done with respect. . . . You hear what other people are going through too."

Fourth, the idiom through which *umbanda* diagnoses a large number of afflictions is itself "domestic." Spirits urge supplicants to speak of

their conjugal travails, and to recognize many other problems as ultimately due to the state of their domestic affairs. Thus, even problems not
clearly linked to the household require spirits to visit the afflicted person's home to "see what's going on there." In one *centro*, spirits requested petitioners' addresses, even when the petitions were about such
seemingly extra-domestic issues as bureaucratic or occupational troubles. When I expressed anxiety about the progress of my research, for
example, the *preta velha* insisted the heart of my problem was that my
guia had a different temperament from that of my wife. As in other
centros, the *preta* encouraged us to attend together as a couple.

Finally, the discourse of *umbanda* allows for a shift of responsibility
away from the woman and her husband, to outside forces like the evil
eye and *despachos*. In Ivanda's case, this was crucial as a way to make sense
of Aldyr's behavior while at the same time minimizing her feelings of
hurt and resentment toward him. Zélia confirmed that an envious neighbor was employing *exús* to turn Aldyr against his wife. "She said it was
a *despacho*," Ivanda explained. Why, I asked her, couldn't it simply have
been Aldyr himself? "No, no," she answered. "He's not like that. It just
wasn't him."

Ivanda liked the *centro* at first. She could speak about her domestic
misfortune there, and the spirit confirmed her suspicion that it was due
to outside powers. Yet Ivanda's Catholic identity would not allow her
to become too settled there. Because she regarded herself as a compas-
sionate Christian, she began to resent the spirits' insistence on identifying
the source of the *despacho*. "I didn't want to take vengeance on anybody,"
she recalled. "There at the *centro* they make you confused, they turn
neighbor against neighbor, they say that you have to do a *despacho*. I
didn't want that. . . . Why should we be angry against our neighbors?"
Moreover, she was afraid that she "might stop going to Church, and start
going only to the *centro*, because it's a religion. I mean: you have to be
either one thing or the other, either with the church or the *centro*."

After some months the *orixás* seemed to be having little effect on
Ivanda's marriage. It was time, according to Zélia, for the spirits to turn
to stronger medicine. Stronger medicine required the investment of
considerable time and money. "She told me to do a *despacho*. She asked
for money, she said I had to return with the money, she told me I had
to buy all this stuff in order to make a *despacho*." The medium's mention
of money aroused Ivanda's suspicions. "If she's helping me only for the
money," she recalled feeling, "it's not for me she's helping. So she has
no loyalty. . . . If she charges me, why can't she charge another person
who wants to hurt me?"

Ivanda had accepted the *centro* because she felt her prejudices against *umbanda* had been unfounded; but when the medium proposed a *despacho,* Ivanda concluded that "everything they said about these spirits is true! They just care about themselves. Not about the people who come to them." The medium's legitimacy in tatters, Ivanda ceased attending the *centro.* But what had troubled her most was the attitude of the spirits, which struck her as distinctly un-Christian. "I didn't want to take vengeance on anybody. . . . There at the *centro* they make you confused, they turn neighbor against neighbor, they say that you have to do a *despacho.* I didn't want that. . . . Why should we be angry against our neighbors? That's no way to feel, that's not what the Lord wants."

FREQUENTING A PENTECOSTAL
PRAYER-HEALER

Ivanda's problems at home continued. She remained aloof from religious specialists for a time, until her mother-in-law converted to the Assembly of God, and began speaking a good deal about Manuel the prayer-healer. "She told me he never charged, that he refused money." This indifference to money set him in contrast to *umbanda.* She went once, then twice, then a third time.

At this point in her trajectory, Manuel offered her several things. First, he was not concerned with identifying the human sources of her afflictions. She had had her fill of such things at the *centro,* and had seen where they led. She wanted to avoid feeling suspicion and resentment, sentiments at odds with her identity as a Catholic. "I just needed prayer," she said. Prayer she could have from Manuel, in abundance.

Second, like Zélia, Manuel provided Ivanda a safe place to ventilate her feelings about her domestic troubles. She found she could "talk about things . . . There was no judgment, no one criticized . . . I felt the strength of his prayer. There, there's no gossip." Or, as another Catholic woman put it, "there everyone supports you, but in the Catholic Church, everyone just criticizes." Like *umbanda* consultations, prayer-healing is a cult of affliction. The bond of suffering among petitioners permits a temporary suspension of social roles and statuses, forging an arena unencumbered by social sensitivity. As Manuel maintained, "Everyone here is full of problems, so it's not necessary to hide problems from each other. I mean, no one is going to leave here criticizing anyone, because each one has their own problems." Manuel could be quite explicit in this regard about the contrast with the Catholic Church. "People bring their problems to me," he observed, "because I am separated from the world where their problems come up. In the Catholic Church, you're not leaving society. This here is a refuge, there is no gossip, there are no fights or misunderstandings."

Perhaps most importantly, Manuel places ultimate blame for domestic discord on generalized external evil power. "The Enemy works hard to destroy married life," he explained. "The discord that arises in people's homes is the work of the Devil. He came to rob, kill, and destroy. Fights between married people are always due to the Enemy." This diagnosis erodes that individualizing moralism that is one of the foundations for gossip. "In the Catholic Church we felt ashamed of this kind of problem," recounted one woman about her domestic fights. "Now we know it is the vice of the Enemy." The Devil thus became the depersonalized target of Ivanda's anger, allowing her to shift blame away from human agents, including herself, Aldyr, and suspicious outsiders.

Once again, however, Ivanda's identity as a Catholic placed limits on how far she was willing to move into Manuel's orbit. Though she frequented his prayer-healing sessions for nearly a year, she never considered following her mother-in-law's example of conversion. "I'm happy as a Catholic. I was born a Catholic, baptized. Why should I change? God helping, I've learned to accept this burden." After all, she had been disappointed, but not disillusioned by the Catholic Church: Catholicism had at no time lost its moral legitimacy for her.

In the end, God, working in His usual fashion, finally allowed the line between miracle and the natural course of events to blur. Aldyr eventually found a job at a decent wage, and Ivanda withdrew from wage labor. Although they never returned to their former contentedness, their domestic lives began to improve once more. Ivanda stopped going to Manuel and, in typical post-Conciliar fashion, began to judge herself harshly for ever having turned to him. "I wanted things to happen overnight, I thought that maybe by going somewhere else things would happen more quickly . . . all this was weakness of my own faith. I could talk to God, too. I could go into my room and pray."

Umbanda Mediumship and Domestic Conflict

Ivanda's story provides a window onto the conditions under which Catholic women turn for help to *umbanda* centers and pentecostal healers. It does not, however, offer insight into why some Catholic women become *umbanda* mediums or convert to pentecostalism. To understand this, we must turn from the process of frequentation to that of affiliation. The main contrast between women who frequent and those who affiliate with *umbanda* or pentecostalism is that the latter generally have weaker Catholic identities to begin with and they succeed through affiliation not only to articulate but to resolve their domestic troubles. In the case of *umbanda*, mediumship helps women develop coping strategies by introducing spiritual thirds into marriages, redefining suffering, and forging an autonomous sphere of power.

POMBAGIRA AND EXÚ

Everything about Silvia, a dark-skinned, hefty woman in her fifties, conveyed a woman at peace with herself and the world: how she carded her tightly curled gray-black hair unhurriedly as we spoke; how she punctuated the telling of vivid episodes of her life with bursts of vibrant laughter; how during pauses she leaned back to stretch and breathe deeply. As we sat in her pale-blue *sala*, sipping lemonade in the dwindling afternoon light, our bare feet cooled by glistening brown tiles, the picture of her earlier life made her present serenity seem nothing short of miraculous.

Silvia never developed a strong identification with the institutional Catholic Church. Born one of seven children to a poor sharecropping family in Minas Gerais, she was raised on the periphery of the Church. "I didn't have that practicing faith," she recalled. At eighteen she married the son of a neighbor in the countryside, had their first child, then moved with them to Rio, where she remained distant from organized religion, "because I didn't know anyone in the Church, I just went to Mass from time to time."

It was here that her problems with her husband began, eventually growing to critical proportions. "The man wasn't a man," she said. "He didn't like to work, he didn't care about his family, he liked the world. It was very, very difficult. . . . He drank, and we fought." Things went from bad to worse. Falling deep into debt, Silvia's family was forced to move in with her sister-in-law. Then the first crisis occurred. One night, when their second child was about six months old, Silvia's husband bundled him up and left for Minas Gerais. "I went to the judge," she recounted, "to the police, everything. My mother prayed, I went to Mass, and there was nothing, no way of finding my son." Distraught, and without support, Silvia turned, on the recommendation of a neighbor, to an *umbanda* medium.

This woman said to me, "See so-and-so, for he will find your son." I didn't even know that *macumba* existed. There were a lot of people there. When we entered, he took a picture of my husband, he scratched it and put it into the fire. And he said, "Go look for him." So I went home.

Two weeks later, Silvia's son was back in her arms. She paid a high price for his return: his father came with him. "That was a tribulation," she said, "but I wanted my child. If I hadn't accepted him back with him, he would have taken away my son again. For me, my life was like being in hell."

It was in this desperate situation that Silvia began to have a recurrent dream.

I saw a man, without a shirt, white pants, shoeless. When I saw the whole man, I looked, he walked away from the bed, and entered the living room. I wasn't afraid, he looked gentle.

The image was unmistakably from *umbanda,* the classic half-naked white-trousered male. Silvia braced herself to return to the *centro*.

I went back to the *centro* where the man had brought my son back to me. I thought they must be good there. . . . I told the *pai de santo* about my dream. He laughed. He said, "That man is an *exú,* he takes possession of women. You're lucky that he didn't take you." I found that very interesting, a spirit taking a . . . what would a spirit want with a woman? I found that *very* interesting. He said, "Look, you have to be a medium, because you have a *pombagira.* The *pombagira* showed you the way to your son, and now she wants you to develop with her. She will teach you many things." I thought, she has done this for me, so I started to develop, I discovered what it meant for her to possess me, and then for him to possess me, I discovered why I found it interesting, the feel of my flesh, to be used by a spirit.

Once she had become a medium and entered into the *centro,* Silvia claims she "felt better" about her problems at home. To understand why, we must realize that a spiritual "third" can provide the medium with support, counsel, and otherwise inaccessible knowledge. One elderly medium found in her mediumship a source of authority to chastise and renounce her husband.

The *velha* would say to him [husband], either he had to change the way he treated me, or figure out a way to leave, without fighting, without anything.

The *velha* didn't like him spending money on other women. . . . I wouldn't yell, but she would. The *velha* knew that it was no good staying with him, that I had to forget him. My sexual part got cold. The *velha* came, explained that he was with another, that she had discovered him. After that I felt better, more at peace.

Spirits can also act as arbitraters whose authority is recognized by both husband and wife.[9] In one case, a woman in her late forties was married to a very moody man. She learned from her *mãe-de-santo* that her husband's irritability came from his lack of obedience to his *guia*. She prevailed upon him to attend the *centro* with her. Now whenever he feels out of sorts, he admits to his wife that he has failed to fulfil an obligation to his *guia*. She can thus excuse herself for his moods, and has the authority to point out to him that he has not carried out his obligations. She feels happier, she says, in the marriage.

In Silvia's case, what seems to have been most important was that her relation with the *exú* offered her a spiritual substitute for her unloving husband. The dreamy manner in which Silvia spoke of the *exú* suggested a kind of fantasy male, strong, gentle, respectful, sensual, to replace her own. The erotic language she used to speak of the *exú* was less than metaphorical. Silvia was finding, it seems, release from her conjugal hell through an intensely intimate sexual-spiritual bond. "When I felt the spirit arrive, I would forget everything," she said. "At home it was all misery. But there, I didn't think I was miserable."

As important as the *exú* as spiritual third, however, was Silvia's experience of mediumship itself. "The spirit would enter me and work," she said, "and help others who came. I liked that, I thought, 'I'm really helping others, this is good.' . . . For everything I did at home, do you think anyone thanked me for it? All I got was suffering and pain. There, in the *centro*, I worked for good. There, when I helped people, they were grateful." This is, in an important sense, the very essence of *umbanda*'s power for many women: its creation of a parallel household in which they can fulfil their role while receiving, at long last, recognition for it.

In fact, *umbanda* is the only religion in Brazil in which women consistently exercise more official ritual authority than men. Female-headed *terreiros* are more common than male-headed *terreiros,* and while *mães-de-santo* usually enjoy undivided authority, *pais-de-santo* must share theirs with a female medium.[10] In female-headed *centros,* the *mãe* blesses and disciplines mediums, controls access to ritual paraphernalia, confers sacred white clothing, and consecrates shrines. Zélia, for instance, once ordered a *filho-de-santo* who had disobeyed her to cook her meals for a week.

The authority of *mães* tends to be informal, personal, and direct, while that of *pais* tends to be formal, distant, and mediated by women. *Pais* have less of an interactive role than do *mães*: while *pais* remain close to the altar and do not circulate among mediums and guests, *mães* tend to move freely throughout the *centro*, joking, coaxing, coddling, and laughing. More generally, female mediums are more at home in *umbanda* than their male counterparts: they look more relaxed at sessions, chatting boisterously before and after sessions, while male mediums, for the most part, remain subdued.

Women enjoy this authoritative edge in part because *umbanda* discourse assumes they are more spiritually receptive than men. This receptivity is the direct outcome of women's "humility."[11] "Men have more trouble with developing [mediumship]," said Silvia, "because they cut themselves off, they are too proud. We women are humble." The experience of self-sacrifice and intra-household sharing, female mediums claim, prepares them for the charity essential to accruing merit for themselves and the spirits. The reliability acquired through homemaking, in particular, gives them the requisite steadfastness to fulfil obligations to the spirits. "It requires that firmness, responsibility," one medium told me. "Men always vacillate more. Men think they can go out and get into trouble. But a *centro*, like a home, is a lot of responsibility." One medium suggested that as a housewife she had been trained to attend to the cleanliness and detail necessary to make both visitors and human-like spirits feel at home.

Although this model seems to reinforce the patriarchal norms of female humility, self-sacrifice, and domesticity, it in fact subverts these norms in subtle ways. Humility, for example, is not the result of a prescriptive norm but the outcome of daily suffering. "Women suffer more than men," said Silvia, "with all the worrying about the kids, and the house, and the man who comes home drunk, and sickness." It is these experiences, not an arbitrary patriarchal norm, that forge humility. "The man thinks he can do anything," Silvia lamented. "He will run ahead, thinking only of himself. Not women. We know how hard things are. We must think of others, we have to be humble." It is precisely this humility that helps women become mediums. "For the spirit to descend," Silvia explained, "you cannot just think about yourself, you have to stop thinking just about yourself."

In addition, mediumship allows women to accumulate more power in the *umbanda* household than in the secular household, and assigns them important powers beyond the domestic arena. Mediums consult with and influence non-kin; their advice influences powerful men who come for consultations, including employers, bureaucrats, and politicians; they place ritual paraphernalia at crossroads, near streams and waterfalls, in forests, graveyards, on the beach, and in a variety of other extra-domestic locales; and their *guias* move freely through the space between *centros*, thus linking them together and creating an expansive inter-household network.

Most dramatically, to the extent that male mediums depend on *mães-de-santo* for initiation and the right to develop, they also rely on them to participate in a realm of power that transcends the household. The sweetness of this inversion of gender roles is hinted at by Silvia's comment:

A man yells and screams, tells a woman what to do. Could a man do that in the *centro*? No. The *mãe* would stop him right away. There he has to show a woman more respect.

Rather than simply reinforce patriarchal norms, then, *umbanda* is able to draw attention to the suffering inherent in Brazilian womanhood, while simultaneously transforming that suffering into a new source of power.

Pentecostal Conversion and Domestic Conflict

Pentecostalism is usually regarded by local non-*crentes* as oppressive to its female converts. "I would never go to that religion," a Catholic woman said. "The women there are so ground down." The religion does, in fact, enforce a variety of patriarchal norms, including the sanctification of male dominance in the household and the imposition of strict dress codes for women. Women can never become a deacon, presbyter, or pastor. "God," one man said, "did not make it within women's powers to do those other things." Still, a growing number of observers have noted that the gender assymmetries of pentecostalism are different in important ways from those that characterize the larger patriarchal societies in which the religion exists. For example, it has been argued that by challenging the male prestige sphere of alcohol, gambling, adultery, and so forth, pentecostalism makes patriarchy less injurious to women.[12] I will expand upon this point by placing it in the context of the range of discursive and practical resources inherent in pentecostalism that help women cope with and overcome domestic conflict.

I take as my point of departure one of the key rituals among *crente* women: testifying before the congregation. Every day, women testify eloquently, revealing in detail stories of domestic suffering. Possessing great emotional power, the testimonies follow the rules of their genre, demonstrating the *crente* church as a place where women publicly articulate their suffering, and teach each other the *crente* way of interpreting it. In these testimonies are voiced most of the themes that draw and keep women in the Assembly of God.[13]

Testimony at Margarida's

Shortly before eight o'clock on Monday mornings, I would take a ten-minute bicycle ride to a small, unfinished brick building in a neighboring town, where Margarida, a tall, baritoned-voiced *negra* in her forties, would be leading a pentecostal congregation in prayer. At a hundred yards from the humble orange brick structure, I could already hear the ululations of *crente* prayer. Walking through the windowless blue metal portal, I would squeeze onto a long wooden bench, amid the two dozen men who swayed to the rhythms of an electric guitar. Across the aisle, about fifty women would be seated, some with small children on their laps. At the room's center, Margarida would be seated, poised behind a white cloth-covered table, an open ledger before her, assistants at her side. Her husband, a tall, muscular man in a tight-fitting suit, a presbyter in São Jorge's Assembly of God, would be seated behind her on a dais. He would, as usual, be looking slightly bored, for his role at Margarida's sessions was only to open the proceedings with a benediction and close with a prayer. On Thursday evenings Margarida would cede the leading role to him; then he could hold forth in detailed Biblical sermonizing.

In contrast to Manuel's prayer circle, most of the people in Margarida's group are *crentes,* for this is a congregation, complete with offices and membership roster. In this small congregation, in contrast to the larger parent congregation of São Jorge, visions, prophecies, and the recounting of blessings occur frequently and fervently. Here there is no pulpit, no microphone; here, each *crente* sings or testifies or prophesies where she stands or sits. For three full hours every Monday morning, anyone who wishes to has the chance to reveal themselves, while Margarida, with sure and sensitive touch, keeps testifiers and prophesiers within time limits by interjecting an occasional "hallelujah."

One morning, after the first round of hymns, a gray, bespectacled woman in her fifties stood up suddenly, slicing the air. "Hallelujah, Glory be to God!" she cried. The congregation grew quiet. The woman was about to testify. "The Lord worked wonders in my life," she began. "Glory be to God! I have suffered, and suffered mightily. Ah, the Lord had prepared many trials for me." A chorus of hallelujahs rolled majestically around the room.

Stern-faced, clad in a light calico skirt, hair trussed tightly in a bun, surrounded by her sisters in the faith, Nathalia stood and spoke of her tribulations. "There was no trial bigger than my husband," she began.

He made me suffer. Sisters, I would get up at four in the morning so that my house would be clean, lunch ready, clothes clean in the room, everything ready before he went to work. Then he would come back, throw his clothes on the floor, and go off into the street to drink.

She paused. "But I had a very great responsibility with Christ." Bursts of hallelujahs. "He said this to me: 'Honor your husband, smile, receive him, don't let there be any fault in your conduct in the house.' Did I shirk my duties? No! God had a plan in my life!"

Nathalia's litany of wifely duties was met with knowing looks, nods, and tight-eyed sobs. By honoring her husband irrespective of his behavior, Nathalia had done what any self-respecting *crente* woman would do: obey divine dictate, as revealed by the Apostle Paul. Male *crentes* rarely miss an opportunity in sermons and informal conversation to refer to the Biblical passage, "Now as the Church is subject to Christ, so must wives be to their husbands in everything" (Ephesians 5:23). One deacon offered me the following gloss: "If the woman is a true Christian, she is going to want to obey. For the Apostle Paul said: 'Women must obey their husbands.'"

By sacralizing women's subjugation to their husbands, this doctrine undoubtedly reinforces female oppression. And yet, for women tempted by alternative gender roles but still without the social power to fill them, learning to accept a subordinate status in the household is experienced not as oppression, but as bringing relief from domestic conflict. Consider Andrea, a woman in Margarida's congregation. Now in her fifties, Andrea felt from an early age that she would never be fully satisfied in the role of wife and mother. She wanted to "improve herself," to learn to read and write. Later, against her parents' wishes, she eloped with a neighbor's son. Her husband turned out to be domineering and violent. "I always wanted to do what I desired," she said. "I was taught to be obedient to my husband. That was hard. He would prohibit me from visiting neighbors even." She eventually converted to *crença* for a variety of reasons; but the strongest force keeping her in the Assembly of God, she said, was that it helped her resign herself to a submissive marital role. "The Assembly helped me to obey, to accept this situation."

Or take the case of Tatiana, a twentyish mother of two toddlers, also a congregant in Margarida's little church. Tatiana had been ambitious before getting married, hoping to finish school and become a secretary. "I loved school," she said. "I loved learning things." (She now looks upon such ambitions as the worldly fantasies of an unconverted soul.) After marrying, she found herself confined to her husband's house, staring at a future of drudgery. She began having fits while doing housework. "That evil spirit would arrive in me," she recalled. "I'd start to break things. Sometimes I'd throw the stove grill to the floor, I'd throw buckets of mop-water on the floor." Only conversion to the Assembly of God forced the afflicting spirit to leave her. "From that time on," she said, "the Devil has left me alone. When I'm working in the house, doing my chores, I whistle, I feel joy, joy in all the things of life, big and small."

Achieving a measure of domestic peace in exchange for subordination may seem a poor bargain. Yet that very subordination, when inspected more closely, reveals itself as a site of contested models of gender relations. For starters, we need only consider Nathalia's reference to "duties": by counterposing these to her husband's conduct, she effectively recast household chores from expressions of subservience to proofs of moral superiority, drew attention to men's dependence on women's labor, and reminded her listeners that adversity itself is part of God's plan. Paradigmatically, Nathalia's shift from a description of her suffering to "But God . . ." recalls Biblical prophecies that those who are now held low shall be held high. To this extent, pentecostalism's casting of subordination as divinely ordained is part and parcel of Christianity's classic reversal of social signs, its exaltation of what Turner has called "positions of structural inferiority."[14]

One important consequence of this is that *crente* women regard their subordination as an act of obedience to God, not men. I could not find a single *crente* woman who rationalized submission in the household in terms of female moral or intellectual inferiority, for their own everyday experience refuted this. Rather, they saw their obedience as submission to God, like Jews observing the taboos of Leviticus. As one *crente* woman reflected, "It is a kind of law, not because men are better, or stronger. It's just a law we have to obey. That's all."[15]

What is true in the home is also true in church. Though doctrinally excluded from the church's highest offices, *crente* women comment that such positions are only "material" power, and that they would distract them from developing their spirituality. "We are firmer in our faith," proclaimed one woman, "we have no distractions like men do. Women are more spiritual." This is why "it was women who went to the sepulchre of Jesus first." Similarly, pentecostal discourse allows women to turn their high illiteracy rate into a spiritual virtue. Male *crentes*, even those who do not read, are careful never to be seen without a Bible in hand. Women, meanwhile, though agreeing that men know the Bible better than they do, affirm that "the letter kills, but the word revives. Men are so concerned about knowledge, their faith weakens."

Women in the Assembly of God have little patience for what they see as men's self-serving interpretations of the Bible. I was once having a theological discussion with a presbyter and his wife, when the presbyter declared that men led the church because "the prophets were all men." His wife interjected, to his discomfort, that in the New Testament women figured just as prominently. Men consistently pointed to the sin of Eve to explain women's subordination, but women retorted that they do not bear full blame for the Fall. As Margarida insisted, "Adam didn't need to accept the apple!" Another *crente* woman explained,

Men say women are weak, because they're the ones who sinned first. But for me, women are strong. A woman isn't as easily tempted as a man. The dumbest beast is man. Any pretty woman, even an old one, will throw a man into hell . . . Maybe Eve was just testing him! And he failed the test!

Thus, for example, when a presbyter was discovered making sexual advances to a female congregant, the men in church blamed the girl for leading him on; but the women blamed the Devil for having misled the presbyter.

It is not, however, only by promoting an overtly subordinate role that pentecostalism contributes to women's ability to cope with domestic conflict. In a variety of ways, female converts exchange overt submission to men for new sources of power over them. The "love of Jesus" de-centers the husband's authority and provides women with a new focus of confidence and self-esteem. It is no accident that "accepting Christ" in women's testimonies has an adulterous feel. Listen again to Nathalia testifying to her entranced audience. "I had been married many years when I accepted Christ as my savior," she declaimed.

I got home that night, and I told my husband: "I have accepted Jesus, I have known Christ, I don't know what's going to happen, all I care about is that I'm with Christ." [A burst of hallelujahs and glories] He looked at me and said, "Now, are you going to be a *beata*? You're going to be like the rest of them." And I said, "Whatever happens, my life belongs to Jesus."

The threat this spiritual love affair posed to her husband soon became manifest. "My husband, from that moment, when he heard I had accepted Jesus, the first thing he did was to get another woman." Gasps all around. Had she not been a *crente,* Nathalia would have been powerless before her husband's adultery. But listen to how, as a *crente,* she dealt with him.

I saw that I could speak, and I did, I showed him my example, and I shamed him. For God was marking my life, even my dresses bore the imprint of His hand. I would speak, speak, gently, and he would have to listen.

"Speaking gently" at home is among the most vital of abilities forged by conversion. The Holy Spirit and coreligionists' prayers give a woman the confidence quietly but firmly to challenge her husband's conduct. Given the Apostle Paul's rule of female subordination, this confidence may seem paradoxical. Yet it is precisely the *crente* woman's strict observance of a subordinate role, as well as her knowledge of Biblical pronouncements and her feeling of being inspired by the Holy Spirit, that give her the right to "show the man the error of his ways." Her observance and knowledge, furthermore, often erode her husband's ability to dismiss her challenges. Take Carolina, also in Margarida's congregation, who before converting constantly fought with her husband about his drinking.

After becoming a *crente,* I didn't fight anymore, because I had more strength to speak about things, without having to fight. You feel there is always someone praying for you. . . . I'd talk with him [after conversion] with authority, and he would cry. I would talk, quietly, that it wasn't right for us to waste the small salary we had on things that weren't bread, because that's Biblical. . . . Being a member of the church gave me more authority to talk like this at home.

Another woman linked her conversion consciously to an effort to cope with her alcoholic husband.

I thought, on the day that I decided to be baptized, "This is a decision that I have to take, in order to have more strength to control my house." Because being baptized, you feel the Holy Spirit, you feel more energy to converse better at home.

Women are often rewarded for their efforts. I learned of several instances of men moderating their drinking after their wives converted. "Men are very vain," one woman said. "They don't just want obedience, they want their wives to respect them." Indeed, men married to *crentes* often report feeling shame in front of their wives. "I felt ashamed," one man recalled. "I felt that I was annoying her. I'd arrive in the house drunk, and I felt that I was going against her." In another case, a *crente* woman opened her Bible and placed it in a central spot in the *sala,* so that whenever her husband arrived home late from carousing he would have to walk past the open Book. "He couldn't walk past it drunk, so he stopped going out so much," she reported. Why, I asked her, didn't he just close the Bible? "I don't know," she answered. "Maybe he knew, maybe he was afraid."

Sometimes, of course, such devices are of no avail against a stubborn and abusive husband. Still, *crente* women do not despair, for they know God is on their side. When communication finally failed Nathalia, she did what she had never had the courage to do before: take her husband to court.

It got to the point I couldn't take it any longer. The Lord said to me, "Now look for a solution." So I went to seek justice. There I was, without a lawyer, without a witness, without anyone. Just me and God. Hallelujah. When I arrived there, this woman, a lawyer, gave me her card. The first thing my husband did was rip it up! But it's good to have God on your side! It's good to have the lawyer of lawyers! When the day came for my hearing, that lawyer was looking for me! Hallelujah! And there, my husband was called in front of the judge, and said "She's lying!" And the judge said: "No, the real liar is you!"

The room exploded into cries of "Glory to God." That a powerful man—the judge—had sided with this woman against her husband was an irrefutable sign of divine intervention. A discernible gender tension gripped the room. Contrary to the custom that calls upon those present at the recounting of testimony to avert their gaze, all female eyes were riveted on Nathalia. The men, meanwhile, in a stubborn show of piety, kept their heads down and eyes closed, reluctant to lend Nathalia's story more drama than it already possessed.

Its drama, however, was just heating up. "For you to win your husbands," Nathalia cried,

you must make him understand, and make light enter into your home! Hallelujah! For you know, men have very hard hearts. It wasn't till he had a problem, one so bad he couldn't sleep, that his heart started to soften. "How can you sleep?" he'd ask. I'd say: "Look, Waldyr, I have Jesus." And one day, he showed up, my husband was in the church! That man, who used to spit in the face of the church! Hallelujah!

Nathalia was giving voice to the greatest satisfaction a *crente* woman can obtain: bringing her husband to Jesus. Some *crente* women interpret domestic woe as God's way of using them to gain men's hardened souls. "Through my pain," one *crente* woman declared, "God touched me first, so I could go on and win my family for Jesus."

This is not the place to undertake a full analysis of men's conversions. It is sufficient to note that male conversion is double-edged: though a victory for women, it also reflects a man's recognition that the Assembly solidifies his own authority at home. The man who felt "ashamed" before his *crente* wife, for instance, could not stomach allowing her to have the spiritual upper hand at home indefinitely. "I thought that if I went to church too," he explained, "she would respect me again. . . . The man should be the one to lead his family."

We finally arrive at the classic source of female power in pentecostalism: once a man converts, his wife enjoys unparalleled safeguards over his behavior. *Crença* rejects all the elements of the male prestige complex—drinking, smoking, gambling, fighting, and adultery—as the work of the Devil, and subjects men to discipline should they indulge in any of these practices. Yet direct sanctions rarely need to be applied, for cautionary tales are constantly circulating about sinners revealed by prophets in front of the whole congregation. One man, for instance, was considering a clandestine rendezvous with an old flame when he was approached by Margarida; she told him she had dreamt he was about to go against God's will. Naturally he dropped the idea of the tryst at once.

Crente doctrine renders men not only more faithful and tractable, but more solvent: a man who drinks ten bottles of beer per week and smokes a pack of cigarettes a day has already spent over half a minimum salary on these items. By converting, men are able to devote more of their salaries to maintaining the household and providing for the children, including their educations. Women are well aware of the overall result. "I didn't convert from vocation," one confided, "but to see if I could get my husband to live better."

Nathalia finally reached her testimony's climax.

So, sisters, I tell you: it's not easy. But it is not impossible. Today my marriage is happy, brothers and sisters. I have passed through difficulty, but there is one thing I tell you: what the Lord promised, He fulfilled in my life. Take care of your husbands, look for God, have faith, struggle with all your might of your heart, and your desires will be . . .

The room was shaking. The closing words of her testimony, set adrift on the hymn Margarida had called for, were in the end drowned by it.

Where Do "Politics" Lie?

In this chapter, I have suggested that in São Jorge the Assembly of God and *umbanda* offer women richer resources than does the Catholic Church for coping with unreliable and abusive men. For women who wish to articulate their grievances but have no intention of changing their religious identity, the Catholic Church offers little succor: it intensifies gossip and places responsibility for domestic conflict upon the complainant herself. *Crença* and *umbanda*, meanwhile, as cults of affliction, relieve women's fear of gossip by creating socially safe spaces, and assuage their guilt by shifting blame for domestic conflict away from them, fixing it either on the Devil or the ill will and deeds of specific humans and spirits. As cults of transformation, *umbanda* and *crença* allow women to carry with them into their households the mediating power of spiritual thirds, including the Holy Spirit, spirits that have the power to shake husbands to their very foundations.

The failure of the *comunidade* to take arms against the evil that assaults women in their homes is one reason it is losing the battle for souls in São Jorge. The progressive clergy have inherited a theoretical model that defines politics as belonging primarily to the male-centered public sphere. Until the new Church is able to pay full heed to the growing problem of domestic turmoil in the urban periphery, it will, no doubt, continue its own battle in increasing isolation.

5

Escape from the Snake's Nest

Unmarried Youth in the Religious Arena

A Visit to the Snake's Nest

It is Saturday night at the Snake's Nest, the bar that caters to São Jorge's young people. The bar's main smoke-filled room pulsates with the theme song from "O Outro," a popular soap opera. Dozens of young men and women, elbow to elbow, check their finery by glancing at the mirrors that line the walls: the men wear cleanly pressed imitation designer jeans and crisp shirts stamped with blazing colors and English words; the women are in jeans too, brightly colored skirts, and pink, orange, and blue sleeveless blouses with low-cut V-necks. The place echoes with laughter and clinking and buzzing. The sexes remain in their own circles until ten or eleven o'clock, then start to mingle, forming knots of four or five, standing near the bar, or at the door, or around a pillar, or outside, some leaning against the bar's façade just beneath the mural of a grotesque snake, others against a massive motorcycle, smoking, sipping sugarcane brandy and beer, joking, flirting, crossing the swords of repartee, trying to discover where they stand in the crowd. By now some have begun to dance in the back room, stealing kisses in the shadows; others leave to find the darkest stretch of street between streetlamps to indulge in a more serious embrace.

Shortly after one in the morning, someone is drunk, a rumor rushes through the bar that a rival has gained the favor of a young woman, a

117

fight breaks out, fists fly. A nose is bloodied, there is a scream. The bartender turns the music up louder, and a chaotic peace returns, but the crowd has peaked and has already begun to dwindle. Tomorrow everyone will sleep late, and some of the men will play soccer in the afternoon against the team of a neighboring town. By two-thirty the last broken glass is swept up, and by three o'clock the only reveler at the Snake's Nest is the moon.

Young People in the Religious Arena

Brazil, like much of the so-called Third World, is a very young society. In 1980, nearly 40 percent of its population was under the age of fifteen, and over half was under twenty.[1] In São Jorge, the predominance of young people is even more pronounced. In 1979, about half of the town's population was under twenty; ten years later, about half was under fifteen.[2]

São Jorge's churches have fared poorly in appealing to this surging, restless, youthful mass. Most youths in town keep their distance from churches of any kind: among the town's roughly two thousand unmarried people between the ages of twelve and twenty-two, no more than one hundred and fifty, or about 7 percent, were active participants in any local church. There are many reasons for this. Churches represent authority and responsibility, signs of the adulthood many youths set themselves against. "I'm not going to go to a church," said one young man, "and have all those duties to attend to. It's time to do other things." Moreover, young people usually have not yet passed through the kinds of life crises, such as sickness or encounters with death, that bring people to a supportive, organized religious community. Perhaps most importantly, for many local youths, the first requirement of any church—moderating their involvement in youth culture—is simply too difficult to accept. "That's for old people," one young man declared, "and for young people who think like old people." Another pointed out that, "it's hard for young people to get involved in the church these days, because now there are so many options: on Sundays, they want to play soccer, go to a movie, a party, the beach." Another youth reminded me that attending church on Sunday morning was hard to reconcile with the schedule of youth culture. "Look," he explained, "I stay up late Saturday night dancing. How can I get up and go to church?"

Of the young people who do participate in church, however, about four times as many are members of the Assembly of God than are active participants in the Catholic *comunidade*. Indeed, unmarried youths represent one of the largest and fastest growing subgroups of the Assembly of God, comprising in 1988 between sixty and seventy of the Assembly's members. At special services held for recent converts, it was common for half of those in attendance to be younger than twenty, and at some recent baptisms, the figure was closer to three-quarters. The pastor was well aware of the trend. "The Lord," he said, "is working to collect His chosen while they are still young." In contrast, there are no more than fifteen to twenty young participating Catholics. A young Catholic recognized the disparity between his church's and the *crentes'* respective appeals to young people. "We have to be careful," he warned, "we have so few young people; they're getting them all."

I cannot possibly do justice to all the forces at work to produce this pattern. Instead, I will focus on the contrast between the two churches' respective stances toward the tension-ridden world of youth culture. The Catholic Church can muster only a partial response to the pressures of youth. Because *comunidade* discourse stresses continuity with extra-religious social identity, its response to the world of young people remains equivocal: while expecting them to remain immune to that world's worst temptations and dangers, it does not call upon them to renounce it. While this compromise seems tolerable to well-adjusted, socially confident youths, it is difficult to swallow for most young people seeking to increase their involvement in youth society, as well as for those who desire to escape it altogether. In contrast, the Assembly of God offers young people a radical break with, and a concrete substitute for, the tension-ridden society of youth.

Being Young in São Jorge

While adolescence throughout the world is a time of high anxiety,[3] in Brazil's urban periphery its vexations have become compounded by tense, burdensome sexual and material competition. In the 1980s, at a time of spiraling inflation and falling wages, the mass media have intensified efforts to induce demand among young people for an ever wider variety of commodities.[4]

In São Jorge, the intensification of this demand began in the early 1980s, when a company installed an antenna on one of the Serra dos Marcondes's foothills, making reception of a clear signal at last possible in this mountain-girt valley. Television—in Brazil a synonym for *O Globo,* the largest TV broadcaster in Latin America—began to disseminate, through advertising and soap operas, costly standards of clothes, records, hairstyles, makeup, electronic devices, and liquor.[5] Competition among young people for such commodities has become fierce.

These commodities are used among young people in São Jorge to mark status in the struggles for courtship and social acceptance. At birthday parties, bars, and other social occasions, young women and men are under pressure to conform to the most recent standards of dress. For both girls and boys, required clothing includes jeans and bright, crisply ironed shirts, with large, ostentatious labels declaring a purer designer pedigree than they have; immaculate white tennis shoes; and, for the boys, imitation fancy watches. For the girls, the most recent styles of nail polish, lipstick, and eye liner as advertised on TV, worn by female newscasters, soap opera heroines, or Xuxa (a popular television personality) are all *de rigueur,* as is being able to comment on where these were bought, at what price, and which media stars wear them. Beauty and hair salons are astonishingly numerous in the urban periphery: in São Jorge alone there were three of them, and they were always busy.

Many of the recreational pastimes of young men are filled with tension. Pick-up games of soccer, either in the street or on the town soccer field, are taken very seriously, and are usually punctuated by rounds of ridicule, cursing, and episodic explosions of anger. Bouts of beer drinking at any one of the local watering-spots can also turn nasty.

Then, of course, adolescents are preoccupied with issues surrounding sex and courtship. Among boys, a major anxiety stems from peer pressure to be sexually aggressive. "My friends would tell stories of having slept with girls," one young man recounted, "so I had to too." Such pressure reinforces competitiveness and can lead to overt conflict. "I'd be with a girl one week," another boy explained,

and the next week a friend of mine would be with her! It was a terrible thing, friends would like the same girls, and that created conflicts. My brother's girlfriend dropped him, and then came to me. That created a fight between us, brothers!

Competitive sexuality and violence can lead young males to alcohol. "Drink was my escape," one young man recounted. "I felt anguish, and drink helped. I wanted to stop drinking, but I couldn't. I was worried about my life in the future, that I would die at eighteen." Occasional violent episodes suggest the presence of harder drugs. One fourteen-year-old lamented that he

went around with kids from here, in the street, but there were always fights happening, it always ended in violence. Violence was the thing that worried me the most. There were always fights, there's always someone who's mad, someone thinks he's better than the other.

Adolescent girls worry, not surprisingly, about finding a husband who will be reliable and not abusive. "I want to get married, but a girl must be very careful," remarked thirteen-year-old Margarida. "I'm afraid of a lot of boys. Who knows how they'll turn out?" Such fears are grounded in the misfortunes of mothers, aunts, cousins, and older sisters. "I'm never going to get married," declared Dania, an eleven-year-old whose father abandoned her mother a few years ago. "They're just a lot of trouble."

Though some girls sympathize with Dania, most still hope to find a man who will, if not cherish them, at least provide for their children and refrain from adultery, excessive drinking, and physical abuse. Handsome, working boys are especially desirable. Girls struggle to improve their chances against each other not only through clothing and cosmetics, but also by potions and love magic, recipes for which may be purchased for a few *cruzados* at any newspaper stand in Rio de Janeiro. Girls sometimes suspect each other of employing evil spirits. "I was with a boy for a long time," Aparecida told me. "Then, all of a sudden, he left . . . and ended up with [another girl]. I knew what she had done. *Macumba*."

Courtship starts for girls around the age of twelve or thirteen, a bit later for boys. Girls still prefer to court boys from town, assuming with some justice that the proximity of the boy's family will act as a check on his conduct. Prospects for marital stability are improved with the son of parents who are already friends, or at least trusted neighbors, of her own family. In such a case, too, the girl knows that getting married will not separate her from her kin.

Yet such pairings are increasingly rare. Local boys often want to take advantage of the proximity of different towns, and prefer to escape the watchful eye of family and neighbors by courting girls from outside the *bairro*. Thus, girls are just as likely to find partners at school, at work, or on the bus—the latter, away from the prying eyes of family and neighbors, is an especially favorite wooing-place. But some girls complain that this pattern contributes to the widespread instability of marriage.[6]

A common arena for flirtation and courtship are parties, especially birthday parties. In São Jorge such parties occur in town at least once a week. Here, the birthday-boy or -girl is helped by the family in serving copious quantities of soft drinks, beer, *salgados,* and cake. The parties are large, loud affairs. Though the family tries to control the number of guests, the food, music, and dancing draw many crashers. After the cake has been served, dancing to amplified music begins. Girls and boys show off their dancing skill, which they rehearse during the week at home with friends, according to the most recent fashions.

Less respectable, but just as common, are the courtship arenas of the dozen bars in town and vicinity. In these, many of the constraints imposed at parties are lifted, and less inhibited drinking and lovemaking can occur. Sometimes a couple will leave the bar and take a room for a few hours at one of the many cheap motels that line the highway. I did not gather figures on the frequency of teenage pregnancy in São Jorge, but I had the impression that it was quite common.

The pressures of the inflationary economy and the low wages earned by parents have increasingly required school-age youngsters to supplement the household income in any way they can. Boys increasingly work part-time in metallurgical factories, as carpenters' assistants, store clerks, and at assorted odd jobs, while girls often work as domestic servants a few days a week and help with cottage industries based in the home. The pressures of a consumption-based youth culture, however, compete for young people's earnings. Up to a third or half of a young person's income may be spent every month on clothes, cosmetics, alcohol, music, and entertainment. The social cost of not spending money this way is high. As one young woman explained,

> You go to a party, and they look at you, studying you up and down, and they'll comment, gossip, say, "Look at what she's wearing! That's not á la mode." So it goes on like that. I try not to pay attention. But I know many girls who'll work extra days just to buy a pair of jeans.

It should come as no surprise that such expenditures create tension with parents, who expect their children to contribute more of their earnings to the household budget. Children's claims to control the money earned with their own labor collide with parents who point out that the child is still under their roof. The latter point, however, rarely sticks. In one household, the son's insistence on buying clothes with his own money led to an unending battle with his father. "He would say I was wasting money that should be helping us out," the young man reported. "But I said it was none of his business. I worked for it, I'll spend it like I want."

Youth and the Catholic *Comunidade*

The discourse and practice of the *comunidade* presents São Jorge's youth with a double, and for some, rather difficult message: to reject many of the values and excesses of youth society while not breaking with it. The first part of this message is familiar fare. *Comunidade* circulars and pamphlets decry alcoholism, drugs, violence, and premarital pregnancy, branding them collectively with the pejorative term "*bagunça*" (trouble). In addition, the priest and pastoral agents denounce the crass materialism purveyed by television, and call on young people to spend more time helping others and less time following the latest fashions.

In practice, however, participation in the *comunidade* does not imply cutting oneself off from youth culture; it means associating with it on new terms. The *comunidade* does not forbid young people to spend money on clothing, makeup, hairstyles, and jewelry; it does not prohibit them from going to parties, soccer matches, dances, and movies, or from listening to "worldly" music. Rather, it calls on them to use judgment and act in moderation. For example, though he stopped attending dances at the Snake Nest bar, Renato, a seventeen-year-old member of the *comunidade,* continued to frequent birthday, wedding, baptism, and holiday parties attended by neighbors and school friends. The Church did not keep him from enjoying himself at the town's annual festival, from playing soccer for the *bairro*'s team of second-stringers, or from occasionally stopping to enjoy a cold beer with his coworkers at the end of his shift at the chemical factory. "God never said abandon your friends!" Renato remarked. "All with moderation, I don't get drunk, but I'll have a beer with the rest of them. We can have fun, all with respect."

The Church's reluctance to enforce a definitive rupture with "the world" is well illustrated by its policy toward marriage. *Comunidade* leaders do not, as I have mentioned, prohibit young Catholics from circulating in dances, the street, bars, parties, and local and regional festivals. Consequently, although young Catholics pay lip service to the importance of marrying practicing Catholics the lack of active sanctions means that religiously exogamous couplings proliferate. Among the half-dozen romantic involvements with which I became familiar that included participating Catholics, I knew of only one pair of Church coparticipants. All the other couples had originated in the non-Church arenas of neighborhood, school, work, and familial friendships. One young Catholic woman, for example, became engaged during my stay to a young man near whom she had grown up, yet who never attended Church, while another young participating man was courting a woman he met at work.

The *comunidade*'s peculiar mix of world-renunciation and world-acceptance calls for a complicated psychological balancing act, in which young Catholics must neither renounce nor abandon themselves entirely to youth culture, but instead strike a compromise with it. The young people of São Jorge who have the greatest chance and strongest drive to pull off this balancing act are relatively better-off, upwardly mobile, and literate, with a strong prior commitment to the Catholic Church.

Most of the dozen members of the youth group[7] grew up in core institutional Catholic families, had displayed from an early age a liking for their parents' Church, and had usually been intimate with religiously

Young members of the *comunidade*

fervent relatives. Délio, a nineteen-year-old leader of the youth group, remembered that

ever since I was little, my mother was very religious, always taking us to Church, I grew up in that rhythm. Studying catechism: I liked it, I always liked religious things. My brothers never felt the way I did. [Why?] Maybe it was because I was so close to my mother, closer than they were. I would always accompany her.

The few participants in the youth group who did not enjoy such strong Catholic backgrounds had become affiliated with the *comunidade* through the patronage of lay leaders who had noticed, in non-church settings, their studiousness, diligence, and calm temperaments. Flávio, a boy of sixteen, reported that his own parents "never practiced anything"; but when he began working in a lay leader's family store,

she'd always say "what a hard worker!", saw I studied my lessons, I was quiet. So she said, "Flávio, you're such a good boy. Wouldn't you like to study catechism?"

Leonora, a girl of fifteen, had a similar experience.

My parents never participated, they hardly had any idea of what a Mass or *celebração* was . . . When I was ten, Rosana put me in catechism because we lived next door, she was always visiting us. She'd say, "What a bright girl!" . . . Because I read well, she invited me to read publicly.

Whether recruited through ties of family or clientage, all the members of the youth group aspired (and were well-situated) to move up in the world. They had all completed or were completing the equivalent of junior high school. Some of the young women worked in office settings as typists or clerks, and hoped to become schoolteachers. Many of the men worked in factories as semi-skilled laborers, but were busily preparing themselves to enter trade school to become skilled machinists, electricians, or pipefitters; a few were even taking home professionalizing courses in order to qualify for low-level white collar occupations such as bank tellers.

Participation in the *comunidade* dovetailed neatly with such worldly social projects. Young *comunidade* participants sought reputations for honesty, industriousness, sobriety, good-neighborliness, and the ability to enjoy a good joke. "I'm a man of God," Renato told me proudly, "so if you give me a centavo, I'll give it back. Look, the Bible said, by the sweat of your brow, and I work every day."

As these men and women expressed it, by helping them avoid *bagunça* the Church was helping them get ahead. "I want to improve my life," Flávio said. "Religion helps you to have family, house, life, stability." Sandra, a girl of seventeen, said, "If I'm going to do something, make something of my life, I can't lose it all now, running around, dropping out of school. The Church helps with that, it helps a lot." These young men and women appreciated the fact that, in contrast to evangelical churches, the *comunidade* imposed no doctrines that might impede the pursuit of higher social status. The men regarded moderate social drinking, taboo in the *crente* churches, as part of the cultivation of male solidarity networks, an important source of job security and advancement. "If I were a *crente*," said one young man,

look what would happen: I couldn't drink even one beer, if I wanted. How can you get ahead? You'd be stuck in the same thing, never change. [What does "getting ahead" have to do with drinking a beer?] Well, all in moderation. I'm against drunkenness. But hey, man, if I'm working somewhere, and someone says, let's have a beer, am I going to say no?

The women not only appreciated the Church for helping them give *bagunça* a wide berth, but also for the fact that it did not disapprove of makeup, styled hair, or fashionable dress, essential ingredients of the "appearance" required of women in the lower echelons of the white-collar world. One of them explained:

The *crentes* of the Assembly, those girls don't want to work, they just want to stay home. If they wanted to be a secretary, or a stewardess, or any kind of career, they'd have to leave that church, because for those jobs you have to have a good appearance. [In the Catholic Church] they don't abandon wearing a soft makeup. . . . It would be difficult to be a pentecostal, wanting to work where I'd have to be well-presented, and wear a little makeup.

The young men and women of the *comunidade* aspired to live in ever-widening circuits of knowledge and power. It is no wonder that they looked with peculiar horror on the fact that some *crente* churches prohibited television-watching, and that some "won't even let you read a newspaper." As one young man exclaimed, "This is the twentieth century!"

THE ALIENATION OF YOUTH
FROM THE *COMUNIDADE*

There are many Catholic youths who would like to participate in the *comunidade,* but who feel awkward and out of place there.

This has partly to do with the youth group's close association with a small circle of friends and relatives, and partly to do with the more general problem of institutional Catholicism's lack of a warm tradition of evangelical outreach. Several people who went to a meeting of the youth group without having been invited told me they had been treated like intruders. "I went to a meeting," sixteen-year-old Matilda recounted, "but they didn't pay attention to me, it was like I wasn't there. It's just for them, the ones who already know each other."

Quite often, such young men and women lack social confidence, a lack aggravated by the *comunidade*'s new, characteristically small groups. Before 1982, young people could mingle with peers from distant *bairros* in a centrally-located *capela*. Now, the Church brings together associates from school and neighborhood. In the absence of a transformative discourse, youthful rivalries, jealousies, and status-rankings from school and street are transferred intact to the religious setting. This transfer provides little social respite for young Catholics beleaguered by uneasy relations with age-mates.

Consider fifteen-year-old Luzia, who completed catechism and First Communion, and went on in the early 1980s to participate in her neighborhood Bible circle and youth group. In her neighborhood and at school, Luzia never felt at ease. In the days before 1982, she had attended Church meetings at some distance from her town. "I loved that," she told me, "meeting girls who didn't know me from school." But when Father Cosme established a *comunidade* in her neighborhood and insisted that locals confine their church attendance to it, Luzia found herself trapped alongside her schoolmates. "They made fun of me," she said, "for being too serious." She stopped participating soon after.

Some young Catholic men and women who are interested in the *comunidade* fail to participate because of strong parental opposition at home. Parents who are themselves peripheral to the Church refuse to accept their children's identification with a religious organization that places their own membership in doubt, a desacralizing Church in the process of usurping the religious authority they, as Catholics, believe they should have over their own children. "They are all snobs now," said one such parent. "Why should my daughter go there, so she can look down on me?" To the extent that nonparticipating Catholic parents refuse to recognize the authority of the new priest, let alone of the laity, it is not surprising that the *comunidade* fails to impart authority to their children.

Parental disapproval makes children's participation in the *comunidade* difficult. "I wanted to participate of my own free will," said Aldio, a seventeen-year-old Catholic. "But when we'd touch on the subject, they'd say I wanted to be better than them, and that led to misunderstandings." Sixteen-year-old Marlúcia recalled that

My father said he didn't like me to be in the Church. He thought the priest was running my life. He said it was better the way it used to be, did I want to be better than other people, like the snobs of the Church, did I want to be better than him?

Marlúcia's situation grew tenser when the progressive priest intruded into one of her father's jealously guarded domains.

He didn't want me to go out with my boyfriend, so I went to talk to Father Cosme. Then someone from the *comunidade* went and told him the priest was encouraging me to disobey him. Now he says I only go to the Church because they're on my side, with my boyfriend, that they're against him because he doesn't participate. He says the priest's only on my side because I participate in Church.

Such tensions take their toll. In both these cases, parental complaints eventually led Aldio and Marlúcia to desist from attending the *comunidade*.

The Church's new aim of remolding parishioners' social consciousness according to elaborate pre-set readings also takes its toll. One Sunday, during the *celebrações,* a selected *comunidade* member read aloud that

The Gospel warns us: it is not enough to prepare ourselves, waiting passively for the manifestation of Jesus. Apathy is against the teaching of Christ. It is necessary to take risks and throw yourself into action so that the received gifts produce fruit. Jesus entrusted to the Christian community the revelation of the will of God and the key to the Kingdom. When we respond affirmatively to the call of Christ, we assume the commitment to place our lives at the service of our brothers . . .[8]

The reader continued for some minutes in this manner, was interrupted by a song, then started again in the same vein. Many young people feel that such readings drain the little emotion left in Mass. Not all young people, of course, emphasize emotionality. Still, I found the complaint of a literate girl of eighteen, from an institutional Catholic background, remarkably common among nonparticipating Catholics:

When I'd go to a Mass, I take one of those guidesheets, I would be sitting there waiting for that to end quickly, I thought it was boring, it felt just like a routine, every Sunday the same thing, the same thing. I wanted an emotional prayer, something from the heart, not something read from a piece of paper.

Aside from the fact that the new emphasis on reading strikes many youths as boring, the content of the readings themselves does not sit well with them. Before Cosme's arrival, the youth group had devoted itself to prayer and the preparation of hymns for Mass; Cosme encouraged members to discuss instead the local neighborhood improvement association. This change led in the early 1980s to an exodus. "They weren't remembering God," said one young man,

just talking about *ganância* [greed], about money. A youth group should participate in the Church, in the songs, the Mass . . . should help old people and children, should read and reflect on the Bible. They shouldn't worry about getting mailboxes.

Those whom ideology drove out of the youth group included not only young people unsympathetic to the new political vision, but also many who attempted to translate that vision into practice. In 1983, for instance, the youth group published a newsletter, invited outsiders to lecture on political topics, and got several of its members elected to the neighborhood association's directorate. These activities resulted in gossip, backbiting, and open disapproval from a large segment of the older upstanding membership. "A youth group is one thing," an old member recalled, "but they were turning it into something else, into something that wasn't the Church." "It came," one ex-member of the youth group remembered bitterly, "so that they wouldn't greet us, wouldn't look at us in Church."

Young activists could not help sensing the hypocrisy in their elders' disapproval, for they used the new Catholic discourse when it suited them. "I thought, there's something wrong with this," an ex-youth-group member recalled.

The Church was changing, but only the priests. The people were changing only in what they said, not what they did. People here in the Church, who didn't help anybody, on Sunday, they'd go to Church, up front, read the Gospel, preach something: "We have to help each other," blah, blah, blah. But they were criticizing us, we who were trying to put things into practice, they could say all they wanted, but didn't practice it at all. . . . How can you stay in Church?

This early experiment eventually collapsed from attrition, its failure becoming a cautionary tale retold by later youthful leaders wishing to justify their return to apolitical prayers and devotions. "They say there once was a group that tried to be political," Délio told me, "a few years back. And it fell apart. So we don't worry about those things now." Now while young participants can use Cosme's language—often with greater fluency than elders long-socialized into the pre-Medellín dialect—they have little desire to translate it into practice. Marisa is typical. "Jesus teaches us simplicity," she declared,

helping others to carry their crosses. Struggling to make the world better for all of us. He teaches us to live in unity and brotherhood, to be always in our community, to do something to help it.

Yet when I asked her whether she participated in a social movement, she replied matter-of-factly, "No, I've never participated in those things."

The apolitical stance of the youth group, not only in São Jorge, but throughout the diocese, according to the parish priests, has led to a loss of the clergy's support. "The real advances nowadays don't come from the young," one priest explained.

They're not really at the cutting edge. Mass culture, *O Globo*, is very strong. Clothing, television, music—they're more alienated now than they ever were. I no longer like to work with them. If we encourage youth groups, they just want to close themselves off. Our experience with them has been negative.

This lack of institutional support has probably further contributed to the youth groups's stagnation in the region. And since it is through such groups that local youth would be recruited, it should come as no surprise that levels of young people's participation in the Church have stagnated as well.

Young People and the Assembly of God

In contrast to the *comunidade,* the Assembly of God calls for a radical break from the society of youth, offering, as well, concrete social alternatives to it. Much of the doctrine of the Assembly of God is premised on the rejection of worldly status competition and courtship practices. Among these is primarily female "vanity": wearing makeup, having one's hair styled, and wearing clothing to enhance sexual attractiveness. As one young *crente* said, "youth nowadays wants all this vanity, they go off to war [to compete]. . . . In the Catholic [Church], the girls just look and look, to see what you're wearing. But in the

Assembly [of God], they don't do this looking." The Assembly of God also denounces young men's displays of toughness, one-upmanship, and obtaining bigger and better material things such as stereos and motorcycles. As failures of humility before God all of these practices are sinful in themselves, and can easily lead to violence, drinking, and drugs. "The Devil," one *crente* said, "makes young people want to be better than each other, they are proud, so when one insults the other, violence results. We have none of that, thank God!"

Once a young person converts to the Assembly, he or she is effectively removed from the company he or she used to keep. Though the new convert may seek out old companions, the latter often keep their distance. As one young convert recounted, "It wasn't me who rejected them, they rejected me. When I converted, they didn't want to have anything more to do with me. See what kind of friends they are?" But this no longer troubles him because "I feel like I have all these new brothers."

Interaction among young men and women in the Assembly is governed by rules that stand in compelling contrast to the competitive lovemaking of the world. While local non-*crente* youths practice courtship beyond the control of any church, courting is closely regulated in the Assembly of God. Young *crentes* must relate to the opposite sex in a "Godly," "wholesome" fashion. The sexes are carefully separated in church on opposite sides of the aisle or in alternating pews, so that, according to one presbyter, "they will keep their minds on God." During bus rides to other churches, chaperones allow girls and boys to sit next to each other. The few opportunities that exist for unchaperoned interaction are church-related, such as the small mixed-sex groups that stand and converse casually in front of the church for several minutes before services, or during choir rehearsals.

Crentes regard premarital sex as a very serious sin. Those who surrender to temptation may be severely disciplined, even excluded from communion for a time, and may suffer the withdrawal of the Holy Spirit. The experience of the Holy Spirit, *crentes* believe, should be more than enough to satisfy young people's libidinal impulses. As one young man explained,

the presence of the Holy Spirit satisfies that desire. If I had less Holy Spirit, the difficulties about sex would be greater. The young person in the Assembly, he is able to overcome the desire for sex. I have been tempted, and turned to the Holy Spirit, which helped me a lot. . . . The Enemy does everything to drag us away: he uses women, temptations to drag Christians from the church.

According to many *crentes*, placing an absolute ban on premarital sex also serves to reduce the jealousies and conflicts that arise when young men fight over women. One *crente*, upon witnessing a brawl, declared, "You see? There is the Devil at work, making young people submit to jealousy and violence. . . . There is always something about a woman, that opens the way for the Devil to darken the hearts of men."

In São Jorge, while non-*crente* boys and girls court beyond the ken of chaperones, the Assembly of God requires the boy to visit the girl only at her home, under her kin's watchful eye. As one presbyter moralized,

Out in the world, you see one going out with one, then another. But in our church it's different: if you like a girl, you go to her father, ask his consent. The relation is different. There's no kissing or hugging. It's decent. Sometimes the girl is outside talking to the boy's sisters, and he's inside with the men!

Crente parents, especially fathers, maintain strict authority over their daughters' relations with men. I knew of *crente* fathers who cut off their daughters' romantic involvements and stood in the way of marriages. In general, *crente* fathers disapprove of extended courtships, because, as one presbyter argued, "The Apostle Paul says that if a man can't remain alone, he should marry. Why drag the thing out?" While non-*crente* courtships frequently last many years (I knew of several that lasted over five years), *crente* courtships usually last no longer than a year. When the boy has proposed and the girl and her parents have accepted, the young people's choir immediately prepares a special hymn, presents a gift to the couple, and arranges for the wedding to take place in church. Weddings tend to be simple affairs: after the ceremony, the congregation and guests gather in the church's *sala* to eat cake and drink soda.

One cannot court and propose marriage to just anyone. A strict interpretation of I Corinthians 7:10–17 obliges *crentes* to marry only other *crentes*. One may remain married to a non-*crente* if the marriage occurred before conversion, but unmarried converts may court only *crentes*. The pastor allows marriages to non-*crentes* only after the latter's conversion. If the non-*crente* does not convert and the marriage takes place anyway (in civil court), the pastor excludes the *crente* from communion until he or she asks forgiveness from the congregation. Though the rule is strict, it is meant more to deter than to punish. After the ordeal, the presbyters readmit the offender, and members henceforth say that the situation now rests in God's hands. "If she is really the one that God prepared for him," one member explained, "she'll pass to the church sooner or later."

CHOOSING BETWEEN THE *COMUNIDADE* AND THE ASSEMBLY OF GOD

There can be no doubt that the Assembly of God's pro-hibitions on dress, conduct, and courting behavior do not weigh lightly on the shoulders of young *crentes,* especially on those of new converts. One convert, for example, was tempted to leave the Assembly when he learned he would no longer be permitted to play soccer. Another convert hid her worldly records for months after her conversion, unable to abandon the music she loved. And several young men confided to me that, while adults might think that rapid courtships simply conformed to Pauline precept, they saw them as the only way to make the Assembly of God's taboo on premarital sex tolerable.

Yet it is precisely these prohibitions, with their promise of release from the competition of youth society, that draw and keep young converts in the Assembly of God. Young people who convert tend to share a strongly negative experience of youth society, including distress about what they call a lack of "sincerity" in school, street, and dances. I found that such youths expressed feeling awkward in the social circles to which they were supposed to belong before conversion. Throughout their conversion accounts, these young people retrospectively construed the social mores that made them feel awkward (generally, sexual and status competition) as the work of the Devil.

Young female converts frequently referred to the "insincerity" of their peers outside the church and to pressure to have sex. These stresses were often associated with fainting spells, depression, "nerves," and attempted suicide. The final straw for these young women often came in the form of a betrayal by a trusted friend.

The story of Madalena, a shy, quiet, young woman of eighteen, is illustrative. She was thirteen when she began feeling estranged by her peers' "lack of sincerity."

I tried to find happiness in dances, but I was disappointed. Sometimes I had that strong desire to go to a dance, make friends. When I'd get back home, I'd feel the void all over again. . . . I was very disappointed by everything: friends, dances, it was all falsity. I wanted to get close, but boys thought I wanted something else. . . . I tried to be sincere, but everyone would just laugh, turn their backs, even take my boyfriends. I was never able to fill that emptiness, that sadness.

Then came the worst sadness of all. "I had a friend I trusted a lot," she recounted, "but she disappointed me, she took away my boyfriend. That made me leave all my friends."

Madalena began to be afflicted not only with depression, but with fainting spells as well. Her mother, a devout Mass-goer, insisted she start to attend the Catholic Church regularly. She did so, but after several months the fainting spells had not ceased. In retrospect, she feels certain why the Church did not help. "Kids were looking at each other there," she remembers, "whispering, holding hands. So they were opening up that place to the Enemy, and he was working in me." I too witnessed ongoing flirtations during services in the Catholic Church; indeed, the Church is notoriously unable to forbid flirtatious behavior in its precincts. It thus confronted Madalena with precisely the kinds of relationships she was trying to escape.

Soon she tried a different tack. Her father, an *ogã* in *umbanda*, told her the fainting spells were due to a spirit demanding she don the sacred white uniform of the *centro*. When she did, however, matters only grew worse. "I just got sick all the time," she recalled. She interpreted her worsening condition as the bitter fruit of her pact with insatiable spirits. Pressing her further on this, she finally said that "something happened" (about which she would not elaborate) at the *centro*, something that convinced her of its members' "lack of sincerity." Whatever happened there, it was exacerbated by her discovery that *umbanda* endorsed Catholic prayers and Masses. "You see," she said, "there's a connection! *Macumbeiros* and Catholics aren't different!"

Longing for surcease, Madalena left *umbanda*, and began "looking around. . . . I was looking, I needed to find sincerity." But the spirits continued to afflict her with fainting spells; these would cease only after she attended the Assembly of God. "My neighbor, inspired by the Holy Spirit, explained everything to me," she recounted. "Saying those spirits were the Devil." At the Assembly she was exorcized. "Jesus finally expelled those spirits for good, and they can't come back, because I have faith in Jesus."

Madalena found evil spirits no longer bothered her because "in the Assembly, no one lets the Devil come to them. There everyone is sincere." If we read "Devil" here as, at least in part, an articulation of insincere, competitive courting relations, we can see that in the Assembly Madalena finally found the "sincerity" she had sought but could not find in either the Catholic Church or *umbanda*. "I saw there something different," she said, "young people sitting quietly, no chitchat, no holding hands in church, I liked that, I found that different."

Like young women, young male converts describe their lives before conversion as fraught with tension about peers' expectations. In some cases, young men's personalities were sensitive and uncompetitive, unsuited to conform to the pressures of sexual and status competition. Such men suffered from chronic anxiety, sadness, and nervousness, leading a few to drink at an early age. In some cases, young men threw themselves with a vengeance into the fray of sexual, physical, and material competition only to be overwhelmed by their own inability to control the intrapsychic and social forces they had unleashed.

Emilio, a slight, olive-skinned *moreno* with intense, penetrating brown eyes, worked as an apprentice pipefitter at a chemical factory. He was nineteen years old when I met him, a year after he had converted to the Assembly of God. He had grown up in São Jorge. His father, an assembly-line operative at the motor factory, insisted that Emilio and his six siblings all receive a Catholic education. He had resented this, and participated in Church until his early adolescence only out of obligation.

Emilio was known in his family and by neighbors for his gentle, sensitive temperament. Although this had won him praise as a child, after turning fourteen he found that it set him at odds with his peers. Most of the time he felt he

couldn't trust anyone. . . . My so-called friends would say one thing; but you never knew what they were feeling in their hearts, they were always lying. I had some disappointments with people in whom I had confided. . . . That saddened me.

He couldn't stomach the rivalries and jealousies that ran rampant through his circle. "Every day it was something else. So-and-so did this, I can do it better, and the swearing, and insults. It was really tiring."

Emilio was also vexed by the constant pressure to seek sexual conquests. "My friends would tell stories of having slept with girls," he said,

so I had to too. There was so much pressure. I accepted it, but with emptiness. I'd be with a girl, and sometimes I'd go beyond the limit, hugging, kissing. . . . But I wasn't satisfied. Tenderness—that's worth much more.

"Tenderness": not exactly a central, organizing value for many young Brazilian males. According to the male prestige complex, Emilio should have surrendered to his sensuality. But he could not. "I was caught," he said, "I wanted sex, but I knew it was a temptation. You always have that thirst, but you must control it!" Worse, in trying to meet his peers' expectations to follow his sexual urges, he found himself entangled in tense, violence-prone situations.

This stuff about having girlfriends brought conflicts between friends, creating anger between us, terrible. Some would beat up someone who had taken away their girl. Always fighting with friends. Sometimes I'd cry, because I saw so many young people fighting around me, all the violence, all over girls and being better than each other.

Emilio longed to escape his peers and the values they espoused. The logical route for him was religion. "I had always been religious, believing in God, going to Church when I was little. So I thought there I could have some peace . . ." The Catholic *comunidade*, however, could not offer him the clear break with youth culture he desired. The very peers he wished to escape

were all Catholics, too, all the kids who were screwing around, they had taken First Communion too. What could I make of that? I felt disgusted, there in the Catholic Church they could be Catholic and do all that.

As far as Emilio was concerned, the only other alternative was *crença*, to which his older sister had already converted. He refused to consider consulting in *umbanda* because, like many other young people in São Jorge, he had imbibed strongly negative images of *macumba*. As he put it, "God can't do good and evil at the same time."

Soon after he turned seventeen, Emilio's older sister invited him to attend the Assembly of God, and he accepted. He rapidly found in *crença* a way to control his sexual urges. His sister

started explaining all about sin, perdition. . . . I heard the pastor preaching about women trying to take away salvation. Women wanted to tempt me, and take away my salvation. I thought that maybe by passing to the *crentes*, that would help me control this temptation. Something touched me deep down. . . . When [I was baptized], I didn't feel so much sexual desire, I was transformed; now it's something I can control, even if I feel it.

Another major pattern among young men is illustrated by the case of Ronaldo, a twenty-year-old son of a retired machinist. By his own account, Ronaldo was a hardened veteran of the worst excesses of youth culture.

I'll tell you, I did everything, everything. There was nothing I wouldn't do, I was so subject to the Devil. Alcohol, drugs. We would go out late and make trouble at dances, shouting, yelling, swearing. And always fights would break out there. I was a fighter! I didn't care, that was what I thought life was about.

By the time he was eighteen, something new began to click in his head: fear.

I don't know how it started . . . seeing buddies die, maybe, that really scared me. In a motorcycle accident, and another from a knife. I started wondering when my turn would come. And when I thought of that, I got scared, I didn't want to die. . . . That kind of life, you think you can do anything, but things start getting out of hand. All the fights, who knew when it would stop? I was afraid of dying. And I thought: if I die now, where will I go? Will I go to hell? I didn't want to go to hell. Death staring me in the face. I had to get out.

He had had little experience of the Catholic Church. His parents had been peripheral to the institutional Church, and all he remembered was having attended a baptism when he was a child. A friend had converted to the Assembly of God, however, and urged him to follow. His decision to do so was clinched by the Catholic Church's reputation as a place "weak in faith" which had "no doctrine or discipline."

I thought I had to be saved from the Devil, that was what was killing me, dragging me to hell. [Why couldn't you be saved from the Devil in the Catholic Church?] [He laughs] They don't worry about the Devil there. Look at the Catholics: they drink, and smoke, and gamble, and do all that. How can the Catholic Church save you? . . . No, in the Assembly of God, God blessed me. There all is purity, no one stabs you in the back. There people are sincere.

CONVERSION AND MARRIAGE

From the viewpoint of numerous unmarried women in São Jorge, the *comunidade* cannot promise that its male members will not be alcoholics, abusive, or sexually promiscuous. *Crente* rules of courtship, in contrast, increase the likelihood of finding dependable spouses. Not only do *crente* men avoid liquor, adultery, and violence; *crente* courtship practices weed out ruffians by reducing shotgun weddings. "The boys in the Assembly," one Catholic woman suggested,

when they want to marry, they are more sincere, they take the sacrament more seriously than Catholic boys do. . . . There you keep your virginity until the day of marriage. It's pure. . . . The boy, if he wants to marry, he has to be sincere with the girl.

Some young *crente* women had no qualms about admitting that the prospect of finding a good husband had been among the Assembly of God's strongest attractions. "I already admired the young men of the Assembly," said one young woman. "I thought: there I will find someone who can make me happy, who will live a life with God." "Outside the church," observed another young *crente,* "all you find are thieves, robbers, men who beat you, drunkards, swearers. Here the boys are good. I will have a happier marriage, I'm sure."

From the male viewpoint, the Assembly of God's courting and marriage rules promise several things: courtships in which their masculinity will not be put on trial; a pool of reliable, "decent," prospective spouses; and the guarantee of patriarchal dominance in the household. The empowering experience of the Holy Spirit seems to provide the confidence needed by young men who have felt frustrated by worldly courtships, either because of their own inadequacy or by what they regard as the wiles of emasculating women. One young convert reported that

before going to the church, I lacked confidence in myself, I was too timid to go near a girl. I thought the only ones who could do that were handsome and smart. Afterward, I had more confidence, I asked God to prepare a girl for me . . . and God would explain to me which one He had chosen for me.

Others recounted stories of "seductresses" who humiliated them and used *umbanda* to bring them to spiritual ruin, from which they could only be saved by the "decent" women of the Assembly of God. Emilio's account has already hinted at this preoccupation. Alberto's story is starker. At the age of eighteen, he became involved with

a very beautiful woman. I am not handsome, she could have had any man, much better than me, rich. I didn't trust her. I wanted her, but I didn't like how she dominated me, I felt sad and confused. She was beautiful, I wasn't. I felt a lot of pressure. I wanted to cut it off. . . . She wanted to destroy me, she was used by the Enemy. She went to *macumba* so that she could keep me. I couldn't separate from her, though I wanted to. I wanted out, but her force was magnetic.

Alberto's liberation from this woman was achieved by his conversion.

I told the pastor everything. Through prayer I freed myself, and she returned to her land. . . . I saw that the women of *crença* are completely different. There they have freed themselves from the Devil, there is love and kindness and respect.

While *crença* promises liberation from the pressures of worldly courtship, it also promises marriages which, according to Pauline law, young men are certain to dominate. One young convert noted that

I used to think, in the *crente* church, the young Christians are more trustworthy, these girls don't go around half-naked. I liked that decency. In the *crente* church, I thought, "this is where I should get a wife."

Emilio, meanwhile, told me happily that

Now we cannot go out with girls unless they are in the Assembly. I liked that idea when I entered. . . . I hoped that going to the Assembly I'd find a spiritual wife, who had a spirituality like mine. . . . The women in the Assembly understand marriage, they take it seriously. They are not going to go running off and sleep with other men.

Indeed, men who have strayed from the Assembly often return to settle down with a *crente* wife, saying they came back because they "needed religion." Similarly, some distanced sons of *crentes* return after having married non-*crentes* in the hope their wives will convert and become God-fearing, obedient women. "A family needs religion," said one returnee, "so that everyone can learn what God wants them to do at home."

In general, the supply of "loving, kind, and respectful" partners plays so pivotal a role in the recruitment of young people to the Assembly of God, that adults indulge in half-serious complaints about it. During a prayer meeting in a small *crente* congregation, a young man wished to take his leave before the service had started. As he approached the pulpit to excuse himself, the pastor, a twinkle in his eye, refused to let him do so. "What is this?" he teased, "Are you going to abandon us? Could it be that the real motive for you coming today is not here?" "No, brother," the youth insisted, "when I come here, my mind is always on God." Only after making the young man squirm for some minutes did the pastor give him leave to go.

CONVERSION AND
FAMILY RELATIONS

It may seem paradoxical that so many young *crentes* are children of Catholics, for one might expect Catholic parents to stand in the way of their children's conversions.[9] After all, the conversion of Catholic children can bring about intra-household tensions, as is suggested by a Catholic father who refused to talk with his *crente* son or by another father who threatened to cast his convert son out of the house. In general, however, non-*crente* parents tend to support their children's new religious identity, especially when they discover that it renders them more respectful in the home, and provides safeguards against their slipping into *bagunça*. One recent convert's father said that, at first, he did not like the idea of his son's conversion, but that soon he felt "no longer worried about [him]."

He used to answer back, but no more. He respects, because in *crença*, there's respect and discipline. There's no lying there. My son is so honest now, he would return a pen. . . . Now I'm more worried about my other son who isn't a *crente!*

Another convert's mother also spoke of the transformation wrought by her daughter's conversion:

Before, she was nervous, swore a lot. And she has more respect for me, she doesn't get mixed up in bad things. . . . Tania has changed a great deal; she used to exalt herself, before, she didn't want to obey me; now she does. Now she knows what's right and wrong.

In some cases, youthful converts' change in conduct impressed parents so deeply that the parents followed them into the *crente* fold. In contrast to young participants in the Catholic *comunidade*, who generally need encouragement, it was often *crente* youths who took the lead, their parents following behind. For instance, one young *crente*'s mother claimed that her daughter's transformation had moved her to convert:

She used to live by crying, tried to kill herself. I saw how different she was, the way she dressed, spoke, stopped running around. I saw all this, the Lord tested me, and I passed [converted].

There is another reason parents convert after their children. Although conversion reinforces outward obedience to parents, it also carries the threat of weakening inward assent to them. This threat raises special concern among fathers. One father, though satisfied by his converted children's obedience, conveyed a certain disquiet about what he suspected might be their unspoken feelings. "My son doesn't say anything against me," he noted,

but I was embarrassed that they knew more than I did. They thought I was without a religion. So I felt embarrassed. They were studying the Word; I didn't even know it. I felt awkward: I didn't have the pretty thing they did. At bottom, though they showed me respect, I knew that they thought they were right, that I was wrong, on the wrong path.

For this reason, he began to consider the possibility of converting. "It's not good for the family," he reflected, "for them to go off one place, me another. A family should be in the place of the father."

The overall role played by Catholic parents' support for their children's conversions to *crença* is well-illustrated by the case of Sandra, a young *negra* of seventeen, whose father, Enrique, was deeply involved in the Catholic *comunidade*. Until she turned sixteen, she had faithfully accompanied her father to Church. She was troubled, however, by his alcoholism. "It was horrible," she recalled, "to live with a father who spent all his time drinking in the street. I'd have to go into the street to get him, it's horrible." Through conversion to pentecostalism, and by conforming to the Assembly's strict rules of dress and conduct, Sandra increased her authority to challenge her father's drinking habits. "After I passed to the church," she recalled,

I had more courage to take him to task, because I was looking for the right path, trying to correct myself, so I was able to take him to task. I said to him: "It's not nice for the head of a family with five children at home to go into the street and drink, it's not nice."

Her forthrightness was rewarded:

When he saw how I had changed, he started to fix his own life. He stopped to think a bit, and saw I was right. That made my faith grow even more. And he understood, and thank God I succeeded . . . He abandoned drink, for my sake, because I asked him, I implored him. My father has changed, he no longer is the one he was before, he used to drink so much. . . . Now he's going to AA, and he has become a new man.

Although Sandra's father never converted, he now sees his own abstinence from alcohol as depending on his daughter's *crente* identity. As she put it, "now, though at first he didn't like me going to the Assembly, now he wants me to stay there, because he sees it helps me and it helps him. He likes me to be a *crente,* he says it gives him the will to keep from drinking. As long as I am a *crente,* he won't drink."

Unlike their counterparts among children of active Catholic parents, children of *crente* parents are taught to regard their religious lives as a matter of individual free will. *Crentes'* insistence on personal conviction leads them, in fact, to exercise less authority over their children's religiosity than many Catholic parents.[10] As one *crente* woman explained, "one cannot be obliged to accept Jesus. When it's their time, they will come." A member of the *comunidade,* in contrast, informed me that

as long as my children are minors they have to respect the religion of their parents. I'd never let a daughter of mine who was only sixteen go to another church. It depends on me, I'm the one who's teaching her.

Pentecostals say that when children reach the age of ten or twelve, they should decide for themselves to what church, if any, they want to go. In an arena with readily accessible religious options, such freedom is hardly a mere formality. When one *crente* mother told her daughter on her twelfth birthday that she could choose her own way, the daughter promptly began attending Catholic Mass.

A common pattern for young people raised by *crente* parents is to distance themselves from the church around the time they are expected to make a decision about baptism, usually in their early to mid-teens. It is precisely at this time that male youths start to leave the home in order to earn wages, enter high school, or join the army. As a result, they find themselves exposed to a variety of new influences, less directly related to kin and neighborhood than to youth culture in general.

Though they hope their children will end up in the Assembly of God, *crente* parents interpret their choices to go elsewhere, even to remain indifferent to all places of worship, as the trials God has set to deepen their faith before they finally return to the true religion. Though I sometimes heard jeremiads about "losing youth to the world," most of the *crentes* I knew took the estrangement of their children in stride, often drawing parallels to the Babylonian Captivity or to Jesus wandering in the desert. For example, when the youth group visited young people who had distanced themselves from the church, no one spoke of perdition; rather, they simply urged the youth to return to church. More often than not, such confidence is justified, for many distanced young people return to the fold around the time of marriage.

YOUTH AND THE FRAGMENTATION
OF THE PENTECOSTAL ARENA

Young people are shaking the very foundations of the pentecostal world. While currently supplying the Assembly of God with its most rapidly growing base, they are also smuggling into it centrifugal tendencies that contribute in the short run to the church's fragmentation, and may in the long run lead to its doctrinal transformation.

The extremism of youth leads some young *crentes* to throw themselves with volcanic energy into the pursuit of spiritual gifts. For example, a disproportionate number of prophets are unmarried or recently married men and women. "Young people are more courageous, more energetic," one young prophet declared.

The older ones are afraid, they swallow the spirit, but they grow sick, and can even die from that! The youngest have more strength to be used, they are more confident! . . . Old people don't make any more room for the Spirit, for them, they just come and sit; for them it's become a routine.

Yet the frequency of youthful prophecy does not sit well with church elders. Committed to maintaining discipline, they commonly reprimand young prophets for overstepping doctrinal limits, and have even begun to identify some prophets as "of the flesh," as manifestors of human pride. Presbyters increasingly choose to interpret Paul's injunction— "The spirit is subject to the prophet, and the prophet is not subject to the spirit"—as demanding controlled, quiet prophecy. "A kid converts, is happy, feels the Spirit of God," the pastor complained, "and then, without preparation, without study, without anything, thinks he can prophesy. Prophecy isn't as easy as that!" Such criticism has prompted some young prophets to turn to the "hot," small churches (e.g., God is Love) where spontaneous prophesy remains unstifled.

While church leaders concern themselves with preserving control over their young "*santificados*," they also remain vigilant against the contrary trend: they know that, while young *crentes* seek to escape the pressures of the world, the world continues to present strong temptations. Among these, two of the most powerful are music and vanity. Church leaders worry about losing young members to churches, such as the Universal Church of the Reign of God or the Baptists, that are more accommodating of worldly music and dress.

São Jorge's pastor and presbyters forbid *crentes* to listen to any music that resembles jazz, folk, blues, samba, or rock, that is, the very rhythms young people find most alluring. It is no wonder the church looks at this music as the work of the Devil: among the most evocative of mnemonics, music transcends rupture, conjuring up the tenderest moments of past, abjured lives. Young *crentes* find few prohibitions more irksome than that against non-church music. A member of the Assembly of God's youth choir admitted,

The world offers many things to young people. So many temptations: music that is so animated that you want to dance, you can't control yourself. I avoid going near parties, because I know that music will tempt me.

Another young *crente* told me,

Young people have a hard time liberating themselves from the music of the world. Because it reminds you of good times. You can only do it [liberate yourself] with fasting and prayer. I threw away my records, I broke them all. But I kept one record that was a memory of an old boyfriend.

Some *crente* pastors, in other towns, have tried to accommodate more diverse musical tastes. In a congregation of the Assembly of God located near Rio de Janeiro, I heard a young electric guitar player hold an audience of three hundred spellbound for fifteen minutes with silvery liquid blues. When I mentioned this to São Jorge's pastor, he listened intently, then remarked,

Yes, I know that place, I understand what the pastor is trying to do. I'm sympathetic, yes. But not here. It's just not in the Bible, I can't bring myself to do it. That's the way they keep the young ones in. I say, keep them by faith or nothing.

Such rigidity has consequences. In the past two years, several young people have left the Assembly of God to attend the Universal Church, which offers, among other things, "better" music, including songs by Roberto Carlos and Caetano Veloso.[11]

Young people's other major temptation is "vanity." In contrast to his rigid policy on music, São Jorge's pastor is more pragmatic when it comes to clothing.

The Bible doesn't change, but if we established today the old way that the people dressed, it wouldn't work at all, young people would just leave. There are other churches they can go to if they're not satisfied. I have to say "let's tolerate it, let's teach, we'll accept it a little." Otherwise we wouldn't have any young people here at all. Now, we don't require that they wear a tie, because sometimes they can't even afford a suit. But to wear a long-sleeved shirt, yes! But they have already transgressed. And I can't punish them, it has to be something that we do slowly, with toleration until they understand.

Young *crentes* take these inches and turn them into miles. One young convert began to go shirtless and short-panted on hot days on the side-street where he lived. When a deacon threatened to discipline him, the boy pointed out that the pastor's own son wore shorts at home. The pastor, realizing the delicacy of the issue, refrained from disciplining the offender. "I decided," he told me, "to let boys wear what they want as long as it's at home or right near where they live. But as soon as they turn the corner onto the main street, they must wear long pants."

The pastor must strike a very delicate balance between the generations. The smallest liberalizing gesture can backfire, leading to the loss of hardliners to more rigid churches. João, a onetime member of the

Assembly of God, left three years ago when the pastor decided publicly to permit the watching of television (though only of "decent" programming), which had in any case by then become a *de facto* practice. "He just wanted the young people to stay!" João remarked angrily. "What about their salvation? Did he think of that?" He was so annoyed that he went to *Deus é Amor*, where, he said, "they know the danger of television."

"They Don't Let Them Play Soccer!"

In this chapter, I have argued that young people who seek escape from the pressures of youth society find the Assembly of God more conducive than the *comunidade* to this end. This point is far from clear to the liberationist clergy in the region of São Jorge, many of whom assume that young people, mired as they are in the pursuit of youth culture, are even more averse to pentecostalism than they are to the *comunidade*. "Look," said one priest, "young people don't convert to *crença*. I'll bet you don't see any young *crentes* over there. They're not going to go to a church where they prohibit soccer. They don't let them play soccer!" He might qualify his opinion if he heard Gilcemar, a recent convert to the Assembly of God, on Brazil's national sport: "I hated it. There were always fights, and if you missed, boy, would they give it to you. Thank God I don't have to do that any more."

6

Slaves and Wanderers

Negros *in the Religious Arena*

"Why Has God Called So Many Dark Souls?"

In the region of São Jorge, both *umbanda* and the Assembly of God are "blacker" than the Catholic *comunidade*. Among the *comunidade*'s forty most active participants, only five call themselves "*preto*" or "*negro*," and among the other fifty regular participants, no more than ten do.[1] In contrast, among the 270 active members of São Jorge's Assembly of God, between a third and a half are *negros*. Among its eight presbyters, half are *negros,* and numerous *negro* deacons and auxiliaries fill positions of visible authority. (The half-dozen other *crente* churches I visited in the region had, if anything, even larger proportions of *negros*.)

The racial disparity between the two churches was so obvious that it frequently gave both Catholics and *crentes* cause for reflection. "This is something we discuss in the [Bible] groups," noted one white Catholic, "that the *negros* frequent other churches more than the Catholic Church." The white pastor of the Assembly of God concurred. "Of course there are more *negros* with us. We were talking about this just the other day: why do they come? Why has God called so many dark souls?"

In estimating the extent of *negros'* participation in *umbanda* I have tried to avoid being influenced by the widespread stereotype of the religion as "black." Most local people agree with Rosana's assertion that "if you meet someone who is *preto,* you can be sure that he is a *macumbeiro.*" My own observations only partially corroborated this image. The people who came for consultations in the *centros* I attended were equally divided between *negros* and non-*negros. Negros* did, however, clearly predominate among spirit mediums. Of the forty-two mediums I saw in these *centros* twenty-five were *negro* or dark *mulato.* Three of the *centros,* in fact, had crystallized around cores of *negro* parents and children.[2]

A chief reason for the strong presence of São Jorge's *negros* in *umbanda* and pentecostalism lies in these religions' discourse of spiritual transformation, which allows them to produce powerful counterdiscourses to racism. The enduring belief among Catholics in the continuity between the secular and sacred realms, on the other hand, unwittingly undermines progressive leaders' efforts to construct a counterdiscourse to racism.

The Myth of Racial Democracy[3]

A rough sketch of race relations in São Jorge is necessary to understand the trajectories of working-class *negros* as they turn to the religious arena for help in constructing their identities. Delicate racial subtexts insinuate themselves into virtually all interactions among townspeople. Jacqueline, a *negra* in her mid-twenties, put it this way:

It's little things, that's why they deny it. But you feel it, you feel it deep down. You try not to care, but you do. You're walking, minding your own business, but you know you're always being watched, they look at you out of the corner of their eye, always watching, but when they pass you they won't smile, they won't greet you. They walk by quickly, fast, they keep their distance. That's the way it is. It's not big things. But it wears you down each day.

Such "little things" cast doubt on Brazil's cherished image as a place where skin color is less important than class insofar as how one is treated. For Jacqueline is speaking, not about wealthy white employers in Rio de Janeiro, but about her lighter-skinned neighbors.

In everyday speech, locals rank Brazil's three "races," placing at the bottom people with the most African "blood," below those with Indian and white "blood," and associating beauty, intelligence, and refinement with light skin and the absence of African traits. Nappy black hair, for example, is usually referred to as "bad hair." Light-skinned locals also

regularly make invidious comparisons between *negros* and Indians that
harken back to images of the brave Indian who resisted slavery and the
negro who submitted to it.[4] One white woman asked me rhetorically
whether I

ever saw a *negro* on TV going and saying, "I am a *negro*, I want such-and-such"?
No, they are ashamed of themselves. But the Indian, you see him go to Brasília
on TV, to demand things from the government. They are proud. They never
were slaves, they were too proud for that.

Lighter-skinned locals more readily note lapses of politeness in *negros* than they do in whites. Once I was standing in a bar with a
light-skinned man who was busy asserting that *negros* expected to be
waited on "puffed up with demands. Whites come here with respect
and decency." Shortly afterwards, both a white and a *negro* bought
drinks. As soon as the *negro* left, my companion leaned over conspira-
torially: "See? Didn't say please, didn't say thank-you. See?" He hadn't
expected such niceties from the light-skinned customer, who had said
nothing more than the *negro*.

Light-skinned people attribute *negros'* "lack of respect" to their
bitterness about slavery. One light-skinned man not only blamed the rise
in local crime on *negros*; he went on to say that

pretos were slaves once, and now they're angry at us. That's why they steal from
us, that's why they shouldn't have high positions. They'll use them for vengeance. If they were teachers, they'd teach our children to hate us.

The ideology of racial democracy has taught light-skinned locals to
mask racial slurs as jokes. For instance, as I was chatting with a white man
on the anniversary of Brazilian abolition, a *negra* he knew passed us by.
Giving me a wink, he raised his voice for her benefit: "The day of the
criollos! [He laughed] I think it's wrong, they should still be under our
whip! Oh, Maria, you should still be our slave, shouldn't you?" Maria
returned his cackle with one of her own. Later I asked her how she felt
about the exchange. "Some people like to make those jokes," she said,
"but it's lack of courtesy. It hurts deep down. But I can't say that, he
would just ridicule even more."

Lighter-skinned locals avoid coming into physical contact with *negros*
in a variety of subtle, and not so subtle, ways. Light-skinned persons
greet light-skinned acquaintances, but not *negro* ones, with a kiss. A
young *negra* who offered to carry a white neighbor's child was met with

Negros in São Jorge

the reply, "No, don't, I don't like *pretos* to touch my children." And an elderly *negra* informed me, when I wiped my brow with a cloth saturated with her sweat, that such behavior was rare, because "whites are afraid of turning into *negros*."

Although light-skinned locals do not all denigrate *negros* to the same degree, virtually all deny being racist, admitting only that racism used to exist "in the time of slaves," or that it exists in Brazil, but "not here." When out of earshot of *negros,* however, many freely discussed their less than racially democratic feelings with me. "Look," one of them explained, "I think all *pretos* are ugly. That's just my prejudice." He smiled. "Everyone is prejudiced. Whites say they aren't in front of *pretos,* but among ourselves, no one denies it."

São Jorgenses sometimes try to rebut claims that their society is racist by pointing to the extent of its interracial marriage and miscegenation. Yet kinship does not erase racial prejudice; it only reshapes it. Darker-skinned children are often called "darkie" by their own parents. Light-skinned grandparents often complain that their grandchildren "are too dark," and, in a few cases brought to my attention, have been known to give them fewer presents than their lighter-skinned siblings. A few dark-skinned women recounted that in their youth they had been expected to do more chores around the house than their lighter-skinned siblings. Light-skinned men and women often refuse publicly to acknowledge their relation to dark-skinned *compadres.* And in interracial marriages, race often arises as a rhetorical weapon during fights and disputes. I was told several times that in mixed couples the lighter partner will resort in anger to the barb that they "should never have married a darkie."

People who are the product of *"mistura de raça"* ("mixture of race") face special problems.[5] In São Jorge, *"mulato"* and *"moreno"* are terms of consideration compared to *"negro,"* which, when spoken by a white, has unmistakably pejorative overtones. Some people speak of the contextual quality of racial usage with striking self-awareness. "I'll say Heloisa [a nun] is *morena,*" one white explained. "But if she were a prostitute, for me she'd be a *negra.* Or Antônio. He's a *mulato.* But if he were a troublemaker, for me he'd be a *negro.*"

When I asked people subject to such terminological fluidity to identify themselves racially, they would invariably begin by reciting the well-known adage, "I'm *preto.* If you're not white, you're black." Yet they never ended with this, recounting instead lengthy narratives about the various bloods and shades of color in their families, drawing attention

The colors of São Jorge

to light-skinned relatives, claiming ignorance of slave predecessors, and asserting Indian ancestry whenever possible. The detail, commentary, and length of such litanies struck me as designed to subvert whatever identifying conclusion one might draw from them. *Negros* resent such efforts to distort ancestry and avoid self-identification. "*Mulatos* are more racist then whites," one *negro* declared.

knowing that the *negro* is a dishonored class, by society, him being *mulato*, he won't even talk about *pretos*. He's no longer *negro*, he only wants to talk about whites. He'll tell you he's Indian, that he never heard of *negros* in his family. But he'll never be able to arrive at the side of the whites.

The Problem of Race in the Catholic Church

As a cult of continuity, the Catholic Church emphasizes the overlap between the world and church, and thus unwittingly reinforces among its members the belief that the stereotypes they hold outside the Church apply within it as well. This belief has contributed to long-standing racial discrimination in the Church and to the formation of a predominantly light-skinned leadership and followership. *Negros* who have achieved positions of leadership in the Church have done so thanks mainly to long-term struggles to transcend racial barriers, and through the patronage of light-skinned lay leaders and clergy.

The peculiar barriers set up by the Church and the means for overcoming them are well illustrated in the story of Enrique, currently one of the few *negro* leaders of the Catholic *comunidade*. I met Enrique, the only local *negro* to coordinate a Bible circle, soon after my arrival in town, in the *salão* of the Catholic Church. The tall, lanky construction worker in his late forties was play-acting the role of a clerk in a skit dramatizing the obstacles to full employment. In front of some fifty members of the *comunidade*, one "applicant" after another presented himself to Enrique to ask for an imaginary job. "Too old!" he said to one. "Can't read!" to another. At one point, an "applicant," upon being dismissed, grumbled aloud, "*Negão danado* [cursed nigger]!", a bit of improvisation that caused general hilarity. Enrique displayed no emotion.

After the skit was over and everyone was munching cookies and sipping coffee, I approached Enrique and introduced myself as the American who had come to São Jorge to study the Church. He said he was glad I had finally sought him out. I asked what he thought of the moment when everyone laughed. His eyes narrowed and the corners of his lips curled into the faintest hint of a smile—whether of pleasure or irony I could not tell.

"Ah. You saw that. Well . . . what can you do? Come and see me."

We began meeting on Saturday afternoons. When I'd arrive, Adalva, a heavy-set, strong-willed *mulata* in her late thirties, to whom Enrique had been married for twenty years, would yell, "Oh, Enrique! Jonas is here for an interview!", then bustle about, snapping orders to her six children, aged six to fifteen, to make beds and sweep floors while she washed clothes and watered the pigs in back.

Enrique was the youngest son of seven children in a sharecropping family in Minas Gerais. His father's land supported the family well enough for him never to know dire need. "My father was a proud man," he said. "He worked hard all his life." He also insisted Enrique learn how to read. "He told me that someday I would show the whites that *negros* can do more than till the soil." Enrique's mother was a devout Catholic. Though the family lived too far away from the chapel for her to participate in Church on a regular basis, she permitted herself to dream that someday her gifted boy would become a priest. "I was close to her," Enrique recalled,

She taught the Ave Maria, she taught the spoken catechism . . . would sit and listen to me to see if I had learned. . . . She would say to me: "You are *negro*, but you can do whatever whites do."

Shortly after his ninth birthday, the landlord's doctor gave him the opportunity of a lifetime: to live with him and study in Muriaé, the largest city in eastern Minas Gerais. He went happily. His experience in attending Church each Sunday, however, was another matter, for it was here that he was first exposed to racial discrimination. "There was this course for choirboys," he recalled,

Sundays, all dressed in red, I got excited about that. I said to myself, "I can be a choirboy too." With those other boys. . . . But when they chose choirboys, they chose the whitest. I was put to one side.

Such treatment did not sit well with his unsinkable temperament. He soon set out to prove to his colleagues at school and in Church that he would not allow them to consider him "just another *negro*."

I made a lot of friends. I had smarts, I was lively. I was always a good student. White boys would even come and say "Enrique, teach me this." So I'd show them, everyone would laugh, that group huddling around like that. That made the color of my skin disappear. . . . They depended on me for many things, I felt myself very responsible, so I didn't feel any difference of color.

Still, in what mattered to him the most, Enrique could not escape the consequences of the color of his skin.

The priest felt I had a greater faith, I was different from the others, I didn't stay in a corner all quiet, whatever I did I was a perfectionist. So finally he let me be the only *preto* choirboy.

The cleric drew the line, however, when Enrique dared to think he might have a vocation for the priesthood. "The priest wouldn't talk to me about that," he recalled. "He opposed my *negro* color, he said I should forget about it." I asked Enrique why he thought the priest had discouraged him.

The priest is like the rest of them. They don't trust the *negro*. They think you give the *negro* a little responsibility, he'll abuse it. [But why? If the *negro* is a good Catholic?] They never think we're "good Catholics." We can't ever be perfect there, for them. They think that if they see *negros* doing bad things in the street, then we may slip into that easily, even if we're in church.

Enrique remained in the doctor's household until he had finished high school. He hoped to continue his studies, and even fantasized about medical school. Soon after turning seventeen, however, he was obliged to return to the countryside to take care of his ailing father; there, he married a neighbor's daughter and had a child. Survival now required forgetting about school. In the late 1960s, he travelled with his family to São Jorge and landed a job as a warehouseman at the motor factory.

Here, try as he might, he could not forget the better life he had tasted in Muriaé. He tried to get involved in the Church. "I went to Marian Congregation," he recounted,

because I had that inclination of the religious person, and the Congregation was a very pretty movement. It was well organized, the members had a lot of commitment to the Church.

But here, Enrique was once again was confronted by racism.

I was one of the few *negros* in the Congregation. There were readings to be done, so many things, and I was always excluded, always left to one side. Whenever there was some representative chosen, they'd always choose other people. A mission would come up, of president, secretary, treasurer, it would never come to me. Even by competence, it would never come to me.

The jokes were even worse. "Those jokes that you had to laugh at, 'the *preto* is the child of the Devil, the white is of God'; and 'the *negro* is in the church like a dog, because he finds the door open.' That would make me shiver." Enrique could not stand it any longer.

I found that the Catholic Church was a place for whites, that it was really for bluebloods. When I would look at Christ at certain moments, I would see that even Christ had blue blood, blonde, with blue eyes. Why? I thought. Aren't we children of God? . . . I arrived at an extreme, to abandon meetings, not to frequent anymore.

It was not until the late 1970s, when Enrique was invited by a light-skinned neighbor to participate in a *cursilhista* Bible circle, that he began participating again. "I knew Antônio," he recounted,

I used to play guitar with him in the bar. When he invited me to participate in the group, I accepted because I respected him, I saw the number of friends he had, the love people had for him. So when he invited me, I wanted to please him. . . . Afterwards, I liked it and kept going.

Later, Antônio invited Enrique to attend the *cursilho,* which led to his eventual appointment as reflection group leader.

THE PROBLEM OF RACE IN
THE *COMUNIDADE*

Enrique now takes pride in having opened the way for a few other ambitious *negros* to arrive at *comunidade* leadership. Yet the *comunidade* has inherited the attitudes of its light-skinned core of followers. Enrique and the others continue to find themselves at the receiving end of a double standard. "You saw how they laughed during the skit," he noted. Enrique's wife reported that whenever her husband took a drink, "they say, 'Oh, that *negro!*' But when Maurício [a white leader] drinks, no one comments." Enrique especially resents never having been selected to represent the *comunidade* to outsiders. "No matter what we do," he sighed, "light people [*as pessoas mais claras*] always find something wrong, they're afraid people will get a bad impression of the *comunidade.*" Only lighter and light *mulato* children, he pointed out, had ever coronated the image of Our Lady during her May festivities. And only rarely were *negros* called upon to read before the assembled *comunidade* during the *celebração.*

Other leaders confirmed these impressions. A *negro* whom Cosme appointed as Minister of the Sick encountered coolness among the families he visited. "I'd arrive in a house," he reported,

the person tells me to enter, I take off my shoes, but they stay there, looking at me funny, you always feel like you're not accepted. . . . They leave me there with the sick person, sometimes I'd say the prayer there almost alone, the others are in the kitchen, in their room, they don't come to be with us. I mean, I'd feel that that was a discrimination. Once, a lady even refused to let me give her the host, she wanted Dona Rosana.

Most seriously, *negros* in Church say that light-skinned leaders deliberately block their access to positions of authority. "People with less capacity than me," one aspiring *negro* complained, "get positions in the Church because they're lighter." Indeed, the two *negros* in the *comunidade*'s council were not elected like the others, but appointed by the priest, and even these, according to the *negros,* had not been safe. When, for instance, Father Cosme appointed a *negra* to the council, a light-skinned leader approached the priest and claimed his appointee did not want the post. "But I did, I did!," the appointee told me. Even now, she says, other council members rarely consult her or inform her of meetings.

Racism also inheres in light-skinned Catholics' views of Our Lady of Aparecida, the patron saint of Brazil. Our Lady is normally represented in chromolithographs and plaster and wood statuettes as *negra* or *mulata*. Most white and *mulato comunidade* members try to deny or minimize Our Lady's color, agreeing with Odilia, a *beata* [strict Church-goer], that "Yes, she was black. But that was because the fishermen found the image covered in mud." Others argue that the image "inside was white, it had a white soul." Still others claim that those who said the image was black were simply mistaken. "That's just a story they tell," one white woman informed me, "the *negros*, because they want to believe it. But it's not so. Nossa Senhora is white, as white as can be."

Again, one reason for the *comunidade*'s failure to undermine racism is that progressive Catholic discourse, like the larger Catholic discourse of which it is a variant, proclaims the continuity between world and church. If someone has certain traits outside the Church, Catholic discourse presumes he will have them inside the Church as well. Thus, Catholics who believe *negros* to be *macumbeiros*, drunkards, lazy, and untrustworthy outside the Church apply such stereotypes to them within the Church as well. "It is hard for *pretos* to be good Catholics," one white *comunidade* member explained. "How could they be, they drink too much, they're always in *macumba*." *Negros* are well aware of such sentiments. "I never felt at home in the Catholic Church," said one. "I always felt everyone was looking at me. You know how it is? 'What's he doing here, that *preto*, that *macumbeiro*?' 'Cause you know, for them, all *pretos* are *macumbeiros*."

THE BROTHERHOOD
CAMPAIGN OF 1988

Liberationist priests have done their best to overcome these prejudices, most notably in 1988, the hundredth anniversary of the abolition of slavery.[6] The Brazilian government's preparations for the centennial galvanized the Association of Black Religious and Seminarians, a group of priests, nuns, and seminarians based in São Paulo and Rio de Janeiro, to call on the National Conference of Brazilian Bishops to declare race the theme of 1988's Brotherhood Campaign.[7] Dioceses headed by progressive bishops such as Dom Mauro Morelli mounted a campaign to bring about change in racial attitudes, most dramatically by urging those of visibly mixed ancestry to call themselves *negros*; by depicting abolition, contrary to its official portrayal as a gift from the white man, as having been a means to better exploit blacks' labor; and by invoking the great black heroes of Brazilian history, such as Zumbi and Anastasia.[8]

Despite these commendable efforts, São Jorge's *negros* stayed away from the Campaign in droves, and reports from elsewhere suggest that such avoidance was typical throughout much of the diocese. In orientation meetings, pastoral agents called on group leaders to make a special effort to invite their *negro* neighbors. Yet in the several *comunidades* for which I was able to gather information, the only *negros* who attended Campaign meetings regularly were those few who already participated in the *comunidade*. The other *negros* who visited the groups tended to remain silent and soon desisted. "The Campaign is frozen," one regional coordinator complained bitterly. "I invited many, many, but they don't come, or they only come once and don't like it."

The problem was not *negros'* lack of sympathy for the Campaign's discourse. *Negros* peripheral to the Church are largely in favor of those who call themselves *mulatos* starting to call themselves *negros* instead, and are well aware of whites' hypocritical use of May thirteenth [the anniversary of abolition]. I met no *negro* who subscribed to the official version of the celebrated day. One *negro's* account was revealing: "The day is always a joke to the whites. That's why I never trusted the day, I thought it's just a joke of the whites."

What then was the problem? Part of the answer is that the Campaign was organizationally locked into preexisting *comunidade* structures, complete with lighter-skinned leadership. Thus, the Campaign's guide-book, designed for preexisting Bible circles, automatically created a light-skinned core of participants. As Enrique observed: "Most of the people who usually participate are white. So most of the people in the Campaign were white, too."

I met a small number of a lighter-skinned Bible circle members whose opinions were indeed influenced by the Campaign. One woman who had always identified herself as a *mulata* declared that henceforth she would call herself "*negra*." Another woman who admitted to having "been afraid of *pretos*" insisted that she felt herself softening, because, she said, "I realize now all the suffering they've been through." And an elderly man proclaimed that he had been convinced that people with darker skins lived harder lives than poor whites.

For most lighter-skinned group members, however, the Campaign accomplished little. Because people with light skins controlled the public interpretation of the guidebook, its lessons were muddied, often beyond recognition. Leaders commonly skipped questions, dismissed parts of the guidebook as irrelevant, and unabashedly encouraged group members to disregard entire passages. In one session I witnessed a leader refuse to discuss the guidebook's pointed question "why do you always offend us *negros?*"[9] When such issues actually found their way into discussion, leaders succeeded in minimizing them with phrases such as "it doesn't happen here," "there's only racism among the rich," or "we are *all* enslaved." Outside the circles, I heard leaders complain vociferously that the Campaign was stoking the fires of racial tension. "The Campaign is stirring up things that shouldn't be stirred up," one of them said. "I don't think much of this thing that it's just the *pretos* who suffer. This all offends the white; don't we suffer too?"

The attitudes of lighter-skinned Church leaders and their followers naturally influenced how *negros* felt about the Campaign. One *negra* I knew attended two meetings, then stopped. "You can tell by looking at their faces," she commented,

how they talk about the *negro*. I saw things, I didn't like it. I saw the whites were just talk. In there *negros* are all their brothers and friends, but you pass one on the street, they wouldn't greet me.

Such mistrust extended to the lighter-skinned militants who led the Campaign at the diocesan level, where the Association of Black Religious was composed largely of people who had once identified themselves *mulatos.*[10] As one peripheral *negro* explained:

Look, *mulatos* have always tried to run away from us. How could they have our culture? They want to use what we have. But it's a lie, because it's not theirs. It's a lie when they say their homeland is Africa, that our religion is theirs, because it isn't.

Enrique felt the issue keenly, for he regarded *mulatos* as the chief obstacle in the way of those *negros* who hoped to enter any door of leadership the Campaign might open. "We don't feel at ease among them," he said. "The movement is just these *mulatos. . . . Mulatos* still think they are better than us. They think the *negro* still needs to look to them as masters."

Perhaps the most problematic effort of the Campaign was its attempt to incorporate elements of African religion and culture into the liturgy.[11]

The Association of Black Religious argued that the time had come for the Church to abandon its antagonism toward African religion and to embrace it as a positive expression of African culture.[12] Pastoral agents attempted to incorporate into the Campaign's ritual what they regarded as the best of African religious traits: the drum and cimbals, hymns with syncopated rhythms, and dancing, all purified of "alienated" practices such as spirit possession.[13]

The attempt proved to have few takers along the racial spectrum. The progressive Church's idealism had simply run ahead of itself. Seeing African-style ritual behavior in Church dismayed many churchgoers. Had they not learned to regard *macumba* as a work of Satan? Such consternation was not limited to light-skinned Catholics: many *negros* feared the Church was trying to taint them, reminding everyone of their special association with the religion of the Devil. As one *negra* noted,

That sent a shiver, a fear that in the midst of us, everything was going to start all over, that there would be a vicious circle, that we were all going to turn into *macumbeiros*.

Moreover, if leaders of the Campaign believed the embrace of "Africanisms" might appeal directly to practitioners of Afro-Brazilian religions, they were, at least in this region, mistaken. The *umbandistas* I spoke with expressed strong mistrust of the Church's newfound liberality. "If they hated me for so long," one medium wondered aloud, "how come all of a sudden they want me now? Can it be that they are losing people?" Perhaps, some *umbandistas* suspected, the Campaign's open-arms policy was a trap. "It's a way of fooling us," one medium declared. "They'll open up, wanting us to demonstrate who we are, and then they'll close up again, but there we'll be, without an out, inside the *comunidade*, exposed."

At the same time, ex-*umbandistas* felt confused by the Church's unprecedented encouragement of a religion that to them represented an evil they had just recently escaped. For Marisa, *umbanda* was implicated in the destruction of her home and the death of her husband. She saw the Church as intent upon making the evil spirits return to haunt her. "I don't agree with this," she told me,

whoever knows what spiritism is, doesn't play with it. The Church is just playing with it, they are showing it a lack of respect. They don't understand that you can't start so easily, because you'll never see the end of it. The spirits will punish you if you don't want to stay with them.

A year after the Campaign ended, I returned to São Jorge. Those who had participated, whether light-skinned or *negro*, admitted to having sighed in relief when the Campaign ended. Some, like Zita, an old white woman, could hardly recall what the Campaign had been about. The great discursive and institutional weight of the Church had ensured, at least this time around, that the effort to forge a counterdiscourse to racism would not get very far. Failing to challenge the premise of continuity between world and church, and falling short of forging a new generation of *negro* leaders, the Campaign simply could not shake light-skinned Catholics out of their deep-seated racism.

The Spirit of Rebel and Docile Slaves

Let us move from the Catholic Church to *umbanda*. *Umbanda* attracts and retains *negros* because, I will argue, it provides a powerful counterdiscourse to racism, and elements for the construction of a strong *negro* spiritual identity. It accomplishes this through its discourse of personal transformation and its recognition of the spiritual specialness of *negros*. For *negros* to become *umbandistas* calls for pride in a mythic *negro* history as well as the renunciation of the project of adapting to white society on its own terms.

My argument is slightly at odds with much recent work on *umbanda*, which views it as a projection onto the spiritual plane of the dominant Brazilian ideology of "whitening" (*embranqueamento*): that peculiar cluster of ideas that foresees the ultimate triumph of light skins over dark ones. In particular, attention has been drawn to parallels between whitening ideology's hierarchy of purity (the less African blood one has, the purer one is) and *umbanda*'s spiritual hierarchy, in which the *preto velho* is at the bottom, followed by the *caboclos* and the white Catholic saints.[14] By presenting the African as docile and humble, and the Indian as proud and powerful, *umbanda* is said to reiterate whitening ideology's claim that the Indian's greater resistance to slavery proved his racial superiority to the African. In addition, the *exús* are, in this view, dangerous and morally ambiguous because they correspond to "uppity" *negros* unresigned to their lot of subordination to the white.[15]

This interpretation of *umbanda* spirits is accurate as far as it goes: that is, it is a fair representation of the views of lighter-skinned mediums. It is, in fact, constructed primarily on the basis of field work in mixed and light-skinned *centros,* as well as on the basis of theology and spell-books written mostly by non-*negros.* However, this interpretation fails to distinguish between *mulato* and *negro* views, presuming that what is hegemonic for lighter-skinned people must be hegemonic for *negros* as well.[16] Thus, according to these writers, *umbanda* represents both the dissolution of black collective memory and the victory of a collective memory defined by white powerholders.[17]

At best, this claim is overstated. When we listen carefully to *negros'* own voices, an alternative version of *umbanda* spirits and spirituality emerges. While overlapping with lighter-skinned and white versions, the *negro* version differs from them in crucial ways. The *negro* version is not, however, a pure, heroic act of cultural resistance. Like all subversive discourses, the *negro* version is not constructed in simple opposition: *negro* mediums flesh out their version of the spirits both abetted by, and in tension with, their lighter-skinned co-religionists. The views of *negro* mediums thus contain elements that draw from the ideologies of whitening and racial democracy. It is crucial, however, to underscore that these elements remain just that: bits and pieces, not systemic wholes.[18]

LUANA'S VACILLATION

Over the course of several meetings, Luana recounted to me how she became a medium, and how this prompted a long struggle with regard to her religious and racial identity. When she first entered the *terreiro* of her mother at the age of fourteen, she felt frightened. "I started to *quebrar cabeça* [develop] there . . . ," she said. "That was a lot of responsibility. Too much for me. But I am a *negra,* it's easier with us."

Luana's claim that "it is easier with us" is far from idiosyncratic; indeed, all the *negro* and white mediums I spoke with agreed that *negros* had a special facility for mediumship. "Whites can go there and learn from them," said a white medium. "We are like their students, the *pretos* are like teachers." In *terreiros* in the Rio area, when men pass through initiation and receive from the *mãe-de-santo* the sacred white clothing of mediumship, the following *ponto* is sometimes sung: "Give the gown to teach the Doctor to dance/Dance, sir, dance sir,/I want to see!"

A *negra* medium interpreted the *ponto* for me: "The one who invented the white clothing was *negro,* it was the *negro* who invited the white to participate. The 'Doctor' is the white man, when he gets the white clothing."

This reading is clearly in tension with the lighter-skinned orthodoxy of *umbanda*, which portrays blacks as crasser and more material, more bound to the earth, and presumably less amenable to spiritual development than those with lighter skins. *Mulatos* give most consistent voice to this orthodoxy. "*Negros* have trouble developing," said one, "they're too thick, too distracted."

At one level, then, *negros'*—and whites'—declarations of *negros'* special spiritual gifts are subversive of whitening ideology. At the same time, *negros* and whites attribute the *negro*'s spiritual receptivity to a greater humility before the spirit—thus reproducing racial democracy's ideal of the passive, humble black. As a *negro* medium put it, "*Negros* are humbler, they don't struggle against the spirit. The white, he's prouder, he'll say, 'No! Don't take my body!'"

Still, if we listen more closely, we hear among *negros* yet another voice. While white mediums rest content with attributing *negros'* peculiar spiritual receptivity to their "humility," without analyzing the concept further, *negros* associate humility with a wisdom born of suffering. "The *negro* opens up more," declared one *negra* medium, "because he is humbler, he has suffered much in life. They do the *trabalho* with greater care and tenderness, because they've suffered." While accepting the dominant image of him or herself as "humble," the *negro* thus reinterprets it in such a way as to challenge racial democracy's contention that *negros* do not suffer. Thus, too, from *negros'* point of view, it is precisely the *mulatos'* arrogance that renders mediumship difficult for them. "It's harder for the *mulato,* because he is proud," Luana remarked matter-of-factly. "They always say 'me, me!' So they have to really struggle with it."

In yet another twist, *negro* mediums turn to their own advantage the stereotype that *negros* have "strong blood." A *negra* medium declared that "the strength of *negro* blood helps, it helps a lot. Our blood has greater resistance, we can receive the spirit—even the most feisty." By this logic, *negros* are able to assert that light-skinned mediums depend for their spiritual strength on darker-skinned mediums. "The white is weaker," one proclaimed. "For him to follow, he has to get his strength from the *negro*."[19] Similarly, *negros* sometimes say that *mulatos'* "weakness of blood" impedes their development as mediums. In part, "weakness" here stands for *mulatos'* notorious ambiguity of identity. "*Mulatos* are depressed all the time," declared a *negra* medium. "They really are sickly, it's their weak blood. They don't know who they are. If they want anything, if they want to do something in *umbc nda,* they must come to us."

Let us return to Luana's account of her entry into the *terreiro.* "I didn't want to develop," she said. "I would go and say, 'no, I'm not going to do it.' But it comes from the slaves, they passed it down to us." This tidbit of historical belief is not Luana's alone. Mediums, irrespective of racial identity, acknowledge the presence in *umbanda* of elements derived from Africa. The religion's published orthodoxy portrays it as a melting pot of African, Indian, and European elements. This orthodoxy depicts such "melting," however, in nonconflictual, diffusionist terms. Elements of *umbanda* were "brought" from Africa, and apparently had little to do with the social relations of slavery itself. As a *mulato* medium explained, "They learned it over there and brought it here. But then it became general, mixed with other things."

In contrast, the speech of *negro* mediums is saturated with allusions to the social relations of slavery. In their version, *umbanda* is not the happy synthesis of European Catholicism and African religion, but a refuge from and a locus of resistance to the slave regime. As one medium put it, "*umbanda* was the religion of the slaves. They were mad against the masters, so they used a lot of magic." Another *negra* medium gave a more elaborate account. "*Negros* were kept out of the whites' church. The slaves, they created *macumba* so they could have their own cult, centuries ago." It is not surprising that some *mães* proudly call their *centros "quilombos,"* the term coined in the seventeenth century to refer to communities of runaway slaves.

Early in our interviews, when we were discussing her *preta velha,* Luana mentioned that she wept much of the time. I was taken aback, since I had long understood the *pretos velhos* to be happy and content. "No," she said firmly, "that's what the whites say, because they want to believe it. But the *pretos* are sad, very sad."

Luana's comment draws us into some of the most important differences between *umbanda*'s race-based versions, those revolving around the nature of the spirits themselves. The discourse of whitening idolizes the Indian for resistance to slavery, pronouncing the Indian superior to the *negro,* who supposedly submitted to the whip. Published *umbanda* manuals spiritualize this ideology by representing *caboclos* (Indians) as purer than *pretos velhos.* Both *mulato* and white mediums articulated this view. As one white explained, "The *caboclo* is more powerful, he is purer than the *preto velho.*" This greater "purity," he added, was due to the *caboclo*'s connection to the pristine forest, away from the temptations of civilization.[20]

Negro mediums, too, say that *caboclos* have greater power than *pretos velhos,* and to this extent they appear to have accepted the dominant discourse. They do not concede, however, that *caboclos* are "purer" than *pretos velhos.* Instead, they speak of the greater "civilization" of the slaves as a source of practical knowledge. One *negra* medium insisted,

The *pretas velhas* brought gardening and seeds from Africa, but the *caboclos* just hunted, they didn't know how to grow things. The *preto velho* knew about manioc and banana. They have lived much in this world, with wisdom. The *caboclos* are powerful, OK, but they yell a lot, they have no *cultura.*

This use of "*cultura*" involves both its collective meaning and individual, moral sense of "upbringing" or "manners." That is, being more "civilized" than *caboclos, pretos velhos* can teach them "manners." This view, I might add, is not shared by light-skinned mediums.

Negros emphasize, furthermore, that the *pretos* have greater compassion than do the *caboclos.* As a *negra* medium explained, "The *pretos velhos* suffered a lot, that's where the force of our religion comes from." Having suffered much in life, *pretos velhos* devote themselves in death to helping others. The *caboclo,* in contrast, "hasn't suffered much, he is indifferent to people. . . . If he doesn't understand you, he'll just turn around and leave."

The contrast between light-skinned and *negro* versions of the spirits emerges also in relation to the *exús.*[21] Repeating the orthodoxy of the published literature, one lighter-skinned medium declared that the *exús* were *negros* who are "marginals, the ones who rob and steal in life, *pretos* from the *favela.* They are angry at the world, they say everyone dislikes them." In contrast, *negros* claim that, though the spirits of *negros* sometimes wander and become *exús,* it is commoner for *mulatos* to do so, because, they say, *mulatos* die angry at themselves for not being white. "Their spirits wander," said one *negra* medium, "until they understand that they are equal to everyone else."

The emotional charge of this image becomes evident in relation to the process of indoctrination, during which *pretos velhos* pass on their wisdom to *exús* who have invaded, uninvited, the ritual space, calming their anger and urging them to undertake good works rather than vengeance. *Negros* take satisfaction in the fact that many *exús* were *mulatos* in life. "In life they made fun of *pretos,*" Luana said gravely. "But later they have to learn from the *pretos.* They don't like that."

Contrasts such as these coexist with at least one assumption held in common by mediums of all racial self-identifications: that the humility of the *pretos velhos* is more complicated than it seems. Lighter-skinned mediums do not elaborate upon this point, but hints of their awareness of it come indirectly through comments such as that *caboclos* "are the purest, because they were in the forest, they're not angry at anyone." Why would this speaker insist that the *caboclos* "are not angry at anyone," unless she was implying that, contrary to their official representation, the *pretos velhos* might actually be angry? *Negros* also feel that the spirits of docile slaves harbor . . . something. I will return to this "something" shortly.

As I have so far presented them, the differences between versions emerge at the level of verbal exegesis. In order to see how the elements of the *negro* version come together to empower *negro* mediums in everyday life, we must again return to Luana's story. In her late teens, she began to work as a domestic servant for a white Catholic family of which she grew very fond. "They gave me food, medicine, everything," she recalled. She was most impressed by the family members' ability to come and go as they pleased. "They were free, really free, got up when they wanted, went away, came back. I wanted to be like them. I wanted to be white."

Living half the week in Rio and the other half in the periphery, Luana began to blame the *centro* for preventing her from partaking in the freedom of white society. The idea of slavery, so central to the collective image of *negros'* spirituality, became the dominant motif in her telling of the growing strain in her relation with her *mãe* at the *centro*.

I'd go to work [as a maid in Rio], and come back only to go to the *centro,* I felt that I was much more a prisoner in there than out there, you know? I felt like a slave. I wanted to be a person full of freedom, like the whites. I thought that a dark person next to me would only dirty me, they would compromise me.

The contrast between Luana's life in Rio among whites and among *negros* in the periphery became condensed for her in the contrast between her white patron family's Catholicism and her own family's *umbanda*. The Catholic Church, she thought, must somehow hold the key to white freedom.

I thought, "I'm going to go to the Church, I must get out of *macumba*." It [the Catholic Church] is the religion of the whites. When I'd go to *terreiros* I'd only see dark people. I thought I should be like the whites: hair nicely done, walk nicely, all pretty, well-dressed. . . . I said to my godmother: "The *negro* doesn't have freedom inside of *macumba*. It's the same thing as being chained as a slave."

As far as Luana was concerned, she was already a Catholic. Like other mediums, she regarded Catholicism as an all-embracing cult of which *umbanda* was but one part. The issue was which religion to participate in. When Luana announced to her grandfather that she planned to attend her white patrons' church, she received a word of caution to which she turned a deaf ear—but which she would later recall.

[He] told me that he had been able to see through this problem of *negros*. "Ah, you, being very intelligent, you are going to discover why it's hard for us to be Catholics."

Ignoring the warning, Luana distanced herself from the *centro*, and began to attend her employer's Church.

At first I felt the difference, going to the Church, I felt like a different person, I felt my body become lighter, I felt freedom among the people there. The Catholic is a white place. I went there to assume my freedom, to take Communion. For me the host was the white man's spirit. I went, I started attending Mass, I started to leave *macumba*. I started to forget those other things.

This tranquillity did not last for long. Within a year, she had begun to understand the import of her grandfather's words. Whiteness, the very thing that had drawn her to the Catholic Church, had begun to reveal itself as part of a Faustian bargain. "I saw that the Catholic Church really was a place for whites. They didn't like to sit next to me, if I said something wrong, they would make fun." Yet Luana could not let go. Thus began a long period of distressing ambivalence.

I felt, I didn't know if I would be better off on the side of the whites, or on the side of the *pretos*. I didn't know what to do, I was caught in the middle. I'd go to Mass and go to the *centro* too. Whenever there was a hard time, I'd run to the *centro*. In the Church I'd be there singing, all educated, but they were looking. When I felt that, I'd run back to the *centro*, "Ah, here they won't look at me that way." . . . I'd go into the Church at night, I'd look at them, the whites, one by one, and think, "Ah! Now I understand why the *negros* go to *macumba*. It's the way they look at us. Now I understand." Then I'd run back.

But far from coming home to a welcoming embrace, Luana found her returns fraught with tension, as her *mãe* insisted on making her squirm for her betrayal.

Mãe would say, "Ah, girl! You're running back! Have you finally seen how things are? Are you finally seeing how whites treat the *preto*? You've felt what they do to the skin of the *negro?*" And I'd say, "Yes." So I was in a state of confusion. My *mãe* would say, "If you don't look for freedom inside of *macumba,* outside you'll never find it. Because freedom for *negros* is here inside." So I would run back to *macumba,* trying to find freedom somewhere. I didn't know where I was.

Luana began to sense in her flights to the *centro* something involuntary, which she interpreted as the demands of her spirit, demands which were, not coincidentally, identical to those of her *mãe.*

I couldn't give up *macumba.* I felt like a prisoner, like a slave, tied with a chain. The *guia* wouldn't let me go. I would faint on my way to Church. The spirit didn't want me going there, it was angry that I left. . . . And every day I went to Church, my mother would come here to fight with me: "Ah, you don't know what you want. You'll never have freedom with the whites."

Luana finally escaped her awful ambivalence in a process that carried her through several moments, the most dramatic of which was her encounter, in her late twenties, with the spirit of Zumbi. As she recounted the meeting, Zumbi descended into another medium to give her a message.

In the *centro,* I saw Zumbi. He said to me, "I am good, and I am bad. But I say one thing to you: you will find your freedom." He was from the days of slavery, but he was different: Zumbi was more on the side of the *negro,* to give freedom. I felt he was the strongest of the *negros* . . . when Zumbi spoke, I felt different about *macumba,* I thought maybe I can be free with the spirits there if I want, I don't have to be enslaved.

It was not long before she translated this thought into practice. She gave up attending both the Catholic Church and the *centro,* and sought a new *centro.* Years later she would return to the Catholic Church, but only for Mass, and without any longer feeling tension with her identity as an *umbanda* medium. Her encounter with Zumbi seems to have been crucial in helping her embrace her *preta velha* wholeheartedly, renounce her fruitless striving for whiteness, liberate herself from institutions that had been straitjacketing her, and find her own way to develop her relationship with her spirit. Quite a plateful. How could a spirit named Zumbi help Luana do all these things?

To begin to answer this question, we must explore the meaning of Zumbi, the pivotal figure in the *negro* version of *umbanda.* This spirit, in its richly mythic form, appears to exist only in this version. The historical Zumbi was one of the chiefs of Palmares, the great maroon society that survived for almost a century in the backlands of Alagoas, until finally being destroyed by the Portuguese in 1697. Zumbi is credited with having rebelled against Palmares' leaders after their ignominious surrender to the Portuguese. Refusing to give up, he is supposed to have staged an internal coup, then fought a hopeless battle against the Portuguese, was defeated, and met a grisly death.[22]

The relation of the figure of Zumbi to the tension between the notions of freedom and slavery in the *negro* version of *umbanda* emerges during a yearly rite on May thirteenth, the secular anniversary of Princess Isabel's 1888 decree of abolition. In *umbanda* centers throughout the urban periphery of Rio, the day is known as "the day of the *pretos velhos.*" On this day, *mães-de-santo* invite all *pretos velhos* to their *terreiros,* in order to feast on rice, black beans, corn mash, chicken, wine, and *cachaça.* Those who interpret *umbanda* as embodying whitening ideology suggest that the cult's ritualization of this date legitimizes the Brazilian state's claim that abolition was proof of whites' benevolence.[23] For lighter-skinned mediums, and for at least some *negros,* the celebration does indeed sacralize the state's version of abolition. "That was the day Isabel freed the slaves," a light-skinned medium explained, "so the *pretos velhos* come to cry for joy." A white medium, too, could state that "The *pretos velhos* are very grateful on that day, they say their thanks to Isabel, who freed their race."

Yet for many *negro* mediums the day of the *pretos velhos* is anything but a celebration of emancipation; rather, it is a day for the spirits of old slaves, oriented by Zumbi, to tell the true story of slavery. "On that day the *pretos* weep for their parents," one medium explained. "It is a day of homesickness. They want to go back to Africa." For Luana, the *pretos* descend to the *centro* feeling very sad. When I asked her about the day she explained,

On that day they come very troubled. "My child, that's the way the time of slavery really was." Then they explain that after Isabel signed the Law, they had to return to the plantations, because they didn't have work, they didn't have houses, they didn't have a roof.

Such mediums regard Zumbi, not Isabel, as the principal figure in their history. Isabel may have signed the law of abolition, they say, but Zumbi commands their greatest respect and loyalty.

Umbanda is one of the few vehicles for transmitting the mythology of Zumbi at the popular level. Official history, as exemplified in grade-school textbooks, rarely mentions Zumbi,[24] and many people unaffiliated with *umbanda* say "zumbi" refers only to tricksterish forest sprites.

Within *umbanda* attitudes toward Zumbi vary. The few *mulato* mediums who acknowledged Zumbi's existence as a spirit called him an *exú*. One *mulato* asserted that "he is dangerous, very dangerous. He kills people. Slavery forced them to eating one another. He was a cannibal." In contrast, *negro* mediums often referred to Zumbi as their "godfather of Angola," and presented him as one of the greatest spirits in the pantheon. When I asked a *negra* medium about May thirteenth, she immediately launched into a rebuttal of Isabel's primacy.

We in *umbanda* have as our main godfather Zumbi of Angola. If you think about it, godfather Zumbi of Angola was already warring a lot for our freedom. Isabel took the credit, but she didn't do it. May thirteenth is not a day of happiness. It is a day of homesickness for their parents.

Other *negra* mediums confirmed the version. "My *mãe* taught me that Isabel only signed the paper," said Rosa, for twenty years a *filha-de-santo* in a *centro* near São Jorge. "She didn't give freedom. May thirteenth is not the day of freedom, it is the day of the *preto velho*, of the arrival of Zumbi. Zumbi comes to protect the *terreiro*." I asked her whether the descent of the *pretos velhos* had anything to do with the liberation of the slaves, since the rite, after all, coincided with the anniversary of abolition. "No," she replied firmly,

it has nothing to do with it. Zumbi explains to them on that day, "Ah, you still are not free." Only on May thirteenth, to tell them he fought to end slavery. If not for him, today everyone would be slaves.

Negro mediums say May thirteenth is the only day of the year that the spirit of Zumbi descends to protect the *terreiro* and transmit his message. When he comes, it is not to possess anyone, but as a hovering presence that instructs and guides the *pretos velhos*. Due to his enormous power, he does not incorporate in any medium. In this respect, he is similar to the *orixás*. As one medium said, "I have never heard of Zumbi incorporating. He would be too strong, he would certainly kill the horse."

Furthermore, Zumbi is the only figure in the pantheon who straddles two spiritual categories. Sometimes I heard him associated with the *pretos velhos*, because he comes to the *centro* on their day as patron and protector; one medium even identified him as "a *preto velho* who comes once each year." Her next comment, however, revealed Zumbi's duality: "At midnight we call him from the *povo da rua* ["street people"], from the *encruzilhadas* [crossroads]." These are terms that refer not to *pretos velhos,* but to *exús.* For, after all, Zumbi died dissatisfied (Palmares was destroyed), and so he resides now in the realm of shadows.

In his dual identity as *preto velho* and *exú,* Zumbi represents not only the overt rebellion of slaves, but their subtler daily rebellion in the various forms of denying legitimacy to their enslavers. There is more to subversion than the *exús'* trickery and deceit. There is a deeper, less tangible subversion: saying "yes" when you mean "no," that quiet, monumental ambiguity that resides in Luana's smile when the white storeowner calls her a "little *neguinha* [nigger]."

There is yet another layer to what Zumbi represents for *negros.* This great slave revolutionary, by appointing himself both guardian of and tutor to the *pretos velhos,* shows that he is aware that at the heart of the slave experience, as of all experiences of subjugation, lies the ambivalence between the desire to resemble and to rebel against the enslaver.[25] In his self-appointed role of putting an end to such ambivalence, Zumbi represents not only passive resistance, or what has recently been called the "hidden transcript" of rebellion,[26] but also the enduring potential of all slaves, even those slipping into docility, to be inspired to rebel.

By pointing to this, the *preto velhos'* secret, the figure of Zumbi sheds light on the multileveled meaning *pretos velhos* have for *negros.* As Luana put it, "the *pretos velhos* suffered much under slavery, they never accepted it, but what could they do? They just nodded and said, 'Yes, sir.' But in their hearts they did not accept it." In view of this, I suggest that to interpret the *pretos velhos* as representing simple docility, as Bastide, Ortiz, Montero, and others do, gives voice only to one version of *umbanda.* For *negros,* the day of the *pretos velhos* is Zumbi's day, the day when he is able to articulate every *preto velho*'s inner sentiments. Zumbi, great wanderer through the astral realm, is not a stranger to the *pretos velhos*; he is one of them.

Luana's encounter with Zumbi was a remarkable bit of religious creativity—no one else I spoke with believed Zumbi could possess a medium. Yet she remembered Zumbi as having spoken directly to her through a medium. Whether she misunderstood what she heard is impossible to know and probably not important. What is important is that, given her agonizing ambivalence, Luana felt she desperately needed to talk to Zumbi. Because of his powerful duality, when Zumbi descended that day and spoke to her, he had the means to alter her vision and persuade her to see *umbanda* both as a place of refuge and as a source of strength. And his legitimation of rebellion sanctioned Luana's desire to leave this particular *centro* and pursue mediumship on her own terms.

This aspect of Luana's story raises serious doubts about the prevailing scholarly opinion of *umbanda,* and suggests that it may be premature to conclude that this religion is yet another vehicle for drawing the Brazilian *negro* into the hegemonic maw of white ideology. Nor was this the end of Luana's story. Her life continues to unfold, and though she may have given up her ambition to enter white society, she continues to suffer from her marginalization from it. It is worthy of note that she keeps her identity as a medium secret (she only revealed it to me after many months of acquaintance). Eventually, she distanced herself from *centros* altogether, contenting herself with private consultations only. Though her maturity as a medium would indicate she should try to found her own *centro,* the reason she gives to the contrary reveals that she is still sensitive to light-skinned opinion.

Look, I could do it. I could. There are many who would come, and many who would become mediums. But I don't need the trouble. What'll they say? They'll just snipe, call me a *macumbeira,* say, "Look at that nigger [*nega*], that darned *macumbeira.*"

Again, though happy to have accepted her *preta,* Luana is distressed by her need for secrecy and the frustration of her ambition to be a *mãe.* Most painfully, she still resents not being accepted for who she is. "I'm as good as anyone," she says. "As good as anyone. But there will always be that thing, you know. They'll say, 'she's a *macumbeira.*'"

"A Place to Call the White Man 'Brother'"

Luana's frustration is diagnostic. As a member of a religion that both *comunidade* Catholics and *crentes* look upon as evil, Luana must resign herself to secrecy or, at most, a narrow social circle. Though *umbanda* helps *negros* to construct powerful spiritual identities, it denies them entry into white society. During Enrique's period of estrangement from the Catholic Church, he never considered frequenting *umbanda.* For him, such a move would have meant abandoning the chance of being accepted into the white man's world. "I think all are equal," he once said to me. "If you go to *umbanda,* whites think you're inferior. And I am not inferior!" His daughter Sandra, even at the height of her disillusionment with the Catholic Church, also remained cold to the *umbanda* option.

If there weren't all this racism, I don't believe *macumba* would even exist. Why should someone give up, and say they can't be like everyone else? Why can't we be? So I think people just get disgusted and go there. But I'm not going to give up, because *negros* are just as good as whites.

In pentecostalism, in contrast, not only do *negros* construct authoritative spiritual identities, they achieve a certain measure of equality with people with lighter skins. As an evangelizing church, the Assembly of God seeks out and makes outsiders feel welcome. It attracts many *negros* initially through its warm invitation, a stark contrast to their reception in society at large. A Catholic *negro* confided that he had been tempted by the solicitude of pentecostals' efforts to convert him:

Let me tell you, they give so much attention to you, they invite you, it's really something. There were times when even I wanted, I even almost converted, because of their invitation, because I felt honored. The welcome they give, they come to you to shake your hand, you really feel at home. . . . Because, man, no one cares about the *preto,* and there, they greet you in the street, they give more attention in the street to black people. Let me tell you, that's a very important thing, that there.

That Catholics and *crentes* recognize the appeal such a church can have for *negros* is revealed in the common local quip that "the black man wants to be a *crente* so he can call the white man 'brother.'" The quip resonates because it seizes upon a real social relation, that between the white proselytizer and the *negro* who feels honored by the attention lavished on him.

Once inside the church, the *negro* is impressed by the number of people of his color both in the pews and on the presbyters' bench. Thus the testimony of a recently converted *negro*: "I felt like I was entering into a *preto* church, really black. I felt at home. I'd never seen a *preto* priest, but here there were those, up there, all of my color." Indeed, during his years of alienation from the Catholic Church, Enrique had been sorely tempted to convert to *crença.*

I wondered to myself: why doesn't our Church have the same opportunity for *negros* as they do? This same acceptance? I wondered that. I'd even go from time to time, when I was invited I'd go. I'd see the opportunity given to them, *negro* pastors, *preto* children singing and all. Talking, preaching, I felt that there. I'd wonder, "Why isn't all that in ours as well?" The difference was that the same treatment they gave to whites they gave to the *negro.* The same opportunity that the white had so did the *negro.* And in our Church no, in the Catholic Church, no.

The only thing that kept him from converting was the weight of his Catholic upbringing. "I had learned from my mother, and from all the years with my patron, I had made that commitment, so I couldn't leave it."

In order to understand better the Assembly's appeal to *negros*, let us return to Sandra's story. We left her in the last chapter having concluded that her religious conversion could be understood as a way of gaining the authority she needed to save her father from disrepute. The racial dimension of her conversion emerged during a later conversation.

There with the *crentes* I could participate in the chorus. In the Catholic, I'm very dark, and when there are opportunities to read, say something, the light girls would go ahead of me. Among the *crentes,* in that religion, I have a chance to sing, to participate in the chorus and the youth group. In the Catholic Church, there's prejudice among the chorus, the youth. That's why I didn't want to participate in the Catholic any more.

As it turned out, there was an intimate link for Sandra between the issues of race and coping with her father. She said she had been upset that other reflection-group members "laughed" at her father. Recall here her own mother's complaint that neighbors criticized her father for drinking while keeping mum about lighter-skinned leaders. The laughter to which Sandra was responding thus carried a powerful racial charge: "I would hear them talk about him," she reported, "calling him names, *'negro'* [nigger] and everything. 'That drunken *negro!*' It was awful." In contrast,

This [in the Assembly] is how I think the world should be, it'd be much better; maybe this, this racism would diminish a bit, because there is a lot of separation [discrimination]. Lots say, "Ah, I'm not going to this church because one is well-dressed, the other is badly-dressed, there are a lot of whites, in the other there are more *escuros* [darkies]." No one would have to say that if we were all equal, if we treated each other as brothers.

AMBIGUITY IN PENTECOSTALISM

Pentecostalism as a haven of racial democracy in a racist land—is it possible? Is it possible, as Regina Novaes has argued, that the ongoing, rapid pentecostalization of mainstream Protestant churches may lead to greater racial democracy in Brazilian society at large?[27] Perhaps. Certainly the presence of *negros* in positions of institutional authority, as well as their access to the charismatic gifts of healing and prophecy, have helped to erode the racism of at least some light-skinned *crentes.* As one of the latter told me,

I used to have more of that thing, that prejudice [*preconceito*]. . . . But you know, it was by going to church with *negros* that I lost a lot of the thing that I used to have. Because, look, how can I say that I am [worth] more than brother Manuel [the prayer-healer]?

Sounds hopeful. Still, if the tortured experience of São Jorge's Assembly of God is any indication, the emergence of racial democracy in Brazil's pentecostal churches will not be easy; rather, it will provoke profound, ambivalent resistance by people with lighter skins. Adherence to pentecostalism, while seeking a rupture with the world, does not put a definitive end to the tendency to interpret experience in racial terms. Possession by the Holy Spirit, that most central of pentecostal experiences, is an important flashpoint for race-based interpretations. To explore these interpretations and their implications for *crente* race relations, I will focus on an episode of possession in church that was particularly controversial.

It was a Sunday when the pastor (who is white) was absent. Hélio, the pastor's son, who had just taken possession of the office of vice-president the preceding week, was the highest authority then present in the church. The trouble began about halfway through the hymns. In the row in front of me, a *negro* in his twenties stood up suddenly and rushed from the pews, down the center aisle, and up to the presbyters' dais, shouting in a high-pitched, unworldly voice. He riveted himself in front of the pastor's son and thundered for several minutes. Though I could not make out the content of his words, of one thing I had no doubt: with his hand outstretched, the prophet's attitude was unmistakeably one of reproof. Then, in mid-shout, he fell in a heap. The church exploded into cries and prayer, and the presbyters leapt from their seats to lay hands upon the prophet's crumpled body. They prayed intensely for several minutes. Finally the young man regained consciousness, stood up shakily, and descended from the dais unsteadily, wiping his brow. The pastor's son seized the microphone and preached with towering indignation that to ascend the pulpit one must be prepared in the sight of God. Yet though he roared, the congregation drowned him out. It was only when another presbyter led a hymn that everyone finally ceased to pray and began to sing in unison. As soon as this show of unity had occurred, the presbyters hastily called an end to the service, half an hour earlier than usual.

In the following weeks I heard different interpretations of this episode, particularly of the fall of the prophet, whose name was Alexandre. Some *crentes* claimed that the young man had fallen because he had been moved, not by the Holy Spirit, but by his own flesh. God had stricken him down before the multitudes. Holders of this view pointed out that his performance had violated Pauline precepts of order and discipline; therefore, he could not have been divinely inspired. Others suggested that because Alexandre had, they believed, some background in *umbanda*, he had fallen as a result of the power of the Enemy. Whether the cause was his flesh or the Devil himself, tellers of both accounts emphasized what they took to be Alexandre's lack of humility before Hélio. As one put it, "he ascended there in an exalted way, but he descended humiliated. . . . If someone exalts himself, God Himself humiliates him." Those who interpreted the prophet's fall in these ways tended to be lighter-skinned *crentes* either within or aspiring to enter the authority hierarchy of the church.

A large number of the *crentes* who were present that night, however, insisted Alexandre had been moved neither by his own flesh nor by the Devil, but by the Holy Spirit. They argued that Alexandre had fallen quite simply because he had been overwhelmed by the power of God. There were two main groups holding this view. The first included lighter-skinned men and women with no pretensions of entering the authority hierarchy of the church. This group's hold on the view proved rather tenuous. When the pastor later preached that Alexandre had been inspired only by his flesh, some of these lighter-skinned *crentes* began to entertain doubts about their initially sympathetic position. The second group were *negro crentes,* among whom I found no waverers: to this very day the *negros* of São Jorge's Assembly of God continue to declare that Alexandre was divinely inspired.

In order to shed light on these interpretations, on the pattern of who holds them, and on their consequences, we must consider the contradictory images about *negro* spirituality that *negros* encounter in the Assembly of God, and the chain of events leading to that Sunday's peculiar tumult.

In the Assembly of God, the *negro* encounters a powerful, flattering image of his or her spirituality. I first realized this when a white *crente* invited me to accompany her to the house of a *negra* prayer-healer. When I told her I could not go with her, she said, "No matter. There's another one who prays for the sick on Thursdays. She's light [*clara*], but her prayers are a blessing too." That little "but" spoke very loudly. There is, it turns out, a widely shared opinion among *crentes* of all racial self-identifications that the *negros* of the Assembly are "closer to God" than anyone else, that they have "greater fervor," speak in tongues, prophesy, have visions, cure, and expel demons far more frequently than do lighter-skinned *crentes*. "We whites," one *crente* explained, "we're lazier in front of God, there are days when we miss church. But not them, they're always there. So you can see, God has more opportunity to work in people of color." *Negro crentes* embrace this image wholeheartedly. Alexandre himself once exclaimed to me, "Just think of it, the Holy Spirit isn't just for us! It can also descend into your white chassis!"

It is worth recalling that such notions remain foreign to the progressive, as to the general Catholic, imagination. In the Catholic Church, the mistrust of the model of personal transformation, as well as the overall scarcity of *negros*, render implausible the idea of *negro* spiritual specialness. I asked over twenty participants in the *comunidade*, of different skin colors, whether they believed the *negro* to be "closer to God" than whites. Their responses ranged from puzzlement, to amusement, to downright hostility. "That idea is ridiculous," said one. "If we're going to get close to God, everyone is going to arrive together"; "I never thought of that. I think that everyone is equal before God, right?"; "Whether black or white, it has nothing to do with how you seek God."

Although light-skinned *crentes* believe that *negros* are "close to God," their reasons are different from those of *negros*. Sometimes they suggest that *negro* spirituality derives from the "fact" that they know better than others how to "humble themselves." Sometimes they point to the "fact" that *negros* "were once in *macumba*." While the widespread stereotype that all *negros* have been at one time or another involved in *umbanda* tends to stigmatize *negros* in the Catholic Church, it allows light-skinned *crentes* to claim that every *negro* in the Assembly is living proof of Christ's saving grace. "If He is willing to save a *macumbeiro*," one white *crente* declared, "certainly He will forgive anything!" *Negros*, in this view, are now especially committed to seeking God because they wish earnestly "to escape that evil." In part, this image accounts for white *crentes*' openness to *negro* leadership in church, for it is consonant with church doctrine to have *negros* stand out and take on special roles. "Seeing them up there," a white explained, "those *pretos*, you really feel the grace of God, how He takes pity on the lowliest of His creatures."

Meanwhile, when accounting for their own evident fervor and spirituality, *negros* stress neither their innate humility nor the dubious heritage of *macumba*; instead, they emphasize the blues of being a *negro* in white-dominated society. A *negro* presbyter explained:

The *negro*, he has more desire, more hunger, more thirst for God. The Bible says, "Blessed are they who hunger and thirst for justice, for they will inherit the Kingdom of God." Because sometimes, you know, they're not well looked upon, you know? They're left to the side, that's why they have more of that desire to seek God. And we are well received.

A young *negra crente*'s testimony was especially lucid:

Negros give more room to the Spirit of God, because we're so often attacked [*apedrejado*], so often attacked. Because if we go walking from here to there, they watch our every step, always watching. So, the best thing we can do is close our eyes and think of God.

Some *negros* go further, and claim their fervor is rooted in the history of slavery. "The *negro* understands spiritual liberation better," a *negro* deacon told me, "because they were liberated once as a people." Some even say *crença* was founded by the slaves themselves. "It was the *negros* who founded the *crente* churches," an elderly *negro crente* reflected.

Crença began as a religion that the slaves liked, because they couldn't go to church, all there was was the Catholic, which was all white. But after liberation, they started to support their own church, and that's how it started.

As in *negros'* version of *umbanda*, in *negro crentes'* reading of their history, they become religious tutors to the whites: "The whites liked the lovely unity of the *negros*," a *negro* deacon proclaimed, "so they went to join them."

For those with lighter skins, however, the image of *negro* specialness has another, more problematic side. Though pentecostalism's nature as a cult of transformation forges the possibility of *negro* spiritual special-ness, it cannot eradicate deep-seated Brazilian racist attitudes. Thus, while not questioning *negros'* claims to spiritual gifts, many lighter-skinned *crentes* still believe *negros* to be more prone to backsliding and temptation than whites. As one light-skinned *crente* said:

I think that *pretos* have to be a bit more vigilant than whites. Because they are weaker when faced with temptation, they can fall much quicker. So they have to be very vigilant, you know? They don't have the instinct for avoiding evil. That's their nature.

Racist attitudes of light-skinned leaders are even more pronounced. Despite the presence of *negros* among its presbyters, the highest offices of São Jorge's Assembly of God continue to be occupied by a white pastor and his clique of white and light *mulato* clients. Those in and around this core do not hesitate to challenge the validity of *negro* spiritual gifts. Here the reverse side of the *macumba* coin reveals itself. "Look," said one white presbyter,

negros always were dedicated to that thing, that spiritism, that manifestation of the spirit. So, when they feel, you know, happy in the church, they already think they can prophesy.

Other light-skinned leaders resort to even more blatant images of racial inferiority. "Receiving spiritual gifts," said one presbyter,

depends a lot on intelligence. And unfortunately, blacks are not as intelligent as whites. . . . The *negro* needs something to bring him to the level of the whites, so sometimes he starts lying, saying that he has gifts.

Negros bitterly resent such attitudes. "It's just when we speak against the white people there on the bench," one young *negra* argued, "that's when they say it's *macumba*! If they like what they hear, 'Ah, let's go to brother so-and-so, he'll help us, he has great spiritual power!' But if they don't like it: 'Ah, brother so-and-so is a silly chatterbox, he's just a *macumbeiro!*'"

Rhetorical battles over the connection between race and spirituality is especially intense between *negros* and *mulatos*. *Mulatos* who aspire to move up in the ranks speak resentfully about how the pastor has accepted *negros* into the prebytery as a concession to avoid accusations of racism. "We can't keep blacks from moving up in the church," one deacon explained, "because people outside will accuse the church of being racist. So we are obliged to let them move up, and to live closely with them in the church. But they themselves know that they don't have the same level as we, they don't have the same capacity." Indeed, some *mulatos* go so far as to say that *negros* are even less spiritual than either *mulatos* or whites, because they are too "proud." As one *mulato* put it, "Whenever they get any little office, they become proud. So it's hard for God to work through them." *Negros* retort that, by trying to be "more than what they are," it is the *mulato* who suffers from spiritual barrenness. In terms similar to those used by *negro umbanda* mediums against *mulato* mediums, a young *negra crente* complained that

a person who is ashamed of themselves, is ashamed of their race, he doesn't make room for the Holy Spirit. If he criticizes, laughs, is ashamed, God doesn't use him. The *mulatos* criticize . . . for them to have a spiritual life like the *negros* have, they have to stop wanting to humiliate others, wanting to be better than *negros*.

Given the ambivalence of light-skinned attitudes, it is not surprising that presbyters apply a *sub rosa* double standard of discipline and exclusion. When a *negro* named Cósimo was accused of having been involved in a fist fight, the prebytery excluded him from church despite evidence that suggested his innocence. The decision to exclude divided the presbyters, with the *negro* presbyters unanimously defending the man. One of them later confided to me,

In the Assembly, the *negro*, he's the one who always has to avoid taking a wrong step. Any little mistake, he's excluded, because he's *negro*. Like with this kid who was excluded. For the white, there's more tolerance. If he makes a mistake today, there's that little bit more of tolerance. *Negros* are always under more pressure.

This discussion of the intersection between racial and spiritual rhetorics in São Jorge's Assembly of God should have prepared us to return to an analysis of the events leading up to Alexandre's church-shaking performance. The story really began the preceding spring, in a confrontation between Alexandre and Hélio, who at the time was still a mere presbyter. During a choral rehearsal, Alexandre was recounting a vision when Hélio told him to "shut up." As one eyewitness testified, "Everyone was pretty shocked. If he had been a white boy, Hélio wouldn't have cut him off."

The second act began a month later, when Hélio was nominated to be the church's new vice-president. The nomination stirred controversy. Hélio had been outside the church for nearly ten years, and had returned to the fold only the preceding year. Congregants of all racial self-identifications had felt the speed with which he had been promoted smacked of nepotism. In addition, it was general knowledge that not only did Hélio lack the gifts of the Holy Spirit, but also that his work as a policeman required him to wear a firearm, something many believed to be contrary to the Word of God.

Negros, it seems, were particularly incensed by the nomination. With so many strikes against him, many *negros* were deeply annoyed that another presbyter, a *negro* named Oswaldo, had not even been considered. Oswaldo had been an active *crente* all his life, and possessed the gifts of prophecy and vision. Yet the pastor had passed over him, it was rumored, because he had once prophesied against a (light-skinned) presbyter.

As the issue finally reached the public arena, it became clear that attitudes toward Hélio were divided along racial lines. When the presbyters voted on his nomination, five of the six voting against him were *negros*, seven of the eight voting for him were whites or *mulatos*.[28] The presbyters' decision was then brought before the congregation for *pro forma* approval, with those opposing the result free to express themselves. A lone voice was raised against the nomination: Alexandre's. His voice no doubt resonated with the secret feelings of many others in the congregation, but he was the only one resentful enough to stand forth in protest. The presbyters, by showing a common front, gave the congregation little choice but to accept the verdict. Still, "the presbyters were not getting along," a deacon told me. "So the pastor called for a week of prayer, to bring unity again."

At the end of that week, a struggle that had been lost in the sphere of human words now entered the battleground of divine speech. For the Assembly's *negros*, Hélio represented authority rooted in whiteness, nepotism, and human privilege rather than in the power of the Holy Spirit. Their resentment of Hélio and all he represented was articulated through taking sides in the interpretation of Alexandre's prophecy. Conditions that Sunday were ripe for Alexandre's fire and brimstone. With the unifying authority of the pastor temporarily gone, it was easier to challenge the authority that remained. The preceding week's collective prayer had rarefied the atmosphere, and undoubtedly was keeping the racial issue uppermost in some minds. It was in this volatile atmosphere that Alexandre exploded.

I do not know why Alexandre fell to the floor that night. I do know that the meaning of his fall went far beyond his own state of mind at that moment. In rising up and feeling God speak through him in reproof of Hélio, Alexandre was joining a battle, part of the long, deep, tortuous struggle between the races in Brazil. In this battle, the pastor claimed victory, as he preached that Alexandre had succumbed to the flesh. Yet it was a victory fundamentally limited both by the large number of *negros* in the church and by popular belief in *negro* spiritual specialness. In the end, the pastor did not exclude or even discipline Alexandre. This failure of nerve was worth a thousand words. The pastor no doubt knew that making too much of an issue of Alexandre's prophesy could divide his church. In the transformative cosmos of *crença*, as in *umbanda, negros* could, on the basis of their distinctive fervor and commitment, make such powerful, legitimate claims to spiritual specialness that to discipline Alexandre would have been playing with holy fire. To this day, *negros* in the Assembly cite the pastor's unwillingness to discipline as proof of Alexandre's divine inspiration. The *negro* prophets of São Jorge's Assembly of God had won another inch of ground.

At the same time, Alexandre's story illustrates the contradictory quality of *negros'* experience in Brazilian pentecostalism. In its vision of personal transformation, the Assembly of God creates the possibility for *negros* to become, at least for a time, better than equal to their lighter-skinned coreligionists. Yet in multiracial congregations such as that of São Jorge, where different ideological cards are still held tensely in the hands of white, *mulato*, and *negro* contestants, pentecostalism's vision of transformation fails to eliminate lighter-skinned people's efforts to maintain their own domination.[29] Though fleeing to *crença* as if to a haven of racial democracy, *negro* converts soon discover that their struggle with white society has not ended. Perhaps their consolation is that this time, at least, they are waging the struggle from within.

Conclusion

I have tried here to convey something of how *negros* in urban Brazil struggle to forge religious identities that give them a measure of peace in a world dominated by people with skins lighter than theirs. I have also tried to suggest that these struggles are never fully completed, that no religious option is ever fully satisfactory. It is thus fitting to give Luana the last word, for her restlessness reminds us of the lack of closure in the *negro* spiritual project. Once, near the end of our interviews, in a quiet, matter-of-fact voice, Luana expressed a judgment that, while devastating the myth of racial democracy, could not quite erect upon its ruins a comparably totalizing myth of spiritual destiny.

Ah, John. The *negro* suffers, so he thinks more about God, with that faith; he's been very hurt, he's still suffering. Nothing is easy for us: just struggle, struggle, struggle. There are days, if I had a gun, my God, I'd shoot myself. But I don't despair, because I have a lot of faith in God, that one day we will be free. [Here on earth or after death?] I don't think it's after death, no. Here on earth. [laughs] And if we are not liberated here, only after death. [laughs] But you know, John, I think that even after death, we will not be free, we will continue to wander, like Zumbi, until we have our freedom.

7

Catholics, *Crentes*, and Politics

In preceding chapters, I have explored some of the social forces that have limited the popular appeal of São Jorge's Catholic *comunidade* and strengthened that of its main competitors. Seizing upon religious discourse as a way to articulate and cope with everyday predicaments is an inherently political process, both because it is empowering and because it nurtures understandings of social relations that question patriarchy, racism, inequality, and the domination of elders.[1] Yet while everyday life may be an ideological battleground, "politics" still refers, as well, to the domain of directed, collective action. In this chapter, I will explore the heated issue of the implications for political belief and behavior, narrowly construed, of membership in the *comunidade* and the Assembly of God.

Catholic progressives and sympathizers assume that the faster growth of *crentes* over that of *comunidades* bodes ill for the future of working-class social movements in Brazil. I hope to cast doubt on this assumption by revealing some of the contradictions and variations in the politico-ideological discourses and practices of both *comunidade* Catholics and *crentes*. I will suggest that the relative weakness and strength of the two churches does not justify easy or foreboding conclusions about the political destiny of Brazil's working class.

Over one year, in an effort to sample patterns of discourse and action, I interviewed almost ninety participating Catholics, mainly from São Jorge, and from a half-dozen other *comunidades* in the parish. I was able

182

to distinguish several general patterns of response to and use of the Church's progressive message in terms of three intersecting contexts: the religiopolitical vision inherent in the kind of Catholicism with which the user came to religious maturity; the peculiar institutional role of the user; and the user's history of class experience.[2] What emerged was the remarkable endurance of pre-progressive discourses, and a widespread discrepancy between progressive discourse, on the one hand, and social movement practice, on the other.

I also interviewed dozens of *crentes* throughout the region about their political beliefs and observed the political behavior of dozens more. By analyzing *crente* participation and leadership in neighborhood associations, labor struggles, and the Workers' Party, it became increasingly clear that portrayals of *crentes'* "apathy" tended to pay little attention to their ideological complexity. By exploring this complexity and the conditions under which *crentes* have been mobilized into progressive social movements, I will also discuss pentecostalism's political limitations as well as its possibilities. In doing so, one conclusion emerges: there may be greater room for dialogue and alliance-building between the progressive Church and the pentecostals than many have supposed.

A cautionary note is in order here. We should remain wary of categories that offer up religiopolitical beliefs and practices as if they came in neat, unchanging packages. Obviously they do not: they are fraught with ambiguity and contradiction, and are constantly evolving. In what follows, then, I have employed terms such as "rights-oriented" or "charity-oriented" as indicators only of what might be more properly called relative centers of gravity within fluid constellations of ideas and fields of language.

The Catholic Church and the Project of Liberation

On the sun-warmed morning of October 12, 1987, the feast day of Our Lady of Aparecida, Brazil's patron saint, nearly two hundred *comunidades* from the diocese of Duque de Caxias marched along the road from the highway to the old seventeenth-century church in Pilar. Three thousand Catholics had heeded the call for a procession to honor Our Lady, making the event the diocese's largest since Dom

Mauro took office. A van mounted with loudspeakers rolled slowly through the crowd as it wended its way along the dusty road, leading us in the hymn, "And there will be a day when all of us "Upon raising our eyes/Will see freedom reigning in this land."

Between each stanza, a scratchily amplified voice intoned a sentence adapted from the Lord's Prayer. "From police violence and death squads, deliver us, O Lord!" "Deliver us!" chanted the marchers. The voice again: "From the lies of the politicians in the Baixada!" The crowd:

> "Deliver us, O Lord!"
> "From unjust and oppressive laws!"
> "Deliver us, O Lord!"
> "From the lack of health, diet and literacy for our children!"
> "Deliver us, O Lord!"
> "From the foreign debt, the IMF, multinational corporations!"
> "Deliver us, O Lord!"

When the throng reached the clearing in front of the stately, white-washed church, Dom Mauro, impressive in a flowing white robe, ascended the dais and preached an electronically-amplified sermon about injustice and the duty to struggle against it. He then led the clergy in distributing Communion to the throng. "With this sacrament," he proclaimed, raising up the host, "we reaffirm our commitment to struggle for the people's liberation." Everyone in the vast gathering repeated the phrase, issuing it forth in an echoing rumble. The following day, the parish newspaper published this notice:

Yesterday all the *comunidades* of the diocese celebrated Our Lady, with faith and love. They together demonstrated the common commitment and faith of the *comunidades* to the liberation of the entire people.

The crowd had indeed been high-spirited, and with every refrain and song it surely seemed that the Catholic people had been united in its commitment to liberation.

Or had it? Had Dom Mauro's phrase meant the same thing to all those who repeated it? I suspected it had not. In what follows, I will do my best to portray the significantly different ideological tendencies shaped by generation, institutional role, and class experience that were present among those who marched that day. Dom Mauro's call for liberation did not enjoy any single meaning, but resonated differently according to the political tendencies of its various audiences.

A PROCESSION OF VISIONS

Liberation as Charity. The most widespread tendency in the *comunidades*, I found, was to interpret "liberation" not in its rights-oriented and this-worldly senses, but as a reminder to perform one's Christian duties to give charity and to seek other-worldly salvation. This tendency was most prevalent among men and women who were socialized into the Church in the years before Vatican II and who, as members of stable, but not elite working-class families, tended to belong to the ranks of followers rather than leaders. While progressive discourse forced some of these men and women to rethink old ideas, in general they tended to use the new discourse haltingly and piecemeal.

Carlita, a soft-spoken woman in her sixties, had lived in São Jorge for forty years, and was married to an assembly-line worker who later entered the construction trade. As a member of São Jorge's Apostolate of Prayer, she had long been dedicated to collecting food and medicine for the sick. She had participated for seven years in Father Cosme's Bible circles, dutifully attended the *comunidade*'s "little courses" and listened attentively to the young priest's sermons.

In some ways, Carlita's response to her Church's new discourse was everything the progressive clergy could hope for. To begin with, participating in the *comunidade* had nurtured in her a broader, more democratic respect for the capacities of all people. "When I started to participate," she said, "I learned how to value people. Even in the bus, in the street, the person who is at your side, talking to you. . . . When I wasn't participating, I was more ignorant, I would always judge others." Working in the *comunidade* had, furthermore, impressed upon her the importance of cooperation. "Every day I learn in the *comunidade*," she reported, "that God did not just make things for me. I have to share everything with my brother. If I know how to knit, or make a different kind of dish, I have to teach it to someone who doesn't know."

Liberation theologians would also have been glad to know that participating in the *comunidade* had fostered in Carlita a feeling of belonging and group identity she had never before experienced. Like many of her comembers, she no longer said "I am a Catholic," but "I am a Catholic of the *comunidade*" or "I am of the *comunidade*." Before the arrival of the new church model, she had marched in diocese-wide processions as part of an undifferentiated mass; now she marched proudly holding a placard emblazoned with the name of her *comu-*

nidade. Recently, on All Saints' Day, when she had missed her own *comunidade*'s morning Mass in the town near the regional cemetery, instead of taking Communion later that morning with another *comunidade,* Carlita had preferred to wait until evening when she could commune along with her own co-*comunidade* members.

Carlita's response to the liberationists' call to join social movements, however, was equivocal. On one hand, seven years of sermons, *cursinhos,* and reflection sheets has made her relatively more, though still often vaguely, aware of social and political issues. "I didn't even want to hear about these things before," she said. "It's only now that I think about them more, I see that there are a lot of people who like to step on the weak. Now I'm more aware of such things." Still, she offered only passive support to social movements. "I think that all movements that are in favor of the victims of injustice are valid," she said, in a phrase I heard repeatedly throughout the region's *comunidades.* "But I don't participate in any movement." Wasn't active participation, I asked, what the new Church was calling for? Carlita did not think so. As she explained,

Look, this "new way of being a church" I understand like this: people have to help each other more. It doesn't help for you to be in church the whole day praying, without helping someone who is hungry, ignoring the person who needs medicine, or a friendly word. . . . The Church is reminding us to help our brother, to practice charity. Some do those other things, but I don't like them. I prefer my way, I like going to houses of the poor, giving things. Those other things, that's for other people.

The core of the progressive message for Carlita, then, was not a call to fight for her own or other people's rights, but to perform charity for those worse off than she. In this view, social movements were but one, not especially important, modality of charitable work. This charity-oriented reading of the Church's new discourse emerged even more clearly when I asked Carlita what Dom Mauro had meant by "struggling for liberation." Though for him the phrase signified a commitment to bring about social justice on earth, for Carlita it meant

helping others. We in the Church have always done this. We must give bread to the hungry, clothing to the naked, visits to the sick. . . . We can take up a collection for someone, we can help the widow, the sick person.

But, I asked, wasn't "liberation" about changing the world into a better place? "Well," she replied, "only God can fix our world, the way it is."

The most one might do was to urge the powerful to be more benevolent, to "convince them to be better Christians."

She had doubts, however, about using language even this politicized. "Sometimes," she complained, "the priests, they mix things together, they get agitated. Sometimes they don't even talk about God! That's why my husband doesn't participate any more." She, however, would never leave the Church, no matter how strange the discourse emanating from the parish. "I have a mission," she said, "to follow Christ and do His work, giving charity."

Liberation as Spiritual Self-Reliance. A second tendency prevailed among nonleading churchgoers who came of religious age after Vatican II, but before the arrival of progressive discourse. In addition to interpreting "liberation" as a call for greater charity, these men and women emphasized liberationism's insistence on "consciousness," which they equated not with the commitment to end social injustice, but with the post-Conciliar rejection of religious images and support for spiritual self-reliance.

Alba, a nonleading Catholic in her forties, was married to a semiskilled factory worker. She had become involved in the Church in the late 1960s. In addition to charity and salvation, she believed the key to the new Church's message was the valuation of spiritual self-confidence and the devaluation of spiritual mediators. These beliefs are well illustrated by the following exchange. When I asked her what she meant by "liberation," her reply was "being *consciente.*"

John: What does that mean?
Alba: That we must understand things, know things.
John: Like what? What things do you have to know?
Alba: All sorts of things. (pause)
John: Like what?
Alba: (pause) Well, the priest, he doesn't turn his back to us any more. We who are *conscientizado*, we understand why he doesn't turn his back, why the Mass is in Portuguese. And that the old saints, the images, we are not supposed to worship them, because there is only God.
John: But what about what Dom Mauro said, that we must struggle for liberation? What does he mean?
Alba: [long pause] That we must love each other. Other than that, I'm not sure, it is the priests who know all that. I say those things, but they are very confusing. Jesus came to liberate us, but all these new things, I don't understand.
John: Doesn't Dom Mauro mean stuff like neighborhood associations and unions?

Alba: I think he means that. And those are good things. We are supposed to help our brother. To do what we can. But for me, it is enough to say a friendly word, and if the beggar comes, I will give him food. The rest of it, I try not to think about too much, but I go along, that's the way they want it. I won't leave the Church like the others I've seen. I'll stick it through. It is good that the priests are trying to help. I am *conscientizada*. I take Communion, I am a good neighbor. What else can I do?

"The Priests Change, But I Am Here Always." Comu-nidade members socialized into the Church before the arrival of progressive discourse but who, as members of elite working-class families, found themselves in positions of institutional authority, learned to recite with varying degrees of consistency the rights-oriented version of liberation yet privately continued to adhere to pre-*comunidade* understandings. Rosana, an important working-class elite woman, was a long-standing Minister of the Eucharist, a leader of the Apostolate of Prayer, and coordinator of the *comunidade*'s pastorals of baptism and catechism. Because of her intercalary role as a leader of São Jorge's Catholic community, she had found it politic over the past thirty years to adapt to successive waves of innovation from the parish. "They changed before, and they'll change again," she told me, "but I stay here always." She had remained calm in the 1960s when the Conciliar priest removed saints' images from *capela*; why should things be different now? If she had to incorporate phrases such as "struggle" and "the oppressed" into her speech, incorporate them she would. Her mastery of the new discourse was impressive. When I asked her to explicate Dom Mauro's call to struggle for liberation, she replied,

Through this new Church we discovered that for the Christian to live out her baptism, she must work for the Kingdom of God to occur here on earth. Before we thought the Kingdom of God would only be in the other life. But God made man to be happy here, to construct the Kingdom here. Because that doesn't happen: some people oppress others, they take away the rights of others. So we must struggle to liberate people from these chains.

What did she mean by this? I pressed her on the question of organized social movements. Were these ways of struggling too? She accepted social movements, she said, as ways to "show the authorities that medicines are lacking, that school is lacking, we must show them that we don't have our eyes shut." At the same time, she acknowledged (in a phrase I heard repeated often from other informants) that she was "pretty disconnected from that stuff." Upon further questioning, she revealed that she didn't approve of the extent to which the Church was getting involved in such things. "The Church was created to preach religion," she declared, in a familiar turn of phrase, "the things of God. Politics has other sectors; it shouldn't be mixed with religion." On another occasion she identified strikes as "just agitation against the government," and complained that "the PT [Worker's Party] is on the side of lazy people." She disliked Leonardo Boff, she said, because she once "saw a picture of him and he looked like a Petista [a militant of the PT]."

Rosana's understanding of the new progressive discourse thus does not differ greatly from the nonleading Catholics indoctrinated in pre-*comunidade* discourse. Women like Rosana can not distinguish struggling for the poor from charitable work such as collecting food and clothing for the needy. When I asked her to specify what she was doing to help "liberate" the poor, she replied,

There was a death near here just a little while back. The person didn't have any will. You know how much the funeral cost? About forty thousand! So, what did we do? We took up a collection, and now we're going to have the funeral.

Far from revolutionizing her own thinking, then, Rosana had simply shifted some of the ways she described charity so as to maintain her institutional identity and authority. She revealed this most candidly when she recounted that she was obliged during a service to read aloud a letter from the bishop calling for a march against violence. "I didn't really agree with that coming into church," she said,

I thought that was mixing politics and religion. But I didn't say anything. There was a man there, though, in church who said, "This is absurd! That's not something to do in church!" I said, "No, I'm going to read the letter, they sent it from the diocese, so I have to read it. The priest brought it to me for me to read, so I'm going to read it!" Because if after all I'm doing something that my superior has ordered me to do, if I do something that the people find wrong, still I'm fulfilling my duty. I have a responsibility to accept the changes. I have to live with everyone.

Nonleading Recent Arrivals. It should come as no surprise that the most consistent users of the rights-oriented lexicon, in both public and private, were a people who became involved in São Jorge's *comunidade* over the past eight years, since Father Cosme's arrival. Yet again we are faced with a paradox. People socialized into the Church after 1982 quite commonly do not connect their consistent progressive discourse with practice. Thus, Carlos, a man in his twenties who had not participated in the Church before 1984, interpreted Dom Mauro's call in the following terms:

There is so much oppression in the world. We Christians have to struggle together, with unity, to make it a better place. That's what Jesus said. Jesus came to give us the message, that we must struggle to improve things here on earth. That is what liberation is. . . . Our *caminhada* [path], the *caminhada* of the Christian people, is the struggle for a better world, a world of justice and equality, where there is no misery.

When, moreover, I asked him how he thought people could accomplish this goal, he replied "by getting involved in these movements that you see all around, by uniting to ask the authorities for our rights."

Yet when I inquired whether he had tried to get involved in a social movement, he replied "that's not something I like. I like religious things, not political things."

DISCONNECTIONS

This last example brings us once again to the more general question of the relationship between participation in the *comunidade* and involvement in social movements. Like most *comunidade* members in the São Jorge region, no matter how they understand the liberationist message, Carlita, Alba, Rosana, or Carlos remain aloof from social movements. Although they do not participate in them, neither do they disapprove of them. In São Jorge, however, the main cause of *comunidade* members' lack of involvement in the local neighborhood association is clear: It is dominated by a coterie of local notables who have little to do with the *comunidade*. In towns where active *comunidade* members came to dominate neighborhood association directorates, *comunidade* members could often be found among the association's participants. It is striking, however, that even these participants tended to explain their involvement not in terms of liberationist ideology of "struggling for rights," but in a variety of other, nonpoliticized terms.

In the early 1980s, for example, in São Judas, a town near São Jorge, an activist Catholic named Maira formed a neighborhood association in order to pressure the state into building a public school. She made sure the association would be democratic and open from the start, and devoted much energy to reaching out to members of her *comunidade*. An elderly Catholic named Camila was so impressed by Maira that she joined several other middle-aged church women from the Apostolate of

Prayer who went to participate in the new association. Like the others, however, Camila saw the association not as a "social movement" (I never heard any of them use the phrase), but as "the same thing as our charity work." Camila entered the association, she said,

because there's mud here. Here there are many children without shoes, who are going to step in the mud and get sick. It is our duty as Christians. We must carry on our work of charity, of helping the neediest.

It might be argued that women such as Camila are carriers of at least some of the "alternative meanings" Melucci has written of as the pre-condition for mobilization into social movements. They had learned greater cooperativeness and sociability in the *comunidade*, had developed a clear identity as members of a bounded community, and had at least some greater tolerance for social movements. These patterns resemble what Melucci calls the "latent dimension" of social movements. Open, democratic neighborhood associations appear to make visible this latent dimension. At the same time, participation in neighborhood associations did not transform the ideological views of people such as Camila, whose pre-progressive beliefs displayed remarkable resilience. Even after three years of active participation in her town's neighborhood association, she could still construe liberation as the effort to "liberate the poor with our prayers and charity." I asked her whether liberation could come through social movements. "Well," she replied, slowly,

the liberation of the world is going to be by grace, it will not depend on our movements. . . . Look, John, Christ came to struggle for heaven, not for the earth. He came to do the will of the Lord, not to give us material things. Wouldn't you rather have eternal salvation than a piece of bread? Jesus told us we have to defend our children and the little ones, to be good. Movements are fine. But they will get you nowhere; they are to improve a little, not to transform anything. The world will only be transformed when Jesus comes.

Perhaps most curiously, I found that many nonleaders who had entered the Church since the arrival of progressive discourse, employed that discourse consistently, and had become involved in a neighborhood association, still failed to connect their involvement to the discourse. Instead, such people often explained their practice as simple conformity to social expectation. Sinza, a woman in her thirties, lived in São Judas and became involved in its *comunidade* after Cosmo's arrival. She had learned, she said, that "Jesus wants us to have plenty. And to be fraternal, like good brothers, and come together. To get what we need." Recently, when the association called on the local population to assemble along the highway and carry banners to demand a new bus line through town, Sinza joined in the fray. While one might assume that she had been motivated in this by the new religious ideology, her reply to the question of why she attended the demonstration places such an assumption into doubt..

> *Sinza:* Because Carmen [another person in the association] asked me to.
> *John:* That was all?
> *Sinza:* Well, I go to these things. I mean, when someone asks me, I go.
> *John:* [pause] What about Jesus' message?
> *Sinza:* Huh?
> *John:* What about what Jesus said?
> *Sinza:* [confused] What did Jesus say?
> *John:* That we have to struggle to make our lives better here and now?
> *Sinza:* [snapping to] Yes, right, that's what Jesus wants us to do.
> *John:* Were you thinking of that when you went to the march?
> *Sinza:* [without hesitating, as if the question was silly] No, of course not. I
went because Carmen told me about it, said we should go. I didn't think about Jesus.

Others who had become involved in the Church since Cosme's arrival and who knew that "Jesus wants us to struggle," similarly did not explain their participation in the neighborhood association in liberationist terms. Their primary motive, they said, was social: as members of the Church, they simply wanted to do what other Church people were doing. A sample:

Informant I.
   Occasion A: *John:* What did Dom Mauro mean when he said "we must struggle for liberation"?
   Informant: That is what we must do, come together to make the world a better place. Join with our brothers.
   Occasion B: *John:* Why do you participate in the association?
   Informant: Because the *bairro* needs to be improved.
   John: But why are you personally involved? Why not just let others do it?
   Informant: It's the Church that's doing it. I go because they announce it in Church, and my friends go there, so I go too. I am a member of the Church.

Informant II.
   Occasion A: *John:* Why do you participate?
   Informant: Because the *bairro* has a lot of problems.
   John: But why do *you* participate?

Informant: I go because when something happens, someone knocks at my door and says, "Let's go!" So, those are my friends.

John: You don't go because of religion, because of something you believe?

Informant: Religion is one thing, going to the march is another. They are totally different. They make announcements in Church, that's all. We go together.

I could continue transcribing similar exchanges, but the foregoing should suffice to illustrate the frequently tenuous relation between liberationist ideology and social movement practice among *comunidade* Catholics.

Comunidade members' continuing conception of social movements as works of charity or sociability, rather than as the implementation of liberation theology, have consequences for the nature and quality of members' political action. For while making possible initial mobilization into neighborhood associations, charity- and network-centered images of social movements render social mobilization fragile and contingent.

Charity thrives on its own definition of success: the rapid response to dire circumstances, the immediate gratification of seeing (preferably grateful) recipients get what they need. This definition is not well-adapted to extended struggles that often end with scant rewards, periodic defeats, and the ingratitude of fellow townspeople. For example, when devastating floods hit the region of São Jorge in February of 1988, the people of the *comunidades* immediately joined neighborhood associations' efforts to collect food and supplies. This mobilization was in perfect keeping with the ideal of charity. One woman expressed the linkage very clearly: "To be a good Christian means helping others in time of need. And this is a time of need." In the months after the flood, when neighborhood association leaders called upon these same people to help pressure the state to implement policies against irrational land use (the condition that had fostered the floods in the first place), the response was mixed. Many *comunidade* members who had mobilized initially simply stopped participating once the crisis was over. Others stayed on for a while as the struggle entered the protracted phase of dealing with local politicians. Within two months, however, these hangers-on had lost their initial enthusiasm and dropped out as well. In part, the problem was the discrepancy between their accustomed time-line for charitable works, and their impatience with the time required to build a collective movement that could pressure municipal officeholders. One woman conveyed her frustration after a few weeks. "Nothing was happening. Politicians say they'll do something, and don't. . . . The

Church gets us all ready to do something, to make something happen, 'We're going to march' and all that—and then nothing happens."

Such frustration was reduced wherever the neighborhood association was led by a directorate whose members were drawn mainly from the *comunidade*. In such cases, the association became "a work of the Church." Yet while this linkage creates strong loyalties, it suffers from a built-in weakness: when the directorate passes out of the *comunidade*'s hands, the glue keeping the group mobilized dissolves. In a town near São Jorge, when several Catholics were elected to the directorate, numerous *comunidade* members began to participate. But when a new non-*comunidade* leadership was voted in, *comunidade* Catholics grew distant once again. When I asked a *comunidade* member why she had stopped participating, she replied, "it was the Church that was doing it. I went because they would announce it in Church, my friends went there." In another *bairro*, as long as Catholics controlled the association's directorate, a major contingent from the *comunidade* attended meetings and participated in association activities. When non-*comunidade* leadership replaced them, however, their participation rapidly dissipated. As one woman explained, the association was "no longer a work of the Church."

THE LIMITS OF CONSCIOUSNESS-RAISING

Why do pre-liberationist discourses remain robust even in *comunidades* thoroughly missionized by the progressive Church? And why do so many *comunidade* participants fail to draw clear connections between liberationist discourse and involvement in social movements? Undoubtedly, the answers to these questions are more complex than I can do justice to here. At least part of the answer, however, has to do with inherent limitations in the Church's model of consciousness-raising. To illustrate these limitations, I will focus on the institution upon which the progressive model has placed the greatest emphasis: the Bible circles.

According to theologians like Carlos Mesters, Bible circles are supposed to be the *comunidade*'s nucleus of consciousness-raising, the place where participants can, through the free exchange of ideas, collectively discover how their faith is connected to everyday life. In practice, however, the Bible circles (at least those with which I became familiar) simply do not create the kind of warm, socially safe atmosphere conducive to the free expression of feelings and ideas. The problem, as I have suggested at various points in this book, is partly due to Catholicism's general discourse of continuity: local people perceive each other in the Bible circles primarily in the roles they occupy outside of them. Because of this, efforts to discuss problems of the "oppressed," "marginalized," or "abandoned" commonly become enmeshed in labyrinthine stories of interpersonal relations, kinship, friendship, bad blood, and personality.

From this perspective it becomes understandable why members of Bible groups do everything they can to *avoid* making concrete connections between the Word "and life," for these only serve to remind everyone of the resentments, judgments, gossip, and rivalries that pervade the neighborhood. Instead, members do their best to keep group discussion limited to abstract exhortations to be virtuous and charitable and to increase participation. Whenever the guidesheet raises issues that threaten such studiously preserved generality, members move swiftly to deflect them. In one instance, the guidesheet asked the group to reflect on the question, "Some *comunidade* councils work better than others. How does our council work?" At the time, there were widespread mutterings about the inefficiency of the council; but while gossip abounded, no one dared mention the issue in the public arena of the Bible circle. The question was met with nearly twenty seconds of silence, until one woman finally murmured: "That's a question for the council to answer, not us." Talk then returned safely to soliloquies about the Church's *caminhada,* and how wonderful it was to be *consciente.*

Here the importance of articulateness and literacy looms large. Leaders in the Bible groups reward with warm responses articulate reproductions of progressive discourse. Despite claims that "everyone has a say" in the circles, in fact far from everyone does. Those who feel unsure of their verbal skills or who "do not know enough" are strongly inhibited from speaking up. In the meetings I attended, the majority of participants remained silent while leaders and the most articulate members dominated both the reading and commentary. As one woman said, "I won't say anything there, I just listen and pray. I don't want to look stupid." Ironically, one of the commonest complaints on the part of group leaders is that "most people stay silent through the whole thing."

A related problem is that progressive Catholicism shares in the Church's tradition of incantation. Just as Catholicism has long valued ritual repetition of Ave Marias and credos as methods of indoctrination, liberation priests seem to believe that getting people to recite politically appropriate words and phrases has an automatic impact on their sociopolitical vision. As one lay leader complained, "The priests think that all they have to do is put a lot of words into people's mouths and on their shirts, and that they'll understand what they mean." Those words, however, are often as unintelligible as the Latin of pre-Conciliar prayer, and often spoken in the same dry, hypnotic monotone.

As with Latin, many members find the best strategy is simply to repeat whatever they hear, without worrying about its meaning. In Bible group meetings I often witnessed people dutifully repeat phrases, even those with no readily apparent sense. In one case, the group's coordinator mistakenly read "We understand the Mother's call" as "We do not understand the Mother's call"; yet without batting an eye everyone repeated the phrase in the negative, as it had been spoken. It should come as no surprise that participants' recall level is very low; this is even true of leaders. When I asked two leaders to speak to me of the theme they had studied just the day before, they had to jog their memories by referring to the pamphlet. "It's true, we don't remember anything," one explained. "I don't even remember what the theme was. . . . We read so much, but we don't understand what we're reading, because there's so much, strange words, just a lot of talk."

Perhaps the deepest obstacle to the ambition of forging *consciência* in the circles is that most participants simply do not attend them with any such object in mind; rather, they go for prayer. When women call each other to attend a reflection group, the phrase they use is "let's go pray." Though reading aloud and commentary take up the lion's share of meeting time, most people, including leaders, prefer prayer to talk. According to one member, "talking just doesn't feel like religion." Another complained that "with all that talk and reading, that weakens the strength of prayer in the group. Why all that talk? We are there to pray." Though they tolerate the talk, many participants said they attend the groups because they have heard that similar groups meet simultaneously throughout Brazil. "That means," one said, "that the Church is uniting all our prayers together. So prayer there is strong." One woman always napped through meetings, bestirring herself only at moments of prayer, when she would stand and fervently move her lips.

ACTIVISTS

Thus far, I have focused on ideological tendencies that encompass the largest numbers of *comunidade* participants in the São Jorge region. I will now discuss an important ideological minority, the *"líderes"* or *"militantes,"* so-called by progressive clergy, in effect, "activists." These are people who speak fluently the language of rights-oriented liberation; are involved in some social movement; and consistently explain that involvement in liberationist terms. In the entire fourth district of Duque de Caxias, there were probably no more than two dozen such people, only two of whom lived in São Jorge.

As a group, female activists bore a striking resemblance to each other. In their thirties and forties and highly literate, they came from families that had nurtured their aspirations for educational and social mobility. They were daughters of small-town shopkeepers or mid-sized landowners who recognized their daughters' intelligence and made it possible for them to stay in school. At some time or other, these women had encountered insurmountable class barriers to social ascension. By the time they were reaching religious maturity, they found themselves in the radical parish of Pilar, where Orlando, the radical priest, helped them to articulate and confront their already developing sense of social injustice. Through leadership in the progressive Church, these women were able to bring together the many strands of their identities: institutional Catholicism, razor-sharp intelligence, education, aspirations for social and material improvement, and resentment of the wounds of class. All these women now have supportive husbands with stable incomes (some were small shopkeepers), and children old enough not to require constant attention.

Maira, mother of two teenage daughters and wife of a metalworker, was a sensitive, cautious woman in her early thirties who took as much care separating pebbles from rice as she did in preparing her candidacy for assemblywoman on the Worker's Party ticket. "The PT," she once told me, "is a real party of the people." She interpreted Morelli's call that day in October by saying that

it was the faith that Jesus had come for us, the poor and oppressed, that gave me courage at the hardest times. You better believe it! Days like when we were spending our last *cruzeiro* to take the bus to the city to make demands at the municipal office for the crosswalks, but we didn't know what would happen, faith in God was our only support. Faith that what we were doing was right. Because the liberation of the people will come only through struggle. We must stay on the path, and remember our liberation only happens if we do it ourselves. . . . There is no Father Christmas, it doesn't fall from the sky. We must organize and struggle for our rights.

Born in 1955 outside a large town in the state of Alagoas, Maira was the eldest of six children of a mid-sized landholder who prided himself in being an upstanding member of the Catholic League. She recalled that from early youth "I had a need, a desire to know things." Fortunately for her, her father, something of an eccentric, recognized the value of female intelligence and against the advice of his peers sent Maira to a private Catholic school. During her time there, she never ceased to consider her schooling a privilege. Still, along with finding her horizons expanded at school, she found herself the victim of class hostility. "I studied," she told me, "among the children of the rich. I had trouble there, they always looked down on me."

Maira was only a teenager when her father began to lose the little land he had.

I didn't understand it, but he said it was the *grileiros* [land-grabbers]. That woke me up [*aquilo me despertou*]: I wondered why he had owned land, and was losing everything he had. My father didn't have any explanation. . . . He sacrificed so I could go to school, but he couldn't any more. So I struggled, worked part-time, and went to school at night.

Maira would not be kept down. By the age of fourteen, she was not only a catechist, but a worker in the local literacy campaign. Here, once again, she suffered the wounds of class.

I was working alongside the children of the mayor and politicians. They received much better salaries for working there than we did, who weren't related. I got mad at that, I felt that was wrong. I was as smart as they were.

By the time she married at nineteen, Maira had developed an acute awareness of the obstacles to her social mobility. Soon after marrying, she moved with her husband to the parish of Pilar, a sprawling *bairro* at the northern edge of Duque de Caxias, where he landed a stable job at the petrochemical plant. Suddenly she found herself confined to the house, caring for two daughters, a role to which she could never entirely accustom herself. "I wanted to get out," she recalled. "I had always thought I would do bigger things. Education, teaching and all."

Before long, Maira approached the lay leaders of the Church in Pilar to inquire into whether she might serve as a catechist. The year was 1976, just at the time Pilar was becoming a hotbed of radical activity under the leadership of the Franciscan priest, Father Orlando. By 1976, Orlando's parish had become a mecca for *assessores* (technical advisors and other urban intellectuals), who arrived every week to give lectures and seminars, while advisory committees organized neighborhood associations, health care, and political instruction. Never before—and, after Orlando left in the early 1980s, never since—had the Church in Pilar been so intimately linked to the formation of political cadres.

Orlando immediately sensed Maira's leadership potential and urged her to become involved in the health and neighborhood pastorals. As she recalled,

I learned something new every day. I became very involved with everything, Father Orlando pushing us all the way. There was a lot of fellowship: all these other people like Laíse, and all, we worked together in the neighborhood association, and in the pastorals. It was very exciting. . . . It all made sense to me, that the people had to organize and fight for its rights.

Militant women like Maira, married to men with relatively stable incomes, typically do not work at full-time wage-earning jobs; when they do, their activism inevitably suffers. Another militant woman helps her husband on a flexible basis in his small watch repair shop; still another works informally in the mornings as an assistant in a nursery school. For her part, Maira has in recent years started working in the mornings as a secretary at the local state school, on a schedule that does not conflict with her Church or political activities. Her work at the school actually contributes to her activism, by keeping her close to the nub of local information networks.

Maira had something else crucially in common with the other women of her cohort: a supportive husband. "I got involved in things," she said, "and my husband encouraged me. While I was off in that fight, he agreed to take care of the children." She seemed exceptional in her ability to balance caring for young children with political involvement. Yet even in her case it was not until her youngest reached the age of about ten that she would be able to organize the neighborhood association of São Judas.

It was partly because she had such a supportive husband that, when the PT of Duque de Caxias offered her the chance to run for assemblywoman in the 1988 municipal elections, she could accept the nomination. It was, however, a decision she would soon regret. She confided that

I'm wondering now about whether I should have accepted this. I mean, I'm like a little fish in a big ocean and there are a lot of sharks. I don't like the way the Party does things. Maybe I just don't like politics. It's all factions, and fighting for your position. I'm used to the rhythms of the Church, to the rhythms of the neighborhood association. Here, we all know exactly what we want: a better life for ourselves and our kids. We all agree: let's go and get water, let's get the crosswalk so children won't die. I am used to working with agreement. But there it's all debate and namecalling. I don't think I'm prepared for it.

Maira's trepidations about politics were not personal idiosyncrasies; they are diagnostic of *"igrejeiros"* in general (as they are often called by their non-*comunidade* political companions): Catholics whose interest in social movements was sparked by the Church, and who now find themselves increasingly involved in non-Church political groups. Such people often feel ill-prepared for the confrontational world, especially of party and labor politics, into which they have been thrust.[3]

There are many reasons for this malaise, most of which are rooted in the progressive Church's own ideology and practice. For all their claims to have a prophetic voice, politicized Catholics continue to have a visceral preference for conciliation over confrontation. This preference stems from their deep commitment to the idea of universal brotherhood. "Whatever party someone is," one *igrejeiro* explained, "they are my brother, they too call God 'father.' I don't care if he is from party A or B." The emotion of anger, even righteous anger, must give way before the attitudes of love and forgiveness. When I asked Maira whether one might feel angry at a landlord who evicted a tenant, she replied,

We shouldn't feel angry. You must feel compassion for the one who lost their land, and try to help them. Pity the landgrabber. You must forgive him, he is a child of God. [Then how can one struggle against him?] You don't struggle against him; you struggle for the poor man. One must not be angry against the exploiters; one must simply show them the truth. We can argue, appeal to their conscience, without aggression. . . . The Bible doesn't permit you to keep anger in your heart. The *patrão,* the boss, he must understand, he must change his ways.

Given such attitudes, it should come as no surprise that Catholic activists feel more at home in movements that struggle over local-level infrastructural and land issues than in the world of party and labor politics. Their political style is well-suited to neighborhood organizations and the Pastoral of Land because there tend to be only minor differences of opinion about the need for new schools, electricity, or secure land tenure. Neighborhood associations and the land pastoral generally employ nonconfrontational legal tactics, including peaceful processions, visits to elected officials, petition drives, and the courts.[4]

In contrast, tough debates over strategy are a constant fact of life for Brazil's progressive parties, especially the PT. Over the past decade, Duque de Caxias's Worker's Party has included numerous Catholic activists. "In the Church," Maira acknowledged, "you speak a lot about brotherhood, love, peace, caring, forgiveness, those things. But when you arrive there in the political party, things are the exact opposite of all that. We are made fun of."

In Duque de Caxias, a plurality of militants in the Worker's Party believe in the occasional necessity of confrontational action. At a recent demonstration, however, when marchers were surrounded by police, the ranking Catholic party member gave the order to retreat. "We left the square," he explained,

so as not to create a conflict with the police, so that no one would leave there injured. . . . We're the ones, in the Church, who always try to soften any potentially conflictual situation.

Non-*igrejeiros*, meanwhile, tell this story with some bitterness. "They wanted to leave," recounted one,

but that wasn't the moment for leaving. We had a right to be there, and we should have advanced, together, to demonstrate that right. . . . They are too soft, all they think about is God, God, God, they say "brother." They think you can change the world through love. But some things aren't that way.

As for labor issues, the Catholics in Duque de Caxias's PT have provided less than enthusiastic support for the new labor movement. At this juncture, the oppositional labor movement often relies on combative, less-than-fully legal tactics such as direct action, pickets, slowdowns, and strikes.[5] Catholics in the PT directorate usually vote against general strikes and, once obliged by the directorate to participate, balk at picketing or, as one non-*igrejeiro* put it,

refuse to yell at the scabs. . . . Look, we prioritize the union movement, but the *igrejeiros* prioritize the associations. . . . There are very few comrades in the unions who are linked to the Church.

It is not surprising that Catholic activists often find themselves caught in a dilemma: their political views, not considered radical enough by militants outside the *comunidades*, are usually considered too radical within them. Carlos, a young metalworker in his thirties, fondly remembered participating in the Church's Worker's Pastoral, where he "learned things about the rights you have entering and leaving a company . . . it was like being in a university." Yet when he became involved in a metalworkers' strike, he felt the Church had not prepared him for the very reality it had urged him to enter. "There in the Pastoral," he complained,

all they talk about is "love, love, love," "we have to change society through love and peace." But in the union I saw that the powerful are not going to change their ways through persuasion. Because they have every trick up their sleeve to keep you down. And then they sic the police on you.

Problems of political style thus often force activists to choose between politics and the church. Carlos chose politics. "I didn't belong in the *comunidade* any more," he said. "I didn't have anything more to learn, and there was just tension. I'd say something about the union in there, and they'd say, 'What does that have to do with us?' It was all too general, too abstract. I wanted to do something more realistic." Others have chosen the church. "I started going to party meetings," one *comunidade* member recounted. "But when the meetings happened at the same time as meetings in the church, I thought, 'which is more important?' I didn't feel like that was my place, so I stopped going."

Yet others, caught between the religious and the political horns of this dilemma, throw up their hands and are sorely tempted to release both. The testimony of Laíse is candid:

I find these days I don't know where I am any more. I go to a meeting of the Church, and there they are all just talking about loving your brother, but they aren't doing anything, so I feel restless there. Then I go to a meeting of the PT, and there they are all screaming at the top of their lungs. So I don't know where to turn any more. I have been feeling sick from this. Some days I think I'm just going to give up everything and go back to taking care of my family, like I should.

A few activists have succeeded in reconciling party or labor politics with continued religious activism but these are the exceptions that prove the rule. They attribute their political consciousness not to the Church, but to non-Church experience and praxis. In two illustrative cases, PT politics evolved out of prior social activism, shaped not by the political style of the Church, but by the confrontational politics of pre-coup industrial unionism and rural workers' movements independent of the Pastoral of Land.

Lírio, a tall, sharply intelligent construction worker in his late forties, was active in the Church's Labor Pastoral, the construction workers' union, and the PT. When discussing his politics, he spoke with the accents of liberation theology. "Our salvation," he once told me, "is here on earth. We must struggle in the movements to bring it about."

He insisted, however, that he had formed this opinion not in the Church, but by thirty long years of experience. As he tells the story of his politicization, in the late 1950s and early 1960s he had worked as an apprentice electrician at Petrobrás, at the very time of the first major autonomous workers' organizations in Brazil. In 1964, at the age of twenty-three, he had seen the military smash all organizing efforts. "That showed me," he recounted, "how powerful and mean the rich really are. You can't trust any of them, they'll never change."

Francisco, a squat man in his late fifties, was active in both the Church's Land Pastoral and the PT. It wasn't the Church, however, that had taught him the basic principles of moral economy. "I knew what was going on," he said, "long before the Church decided to care about the little people." He draws a proud distinction between "the talk of the priests" and what impelled him to "fight the landgrabbers" in the first place.

It was simple disgust at seeing someone lose their land. When I entered the Pastoral of Land, I had fifteen years experience in the rural union! It never had anything to do with religion. . . . The Church didn't teach me anything about that! I felt God had given so much land, so much space, so why all this dishonesty?

Still, although the Church may not have determined Lírio's and Francisco's political styles, it provided them with important material and spiritual support. In Francisco's case, the Church provided courage and a new theological vocabulary to shore up old arguments. "I always thought," Francisco said, "the land should be divided; what is new is that I now say 'land of Christ, land of our brother.'" The Church helped Lírio, too, embed his political commitment in theological language. "Jesus came for the smallest of us," he said. "He [Jesus] said to struggle hard, not to cross our arms. And he came so that we would have life, and life in abundance. I am carrying out that mission in the union."

At the same time, activists like Lírio and Francisco whose political roots push deeper than their years in Church express strong reservations about the extent of the Church's own political commitment. "Where will the Church be tomorrow?" Lírio asked rhetorically. "The priests mean well, but they talk, talk, talk. There are a lot of priests who are *for* the people, but how many are *of* the people?" Francisco also remained trenchantly skeptical. "They say they opted for the poor," he remarked, "but they can choose! . . . But I can't choose, I can't opt."

THE ALIENATED

There was yet one more group of Catholics that made an impact on the size of the march that October morning: those who did not go at all. Most of my informants maintained that large numbers of Catholics who once participated in just such processions had grown alienated from the Church since the introduction of progressive discourse. "The church used to be chock full," said one woman, "but now there's hardly anyone. People don't like the changes." It is difficult to characterize the alienated in generational terms. Young people as well as old have reacted negatively to the new Catholic discourse. Still, my overall impression was that most of the people who stopped going to Church since Father Cosme's arrival were older, pre-Conciliar and Conciliar Catholics.

The new Church, many of these people complained, was "mixing things together," spending too much time talking about "material things," and slipping away from its role as promiser of other-worldly salvation. "I go to Church to hear the Gospel," said one man. "There all I heard was about fighting, politics. So I said, I'm not going back." Talking about poverty and injustice in the Church, he said, "takes away time from praising God . . . Talking about unions and all, that's slipping away from the word of God." Another woman recalled that "when they started talking about neighborhood associations, unions, politics, I left right away. . . . The Church is for praying, for speaking about the Word of God, not for talking about potholes."

Moreover, in regard to the progressive Church's liturgical changes, I found an equally strong negative response. In some *comunidades*, priests who were trying to make *celebrações* carry a stronger social message decked the chapel with sugar cane, coffee branches, fruits of the earth, and farming tools. One elderly man wondered, "what is sugar cane? It's just sugar cane!" Such things signified not the realm of the absolute, but only themselves. By sacralizing almost everything, the new Church seemed to be sacralizing almost nothing. Older *misseiros* were the most likely to jump ship. "In the time of Linz [previous priest]," complained one woman, "there was more respect. Now women can go in there in short pants! Now they let women go and take Communion with short sleeves! Lack of respect!"

Luís, another old Catholic, complained that "these new priests, they level everything, they make everything the same as us." A most dramatic example of this kind of levelling occurred on Mother Mary's feast day. Traditionally, the day's highlight was the crowning ceremony of a figurine of Mary. Cosme called upon locals to replace the statue with the oldest living woman in town. This was, for some people, the last straw. "I'd never seen anything like it!" one woman complained. "When they put that old woman as Our Lady! You shouldn't do that! People shouldn't crown humans, they're not pure enough. And that woman was a *macumbeira*! To turn a human into an image! Error! I'd never seen anything like it. . . . I couldn't keep going there."

Carlita's husband, Edson, had once been very active in the Church. A round, balding construction worker in his sixties, he had been born and bred according to the traditions of the pre-Conciliar Church, and was deeply offended by the progressive Church's newfangled ways. With the exception of monthly Mass, he stopped attending Church functions since Cosme had arrived. He had been especially irritated by Cosme's liturgical innovations. "He started telling us to do strange things," he recalled,

It was raining, he asked us to go out of the church, walk under the rain, get wet, as the "grace of God." That's not in the Bible. There are so many improvised things, that they just mess things up.

Of course, Edson had not shown up at the march in October. He knew the bishop was planning to turn the procession for Mary into a "bunch of stuff that doesn't belong there, about the government, and rights, and I don't know what." "The bishop talks about liberation," Edson complained, "but he just means material things. That's the problem with these new priests. They're mixing religion and politics."

Father Cosme was acutely aware of these attitudes and of how widespread they were. From early on, he sensed that his message of struggle and liberation was not striking a chord with a large segment in the *comunidades.* "When I first arrived," he recalled,

I could see how the people were reacting to an explicitly politicized celebration. And that my focus, my way of seeing problems, didn't always correspond to that of the people. What struck me most was a kind of deafening silence. A lot of the poor felt awkward with the celebrations, because they were there to meet with God, not receive a lecture or listen to talk of this world. . . . I saw that people were remaining silent, that the vision of the world I wanted to transmit to them, wasn't so easy to transmit after all.

The Assembly of God and Politics

Pentecostal services and prayer meetings contain precious little "mixing of religion and politics." Here, the highest value is placed not on material, but spiritual liberation. Some pentecostals actually attribute their conversions to the politicization of the Catholic Church. One young man who had been raised in a Catholic family recounted that when "the Church got mixed up with politics, that was mixing things too much. We know so little of the Word of God, why waste time with politics? The Church is concerned about spiritual life, not material things. In the groups, they would talk so much about politics. So I left. In the Assembly, they don't mix things: what is material is material, the spiritual is spiritual."

On the other hand, there can be no doubt that the religious logic of pentecostalism includes a number of tensions, contradictions, and sources of empowerment that facilitate rather than hinder participation in social movements. In some cases, these may even nurture the development of a highly critical social consciousness. In order to explore such tensions and contradictions, I will examine more closely whether, when, and how pentecostals come to participate in collective action for social change.

PENTECOSTALS IN NEIGHBORHOOD ORGANIZATIONS

At first glance, anyone concerned with the political consequences of pentecostal identity would take little solace in the level of pentecostal participation in São Jorge's neighborhood organizations. Here, of the many dozens of men who have participated over the past decade as directors of the Association, only two have hailed from the Assembly of God. Furthermore, in the 1988 election for directorate members, only a dozen pentecostals cast votes, compared to the three hundred votes cast by non-pentecostals. How to account for such apparent alienation?

If one poses this question to a non-pentecostal, he will offer a favorite explanation: pentecostals care little for material improvement. "Pentecostals," one association director told me, "don't care about sewage or streets. They feel they can walk in the mud." The explanation continues:

crentes think they need only pray to get what they want; therefore, they have little use for worldly, collective efforts. "They think if they stay at home and ask God," said another director, "it will just fall from the sky."

Accounts such as these are not entirely wrong. Pentecostals do cite Jesus' remark that "My Kingdom is not of this world." They also are quick to rationalize much of their material deprivation as God's way of bringing His chosen closer to Him. Yet the contention that pentecostals are indifferent to the material world is simply off the mark. *Crentes* denounce the world for its corruption; they do not denounce the world *tout court.* Most pentecostals studiously avoid the dogmatic world-renunciation of the few converts who attract such a disproportionate amount of attention; I often heard pentecostals call such people "*fanáticos.*" Rather than such world-renouncing mysticism, most *crentes* seek the Christian life envisaged by the Apostle Paul, one implicated in such worldly relations as marriage, family, work, neighborhood, and the maintenance of physical health. From this viewpoint, whatever permits these to be nurtured and maintained is good; whatever threatens them is bad.

Crentes express this worldview by pointing to their commitment to living "correctly" and "decently" in the here and now; for example, it is especially important to *crentes* to strive for "improvement" and "cleanliness." The pentecostal can thus be heard as often as anyone else decrying bad drinking water, dangerous buses and roads, unstable tenure of houseplots, and the lack of electricity. As one pentecostal presbyter explained, "We have salvation,"

but salvation is in heaven. We are here on earth. Jesus will come, but he's not here yet. Look, this road here was bad: wasn't it better to asphalt it? Didn't that benefit people? If you don't improve things, they worsen. When I arrive at home after work, I have to take my bath: I've improved! I'm not going to lie down in a bed all dirty. God loves improvement, and everything that improves is clean.

Even those observers who acknowledge pentecostals' appreciation of material benefits sometimes claim that *crentes* believe the only way to obtain them is through prayer. This may characterize the attitudes of some pentecostals (as it does some non-*crentes*), yet most pentecostals I spoke to embraced the dictum that God helps those who help themselves. The following statement by a deacon illustrates the logic.

Let's suppose there is an empty glass here, and I say, "Let's pray for water to fill it up." That won't happen! We have to go over there and fill it. So they have to go to CEDAE [the water authority] and ask and talk. They need to pray for strength to walk and speak. You have to form those groups and go to the mayor and ask for things. To make a meal, you can't ask God, you have to build your own house. Is He going to pave your street? No, you have to go to the mayor. Look at Nemias, he was a servant of the king in Jerusalem. He went to demand from the king, and prayed, he didn't just fold his arms.

If we take such views seriously, it becomes difficult to maintain that *crentes* remain uninvolved in neighborhood associations simply as a result of indifference or overweening reliance on prayer. While these may be contributing factors, we must also consider the fact that pentecostals usually feel socially marginalized from the groups that tend to dominate neighborhood associations.

This marginalization has several dimensions. First, *crentes* rarely see their coreligionists in positions of leadership in neighborhood associations. The associations of most towns in Duque de Caxias are run by closely-knit cliques of local notables who promise to deliver votes to local politicians in exchange for infrastructural improvements. In São Jorge, the association has rotated posts among such notables for over twenty years, with decision making monopolized by factions that crystallize in the street and bars. The result is a back-room faction politics that requires skill in saying things one does not mean and making promises one does not intend to keep. It should thus not surprise us that non-pentecostal leaders hesitate to ask pentecostals to run on slates with them: they clearly wish to avoid constraints on practices they deem essential to local male-dominated politics, including smoking, drinking, swearing, and swapping of adulterous stories. Such activities are not acceptable for practicing *crentes*; pentecostals are forbidden to frequent the bars where much factional caucusing takes place. When a pentecostal attends association meetings, he becomes quickly frustrated. "Sometimes," one of the two *crentes* who entered the directorate told me,

you have a good plan, but you get lost. There at the table, they don't call on you, they don't respect your opinion, they won't even listen. The *crente* isn't shrewd, he doesn't know how to get support, go out drinking, give favors, lie. He can't! He's not around, hanging out on the street and in the bars, getting people on his side.

This man was a presbyter in his church. His annoyance thus offers a clue to another problem: as proud members of a church with its own hierarchy, pentecostal deacons and presbyters balk at subjecting themselves to people who do not respect their opinion. The presbyter recounted bitterly that the current directors had asked him to run for office with them, but once he had brought in pentecostal votes they ceased consulting him at all. "They wouldn't even tell me when the association was meeting!"

Non-pentecostals' lack of solicitude for *crentes* is further manifested in their insensitivity to pentecostal religious schedules. Whenever the directors set dates for town meetings, they carefully consider the possibility of conflicting with Catholic, but never pentecostal, weddings. Moreover, elections for new directorates always take place in the *salão* of the Catholic Church. "I won't attend there because they will treat me differently," one pentecostal explained. "They are Catholic, I am *crente*."

That the obstacles to pentecostal participation in local neighborhood associations are mainly social and practical, not doctrinal, is suggested by the fact that, in several associations, pentecostals have become actively involved to the point of outnumbering progressive Catholics. *Crentes* have a better chance of becoming involved in associations in places with newer, more heterogenous populations where the association has not been dominated by a Catholic clique.

Consider Sarapuí, a far-flung town of about fifteen thousand inhabitants located on the outskirts of Duque de Caxias. Here, pentecostals stepped into an organizational vacuum. By the mid-1970s, no associ-

The directorate of São Jorge's neighborhood association

ation had yet been founded there. In the late 1970s, a middle-aged pentecostal named Dalila who had lived in town for nearly fifteen years found herself and her neighbors threatened with eviction.

They sent us a paper saying we had only ninety days to get out. We were worried, it was a Wednesday, we were in prayer. Then God said to me, "I will show you that here at home there will be a person behind the Word."

Emboldened by this voice, Dalila sought the assistance of a lawyer; impressed by her energy, neighbors heeded her call when she convened a meeting in her house. There the lawyer explained that "we had a better chance if we were organized into an association. My husband became president . . . we had lots of *crentes* there in the association, because we founded it." In the association, she had to meet on equal terms with people of all religions, including *umbanda*. The Bible inspired her: "When Jesus walked upon the earth, he sat down and ate with sinners," she reminded me. "He cured the sick. He worked and helped all without exception. He said, 'I have not come for the healthy, but for the sick.'" Dalila never wavered from the conviction that she was doing God's will. "We have two struggles in life: material and spiritual," she declared. "In anything material, when things are good, God is acting." The struggle dragged on for four years. "And I was always talking to the people, saying 'don't lose heart, because nothing is going to happen.' God was always speaking to me, you know? 'Do not fear,' He would say, always inspiring me."

In 1978, in a victory that solidified Dalila's own commitment the state government finally settled in favor of the association. She then persuaded the pastor to give her release time from church services to attend the conferences of the regional confederation of neighborhood associations. During this time, she and her husband also inspired dozens of their coreligionists, as well as non-*crente* neighbors, to participate in the organization. "The people around here believe a lot in us, they support us. They trust us." Such expressions of trust are common whenever pentecostals take on roles of political leadership. Non-pentecostal small-holders who support a local pentecostal as the leader of their peasant union, for example, spoke of his honesty.[6] Elsewhere, non-*crentes* voted for pentecostal candidates for assemblyman on the grounds that "they won't rob and steal."

While pentecostals in Sarapuí stepped into an organizational vacuum, in Pilar, a larger and more heterogeneous town than either São Jorge or Sarapuí, the *crentes* encountered, not a lack of preexisting organization (the place had had a neighborhood association for almost ten years), but a crisis of Catholic leadership. This crisis, which illustrates some of the rigidities of the Catholic Church's relation to social movements, opened a window through which pentecostal leaders stepped, bringing other pentecostals in their train.

Pilar was home to Father Orlando, who in 1983 persuaded his protégés to run for the local association's directorate. After winning, the Catholics gained improvements for the geographic center of town (where most of them happened to live), rather than for the area at the town's margins, largely inhabited by *crentes,* who live near their own churches. Consequently, during the Catholics' tenure, pentecostals burned a slow fuse. Then scandal struck: Orlando had an affair with a married woman and was forced to abandon the Church. Recalled one Catholic: "Many people lost heart when he left and desisted from the association."

Soon after, the Catholic hierarchy's paternalism—a tendency to abandon any movement it cannot dominate or engineer—reared its ugly head. A nonpracticing Catholic won the presidency of the association, no doubt in part due to general disillusionment with the Church after Orlando's scandal. No longer in control of the association, the progressive bishop promptly expelled its members from the Church-owned building where they met, forcing them to convene at the public school, which happened to be located near the residential concentration of *crentes.* Many pentecostals jumped at this opportunity to redress the inequity of past directorates, seeing the arrival of meetings in their neighborhood as a way to gain access to the improvements from which they had so long been excluded. They began attending meetings in large numbers. During this crucial period, water pipes were installed throughout the town, the first major improvement to affect the *crentes'* neighborhood. Though this benefit had already been in the works before the arrival of the pentecostals, for many it seemed hardly coincidental. The *crentes,* some began to say, get results for the whole town, not just one part of it. When the pastor of the Assembly of God threw his weight behind a bloc of his congregants running for office in the new directorate in 1985, they had little difficulty getting elected. "In many pentecostal churches," the pastor told me,

they think it's a sin to work in things. But not here, I teach differently. I let the neighborhood association use this *sala,* and I give them a word of support. And we are setting up a medical consultation room upstairs. We are preparing a little school.

The Catholic leaders in Pilar, demoralized by the collapse of Church support, eventually resigned. By 1988, pentecostals were still so active in the association that its two remaining Catholic leaders freely admitted that "we now rely more on the people of the Assembly of God than on the Catholics." The presence of *crentes* in the directorate of a neighborhood association does not come without contradictions. In another town, where the federal government named a Kardecist center as an official distribution point for milk, a municipal truck arrived with a hundred liters. When the center tried to deliver the milk to the neighborhood association, the latter's *crente* president refused to accept it, saying it had been tainted by the Devil.

CRENTES IN LABOR STRUGGLES

If under some circumstances *crentes* throw themselves into neighborhood improvement, they seem rather less inclined to translate experience of the more direct contradictions of capital into collective action. Local labor organizers, who point to pentecostals as major culprits in undermining union strength, remark on the low levels of involvement among pentecostal industrial workers in newer, more combative labor organizations.[7] Among Rio's municipal transport workers, for example, pentecostals are said to "keep their distance" from the union; in Rio's metalworkers' union (which recently elected a militant directorate),[8] an organizer told me that

we invited the *crentes* and the pastors, but they say that we fight too much. A master craftsman who is a *crente* said that Christians cannot fight. He didn't like that we spoke badly of the current president [of the union].

As with their account of pentecostals' passivity in regard to neighborhood associations, non-pentecostal critics commonly attribute this political apathy to lack of material ambition. "*Crentes* are not excited by material things," explained a metalworkers' organizer. "They don't want to get ahead, they don't have that drive [*pique*]. They don't think they need to go on strike, because they think they've got it made in heaven."

There may be some truth to this. Religious ideology may influence the conduct of pentecostals engaged in industrial labor, especially among operatives not engaged in precision work. For example, I heard that in factories pentecostal operatives sometimes left machines running while going off to pray, sing, or read the Bible. Though such tales undoubtedly involve a dose of malice, I did meet several *crentes* who had been

fired more than once for loafing. At any rate, pentecostals seem better
equipped spiritually to deal with unstable employment than Catholics.
They say they do not worry about losing their jobs, for unemployment
is a Jobian trial. "God is working His will," a pentecostal told me after
being fired. "He didn't want me to stay there. He has another plan for
me." *Crentes* point to Isaiah's prophecy that in the final days man shall
receive his salary "in a bag with a hole in it," which they say accounts
for the high inflation rate and the low minimum wage in Brazil.

Yet the opinions of pentecostal industrial workers on wages and
unemployment are contradictory. The meaning of such contradictions
has generally been missed because of Brazilian scholars' excessive reliance on the statements of pastors.[9] In fact, major differences separate the
views of working-class pentecostals from those of salaried pastors. "The
employer is the worker's brother before God," insisted pastor Alcyr, who
receives five minimum salaries and owns a car, "and Jesus said, 'Do not
hurt your brother.' But strikes hurt them!" What of Christ's denunciations of wealth? "You can be as rich as you want," he argued, "but if
you are humble of spirit, you are a servant of God." The pastor even tried
to downplay the thrust of Christ's "eye of a needle" pronouncement by
saying "Jesus was talking about those who were greedy and valued
money above Him. Sometimes a person isn't even rich, but has an
ambition for money, he'll kill for money." Such apologetics ring hollow
for working-class *crentes*. "Most pastors," one explained,

earn a salary, so they don't need to strike. They earn two or three salaries, with
a pension. They don't need to enter the fray, they stay cozy in their churches.
So of course they don't think it's necessary to go there. But whoever earns only
enough for his daily bread is obliged to go! It is Biblical that we must work by
the sweat of our brow. The *crente* doesn't go there to create fights or anarchy;
he goes to offer his help.

It is as much of an error to attribute pentecostals' avoidance of labor
struggles to indifference to wages as it is to argue that *crentes* like walking
in mud in their towns. Brazil's inflationary economy obliges the working
class, whether pentecostal or non-pentecostal, to be all too aware of the
wage-price squeeze. Like other workers, pentecostals need no lectures
to grasp that, unless wages keep up with the cost of rice and beans, misery
quickly results.

The crucial point is that while pentecostals accept poverty, they do not
accept immiseration. If *crentes* see poverty as nurturing virtue, beggary
signifies disobedience to God, as implied by the psalm, "I have never

seen a servant of God beg for bread." Pentecostals hesitate to turn to each other for financial help, lest their obedience to God be placed into doubt. "God said that by the sweat of your brow you would make bread," said one. "So He wanted you to make bread!" Another argued that "God doesn't want things to become super bad. He wants them to be a way that we can tolerate. God does not like misery!"

If God does not approve of misery, neither does He look favorably upon the lifestyle of rich bosses. The sacralization of poverty carries with it a compelling denial of legitimacy of the rich and powerful. The less well-off members of pentecostal congregations have no illusions as to why they see so few persons of wealth in their church. "You never see merchants in our church," remarked one,

because they think "we have our money!" Money is everything for them, and the church isn't going to give him any money. It is harder for a rich man to be saved, because he thinks he has everything. Our everything is God. We need work and all, but the rich man already has that.

Crentes do not hesitate to denounce rich pentecostals as hypocrites. "They are wasting their time," said one,

when they really convert, they won't want that wealth and vanity any more! They give it all up. Job lost all of his wealth, and all the prophets in the Bible are poor. The rich cannot save themselves.

This denial of legitimacy, combined with the pentecostals' awareness that misery is due at least in part to the wage-price squeeze, opens the way for an interpretation of economic deprivation as resulting not from workers' sins, but from employers' and government sins. "There is misery because the employer has no love for his employee," one pentecostal declared. "He treats him like an animal, an object, he doesn't care if he lives or dies." Many working *crentes* point out that employers, by firing them, make it impossible to fulfil the Biblical injunction to work by the sweat of their brow and not burden their neighbors. Another pentecostal argued,

The Bible said we must work, that by the sweat of our brow shall we live. But when the employer fires you, you become a burden, you have to get INPS,[10] that is a burden on your neighbor.

At the same time, working-class pentecostals understand that only organized pressure will induce employers to raise wages to keep pace with inflation. "Without strikes," said one, "there is no raise in salary, so there have to be strikes. They won't give it to you any other way."

Biblical prophesies do not obviate the need for workers' action: As one pentecostal worker said,

You have to live, you have to survive. That saying about receiving salary in a sack with holes, that's true, but that doesn't mean you have to accept misery! No! We must survive, stay healthy, so we can preach the Word.

One deacon simply sidestepped Isaiah's prophesy altogether, justifying strikes by the divine injunction to help oneself. "Without strikes," he declared,

you can't get anything. And we can't just sit back with our arms folded while others are struggling there in battle! God told us to help ourselves. So we have to bring our strength together, because in unity there's strength. Without unity how can we win?

Given these attitudes, why do *crentes* so often avoid union militancy? The first part of an answer may be gleaned from the fact that many pentecostals explain their apathy about organizing in the same non-religious terms used by non-*crentes*: hard experience proves that employers still hold the cards and use strikes to get rid of troublemaking or unprofitable workers. One pentecostal disavowed any theological rationale for his skittishness about strikes. "My opinion on this has nothing to do with me being *crente*," he insisted. "I always felt this way, even before I converted. I'm against the strike because when it doesn't work out, it's the little guy who always has to pay, he's the one who suffers!"

From this viewpoint, pentecostals' lack of participation may partly be a matter of perception. I have not come across any statistical analysis that compares rates of participation of *crentes* with non-pentecostals, but to the extent that most workers, irrespective of religion, do not participate in labor activism of any kind, it is quite possible that pentecostal participation may not differ dramatically from that of non-*crentes*. In terms of the percentage of any given work force, pentecostals are always less numerous than peripheral and participating Catholics, thus making up only a small percentage of unmobilized workers. Because of their dress and demeanor, however, *crentes* stand out perceptually. By remaining outside union drinking and politicking networks, it is possible that pentecostals provide organizers a scapegoat to account for the weakness of organizing drives.

When pentecostals *do* participate in labor struggles, their conduct provides backbone to work stoppages and other actions. In some factories, pentecostals can comprise up to a tenth of the workforce. "*Crentes* are very firm in a strike," explained one non-pentecostal organizer. "They give credibility to the movement." A pentecostal confirmed this. "We won't scab, we won't vacillate. When they want our support, we say, 'OK, but without any violence.'" Indeed, because of their tactical importance, organizers often rely on pentecostals' support as a way of building legitimacy for the action both among workers and in negotiating with employers. In a strike of metalworkers in one plant, for example, the strike committee nominated a pentecostal to approach the employer. Those with him clearly recall the effect this had on the climate of negotiations. "He spoke calmly," one remembered. "He said, 'Look, we're not able to tolerate these wages.' He was right, because the salary was low. That gave the workers a real boost, and the manager got the rug pulled right under his feet."

For all this, there is no denying that working-class pentecostals impose conditions for supporting union militancy. Above all, to be legitimate, a strike must not have any "*baderna*"—confusion, violence, disorder. Thus, in 1988, local *crentes* supported the municipal teachers' strike in Rio because of its nonviolence, but were horrified by the picketline confrontations that same year in the retail workers' strikes. To the extent that government and business have been willing to use police to break strikes, many of the most visible Brazilian labor conflicts in recent memory have involved "*baderna*," and the resulting climate of tension and polarization contributes to quickly flaring tempers on picketlines and the shop floor. Yet *crentes*' sense of what is required for survival continues to intervene. I met numerous pentecostals who approved of passive resistance. Under some circumstances, they were willing to accept nonviolent civil disobedience. "It's a legitimate weapon of the worker," said one retired man,

Look, they were going to take away our pension; and there was a whole bunch of people who went to Brasília to invade the office of INPS. I couldn't go because it's so far. We achieved an 80 percent increase in INPS, through an invasion of the INPS office there in Brasília. I saw that on TV. That was right. The *crente* can't throw stones; he can strike and support his brothers, though.

Crentes in Radical Party Politics

Analyses of the relations between pentecostals and political parties generally support Gomes' assessment[11] that *crentes* tend to vote for conservative parties (especially in 1982) guided primarily by self-interest, or religious group or local interests, rather than by class interest or ideology.[12] At the same time, these writers acknowledge the sizeable presence of pentecostals in the Workers' Party.[13] What can this presence mean?

According to estimates from different sources, roughly one-tenth of the almost thirty-five hundred members of the Duque de Caxias branch of the Worker's Party are *crentes* of the Assembly of God. Three-quarters of these have been members for nearly ten years. Working-class pentecostals began to enter the party during its founding period between 1979 and 1982 for the same reasons non-pentecostals did: the PT was new on the political scene and free from any taint of corruption and unfulfilled promises.[14] Many of the original pentecostals in the party were active in neighborhood associations—like Dalila, whom we met earlier—an experience that persuaded them of the importance of electing trustworthy politicians. Through her work in the neighborhood association, Dalila met regional leaders who offered advice and support. Their honesty impressed her, so that when they campaigned for the PT ticket in 1982, she entered the party. "They were very good," she reported, "very honest, they wanted to help the poor people, not just get their vote."

Dalila and other *crentes* found support from Libôrio, the president of the regional convention of Assemblies of God. As a town councilman, Libôrio decided to abandon his centrist party label in 1982 and take advantage of the vote-getting appeal of the new party's still unblemished record. The PT's directors welcomed the pastor as their standard-bearer, judging that the party could use an established politician to attract pentecostal votes. Not only did Libôrio do this, he also drew and reinforced a core of pentecostal party activists who otherwise might have stayed away.

Though the PT's reputation for confrontation frightened pentecostals, by the late 1980s a softer-spoken Catholic leadership and improved linkages to neighborhood movements had drawn numerous pentecostals into the party. As an increasing number of the region's union directorates passed to the militant labor central (CUT) and began winning improvements in the workplace, the PT's legitimacy also increased. A member of the Assembly of God and leader of the Civil Construction Union has personally recruited numerous other *crentes* into the PT.

Yet in light of Romans 13 (the Apostle Paul's injunction to obey worldly authority), how could pentecostals stomach the PT's antigovernmental stance? The prophetic tradition of the Old Testament came in handy here. When I asked whether the military in Brazil had been placed in power by God, one *crente* replied "Yes, placed by God,"

but then they got corrupt. There is a lot of money there. Man is very drawn to things of the flesh. They want to fill their pockets. When they turn into "maharajahs" [corrupt high officials], God starts to distance Himself from them, He doesn't give them any more grace. They're like Judas. Sarney fell into the corruption of his ministers. "Woe unto you who afflicts my people with unjust laws."

Dalila, meanwhile, quoted Isaiah 10 to the same effect: "Woe unto they who decree unjust laws, and unto scribes who write perversity." She was reinterpreting Pauline obedience as a way for God to protect the weak from the powerful.

God tells us to respect them, so they won't attack us. If an authority comes along and the police comes, how is it going to be? With a lawyer by your side it's better, because if we just do it on our own, disasters will occur.

Although the theoretical and ideological clarity of the *crentes'* political vision may be doubted, its combativeness cannot. To place their peculiar sense of militancy in greater relief, let us compare it with the surprisingly conciliatory stance of leaders from the Catholic base communities in Duque de Caxias. Although Catholics comprise a large majority of the local branch of the PT, those pentecostals who have become involved as leaders appear firmer and more ideological than Catholics. "Once they are in the party," a non-pentecostal director of the PT observed,

the evangelicals are really very combative. The people of the Catholic Church have a very vague vision; but not the evangelicals. They have a vision of transformation of society. The evangelicals are able to develop a clear socialist class vision; but the Catholics cannot. That much is very clear.

What is going on here? To put the matter briefly, while Catholics are taught to think in conciliatory terms, pentecostals see the world as a battleground in which the Devil plays a constant role. *Crentes* are thus able to claim with relative ease that many of the rich are in league with the Devil.[15] The pentecostal in politics speaks of the politician or captain of industry as a "tool of the Devil," while, as we have seen, the Catholic emphasizes that "we are both children of God." "There are employers," one pentecostal affirmed, "who sell their souls to the Devil for money. Most of the rich people, the merchants around here, they seek out the

Devil to make compacts, there in *macumba*, to make money." As Dalila explained,

The Enemy only wants to see us thrown to one side. He doesn't want to see anyone doing well. He's only satisfied with destruction. When we don't have any electricity, no drainage, that's the work of the Devil, because God is light. From the moment we are concerned with improving, I believe we are struggling against the Devil.

And according to a pentecostal in the civil construction workers' union,

ninety percent of wealth is contributed by the Devil. Because they are constructed in fraud. All action against society is made by him. Whenever someone sins against God and the nation, that comes from the Devil, fraud, robbery.

The association of the middle class and business people with the Afro-Brazilian spiritist religions also has widespread notoriety among the working class. It dovetails with pentecostals' images of the wealthy as entering into pacts with the Devil. As one pentecostal in the PT declared, "The great capitalists serve the Devil, they come from *candomblé*, spiritism, buddhism, magic."

Perhaps the clearest evocation of this connection came from Murão, a pentecostal construction-workers' leader who is also currently on the board of directors of the PT in Caxias. Though Murão's political stances are clearly heterodox, they are rooted in basic premises of pentecostal theology. "When I struggle against capitalism," he told me,

I feel that I am struggling against the Devil. I struggle against the capitalist because he is the Devil's partner. I struggle so as not to give in to the Devil. Capitalists don't believe or trust in God. The rich man doesn't need to distribute things; he just has pride.

Murão's reference to "struggle" brings us to the very heart of pentecostalism as a religion of overcoming adversity. "With *crentes*," he explained, "the struggle against evil is a very large, a very great struggle. The Apostle Paul said, 'struggle ferociously against the spirit of the Devil.' So our daily life is a struggle." No fatalism or quietism here.

You only achieve some victory through struggle. Life is a struggle. Our struggle must be tireless, because God is going to judge us. The Bible says, "Do not accept this world." And another part says, "Do not be quiet, because your rest is not here!" So why should we be quiet in front of a situation that enslaves us?

It is possible that Murão's heterodoxy will begin finding adherents among his coreligionists.[16] He is, after all, well-situated institutionally:

in the PT, his union, and his church. If the objective conditions of the Brazilian working class continue to decline at the current rate, Murão may be able to tap into the widespread, deep-seated *crente* rejection of immiseration. Perhaps he will even be able to persuade some pentecostals that socialism is a precondition for spiritual liberation. For Murão, true liberation means living in a world in which one is free to discover Christ; and this means living in a socialist world. "Through changes in society," he prophesied,

man will be able to improve himself religiously. Improvement only comes through a transformation, whether material or spiritual. Because if you don't have a transformation in your material life, you can't get one in the other. The system doesn't let man liberate himself from things. The corrupt system doesn't let people become *crentes.*

It is not too far-fetched to hypothesize that in Brazil's deepening crisis, Murão's pentecostal socialist vision might actually catch on. Though Brazilian Catholics may go only so far politically before breaking with the Church, pentecostals have no specific political line for their members to toe. *Crentes* are thus freer than progressive Catholics to develop their own political thinking. Unrestrained by the official political position of a church, the pentecostal can maintain his religious identity even while becoming radical. If the miraculous signs of salvation that Jesus foretold would "accompany those that believe," they might also include the ability to remake the world. We have yet to hear the *crentes'* last word.

Conclusion

Looking for Liberation

Reassessing CEBs

From the late 1960s, when Brazil's Catholic Church had just begun to promote the spread of *comunidades de base*, to the late 1970s, when the formation of new CEBs was at high tide, the nearly-universal consensus in the Church was that the *comunidades* represented an irresistible mass movement that would soon transform Brazilian society. In the late 1970s and early 1980s, when the military government handed over the reins of power to civilians, this prognosis appeared to be at least partly confirmed. Various observers, in fact, have attributed the transition to democracy in the mid-1980s as owing a great deal to the pressure of the CEBs.[1]

In the 1980s, this consensus began to fray at the edges. During the 1970s, while military rule was still in force, the progressive clergy could still explain adherence to religious groups other than the CEBs as resulting from fear of repression. In the 1980s, however, when the "sects" continued to grow by leaps and bounds and the CEBs stagnated this explanation because increasingly difficult to sustain. It was clear to most observers that the lack of dynamism among CEBs in the 1980s reflected a growing conservatism at the highest levels of the Church, under pressure from the Vatican.[2] Still, at the local level, many clergy were well aware that even in dioceses with firmly entrenched progressive bishops and longstanding "Popular Pastorals," CEBs still lagged far behind their competitors. Late in my stay in São Jorge, Father Cosme said to me,

we are witnessing a crisis in the euphoria we once had. Over the past twenty years, the one who has been producing the discourse has not been the people. The one who "chose for the poor" was not the poor, it was us, the pastoral agents. The more we recognize that the discourse is our own, the more honest we will be. . . . Liberationist spirituality is still very directed toward the militants, not the masses. We say that the people have to participate, but they aren't there participating! The more we say "participation," the more they distance themselves from us. The pentecostals are much more attractive to the Catholic masses than are our CEBs.

In addition to the issue of participation, there was the problem of CEBs' politics. In the 1960s and 1970s, the CEBs had been one of the few organizational spaces available for demanding improvements in infrastructure, health, education, and social services. With redemocratization, however, many such political functions passed to secular neighborhood organizations, social movements, and political parties. Many of those who had participated in CEBs because they regarded them as vehicles for social action left altogether, while many of those who remained became demobilized.[3] A premonition of this process came in 1982, when the CEBs did not vote *en masse* for the PT, as the progressive clergy assumed they would.

In the mid- and late 1980s, on the occasions when progressive clergy openly conceded that their high expectations, formed during the first flush of CEB growth, were not being realized, they generally blamed the problem on the growing number of conservative bishops who refused to support them.[4] Although the changing political complexion of the bishopric was certainly a factor, it cannot explain why CEBs were so easily demobilized, nor why so many people preferred other religions even before the concerted attack on liberation theology. Many clergy simply resorted to blaming the "alienation" of the people.[5]

At the same time, an awareness began to dawn on some priests that the *comunidades'* relative demographic inertia and fragility of "consciousness" could not all be blamed on the Vatican or the people. Small groups of clergy began to turn their gaze back on themselves and to reconsider their earlier certainty that the masses wanted eagerly to drink at the well of progressive discourse.[6] It was in this evolving climate of reassessment that I conceived the questions motivating this book. How to account for the paradoxes of Brazil's CEBs? How to explain their inability to "keep up" with other religions and the surprisingly widespread disinclination among their members to become involved in non-church social movements?

Summarizing the Argument

In this book, I have attempted to offer a partial answer to the questions noted above by breaking with the traditionally narrow focus of CEB studies on only those individuals who participate actively in the CEB and speak its language fluently. Rather, I began my study by broadening my field of vision to embrace the wider contested arena of religious and ideological alternatives, in which the CEB, as religious group and specific ideological message, was but one contender. My next step was to focus on clusters of people in the process of encountering, interacting with, and choosing between the arena's alternatives. This approach allowed me to argue that, in São Jorge, various religious groups were more effective than the CEB in helping the less stable segments of the working class, married women facing domestic conflict, unmarried youths, and *negros* all cope with their experiential predicaments. It also made it possible to see that, far from being ideological monoliths, São Jorge's *comunidade* and Assembly of God contained ideological subgroups, shaped by the timing of religious socialization, institutional position, and histories of class experience.

I do not intend here to characterize São Jorge's religious arena once again in all its complexity; I want only to remind the reader of one contrast that helps to explain the differential appeal of religions in that arena. Observers who contend that the CEBs are the best answer to the *crentes* believe they enjoy the same personalized religious environment, and equality as do the *crentes*.[7] These writers assume that the small size of the CEBs nurtures the same kind of mutual trust and egalitarianism that exists in *crente* churches; that is, that both the CEBs and *crentes* are what Weber would have called "congregations."[8] It is possible, however, that the CEBs' and *crentes'* religious structures resemble each other only at the superficial level. At a deeper level, the CEB, like the institutional Catholic Church of which it is but the latest expression, remains aloof from notions of radical rupture in the self, emphasizing instead continuity between religious and nonreligious roles and statuses, and the allocation of responsibility to adepts for both causing and alleviating misfortune. To this extent, the CEB may be regarded as a cult of continuity. In contrast, both pentecostalism and *umbanda*, as cults of discontinuity or transformation, conceive of radical ruptures in the self as both possible and desireable; thus, they have an inherent potential to suspend and invert nonreligious roles and statuses. In addition, as cults of affliction, these religions shift responsibility for both the causes and treatment of misfortune away from the sufferer.

In the context of this contrast, I have argued that the emphasis placed by the *comunidade* on reading, small-group interaction, and intense levels of participation have lowered the religious status of people who have relatively less literacy, are less well-off, and have relatively heavier and more inflexible work schedules. São Jorge's *comunidade* has thus reinforced a process of elitization, shoring up the institutional Church's rootedness in the stabler, better-off, and more literate segments of the local working class, as well as pushing an increasing number of the less stable or well-off segments onto the margins of Church life. Pentecostalism, on the other hand, by accommodating illiteracy and heavy, inflexible work schedules, has been able, I suggest, to attract many of those alienated by the CEB's elitization.

Yet economic differentiation is not the most important source of distinction in São Jorge's religious arena. Both as a cult of continuity and because it sees women's empowerment mainly as a consequence of class liberation, the new Catholic Church does not encourage the creation of spaces in which women might speak of their domestic turmoil without fear of gossip or without reinforcing their own feelings of guilt. Liberationist priests retreat from the domestic arena, fearing "alienation," and in the process alienate women who seek an outlet for their grievances. Pentecostalism and *umbanda*, as cults of affliction, shift responsibility for domestic conflict away from women themselves and encourage them to articulate their domestic tensions; and as cults of transformation, they provide women with the ideological means to increase their authority within their households.

Unmarried youths, faced with the strains of an increasingly competitive consumerist culture, find the *comunidade* less helpful than pentecostalism in dealing with those strains: for while the *crentes* provide a clear break with youth culture, the *comunidade* perpetuates the overlap between Church and non-Church social circles. Pentecostalism also provides young people with other major advantages over the Catholic Church: increased spiritual authority in relation to parents and potential spouses that promise futures of relative domestic tranquility.

In the context of profoundly troubled race relations within the Brazilian working class, the *comunidade*'s lack of transformative discourse has stymied its efforts to develop a counterdiscourse to racism. In 1988, the progressive Church's effort to erode racism met with resistance from *negros* at the local level because it did not touch upon the continued domination of the Church by lighter-skinned Catholics. In contrast, both *umbanda* and pentecostalism create, through the logic of transformation, the possibility of powerful counterdiscourses to racism. At the same time, these are replete with their own ambiguities and exist tensely and in contestation with lighter-skinned resistance to them.

If the *comunidades* are in fact "losing the battle for souls" in the urban periphery, it becomes all the more urgent to clarify their and their rivals' practice with regard to the collective struggle for social justice. This book joins the company of those who argue that the images of *comunidades* as the natural voice of the poor's liberationist impulses, and the pentecostals as alienators of the Brazilian masses, fail to do justice to their more complex and contradictory practice. On the one hand, the *comunidades* of São Jorge and its vicinity have nurtured among many of their participants heightened feelings of self-worth, greater awareness of social issues, and increased sympathy for social movements. In some places, under the right kind of leadership and for temporary periods, they have even stimulated some members to enter social movements. On the other hand, far from being unanimously welcomed and internalized in the *comunidade,* the progressive Church's message of rights-oriented liberation has met with an uneven and uneasy reception. Most participants in the CEB nominally embrace the discourse but interpret it according to a model of charity which, while stimulating some to enter social movements, renders their political commitment dependent upon activist Church leaders. Even among committed activists, the Catholic value of conciliation has fostered emotional and social tensions with the confrontational world of party and labor politics.

Other local people have reacted negatively to progressive Catholicism's call to people to struggle to change the world. Many resent having their suffering attributed to their own failure to struggle; they feel they "struggle enough" and prefer to luxuriate in a bit of divine intervention. At an even deeper level, however, many local people resent what they perceive as progressive Catholicism's overemphasis on material welfare, to the neglect of eternal salvation. This would not be a problem, perhaps, if the CEBs constituted a proper cargo or millennial cult, promising a reversal of the world order and divine intervention in the near future. But the progressive Church says only that it is up to humans to transform the world, a truth which on its own appears to have rather limited religious appeal. "It's as though," Cosme once observed,

between having complete confidence in the power of God, and having total confidence in the political, that there was no possible midway point. . . . The people often limit themselves to silence before our sermons. Only a few, the agents, a very small number in the community goes along.

Pentecostalism, usually regarded as a "religion of the status quo,"[9] is actually more politically ambiguous than this. Depending on circumstances, railing against "the world" can foster both passivity and activism. In propitious circumstances, *crentes* have not only become involved in social movements, but have developed a surprisingly radical and confrontational social vision. To the extent that it provides space for the experience of radical egalitarianism, *crença* carries as much long-term potential for becoming a religion of revolution as does liberationist Catholicism.

Applying the Model to Social Movements

The model I have employed here, that of religious arenas encountered by clusters of people, is without a doubt applicable beyond the confines of the urban periphery of Rio de Janeiro. From a global perspective, locales in which single religious groups or discourses remain unchallenged have become increasingly rare. What we usually find, especially in urban areas, are polyreligious fields in which a host of religious groups and specialists jostle cheek by jowl, vying for the attention and loyalty of local people.[10] Examining how specific clusters of people encounter and move through these fields should bring to the study of polyreligious arenas a new level of depth and precision.

The model may have the advantage of helping to shed light not just on religious movements, but on social movements more generally. Anthropological writings on social movements have tended to present the movement's social base as composed of entire groups, such as "women," "small holders," and so forth.[11] In reality, of course, only some fraction of such groups actively support the social movement at the local level. Indeed, in many instances, a social movement succeeds in aggregating only a small percentage of its target social group or groups. In a community in Morelos, Mexico, large enough to have a tourist industry, for example, the women's movement could depend on only ten to twenty women.[12] An oppositional union movement could bring together only 15 percent of Mexico's national teacher's union.[13] In Madrid in the late 1970s, only a little more than 1 percent of the population was involved in its neighborhood associations.[14] In towns of nearly ten thousand people in Brazil, one is often lucky to get fifty to come to a meeting of the neighborhood association.

Of course, smallness does not negate the political importance of such movements, for small groups can influence larger populations through strategic mobilizations, the media, and the state. Still, by restricting their focus to "groups of militants who are all aware of belonging to a movement,"[15] observers fail to investigate those people in the movement's targeted social group who remain unmobilized by it. Unless we broaden our focus to include such "outsiders," we will fail to pose, let alone answer, the politically crucial question: What features of the social movement's discourse or practice fails to appeal to them?

The question has another, equally important side: what activities *do* mobilize outsiders? It is in the effort to answer this question that the model of a contested arena encountered by various clusters of people becomes useful. Social movements do not exist as isolated messages and practices but alongside a variety of discursive and practical alternatives—including sports, bars, the male prestige sphere, street-corner crews, family, religion, television, and so on—that vie, in different ways, for the time, energy, and loyalty of different clusters of people. It would be illuminating, for example, to compare the Mexican women Martin studied in the women's group alongside others who are busy going to an evangelical church, a Catholic prayer group, or watching a television soap opera. Why are these other women doing these things and not going to the women's movement group? Are there patterned social differences that may help us to distinguish those who attend from those who do not? Is it possible that some women gain benefits from these other activities they feel are not available in the women's group? What then might the women's group do to attract them?

Studying different clusters of people as they encounter and interact with the complex field in which the social movement is but one entrant allows us not only to better assess why a social movement is growing, stagnating, or flopping (or something in between), but also to explore the differences among movement participants in their understanding and interpretation of its discourse and practice. In this connection, we would do well to develop a kind of political economy of polyphony: the exploration of how differently-patterned understandings are embedded in differences of class fraction, racial identity, gender, age, and institutional power, and of the consequences such differences have for political and social action.

The Path to Liberation

Perception is structured by point of view. This book has examined the CEB phenomenon not from the aerial view of the cartographer but from the view on a winding dirt path; other, equally winding paths must be travelled to see how they differ from and resemble the path I walked. Furthermore, the perception of CEBs in Brazil, as viewed from a path in space, should be complemented by a view from a path in time. After all, from the point of view of those seeking liberation, the Church must forever move on its cosmic pilgrimage—slowly, gradually, haltingly, but move nonetheless—toward the Kingdom.

By the end of the 1980s, the sentiment that the strategy of the Popular Pastoral should be rethought had become fairly widespread in Latin America. After 1989, such soul-searching was sharpened by the global crisis of socialism, such that by the start of the 1990s liberation theology and the program of the Popular Church has begun to undergo dramatic evolution. A number of theologians, recognizing that their category of "the poor" was too monolithic, have begun to expand that category to include difference as well as similarity. As Luiz de Souza wrote,

There is, indeed, a reality of the poor. But the poor are also women, the poor are also blacks, the oppressed.[16]
The theology of liberation deals with the poor, but also with women, with Indians, with blacks. It is opening up a series of "new departments."[17]

The translation of this "opening up" into concrete practices that may effectively draw women and blacks, among others, back into the fold of the *comunidades* will be among the greatest challenges of the People's Church as it enters the twenty-first century.

At a deeper level, however, leading members of the People's Church have begun to see the inherently limited appeal of a religious project that calls upon "the People," even in all their diversity, to think about themselves primarily in their secular capacities as the poor, oppressed, blacks, women, Indians, workers, and so forth. "For me," de Souza writes,

the problem of the sects is much more important for its causes than for its consequences. What brings people to look for God? . . . I think that we, without realizing it, frequently secularized ourselves more than we thought. We secularized ourselves in our liturgies, emptying them of the sacred; we secularized ourselves in a mass of debates—people gather for a celebration and talk, talk, talk, and end up discussing political problems, they end up doing ideology, and not celebrating God. And then they complain that people are going to other sects, where they sing to God. We don't know how to sing to God. We don't know how to live a profound spirituality.[18]

Such new thinking has an impact. In the summer of 1989, the Intereclesial Conference of CEBs in Duque de Caxias set forth extensive proposals for shifting the emphasis of the Popular Pastoral away from purely sociopolitical, and toward spiritual matters. Liberation theologians are now busy writing books and articles about the rediscovery of spirituality, ritual, and popular religiosity. Clodovis Boff has recently suggested that the progressive Church put aside its focus on CEBs, and "work with the masses" through "new forms of meetings, of experiencing mystery, the transcendent, finally, the mystical question, the question of spirituality."[19] It was thus perhaps no accident that the last time I saw Father Cosme he had given up pastoral work, and was planning to devote himself to studying the theology of baptism.

A greater challenge, however, lies ahead. The promised "spiritual" renovation of the progressive Church continues to suffer, I would argue, from its competitive tinge. In current publications on the "sects," progressive Catholic writers continue, even while announcing their own new spirituality, to denounce their rivals' "alienation," "apathy," and "massification."[20] This book has, I hope, raised serious doubts about the adequacy of such characterizations, for either the *comunidades, crentes,* or, for that matter, *umbandistas.* All three religions, I have argued, include what theologians of liberation would call liberatory, as well as nonliberatory tendencies, with regard not only to issues of class, but to those of gender, race, and age. By replacing the notion of such religions as ideologically homogeneous, by a more nuanced, dialectical understanding of each, new opportunities for political dialogue should be created. A *comunidade* leader active in neighborhood associations once told me he had never considered asking the pastor of the Assembly of God to allow him to announce association activities and events in church. "Why should I?" he asked. "He would just say no. And even if he said yes, do you think anyone there would listen? They are just saying 'Holy, holy, holy!' " Whether or not this leader was right about this particular congregation, such attitudes help perpetuate a cycle of mistrust. The only winners are Brazil's ruling elites, who benefit from a divided and weakened popular movement. Efforts toward a limited ecumenicism across this particularly troubling divide thus might be among the most worrisome political developments the Brazilian ruling class ever saw.

In a larger sense, however, the challenge of the transition to the twenty-first century, and not only for the progressive Church, is to continue to probe what we mean by "liberatory politics." Whenever we write of a discourse or practice as either "reinforcing" or "resisting" domination, we run the risk—imperceptibly, even unconsciously—of squeezing complex and contradictory understandings of the world into Procrustean beds, making it difficult for ourselves to understand why someone who was "resisting" domination yesterday appears to be "reinforcing" it today. We would do better to realize that every gesture of resistance carries a seed of reinforcement, every act of reinforcement a seed of resistance. When we do, we remember the importance of discovering how others themselves talk, feel, and think about the relationship between what they do and how they experience domination. And when we remember that, we will stop expecting others to fit into our, rather than their, vision of the world.

Notes

Notes to Preface

1. I have adopted the Portuguese- and Spanish-language acronym rather than the English-language "BECs" or "CBCs."

2. Articles in *The Nation* and *The Guardian* on the Catholic Church in Latin America consistently worked from these premises, and European socialists made similar deductions. See, for example, the articles in *Le Monde Diplomatique*, June 1984, 5–9.

3. *New York Times*, 10/10/84; for the roots of the counter-offensive, see Ralph Della Cava, "A ofensiva vaticana," *Religião e sociedade* 12/3 (December 1985): 34–53. For Boff's response, see "O caso Boff: o sentido da obediência," *Religião e sociedade* 12/3 (December 1985): 110–136.

4. See Affonso Gregory, *CEBs: utopia ou realidade?* (Petrópolis: Vozes, 1973); Cláudio Perani, "Pastoral Popular: serviço ou poder?", *Cadernos do centro de estudos e ação social* (CEAS) 82 (November–December 1982): 7–19; Idem, "Comunidade eclesial de base e movimento popular," *CEAS* 75 (September–October 1981): 25–33; Idem, "Igreja de nordeste: breves notas histórica-críticas," *CEAS* 94 (November–December 1984): 53–73; and José Comblin, "Os leigos," *Comunicações do ISER* 26 (July 1987): 26–37.

5. Edmund T. Gordon, "Anthropology and Liberation," in Faye V. Harrison, ed., *Decolonizing Anthropology* (Washington, 1991), 162. For other recent discussions of the problem of relating anthropology and history to popular social movements, see Arturo Escobar, "Culture, Practice and Politics: Anthropology and the Study of Social Movements," *Critique of Anthropology* (1992); Faye V. Harrison, "Anthropology as an Agent of Transformation," in Fay V. Harrison, ed., *Decolonizing*, 1–10; Trinh T. Minh-Ha, *Woman, Native, Other*

(Bloomington: Indiana University Press, 1989); bell hooks, *Yearning: Race, Gender, and Cultural Politics* (Boston: South End Press, 1990); Sherna Gluck and Daphne Patai, eds., *Women's Words: The Feminist Practice of Oral History* (New York: Routledge, 1991); Popular Memory Group, "Popular Memory: Theory, Politics, Method," in Richard Johnson, Gregor McLennan, Bill Schwarz, and David Sutton, eds., *Making Histories: Studies in History-Writing and Politics* (Minneapolis: University of Minnesota Press, 1982), 205–252.

6. See Alain Touraine's discussion of "intervention" and "permanent sociology" in *Anti-Nuclear Protest: The Opposition to Nuclear Energy in France* (Cambridge: Cambridge University Press, 1983), 147–173; Idem, *The Voice and the Eye: An Analysis of Social Movements* (Cambridge: Cambridge University Press, 1981), 139–222.

7. This echoes Touraine's insistence that academic intervention challenge totalizing official discourses that admit of no refinement. As he puts it,

intervention reacts against *activism* and the preference accorded to desire for breakdown [of the movement] over the always suspect counter-projects of reformism. This it does in particular by entering at the base of the movement, by refusing to identify the movement with the strategy of the leaders, and by causing the voice of the people to be heard . . . (1981: 216)

8. Thus, too, Harrison was motivated by the desire to understand why so many people in a Jamaican ghetto were turning away from a radical to a conservative party. "I believed," she writes, "that the forces of change could learn from their mistakes and deficiencies as well as from their noble visions and successes." Faye V. Harrison, "Ethnography as Politics," in Faye V. Harrison, ed., *Decolonizing*, 97.

9. Cf. Orin Starn, *"Con los llanques todo barro": reflexiones sobre rondas campesinas, protesta rural y nuevos movimentos sociales* (Lima: Instituto de Estudios Peruanos, 1991); David Sutton, "Is Anybody Out There? Anthropology and the Question of Audience," *Critique of Anthropology* 11/1 (1991): 91–104.

Notes to Introduction

1. François Houtart, "Religion et champs politique: Cadre théorique pour l'étude des sociétés capitalistes peripheriques," *Social Compass* 24 (1977): 265–272; Idem, "Religion et lutte des classes en Amérique Latine," *Social Compass* 26 (1979): 195–236; Brian Smith and Sanks Howlands, "Liberation Ecclesiology: Praxis, Theory, Praxis," *Theological Studies* 38/1 (March 1977): 3–38; Michael Dodson, "Liberation Theology and Christian Radicalism in Contemporary Latin America," *Journal of Latin American Studies* 2/1 (May 1979): 203–222; John Eagleson and Philip Scharper, eds., *Puebla and Beyond: Documentation and Commentary* (Maryknoll: Orbis Books, 1979).

2. John Eagleson and Sérgio Torres, eds., *Theology in the Americas* (Maryknoll: Orbis, 1976); J. L. Idigoras, *Vocabulário teológico* (São Paulo: Edições Paulinas, 1983).

3. Gustavo Gutierrez, *A Theology of Liberation* (Maryknoll: Orbis, 1973), 167, 227, 291–293; Carlos Mesters, *O profeta Elias* (São Paulo, 1986), 11.

4. Paulo Freire, *A Pedagogy of the Oppressed* (Myra Bergman Ramos, trans., New York: Seabury Press, 1970); Almir Ribeiro Guimarães, *Comunidaes eclesiais de base no Brasil* (Petrópolis: Vozes, 1978), 89–91; Clodovis Boff, *Comunidade eclesial,* 131–133; Carlos Mesters, *Palavra de Deus na história do homem* (Petrópolis: Vozes, 1971); Ronaldo Muñoz, "Sobre a eclesiologia na America Latina," in Sérgio Torres, *et al., A igreja que surge da base* (São Paulo: Paulinas, 1982), 242–254. Analyses of the episcopal conference at Medellín in 1968 that legitimated these views among the Latin American hierarchy include Penny Lernoux, "The Latin American Church," *Latin American Research Review* 15/2 (1980): 201–211; Renato Poblete, "From Medellín to Puebla," *Journal of Interamerican Studies* 21/1 (February 1979): 31–44; Brian H. Smith, "Religious and Social Change: Classical Theories and New Formulations in the Context of Recent Developments in Latin America," *Latin American Research Review* 10/2 (1975): 3–34.

5. Gustavo Gutierrez, "A irrupção do pobre na América Latina e as comunidades cristãs populares," in Sérgio Torres, *et al., A igreja,* 186–126; Leonardo Boff, *Eclesiogênese: as comunidades eclesiais de base reinventam a igreja* (Petrópolis: Vozes, 1977); Idem, *O caminhar da igreja com os oprimidos* (Rio de Janeiro, 1980); Idem, *A fé na periferia do mundo* (Petrópolis: Vozes, 1978); Idem, *Igreja: carisma e poder* (Petrópolis: Vozes, 1981); Clodovis Boff, *Comunidade eclesial, comunidade política* (Petrópolis: Vozes, 1979); Almir Guimarães, *Comunidade eclesial de base no Brasil: uma nova maneira de ser igreja* (Petrópolis: Vozes, 1978); Faustino Luiz Couto Teixeira, *Comunidades eclesiais de base: bases teológicas* (Petrópolis: Vozes, 1988), 117–121; Alvaro Barreiro, *Comunidades eclesiais de base e evangelização dos pobres* (São Paulo: Loyola, 1977). For reports on CEBs throughout the continent, see Scott Mainwaring and Alexander Wilde, eds., *The Progressive Church in Latin America* (Notre Dame: University of Notre Dame Press, 1989); Daniel Levine, *Popular Voices in Latin American Catholicism* (Princeton: Princeton University Press, 1992); Idem, "Popular Groups, Popular Culture, and Popular Religion," *Comparative Studies in Society and History* 32/4 (October 1990): 718–764; Brian Smith, *The Church and Politics in Chile* (Princeton: Princeton University Press, 1982); Philip Berryman, *Religious Roots of Rebellion* (Maryknoll: Orbis, 1984).

6. Leonardo Boff, *Igreja,* 197; cf. Idem, *E a igreja,* 21.

7. This paragraph is based on Thomas Bruneau, *The Political Transformation of the Brazilian Catholic Church* (London: Cambridge University Press, 1974); Scott Mainwaring, *The Catholic Church and Politics in Brazil, 1916–1985* (Stanford: Stanford University Press, 1986); Emanuel De Kadt, *Catholic Radicals in Brazil* (London: Oxford University Press, 1970); Madeleine Adriance, *Opting for the Poor* (Kansas City: Sheed and Ward, 1986); Ralph Della Cava, "Catholicism and Society in Twentieth-Century Brazil," *Latin American Research Review* 11/2 (1976): 7–50; Idem, "Política á curto prazo e religião a longo prazo," *Encontros com a civilização Brasileira* I (1978): 242–258; Márcio Moreira Alves, *A igreja e a política no Brasil* (São Paulo: Brasiliense, 1979); Luiz

Gonzaga de Souza Lima, *Evolução política dos católicos e da igreja no Brasil* (Petrópolis: Vozes, 1979); Luiz Alberto Gomez de Souza, *A JUC: os estudantes católicos e a política* (Petrópolis: Vozes, 1984); José Oscar Beozzo, *Cristãos na universidade e na política* (Petrópolis: Vozes, 1984).

8. *Estudos da CNBB* (1979): 22–23; Thomas C. Bruneau, "The Catholic Church and Development in Latin America: The Role of the Basic Christian Communities," *World Development* 8 (July/August 1980): 536; Leonardo Boff, *Igreja: carisma e poder,* 197; Maria Helena Moreira Alves, *Estado e oposição no Brasil* (Petrópolis: Vozes, 1984), 231; for a critical review of these statistics, see W. E. Hewitt, *Base Christian Communities and Social Change in Brazil* (Lincoln: University of Nebraska Press, 1991), 6–10.

9. In Brazilian politics, the image of a progressive Church endowed with compelling mass appeal has become a social force in its own right. Lula, the national leader of the Workers' Party (PT), rarely misses an opportunity to appeal to "the struggling people of the CEBs, the beacons of hope for a society of justice and rights," as at a campaign rally in December 1987. On the other side of the political divide, Ronaldo Caiado, president of the neofascist Rural Democratic Union (UDR), advised the president of Sao Paulo's stock exchange that "we must crush the CEBs . . . We must overpower them ten to one," *Jornal do Brasil,* 2/7/88.

10. In favor of the "top-down" thesis, see Roberto Romano, *Brasil: igreja contra estado* (São Paulo: Kairos, 1979), 191; Thomas Bruneau, *The Political Transformation of the Brazilian Catholic Church* (New York: Cambridge University Press, 1974); Vanilda Paiva, "A igreja moderna no Brasil," in Vanilda Paiva, org., *Igreja e questão agraria* (São Paulo: Loyola, 1985): 52–67; Idem, "Anotações para um estudo sobre populismo católico e educação popular," in Paiva, ed., *Perspectivas e dilemmas de educação popular* (Rio de Janeiro: Graal, 1984), 227–266. In favor of the "bottom-up" thesis, see Luiz Gonzaga de Souza Lima, "Comunidades eclesiais de base," *Revista de cultura vozes* 74/5 (June–July 1980): 61–82; Pedro A. Ribeiro de Oliveira, "Oprimidos: a opção pela igreja," *Revista eclesiástica Brasileira* 41/164 (December 1983): 643–653; Helena Salem, ed., *A igreja dos oprimidos* (São Paulo: Editora Debates, 1981); Luiz Alberto Gomez de Souza, *Classes populares e igreja nos caminhos da história* (Petrópolis: Vozes, 1981); Eduardo Hoornaert, "Comunidades de base: dez anos de experiência," *Revista eclesiástica Brasileira* 38 (1978): 474–502; Clodovis Boff, "'E uma pedrinha soltouse': as bases do povo de Deus," *REB* 42/168 (December 1982): 661–687; João Carlos Petrini, *CEBs: um novo sujeito popular* (Rio de Janeiro: Paz e Terra, 1984), 43–44.

11. Ralph Della Cava, "A igreja e a abertura, 1974–1985," in Paulo Krischke and Scott Mainwaring, eds., *A igreja nas bases em tempo de transição* (Porto Alegre: LPM, 1986), 21.

12. Some Church leaders define as CEBs all congregations with elected councils; some include all congregations with a Minister of the Eucharist; others include only those congregations with politically activist leadership. See the discussion of this definitional problem in Marcello Azevedo, *Basic Ecclesial Communities in Brazil* (Washington: Georgetown University Press, 1987), 80–87.

13.   On Vitória, see Pedro A. Ribeiro de Oliveira, "Comunidade, igreja e poder: em busca de um conceito sociológico de 'igreja'," *Religião e sociedade* 13/3 (November 1986): 46; on Goiás, see Carlos Brandão, "A partilha da vida," 7th. Caderno de *Condições de vida e situação de trabalho do povo de Goiás: as pessoas e as famílias* (Goiânia: Universidade de Goiás, 1988), 13; Cecilia Mariz, "Religion and Coping with Poverty in Brazil," Ph.D. dissertation, Boston University, 1989, 57; Carmen Macêdo, *Tempo de gênesis* (São Paulo: Brasiliense, 1986), 112–113.

14.   Hewitt, *Base Christian Communities*, 42.

15.   José Comblin, "Os leigos," *Comunicações do ISER* 26 (July 1987): 33.

16.   Frei Betto, *O que é comunidade eclesial de base?* (São Paulo: Brasiliense, 1981), 17. It is possible that Hewitt and Betto counted only highly active participants. In the *comunidades* with which I became familiar, the total number of participants usually exceeded fifty.

17.   This is also the assessment of Alberto Antoniazzi in "O catolicismo no Brasil," a paper presented at the Meeting on Religious Diversity of the Instituto de estudos da Religião (ISER) in 1986. Other estimates of CEB participants have been even lower: Edward Cleary, for instance, guesses at one million. Edward Cleary, *Crisis and Change: The Church in Latin America Today* (Maryknoll: Orbis, 1985), 104.

18.   Delcio Monteiro de Lima, *Os demônios descem do norte* (Rio de Janeiro: Francisco Alves, 1987), 75.

19.   Francisco Cartaxo Rolim, *Pentecostais no Brasil* (Petrópolis: Vozes, 1985), [20]; José Gomes, "Religião e política: os pentecostais no Recife," unpublished Ph.D. dissertation, Federal University of Pernambuco, 1985, 134. These figures are echoed in the revolutionary context of Nicaragua. As Lancaster has observed,

it may seem surprising in a revolutionary state whose "overarching ideology" is liberation theology, but evangelical Protestantism has grown rapidly since the late 1970s, and especially since the 1979 revolution: from approximately 5 percent of the population in 1979 to more than 15 percent of the population in 1985. It seems altogether plausible that a fifth of the population will be evangelical by the end of the decade.

Roger Lancaster, *Thanks to God and the Revolution* (New York: Columbia University Press, 1988), 101.

20.   Diana Brown, *Umbanda: Politics and Religion in Urban Brazil* (Ann Arbor: University of Michigan Press, 1986); the 50 percent figure comes from the documentary by Madeleine Richeport, "Macumba: Trance and Spirit Healing" (1984).

21.   Levine, "Popular Groups," 718. See, too, Ireland, *Kingdoms Come*, 216.

22.   José Comblin, "Os leigos," *Comunicações do ISER* 26 (July 1987): 32. See, too, the commentaries on "the sects" in Leilah Landim, org., *Sinais dos tempos: igrejas e seitas no Brasil* (Rio de Janeiro: ISER, 1989); Clodovis Boff, "É preciso trabalhar com as massas," *Vermelho e branco* 26 (March 1992): 6–7; and Eduardo Hoornaert, "Os três fatores da nova hegemonia dentro da igreja católica no Brasil," *REB* 26 (1986): 371–384.

23. Carlos Brandão, "Crença e identidade: campo religioso e mudança cultural," unpublished manuscript, 22.

24. Macêdo, *Tempo de gênesis,* 150–151.

25. Ana Maria Doimo, "Os rumos dos movimentos sociais nos caminhos da religiosidade," in Paulo Krischke and Scott Mainwaring, eds., *A igreja nas bases no tempo de transição* (Porto Alegre: CEDEC, 1986), 122–123; also see Idem, *Movimento social urbano: igreja e participação popular* (Petrópolis: Vozes, 1984); Silvio Caccia Bava, "O movimento do ônibus: a articulação de um movimento reinvindicatório de periferia," *Revista espaço e debates* 1 (1981); Luís Inácio Gaiger, *Agentes religiosos e camponeses sem terra no sul do Brasil* (Petrópolis: Vozes, 1987); Laura Maria Duarte, *Isto não se aprende na escola* (Petrópolis: Vozes, 1983); Scott Mainwaring, "Grassroots Popular Movements and the Struggle for Democracy: Nova Iguaçu," in Alfred Stepan, ed., *Democratizing Brazil* (New York: Oxford University Press, 1989), 168–204; Idem, "Brazil: The Catholic Church and the Popular Movement in Nova Iguaçu, 1974–1985," in Daniel Levine, ed., *Religion and Political Conflict in Latin America* (Chapel Hill: University of North Carolina Press, 1986), 124–155; Daniel Levine and Scott Mainwaring, "Religion and Popular Protest in Latin America: Contrasting Experiences," in Susan Eckstein, ed., *Power and Popular Protest: Latin American Social Movements* (Berkeley: University of California Press, 1989), 203–240.

26. Ribeiro de Oliveira, "Comunidade, igreja e poder," 51.

27. W. E. Hewitt, "Religion and the Consolidation of Democracy in Brazil: The Role of the Comunidades Eclesiais de Base (CEBs)," *Sociological Analysis* 50/2 (1990): 146.

28. Ireland, *Kingdoms Come,* 190.

29. Comblin, "Os leigos," 37. Other discussions of tendencies against political activism in the CEBs include Lygia Dabul, "Missão de conscientização: agentes e camponêses em experiências comunitárias," in Neide Esterci, org., *Cooperativismo e coletivização* (Rio de Janeiro: Marco Zero, 1984), 99–136; José Ivo Follman, "O 'ser católico': diferentes identidades religiosas," *Comunicações do ISER* 26 (1987): 17–25; Rowan Ireland, "The Prophecy that Failed," *Listening: Journal of Religion and Culture* 16 (1981): 253–264; Eduardo Hoornaert, "Os três fatores da nova hegemonia dentro da igreja católica no Brasil," *Revista eclesiástica Brasileira* 26 (1986): 371–384; Affonso Gregory, *CEBs: utopia ou realidade* (Petrópolis: Vozes, 1973); Claudio Perani, "Pastoral Popular: serviço ou poder?", *Cadernos no centro de estudos e ação Social* 82 (November/December 1982): 7–19; Thomas Bruneau, *The Church in Brazil* (Austin: University of Texas Press, 1982).

30. *Jornal do Brasil,* 5/18/88.

31. Sandra Stoll, "Púlpito e palanque: religião e política nas eleições de 1982 num município da grande São Paulo," Ph.D. dissertation, Universidade Estadual de Campinas, 1986; Cecilia Mariz, "Religion and Coping," 188–189; Jether Pereira Ramalho, "Algumas notas sobre duas perspectivas de pastoral popular," *Cadernos do ISER* 6 (1977): 31–39; Rubem Alves, *Protestantismo e repressão* (São Paulo: Atica, 1980); Pedro Ribeiro de Oliveira, "Comunidade e massa: desafio da pastoral popular," *Revista eclesiastica Brasileira* 44 (1984);

Francisco Rolim, "Afinal, o que estaria levando as pessoas ao pentecostalismo?", paper delivered at ISER seminar on Religious Diversity, ANPOCS, 1987; Judith Hoffnagel, "The Believers: Pentecostalism in a Brazilian City," Ph.D. dissertation, Indiana University, 1978; Beatriz Souza, "Protestantismo no Brasil," in Cândido Camargo, *Católicos, Protestantes, Espíritas* (Petrópolis; Vozes, 1973), 134–154; Gary N. Howe, "Representações religiosas e capitalismo: uma 'leitura' estruturalista do pentecostalismo no Brasil," *Cadernos do ISER* 6 (1977): 39–48. Lalive D'Epinay makes this argument for all of Latin America in "Religião, espiritualidade, e sociedade," *Cadernos do ISER* 6 (1977): 5–10, and in his *Haven of the Masses* (London: Lutterworth Press, 1969).

32. Ramalho, "Algumas notas," 39–40.

33. Delcio Monteiro de Lima, *Os demônios descem do norte* (Rio de Janeiro: Francisco Alves, 1987), 25, 50.

34. Paul Freston, "Protestants and Brazilian Politics Since Redemocratization," in David Stoll and Virginia Burnett, eds., *Pentecostals and Politics in Latin America* (Philadelphia: Temple University Press, 1993); Rowan Ireland, "The Politics of Brazilian Pentecostals," in Stoll and Burnett, eds., *Pentecostals*; Oneide Bobsin, "Produção religiosa e significação social do pentecostalismo á partir de sua prática e representação," Ph.D. dissertation, Pontífica Universidade Católica de São Paulo, 1984; José Francisco Gomes, "Religião e política: os pentecostais no Recife," Master's thesis, Universidade Federal de Pernambuco, 1985; David Martin, *Tongues of Fire* (Oxford: Basil Blackwell, 1990); David Stoll, *Is Latin America Turning Protestant?* (Berkeley: University of California Press, 1990). For the changing political backdrop of the study of pentecostalism, see Rubem Cesar Fernandes, "O debate entre sociólogos," in "'Religiões populares': uma visão parcial da literatura recente," *Boletim informativo e bibliográfico de ciências sociais* 18 (1984): 13–14; Idem, "Conservador ou progressista: uma questão de conjuntura," *Religião e sociedade* 9 (1983).

35. Regina Novaes, *Os escolhidos de Deus* (Rio de Janeiro: Marco Zero, 1985), 131.

36. Ethnographies of religion tend to focus on one religious group at a time (e.g., Evans-Pritchard 1956; Lienhardt 1961; Reichel-Dolmatoff 1971; Jules-Rosette 1975; Schieffelin 1976) or, at most, on the conversion from one religion to another (Firth 1967; Nicolas 1975; Beidelman 1982; Horton 1971; Daneel 1971; Wallace 1970; Field 1987; Worsley 1957; MacGaffey 1983).

37. E.g., João Carlos Petrini, *CEBs: Um novo sujeito popular* (Rio de Janeiro: Paz e Terra, 1984); Cândido Procópio Ferreira de Camargo, *et al.*, "Comunidades eclesiais de base," in Paul Singer and Vinioius Brant, eds., *São Paulo: povo em movimento* (Petrópolis: Vozes, 1980).

38. Even in Geertz's and Werbner's work, religions are portrayed as self-contained packages, with the flow of people between them remaining unanalyzed. Clifford Geertz, *The Religion of Java* (New York: Free Press, 1960); Richard Werbner, *Ritual Passage, Sacred Journey* (Washington: Smithsonian Institution Press, 1989).

39. Arthur Kleinman, *Patients and Healers in the Context of Culture* (Cambridge: Harvard University Press, 1980).

40. Judith Lasker, "Choosing Among Therapies: Illness Behavior in the Ivory Coast," *Social Science and Medicine* 15A (1981): 157–168; A. Minocha, "Medical Pluralism and Health Services," *Social Science and Medicine* 14B (1980): 217–223.

41. M. A. Loyola, "Cure des corps et cure des âmes: les rapports entre les medicines et les religions dans la banlieue de Rio," *Actes de la recherche en sciences sociales* 43 (1982); Duglas Teixeira Monteiro, "Igrejas, seitas e agências: aspectos de um ecumenismo popular," in Carmen Macêdo, *et al.*, *A cultura do povo* (São Paulo: Cortez e Moraes, 1979), 81–111; Luis Fernando Dias Duarte, "Pluridade religiosa nas sociedades complexas e religiosidade das classes trabalhadoras," in *Boletim do museu nacional* 41 (1983); Renato Ortiz, "O mercado religioso," *Comunicações do ISER* 5 (1983); Idem, *A morte branca de feitiçeiro negro* (Petrópolis: Vozes, 1978), 185–191; Novaes, *Os escolhidos*, 146–147; Carlos Brandão, "Religião, campo religioso e relação entre religião erudita e religião do povo," in Riolando Azzi, *et al.*, *Religião e catolicismo do povo* (Curitíba: Cadernos da Universidade Católica do Parana, 1977), 7–38; "O número dos eleitos," *Religião e sociedade* 3 (1977); Idem, *Os deuses do povo* (São Paulo: Brasiliense, 1980); Idem, *Memória do sagrado* (São Paulo: Paulinas, 1985), 92–126. Even Peter Fry and Gary Howe's celebrated article, "Duas respostas á aflição: umbanda e pentecostalismo," *Debate e crítica* 6 (1975): 75–95, fails to deal with religious mobility.

42. Macêdo, *Tempo de gênesis*, 125, 127.

43. Monteiro, "Igrejas, seitas," 107–108.

44. Johann Janzen, *The Quest for Therapy in Lower Zaire* (Berkeley: University of California Press, 1978); Ursula Sharma, *Complementary Medicine Today* (New York: Routledge, 1992); Lola Romanucci-Schwartz, "The Hierarchy of Resort in Curative Practices: The Admiralty Islands, Melanesia," *Journal of Health and Social Behavior* 10 (1969): 201–209; A. Beals, "Strategies of Resort to Curers in South India," in Charles Leslie, ed., *Asian Medical Systems* (Berkeley: University of California Press, 1976).

45. Victor Turner, *A Forest of Symbols* (Ithaca: Cornell University Press, 1967); Idem, *The Drums of Affliction* (Oxford: Clarendon Press, 1968); Pierre Bourdieu, *Outline of a Theory of Practice* (Cambridge: Cambridge University Press, 1977). M. E. Combs-Schilling argues, for instance, that Islamic ritual etches patriarchal values upon the individual's mind. See *Sacred Performances* 1989: 27–28. For other work in this vein, see Maurice Bloch, *From Blessing to Violence* (Cambridge: Cambridge University Press, 1986); Talal Asad, "Anthropological Conceptions of Religion: Reflections on Geertz," *Man* 18/2 (1983): 237–259.

46. The notions of "voice," as I use it here comes from Mikhail Bakhtin, *Speech Genres and Other Late Essays* (Austin: University of Texas Press, 1986); Idem, *The Dialogical Imagination* (ed. Michael Holquist, Austin: University of Texas Press, 1981). See also Michael Holquist, *Dialogism* (New York: Routledge, 1990) and Robert Hodge and Gunther Kress, *Social Semiotics* (Ithaca: Cornell University Press, 1988). Abu-Lughod reminds us of the importance of "reconstructing people's arguments about, justifications for, and interpretations of what they and others are doing" in order to show how within the limits of

discourses "people contest interpretations of what is happening." Lila Abu-Lughod, "Writing Against Culture," in Richard Fox, ed., *Recapturing Anthropology* (Santa Fe: School of American Research Press, 1991), 153–154. Rebel has made the same point in his critique of Gerald Sider: "By turning away from what the singers and storytellers have to say both in and out of performance, Sider missed an opportunity to discover and contemplate what takes place at this nexus between class and culture, between the private and public experiences of his singers, and what happens as a result." Hermann Rebel, "Cultural Hegemony and Class Experience: A Critical Reading of Recent Ethnological-Historical Approaches," *American Ethnologist* 16 (1989): 362, 363.

47.   Jean Comaroff, *Body of Power, Spirit of Resistance* (Chicago: University of Chicago Press, 1985), 226.

48.   Ibid., 226

49.   Successful examples of what I would call a "political economy of polyphony" include Robert Fardon, *Between God, the Dead and the Wild* (Washington, D.C.: Smithsonian Institution Press, 1990); Candace Slater, *Trail of Miracles* (Berkeley: University of California Press, 1986); Idem, *City Steeple, City Streets* (Berkeley: University of California Press, 1990); Michael Sallnow and J. Eade, eds., *Contesting the Sacred* (New York: Routledge, 1990). More generally, see Loretta Fowler, *Shared Symbols, Contested Meanings: Gros Ventre Culture and History, 1778–1984* (Ithaca: Cornell University Press, 1987); K. Basso, *Portraits of the "Whiteman": Linguistic Play and Cultural Symbols among the Western Apache* (Cambridge: Cambridge University Press, 1979); A. T. Bennett, *et al.*, "Discourse, Consciousness and Literacy in a Puerto Rican Neighborhood," in R. Kramarae, M. Schulz, and W. M. O'Barr, eds., *Language and Power* (Beverly Hills: Sage, 1984), 243–259; Roger Keesing, "Kwaio Women Speak: The Micropolitics of Autobiography in a Solomon Island Society," *American Anthropologist* 87 (1985): 27–39; M. Trawick, "Spirits and Voices in Tamil Songs," *American Ethnologist* 15 (1988): 193–215; K. Woolard, "Language Variation and Cultural Hegemony: Toward an Integration of Sociolinguistic and Social Theory," *American Ethnologist* 12 (1985): 738–748.

50.   Rebel, "Cultural Hegemony," 362; also see Daphne Patai and Sherna Berger Gluck, *Women's Words* (New York: Routledge, 1991); and Lawrence C. Watson and Maria-Barbara Watson-Franke, *Interpreting Life Histories* (New Brunswick: Rutgers University Press, 1985).

51.   José Lustosa, *Cidade de Duque de Caxias* (Rio de Janeiro: IBGE, 1958), 84; Israel Beloch, *Capa preta e lurdinha* (Rio de Janeiro: Record, 1986), 23–25; FUNDREM, *Unidades urbanas integradas do oeste: plano diretor*, Vol. II (Rio de Janeiro: SECPLAN, 1979), 109; Lygia Dabul, "Um tanto da história de Xerém: análise social e eclesial," in *Unidade e prática da fé: pastoral ecumênica da terra em Xerém* (Rio de Janeiro: CEDI, 1987), 11; Leonilda Sêrvolo Medeiros, "Lutas sociais no campo no Rio de Janeiro," Ph.D. dissertation, CPDA/UFRJ, 1983, 17; José Pureza, *Memória camponesa* (Rio de Janeiro: Zahar, 1982), 27; Frederico G. B. Araújo, "As lutas pela terra na Baixada da Guanabara," Ph.D. dissertation, Rio de Janeiro: COPPE/UFRJ, 1982, 160–170.

52. Monica Kornis and Dora Flaksman, "Fábrica Nacional de Motores," in Alzir Alves de Abreu and Israel Beloch, coords., *Dicionário histórico-biográfico brasileiro,* Vol. 2 (Rio de Janeiro: Forense-Universitária/Finep, 1984), 1211–1212.

53. "Modificação e retificação do loteamento da Vila Beira Serra, situada no município de Duque de Caxias," Archives of Land registry, Ministry of Public Works, Municipality of Duque de Caxias.

54. 1988 local census of São Jorge. On the rise of Petrobrás, see FUNDREM, "Sumário de dados," based on IBGE censuses from 1960, 1965, 1970, 1975, and 1980. Also, Rilza Ferreira Saldanha, "Duque de Caxias, aspectos históricos," *Coleções de monografias,* No. 446 (Rio de Janeiro: IBGE, 1969), 13.

55. FUNDREM, "Sumário de Dados," based on analyses of IBGE census data from 1960 and 1970.

56. IBGE, "População residente, por situação do domicílio e sexo, segundo as grandes regiões e unidades da federação, 1940–1980," *Sumário de dados dos censos, 1940–1980* (Rio de Janeiro: IBGE, 1982), 35. According to my census of 350 local households, the average age of new arrivals in the valley in the 1970s dropped to twenty-two. And according to a local census carried out in 1979 by São Jorge's neighborhood association, ABESA, by the end of the decade, *mineiros* had become a minority, with nearly 60 percent of the 1835 people censused hailing from Rio, Espirito Santo, or the northeast. My thanks to José Aparecida de Oliveira Dias, who participated in the original collection of this data, for his assistance in analyzing it.

57. Cf. John Humphrey, "The Growth of Female Employment in Brazilian Manufacturing Industry in the 1970s," *The Journal of Development Studies* 20 (1984): 224–247.

58. 1988 census, São Jorge.

59. W. E. Hewitt, *Base Christian Communities and Social Change in Brazil* (Lincoln: University of Nebraska Press, 1991), 46–47.

60. In brief surveys of a half-dozen other *bairros* in the region, I found proportions generally parallel to these: based on interviews rather than direct counting, the ratios varied from 1:2 to 1:5, always in the pentecostals' favor. So as not to overburden this book with themes, my focus in the pentecostal arena will be on the Assembly of God.

Notes to Chapter One

1. Though about thirty-five hundred children fifteen and under live in town, the two local state-run schools have room for only six hundred of them. For these students, the unwillingness of the post-Brizola state government to increase the education budget means an average loss of over half the year to teachers' strikes. Many parents, in any case, cannot afford to pay for uniforms, paper, or schoolbooks.

2. Though the state and municipal governments were reluctant to allocate money to public hospitals, they had established mobile medical units such as this one, known as *consultórios*, which provided cursory consultations. Entirely inadequate for long-term preventive care or major illnesses, the *consultórios* yet served to weaken popular demand for a good public health system.

Notes to Chapter Two

1. For similar cases, see Alba Zaluar, *Os Homens de deus* (Rio de Janeiro: Zahar, 1983), 38–58; Carlos Rodrigues Brandão, *Os deuses do povo* (São Paulo: Brasiliense, 1980), 98–111; Rubem Cesar Fernandes, *Os cavaleiros do bom Jesus* (São Paulo: Brasiliense, 1982), 134–140.

2. Evil eye is the power of a jealous person to inflict, through visual contact, malaise or minor misfortune directly upon another adult, or upon the envied adult's children, animals, or plants. See Raymundo Maués, "A tensão constitutiva," Ph.D. dissertation, Universidade Federal de Rio de Janeiro, 1987, 197–216.

3. Carlos Brandão, *Os sacerdotes de viola* (Petrópolis: Vozes, 1981); Idem, *Os deuses,* 150–213.

4. For information on these organizations, see Lisette Van Den Hoogen, "The Romanization of the Brazilian Church: Women's Participation in a Religious Association in Prados, Minas Gerais," *Sociological Analysis* 51/2 (1990): 171–188; Marjo De Theije, "'Brotherhoods Throw More Weight Around Than the Pope': Catholic Traditionalism and the Lay Brotherhoods of Brazil," *Sociological Analysis* 51/2 (1990): 189–204; Caio César Boschi, *Os leigos e o poder: irmandades leigas e política colonizadora em Minas Gerais* (São Paulo: Editora Atica, 1986).

5. *Promessas* are requests for a miracle in exchange for a promise to perform a sacrificial act, such as making a barefooted pilgrimage, or lighting a candle. On the *promessa,* see Maués, "A tensão constitutiva," 316–343; Maria de Cáscia Nascimento Frade, "Santa de casa: a devoção á Odetinha no cemitério São João Batista," Ph.D. dissertation, UFRJ, 1987; Fernandes, *Os cavaleiros,* 41–47.

6. For the history and background of the *cursilho,* see Márcio Moreira Alves, *A igreja e a política no brasil* (São Paulo: Brasiliense, 1979), 114ff.; Dana Otto, "A conversão no contexto dos cursilhos de cristandade," *Cadernos do ISER* 1 (1974): 3–20.

7. A good example of the post-Conciliar vision, as articulated by a writer often used in the *cursilho,* is Neimar de Barros, *Os fantoches* (7th ed., São Paulo: O Recado, 1979).

8. The Council's effort to downgrade saintly devotions is well-documented. See, for example, Carlos Brandão, *A memória do sagrado* (São Paulo: Paulinas, 1985), 135ff.

9. Morelli had entered the national spotlight during the 1978 metalworkers' strike in São Paulo, when he had given leaders safe haven in his church.

See Solange dos Santos Rodrigues, "Comunidades eclesiais de base: 'rumo á nova sociedade?'," Master's thesis, State University of Rio de Janeiro, 1985, 39–40.

10. In liberation theology, earthly sovereignty should no longer reside with the clerical hierarchy, but must devolve to the People of God assembled in the *comunidades*. In the old ecclesial model, according to Boff, "the church-goer doesn't have anything. He only has the right to receive. The bishops and priests received everything: it is a true capitalism. They produce religious products, and the People consume them. It has a monarchical and pyramidal structure."

In contrast, in the liberationist vision, "all the objectives of the Church are of the People of God, in the People of God, for the People of God. The authority comes from the *comunidade* itself." Leonardo Boff, *Igreja: carisma e poder* (Petrópolis: Vozes, 1981), 207.

11. In this ministry, unordained local leaders were given the power to distribute pre-consecrated Hosts. The earliest references to Brazilian experiments in having Sunday religious celebrations without the presence of a priest appeared in clerical reports printed in the *Revista da Conferência dos Religiosos do Brasil*: Bernardo Leers, "A estrutura do culto dominical na zona rural," *RCRB* 99 (1963): 521–534; and Antonio Rolim, "O culto dominical e os religiosos," *RCRB* 100 (1963): 631–636.

12. Diocesan pamphlet on baptism, Duque de Caxias, August 1987.

13. Carlos Mesters, *Círculos bíblicos: guia do dirigente* (8th ed., Petrópolis: Vozes, 1985); Idem, *Círculos bíblicos: a sabedoria do povo* (8th ed., Petrópolis: Vozes, 1984); Leonardo Boff, *E a igreja se fez povo* (Petrópolis: Vozes, 1986).

14. Max Weber, *The Sociology of Religion* (Boston: Beacon Press, 1964), 187.

15. From this viewpoint, the sacraments themselves, by serving as a permanent, reliable means to seek and be reassured of God's forgiveness, may be understood as explicitly acknowledging the inevitability of sin. They define the Christian life as a journey, a progressive movement through which one becomes increasingly incorporated into the body of Christ. As such, they are partly pedagogical devices to assist sinful men and women to develop rational ethics.

16. *Chefes* are the heads of the *terreiros* (*umbanda* cult center); *ogãs* are ritual leaders who sing to bring down the spirits but do not become possessed.

17. Kardecism is the spiritualist religion founded in mid-nineteenth century France by Allen Kardec (a pseudonym) and imported to Brazil at the end of the century, where it was adopted by those members of the upper classes eager to identify with French culture. The religion revolves around séances in which the dead return through mediums, and give the living advice. The practice involves no music, dance, or other ritual that focuses on the body. Kardec's philosophy of reincarnation may be found in Allen Kardec, *O livro dos espíritos* (67th ed., Rio de Janeiro: Federação Espírita Brasileira, 1987). *Candomblé* is a Yoruba-derived religion of Bahia, in which initiates become possessed by one of the pantheon of Yoruba gods, including Shango, Ogun, Obatalá, Oxum, and Ye-

menjá. See Roger Bastide, *The African Religions of Brazil* (Baltimore: Johns Hopkins University Press, 1978).

18. Paula Montero, *Da doença á desordem* (Rio de Janeiro: Graal, 1983); Horst H. Figge, *Umbanda: religião, magia e possessão* (Teresópolis: Jaguary, 1983).

19. On *umbanda* possession behavior, see Esther Pressel, "Umbanda Trance and Possession in São Paulo, Brazil," in Felicitas Goodman, *et al.*, *Trance, Healing and Hallucination* (New York: Wiley, 1974); and Idem, "Umbanda in Sao Paulo: Religious Innovation in a Developing Society," in Erika Bourguignon, ed., *Religion, Altered States of Consciousness, and Social Change* (Columbus: Ohio University Press, 1973).

20. The *guias* are in this sense very different from Catholic saints, to whom they are sometimes mistakenly compared, for unlike saints the spirits of *umbanda* require human assistance.

21. Brown has pointed out that the poetry of nineteenth-century Indianist writers appears in the songs chanted in order to call down the spirits. See Brown, *Umbanda*, 66.

22. Brown, *Umbanda*; also see Birman, *O que é umbanda* (São Paulo: Brasiliense, 1983), 44–45.

23. Montero, *Da doença*; Renato Ortiz, *A morte branca do feiticeiro negro* (Petrópolis: Vozes, 1978); Patricia Birman, *O que é umbanda* (São Paulo: Brasiliense, 1983).

24. Cf. Rubem Cesar Fernandes, *Os cavaleiros*, 124–140.

25. The gloves were a sign of her *guia*'s "purity." There are important variations among *centros* in terms of the elements reminiscent of the more Africanized *candomblé*. Zélia avoids gunpowder (usually used to frighten away *exús*), as well as the public sacrifice of chickens, cats, or snakes, she says, except "under very unusual circumstances, when the work is very complicated." Reflecting her Catholic upbringing, she also insists on beginning the *sessão* or *gira* with a series of Ave Marias. In addition, she is reluctant to feed spirits except on their special days, when *caboclos* receive corn pudding, coconut, and salad, and *pretos velhos* rice, beans, and chicken, all served in earthenware bowls.

26. On *umbandista* diagnoses of affliction, see Rosine Perelberg, "Umbanda and Psychoanalysis as Different Ways of Interpreting Mental Illness," *British Journal of Medical Psychiatry* 53 (1980): 323–332; Esther Pressel, "Negative Spiritism in Experienced Brazilian Umbanda Mediums," in Vincent Crapanzano and Vivian Garrison, eds., *Case Studies in Spirit Possession* (New York: Wiley, 1977).

27. Birman is incorrect, I believe, when she claims that mediums do not admit to serving the *exús* in this capacity. See *O que é umbanda*, 64; and cf. Yvonne Velho, *Guerra dos orixá* (Rio de Janeiro: Zahar, 1975).

28. Personal communication, August 1990.

29. A head church, the permanent seat of a pastor, is in any given region the largest and most centrally located congregation. The head church collects tithes from its dependent congregations, then redistributes the funds in the form of construction, maintenance, Bibles, and salaries. Head churches also make sure congregations preserve doctrinal and disciplinary orthodoxy.

30.   Like many other illiterate *crentes,* Manuel claims to be able to read the Bible through the action of the Spirit, though most likely he is simply reciting memorized passages.

31.   The rules are often acknowledged to involve inconsistencies. Why, some would ask from time to time, can men wear moustaches but not beards or sideburns? Why is long flowing hair any more "decent" than closely cropped hair? In such cases presbyters insist that the function of *doctrine* is to instill a spirit of humble submission. "God has His reasons," they say, "which we cannot always understand but must obey."

32. . The prayer services of pentecostalism are referred to as *obras* (works). *Obra* carries with it an implication of directedness, certainty, and the assurance of immanent finality. One refers to a finished house, book or artwork as an *obra*—in the sense of *ouevre;* one also refers to the actual construction site of a house as an *obra.* The contrast with sessions of *umbanda,* referred to as *trabalhos,* is instructive. *Trabalho* carries with it the connotation of ongoing labor, of daily work, not necessarily with an end in sight. *Obra* thus images humans as vehicles for a certain, finished product, while *trabalho* emphasizes human agency, with all its uncertainties.

33.   The notion of cults of affliction comes from Victor Turner, *The Drums of Affliction* (Oxford: Clarendon, 1968). Peter Fry and Gary N. Howe have suggested the utility of applying the phrase to *umbanda* and pentecostalism in "Umbanda e pentecostalismo: duas respostas á aflição," *Debate e crítica* 6 (1975): 75–95.

34.   On allocating responsibility, see Ursula Sharma, "Theodicy and the Doctrine of Karma," *Man* 8 (1973): 347–364.

Notes to Chapter Three

1.   Cited in Marcello Azevedo, *Basic Ecclesial Communities in Brazil* (Washington: Georgetown University Press, 1987), 139.

2.   Conferência Nacional dos Bispos do Brasil (CNBB), *CEBs no Brasil* (São Paulo: Paulinas, 1979), 47; Azevedo, *Basic Ecclesial,* 139.

3.   Cf. Leonardo Boff, *E a igreja,* 93.

4.   The data I collected directly about income levels was not very useful, since informants' reports of income were unreliable, and it was not clear from the household survey how many individuals depended on a given salary. I had therefore to rely on sociomaterial self-identification and occupation as the most readily available indicators of income.

5.   In the town at large, 8 percent of 256 men reported working in skilled factory positions (*profissionais*), while 9 percent reported working in factories as either *serventes* or *operadores.* In the *comunidade,* meanwhile, 15 percent of the men worked in skilled positions as machine-tenders, crane operators or machinists, while only 5 percent worked as *operadores.*

6. Progressive Catholics would of course immediately point out that, while it may be that *crença* has easier access to the poorest people in part because they "do not look around and say 'he should live in a finer house,'" this very neglect of the material realm condemns its members to continuing in their unfortunate circumstances. In the place of such fatalism, the progressive Church offers *consciência* of rights and the importance of struggling to change worldly things. Many local people refer to this message, as purveyed in sermons, lectures, pamphlets, and so on, as "mixing religion and politics." I treat this issue in detail later.

7. Boff, *Igreja,* 199.

8. See, for example, the diocesan document, "O serviço da comunidade," November 1987, 3.

9. "CEBs: rumo a nova sociedade," booklet, 1986, 12.

10. As with my figures for women, these figures about men are only suggestive, and should be taken very cautiously, because of the small size of my samples: forty active Catholic men, forty *crente* men; and about three hundred fifty men overall.

11. On this pattern, see Cândido Procópio Ferreira de Camargo, *et al.*, *Católicos, protestantes, espíritas* (Petrópolis: Vozes, 1973), 44–50; Carlos Brandão, "Catolicismo popular: etica, ethos e sentido de vida," (1988), 26 ff.

12. Fully 42 percent of active Catholic men are older than fifty (compared to 20 percent of local men overall), and a third are on social security (compared to 23 percent of local men overall).

13. Forty-two percent of participating Catholic males were in these trades, compared to only 32 percent of all local males.

14. While 35 percent of the local adult women worked outside their homes, only 25 percent of participating Catholic women surveyed did so.

15. There are, of course, limits to the Assembly of God's liberality. If one continuously fails to appear even once a week in church, one's commitment to the religion may become a matter of open debate. I knew one woman who, because of a job as a domestic servant in Rio, failed to attend church for two months in a row. She was visited by a group of *crentes* who took her to task. Significantly, however, they did not threaten her with ex-communication. In addition, the Assembly of God has no tolerance for specific occupations deemed inconsistent with doctrine such as waiters, owners or employees at bars, armed policemen or night watchmen or, among women, cooks, clerks, or maids in the houses of ill repute along the highway.

16. Forty-two percent of the men in the *comunidade* were in the construction trades, compared to only 28 percent of the *crente* men I surveyed.

17. One-fifth of the *crente* men I surveyed worked such schedules, compared to one-tenth of the active Catholic men.

18. Mariz, "Religion and Coping," 54, 84.

19. Carlos Rodrigues Brandão, *A memória do sagrado* (São Paulo: Paulinas, 1985), 105; also see Brandão, *Os deuses*, 77–78. For examples of petit bourgeois dominance of European popular Catholicism, see William Christian, *Person and God in a Spanish Valley* (New York: Semina Press, 1972), and Caroline Brettell,

"The Priest and His People: The Contractual Basis for Religious Practice in Rural Portugal," in Ellen Badone, *Religious Orthodoxy and Popular Faith in European Society* (Princeton: Princeton University Press, 1990), 55–73.

20. Hewitt, Rolim, 75.

21. Daniel Levine, *Religião e classes*, 732. On this point see too Bruneau, 1982, 1986, "Popular Groups," and for Nicaragua, Lancaster, *Thanks to God.*

22. José Comblin, "Os leigos," *Comunicações do ISER* 26 (1987): 33.

23. Brandão, *A memória*, 101.

24. Rolim, *Religião e classes*, 75. The pattern is not confined to Brazil; in Nicaragua, Lancaster found the poorest of the poor tended to be pentecostals. *Thanks to God*, 101.

25. Clodovis Boff, "É preciso trubalhar com as massas," *Vermelho e branco* (March 1992): 10.

Notes to Chapter Four

1. For these and other affinities between women's experience and religiosity in complex societies, see Robert J. Fornaro, "Supernatural Power, Sexuality, and the Paradigm of 'Women's Space' in Religion and Culture," *Sex Roles* 12/3–4 (1985): 295–302; Judith Hoch-Smith and Anita Spring, eds., *Women in Ritual and Symbolic Roles* (New York: Plenum, 1978).

2. Among São Jorge's ninety *comunidade* members, fifty are women, while among the two hundred and seventy *crentes* in the Assembly of God, one hundred and eighty are women.

3. Cf. Lourdes Beneria and Martha Roldán, *The Crossroads of Class and Gender: Industrial Homework, Subcontracting, and Household Dynamics in Mexico City* (Chicago: University of Chicago Press, 1987), 121–122. Also see Evelyn Stevens, "Machismo and Marianismo," *Society* 10 (1973): 57–63.

4. In this São Jorge typifies the national trend. On women's increasing presence in the wage labor market in urban Brazil, see Marianne Schmink, "Women and Urban Industrial Development in Brazil," in June Nash and Helen Safa, eds., *Women and Change in Latin America* (South Hadley, Mass.: Bergin and Garvey, 1986), 161; Heleieth Saffioti, *Mulher brasileira opresão e exploração* (Rio de Janeiro: Edições Achiame, 184); John Humphrey, *Gender and Work in the Third World: Sexual Divisions in Brazilian Industry* (London: Tavistock, 1987).

5. Setha Low and Dora L. Davis, eds., *Gender, Health and Illness: The Case of Nerves* (New York: Hemisphere, 1989); Luiz Fernando Duarte, *Da vida nervosa das classes trabalhadoras urbanas* (Rio de Janeiro: Zahar, 1986).

6. Sonia Alvarez, "Women's Participation in the Brazilian 'People's Church': A Critical Appraisal," *Feminist Studies* 16/2 (1990): 386. For an overview of liberation theologians' stances on women, see Elsa Tamez, ed., *Against Machismo* (Oak Park, Ill.: Meyer Stone Books, 1987).

7. Sonia Alvarez, *Engendering Democracy in Brazil* (Princeton: Princeton University Press, 1990), 60–70.

8. This term is frequently substituted now for "*benzedeira*," although in practice they mean the same thing in São Jorge.

9. Cf. Esther Pressel, "Spirit Magic in the Social Relations between Men and Women (São Paulo)," in Erika Bourguignon, ed., *A World of Men* (New York: Praeger, 1980).

10. Patricia Birman, "Fazendo estilo criando gêneros," Ph.D. dissertation, Universidade Federal de Rio de Janeiro, 1988; for *candomblé*, see Ruth Landes, *The City of Women* (New York: Macmillan, 1947).

11. Cf. Patricia Lerch, "An Explanation for the Predominance of Women in the Umbanda Cults of Porto Alegre, Brazil," *Urban Anthropology* 11/2 (1982): 249.

12. For comparative cases, see Elizabeth Brusco, "The Household Basis of Evangelical Religion and the Reformation of Machismo in Colombia," Ph.D. dissertation, City University of New York, 1986; Salvatore Cucchiari, "Between Shame and Sanctification: Patriarchy and its Transformation in Sicilian Pentecostalism," *American Ethnologist* 17 (1990): 687–707; Lesley Gill, "'Like a Veil to Cover Them': Women and the Pentecostal Movement in La Paz," *American Ethnologist* 17 (1990): 708–721; Susan Rose, "Women Warriors: The Negotiation of Gender in a Charismatic Community," *Sociological Analysis* 48/3 (1987): 245–258.

13. For comparative cases on women's testimonies, see Elaine J. Lawless, *Handmaidens of the Lord* (Philadelphia: University of Pennsylvania Press, 1988); Cheryl Townsend Gilkes, "Some Mother's Son and Some Father's Daughter: Gender and Biblical Language in Afro-Christian Worship Tradition," in Clarissa Atkinson, ed., *Shaping New Vision* (Ann Arbor: UMI Research Press, 1987), 73–100.

14. Victor Turner, *Dramas, Fields, and Metaphors* (Ithaca: Cornell, 1974).

15. For comparative cases of how patriarchal norms can be turned on their heads through religious discourse, see Catherine Thompson, "The Power to Pollute and the Power to Preserve: Perceptions of Female Power in a Hindu Village," *Social Science and Medicine* 21/6 (1985): 701–711; and Roger Keesing, *Kwaio Religion* (New York: Columbia, 1982).

Notes to Chapter Five

1. Instituto Brasilerio de Geografia e Estatísticos, *Estatísticos anuários* (Brasília: IBGE, 1982), 33.

2. Censuses of São Jorge, 1979, 1988.

3. Paul Spencer, "The Riddled Course: Theories of Age and its Transformations," in Paul Spencer, ed., *Anthropology and the Riddle of the Sphinx: Paradoxes of Change in the Life Course* (New York: Routledge, 1990), 1–34.

4. Discussion of the standards of working-class consumption both in the

urban periphery and the inner-city *favelas* may be found in Carmen Cinira Macêdo, *A reprodução da desigualdade* (São Paulo: Vertice, 1985), 39–49; Idem, *O tempo de gênesis* (São Paulo: Brasiliense, 1986), 183–233; Alba Zaluar, *A máquina e a revolta: as organizações populares e o significado da pobreza* (São Paulo: Brasiliense, 1985), 100–111; Teresa Pires do Rio Caldeira, *A política dos outros* (São Paulo: Brasiliense, 1984), 104–140.

5. On *O Globo,* see Joseph Straubhaar, "Television and Video in the Transition from Military to Civilian Rule in Brazil," *Latin American Research Review* 24/1 (1989): 140–154.

6. Some parents speak nostalgically of earlier times, when marriages were arranged entirely by the families involved. Then, the parents of the boy would propose marriage to the parents of the girl. The girl's parents would have a fortnight to consider the proposal, and then would signal their acceptance by gathering together the trousseau. Some parents, however, continue to retain symbolic control of marriage at the engagement party, where the mother of the bride places the ring on the groom's finger, and the father of the groom places a ring on the bride's.

7. Membership in the youth group is mandatory for young, unmarried persons who wish to be members of São Jorge's *comunidade.* Father Cosme established youth groups as a way to replace traditional young people's associations such as *Filhas de Maria,* as well as those of altar- and choirboys. Now São Jorge's youth group meets in the church's *sala* every Sunday evening for an hour, during which members pray, discuss Bible passages, and play games like "telephone" as a way of learning moral lessons. In addition, the group is responsible for rehearsing and presenting to the congregation weekly readings and new hymns. Occasionally, the group invites outsiders, such as nurses and teachers, to give talks on special topics in the *sala.*

8. *Domingo,* November 15, 1987, 2.

9. Among the twenty-five unmarried male and female *crentes* with whom I became acquainted, ten had pentecostal parents at the time of their conversion, and the rest came from *misseiro,* peripheral Catholic, and institutional Catholic backgrounds.

10. Cf. Regina Novaes, *Os escolhidos de Deus* (Rio: Marco Zero, 1985), 48–53.

11. Roberto Carlos is currently the most popular singer in Brazil. His brand of pop-syrup-rock is filled with strings and predictable melodic forms resembling those of Julio Iglesias or Barry Manilow. Caetano Veloso is more adventurous musically, incorporating elements of samba, jazz, and blues.

Notes to Chapter Six

1. When I refer to an individual as *negro, moreno, mulato,* or *branco* ("white"), in general I do so because he or she referred to him or herself in this manner. I have, however, occasionally used *negro* to denote a phenotype, in-

cluding nappy dark hair and very dark skin that, in the cases with which I was familiar, was always self-identified and identified by others as *preto, escuro,* or *negro.* I adopt this taxonomic approach advisedly. As Fontaine has pointed out, claims about the "fluidity of racial identity in Brazil" notwithstanding, "the number of those with unambiguous phenotypical characteristics is rather substantial." Pierre-Michel Fontaine, "Research in the Political Economy of Afro-Latin America," *Latin American Research Review* 15 (1980): 128. See also Anani Dzidzienyo, *The Position of Blacks in Brazilian Society* (London: Minority Rights Group, 1971).

2. Because most research on Rio's *umbanda* has not investigated the matter, I do not know whether this pronounced *negro* presence in *umbanda* is typical of the urban periphery and *favelas* as a whole. One must keep in mind *umbanda*'s variability according to social context. Diana Brown's focus on middle-sector and lighter-skinned clienteles, for instance, reflects the specific contexts in which she worked, where *negros* were a minority. Diana Brown, *Umbanda: Religion and Politics in Urban Brazil* (Ann Arbor: University of Michigan Press, 1986), 221. For exemplary work on racial self-identifications among *candomblé* mediums, see Maria Lina Leao Teixeira, "Lorogun: identidades sexuais e poder no candomblé," in Carlos Eugênio Marcondes de Moura, org., *Candomblé: desvendando identidades* (São Paulo: EMW Editores, 1987), 33–52.

3. For variations on the myth of racial democracy, see Gilberto Freyre, *Brazil: An Interpretation* (New York: Alfred Knopf, 1945); Idem, *New World in the Tropics: The Culture of Modern Brazil* (New York: Alfred Knopf, 1959); Charles Wagley, ed., *Race and Class in Rural Brazil* (New York: Columbia University Press, 1952); Marvin Harris, *Patterns of Race in the Americas* (New York: Walker and Company, 1964); Donald Pierson, *Negroes in Brazil: A Study of Race Contact in Bahia* (Carbondale: University of Illinois Press, 1967). Many writers since WWII have critiqued the myth of racial democracy, amassing evidence that political and economic opportunities in Brazil decline in direct relation to darkening skin color. See Florestan Fernandes, *The Negro in Brazilian Society* (New York: Columbia University Press, 1969); Octavio Ianni, *Raças e classes no brasil* (2nd ed., Rio de Janeiro: Editora Civilização Brasileira, 1972); Nelson do Valle Silva, "Black-White Income Differentials: Brazil, 1960," Ph.D. dissertation, University of Michigan, 1978; Carlos A. Hasenbalg, *Discriminação e desigualdades raciais no brasil* (Rio de Janeiro: Graal, 1979); Peggy Lovell Webster and Jeffrey W. Dwyer, "The Cost of Being Non-White in Brazil," *Sociology and Social Research* (January 1988); Pierre-Michel Fontaine, *Race, Class and Power in Brazil* (Los Angeles: University of California Press, 1985). On everyday racism in Brazil, see Ana Lucia Valente, *Ser negro no Brasil hoje* (São Paulo: Editora Moderna, 1987); Anizio Ferreira dos Santos, *Eu negro: discriminação racial no Brasil, existe?* (São Paulo: Edições Loyola, 1988); Irene Maria F. Barbosa, *Socialização e relações raciais* (São Paulo, 1983); Haroldo Costa, *Fala, crioulo* (Rio de Janeiro, 1982).

4. For the roots of the Indian/*negro* complex in popular Brazilian thought, see Thomas Skidmore, *Black into White: Race and Nationality in Brazilian Thought* (New York: Oxford, 1974).

5. On the problem of the ambiguity in *mulato* identity in Brazil, see Robert Brent Toplin, *Freedom and Prejudice: The Legacy of Slavery in the United States and Brazil* (Westport: Greenwood Press, 1981), 91–120; Thales de Azevedo, *Democracia racial: ideologia e realidade* (Petrópolis: Vozes, 1975); Neusa Santos Souza, *Tornar-se negro* (Rio de Janeiro, 1983). Some of the torturous ambiguity of *mulato* identity is suggested in Pierre-Michel Fontaine's own surprise that leaders of the Black Consciousness Movement in São Paulo have been identified as *mulato* rather than black: "It came as a surprise to this author," he reports, "to learn that two of these leaders, whom he knows personally, are labelled mulattoes, and not blacks," "The Political Economy," 134. The question is who is labelling whom, and under what social/political circumstances. For a discussion that places the phenomenon of the *mulato* in global perspective, see Luiz Felipe de Alencastro, "Geopolítica da mestiçagem," *Novos estudos CEBRAP* 11 (January 1985): 49–63.

6. On May 13th, 1888, Princess Isabel, the daughter of the emperor of Brazil, signed the law of abolition, bringing to a close more than three centuries of legal slavery. After WWII, various state governments established commemorations of the day, but it was not until 1988, the centenary year of abolition, that the federal government proclaimed the day a national holiday. Micenio Santos, "O 13 de maio," in *Comunicações do ISER* 28 (1988): 72–78; George Reid Andrews, *Blacks and Whites in Sao Paulo, Brazil, 1888–1988* (Madison: University of Wisconsin Press, 1991), 211–233; Suely Robles Reis de Queiroz, *A abolição da escravidão* (São Paulo: Brasiliense, 1982).

7. Under the rubric of "Brotherhood Campaign," each year since 1964 the CNBB has selected a theme to be celebrated during the forty days between Lent and Easter. On the 1988 Campaign, see Caetana Damaeceno, "Cantando para subir," Master's thesis, UFRJ, 1990; Flavio Lenz, "Três versões da fraternidade," *Comunicações do ISER* 28 (1988): 84–89; John Burdick, "Observações sobre a campanha da fraternidade de 1988 na Baixada Fluminense," *Comunicações do ISER* 40 (1991): 42–47.

8. CNBB, *Caderno da campanha da fraternidade, 1988*, 13, 24–26. Though not canonized, Anastásia enjoys a following among older *negras*, who visit her shrine at the Church of the Rosário in Rio de Janeiro. These *negras* recount that the jealous wife of a slaveowner unjustly accused the virgin Anastasia of seducing her husband, and forced her to wear a face-iron for the rest of her life. Pictures, prayer-booklets and other paraphernalia connected to Anastasia's devotion may be bought at any one of the hundreds of newsstands in downtown Rio de Janeiro.

9. CNBB, "Caderno de grupos de família [Bible-group reflection guide for the Brotherhood Campaign]," 1988, p. 7.

10. *Mulatos* have long been fertile soil for the *negro* movement: having achieved institutional positions within the Church, they have often been treated as second-class citizens within it. See the explicit discussion of the "discrimination inside the Franciscan order against *morenos*" in the mimeographed summary, Association of Black Religious and Seminarians, "Encontro de Franciscanos Negros do Brasil," Rio de Janeiro, 1988.

11. This effort parallels earlier Catholic efforts to purify African religion by

approving selected elements in it. For precedents, see Roger Bastide, *The African Religions of Brazil* (Baltimore: Johns Hopkins University Press, 1978), 109–125; Joao Fagundes Hauck, *et al.*, *História de igreja no Brasil: ensaio de interpretação a partir do povo* (Vol. II, part 2, Petrópolis: Vozes, 1985), 286–287.

12. CNBB, *Ouvi o clamor*, 53. The Church had catechized against *umbanda*, spiritism, and *candomblé* for decades, especially since their rapid growth in the postwar period. Several informants remembered having been taught in their catechism of the 1940s that spiritism and *macumba* were the work of the Devil. Also see Renato Ortiz, *A morte branca do feiticeiro negro* (Petrópolis: Vozes, 1978).

13. The ambiguities in the progressive vision of African religion, which approved of song and dance as "expressive," while rejecting spirit possession as "alienated," may be gleaned from Raimundo Cintra, *Candomblé e umbanda: o desafio brasileiro* (São Paulo: Paulinas, 1985), 140–156; Idem, "Algumas pistas para a pastoral dos cultos afro-Brasileiros," in B. Beni dos Santos, org., *A religião do povo* (São Paulo: Paulinas, 1978), 124; Mauro Batista, "Abordagem pastoral da religiosidade do povo," in José Quieroz, org., *A religiosidade do povo* (São Paulo: Paulinas, 1984), 109–122; Helcion Ribeiro, *Religiosidade popular na teologia latino-americana* (São Paulo: Paulinas, 1985).

14. Roger Bastide, *The African Religions of Brazil* (Baltimore: Johns Hopkins University Press, 1978 [1960]), 342.

15. Paulo Montero, *Da doença a desordem*, 269; Patricia Birman, *O que é a umbanda*, 57; Renato Ortiz, *A morte branca*.

16. E.g., Bastide, *The African Religions*, 317.

17. Ortiz, *A morte*, 33; Montero, *Da doença*, 279.

18. For a similar analysis of another arena of Afro-Brazilian culture, see J. Lowell Lewis, *Ring of Liberation: Deceptive Discourse in Brazilian Capoeira* (Chicago: University of Chicago Press, 1992).

19. Similar observations have been made by Pedro Oro, "Negros e brancos nas religiões afro-brasileiras no Rio Grande do Sul," *Comunicações do ISER* 28 (1988): 33–44.

20. Cf. Birman, *O que é umbanda*, 67.

21. Cf. Liana Trindade, "Exú: reinterpretações individualizadas de um mito," *Religião e sociedade* 8 (1982).

22. R. Kent, "Palmares: An African State in Brazil," in Richard Price, ed., *Maroon Societies* (Baltimore: Johns Hopkins University Press, 1979); Joel Rufino dos Santos, *Zumbi* (São Paulo: Editora Moderna, 1985).

23. Diana Brown, for example, states that "This tradition started in the first years of the 1960s, with the government's inauguration of a statue in honor of an ex-slave." Diana Brown, "Uma história da umbanda no Rio," in Diana Brown, *et al.*, eds., *Umbanda e a política* (Rio de Janeiro: ISER, 1985), 38. Yet many of my elderly informants remember the day of the *pretos velhos* as having been celebrated in their youth.

24. I examined about half a dozen such texts from the local grade schools. Recently, the figure of Zumbi has become better known, because he appeared in a widely-watched television drama on *O Globo* (the largest TV station in Brazil).

25. Cf. Eugene Genovese, *Roll, Jordan, Roll* (New York: Pantheon, 1974), 252; Bertram Wyatt-Brown, "The Mask of Obedience: Male Slave Psychology in the Old South," *American Historical Review* 93 (1988): 1228–1252; Orlando Patterson, *The Sociology of Slavery* (Fairleigh Dickinson University Press, 1967).

26. James Scott, *Domination and the Arts of Resistance* (New Haven: Yale University Press, 1990).

27. Regina Novaes, "Os negros entre os episcopais: cor e lugar social," in Regina Novaes and Maria da Graça Floriano, *O negro evangélico* (Rio de Janeiro: Marco Zero, 1985), 45.

28. The actual vote included presbyters from the various dependent congregations in the area, of which São Jorge is the head church.

29. In pentecostal churches in the greater Rio area which are predominantly dark-skinned, the ideological struggles I have documented undoubtedly have given way to entirely new racial-religious visions, as in black Protestant churches in the United States. See, for example, Arthur Huff Fauset, *Black Gods of the Metropolis: Negro Religious Cults of the Urban North* (Philadelphia, 1971); Albert Raboteau, *Slave Religion* (New York: Oxford University Press, 1978); and Genovese, *Roll, Jordan, Roll*, 245–253. Research on this question, however, has unfortunately yet to be undertaken.

Notes to Chapter Seven

1. On the politics of counterhegemonic discourse, see Michael Taussig, "Violence and Resistance in the Americas: The Legacy of Conquest," in *The Nervous System* (New York: Routledge, 1992), 37–52; Idem, *Shamanism, Colonialism and the Wild Man* (Chicago: University of Chicago Press, 1987); James Scott, *Domination and the Arts of Resistance* (New Haven: Yale University Press, 1990); June Nash, *We Eat the Mines and the Mines Eat Us*; Aihwa Ong, *Spirits of Resistance and Capitalist Discipline* (Albany: SUNY Press, 1987); Dick Hebdige, *Subculture* (New York: Routledge, 1979); Robert Weller, "The Politics of Ritual Disguise: Repression and Response in Taiwanese Popular Religion," *Modern China* 13/1 (1987): 17–39; Reynaldo Ileto, *Pasyon and Revolution;* Deborah Heath, "Fashion, Anti-fashion and Heteroglossia in Urban Senegal," *American Ethnologist* 19/1 (February 1992): 19–33; John Fiske, "Cultural Studies and the Culture of Everyday Life," in Lawrence Grossberg, *et al.*, eds., *Cultural Studies* (New York: Routledge, 1992), 154–173. "Resistance," however, is not univocal. Abu-Lughod reminds us that counterhegemonic discourses and action often incorporate elements of and are energized by dominant discourses. Lila Abu-Lughod, "The Romance of Resistance," *American Ethnologist* 17/1 (1990).

2. The patterns I discovered represent only some, not all, political possibilities in the Church. Research of this type in other locales would undoubtedly reveal other tendencies.

3.   There are few questions debated as heatedly today in progressive Catholic circles as why so many of the militants who emerged from the CEBs have lost the momentum they had in the 1970s: why have so many of them distanced themselves from the Church, or from the popular movements, or from both? See Clodovis Boff, *et al., Cristãos: como fazer política* (Petrópolis: Vozes, 1987).

4.   See Lygia Dabul, *et al., Unidade e prática da fé* (Rio: CEDI, 1987); for some analyses of the tensions between cooperativism and small-ownership ideals in the Church, see Neide Esterci, ed., *Cooperativismo e coletivização no campo: questões sobre a prática da igreja popular* (Rio de Janeiro: Marco Zero, 1984).

5.   Margaret Keck, "The New Unionism in the Brazilian Transition," in Alfred Stepan, ed., *Democratizing Brazil: Problems of Transition and Consolidation* (New York: Oxford, 1989), 252–296.

6.   Cf. interview with Chico Silva, *crente* leader of the *Núcleo Agricola Fluminense,* rural union of Duque de Caxias; also see works on Julião, the *crente* leader of the Peasant Leagues in the 1950s.

7.   In the state-controlled clientelistic unions, few workers of any religion participate. In these, there is room only for the *pelegos,* the "saddles" ridden by the managers. On the tensions between clientelistic and independent unionism in Brazil, see Celso Frederico, *Consciência operária no Brasil* (São Paulo: Atica, 1979).

8.   It was dominated by the Central Unica dos Trabalhadores (CUT). This is Brazil's largest national federation of combative unions, standing in contrast with the Central Geral dos Trabalhadores (CGT), associated with *pelego* unions. The CGT supported Collor in the last elections while the CUT supported Lula.

9.   E.g., Judith Hoffnagel, "The Believers: Pentecostalism in a Brazilian City," Ph.D. dissertation, Indian University, 1978; Beatriz de Souza, *A experiência de salvação* (São Paulo, 1969); Jether Ramalho, "Algumas notas sobre duas perspectivas de pastoral popular," *Cadernos do ISER* 6 (1977): 30–39; Rubem Alves, *Protestantismo e repressão* (Petrópolis: Vozes, 1980); Pedro Ribeiro Oliveira, "Comunidade e massa: desafio da pastoral popular," *Revista eclesiastica Brasileira* 44 (1984); Francisco Cartaxo Rolim, *Religião e classes populares* (Petrópolis: Vozes, 1980); Gary N. Howe, "Representações religiosas e capitalismo: uma 'leitura' estruturalista do pentecostalismo no Brasil," *Cadernos do ISER* 6 (1977): 39–48; Willems; Delcio Monteiro de Lima, *Os demônios descem do norte* (Rio de Janeiro: Francisco Alves, 1986).

10.   Instituto Nacional de Previdência Social, Brazil's federal bureau of social security.

11.   José Gomes, "Religião e politica: os pentecostais no Recife," Ph.D. dissertation, Federal University of Pernambuco, 1985, 256.

12.   See also Sandra Stoll, "Embu, eleições de 1982: a mobilização politica de CEBs e pentecostais," *Comunicações do ISER* 3 (1982); Idem, "Púlpito e palanque: religião e política nas eleições de 1982 num município de grande São Paulo," Ph.D. dissertation, Universidade Estadual de Campinas, 1986, 313–314; G. U. Kliewer, "Assembléia de Deus e eleições num município do interior de Matto Grosso," *Comunicações do ISER* 3 (1982); Regina Novaes, "Os

crentes e os eleições: uma experiência de campo," *Comunicações do ISER* 3 (1982); Oneide Bobsin, "Produção religiosa e significação social do pentecostalismo a partir de sua prática e representação," Master's Thesis, Pontifical University of São Paulo, 1984.

13. See, for example, Stoll, "Púlpito e palanque"; Francisco Cartaxo Rolim, *Pentecostais no Brasil* (Petrópolis: Vozes, 1985), 246; Mariza de Carvalho Soares, "É permitido distribuir 'santinho' na porta da igreja?", *Comunicações do ISER* 4 (1983): 57; Paul Freston, "Protestants and Brazilian Politics Since Redemocratization," in David Stoll and Virginia Burnett, eds., *Pentecostal Politics in Latin America* (Chapel Hill: University of North Carolina Press, 1993). A related, still unanalyzed phenomenon was the Assembly of God's official support for Brizola—a social democrat—against Collor de Melo—a conservative—at the national level in the 1989 presidential elections.

14. For a history of the foundation of the Worker's Party in the late 1970s and early 1980s, see Isabel Ribeiro de Oliveira, *Trabalho e política: as origens do partido dos trabalhadores* (Petrópolis: Vozes, 1988).

15. Michael Taussig has found that the Devil plays an important role in how sugar workers in Colombia diagnose social differentiation. See his *The Devil and Commodity Fetishism in South America* (Chapel Hill: University of North Carolina Press, 1980). Certainly the Devil, or some refraction of him, is invoked with great frequency throughout the world to account for clearly visible differences in fortune. In Christianity, however, he loses any vestige of moral ambiguity and takes on an absolute quality. The problem then becomes what to do about the Devil: resign oneself to his wiles or take arms in a millennial battle against him?

16. According to Roger Lancaster, this occurred among a segment of evangelicals in revolutionary Nicaragua, *Thanks to God and the Revolution* (New York: Columbia University Press, 1988), 100–126. It is impossible to predict how the shifting constellation of forces accompanying the new Chamorro government will affect the political alignment of evangelicals. Still, it is significant that in studies of the February 1990 electorate (see, especially, the analyses of LASA's Commission), the evangelicals *were not* singled out as a distinctive voting bloc.

Notes to Conclusion

1. See, for example, Maria Helena Moreira Alves, *Estado e oposição no Brasil* (Petrópolis: Vozes, 1984); for a more skeptical view, that attributes the transition to conflicts within the military itself, see Alfred Stepan, *Rethinking Military Politics* (Princeton: Princeton University Press, 1988).

2. Ana Maria Doimo, "Social Movements and the Catholic Church in Vitoria, Brazil," in Scott Mainwaring and Alexander Wilde, eds., *The Progressive Church in Latin America* (Notre Dame: University of Notre Dame Press, 1989); Ralph Della Cava, "The 'Peoples' Church,' The Vatican, and the *Abertura,*" in

Alfred Stepan, ed., *Democratizing Brazil* (New York: Oxford University Press, 1989), 143–167.

3. The impact of redemocratization on CEB politics has been described by Scott Mainwaring, *The Catholic Church and Politics in Brazil, 1916–1985* (Stanford: Stanford University Press, 1986); W. E. Hewitt, *Base Christian Communities and Social Change in Brazil* (Lincoln: University of Nebraska Press, 1991), 91–105; Della Cava, "The 'Peoples Church'"; and the contributors to Paulo Krischke and Scott Mainwaring, eds., *A igreja nas bases em tempo de transição, 1974–1985* (Porto Alegre: LPM, 1986).

4. See the testimony in W. E. Hewitt, *Base Christian Communities,* 103. I heard a good deal of such testimony myself.

5. See, for example, the interview with Dom Angélico, longtime progressive in São Paulo, in the *Jornal do Brasil,* 5/18/88.

6. One of the first and most clearly self-critical voices was that of Claudio Perani. See his "Igreja de nordeste: breves notas histórica-críticas," *Cadernos de centro de estudos a ação social* (CEAS) 94 (November/December 1984): 53–73; Idem, "Pastoral Popular: serviço ou poder?" *Cadernos do CEAS* 82 (November/December 1982): 7–19; Idem, "Comunidade eclesial de base e movimento popular," *Cadernos do CEAS* 75 (September/October 1981): 25–33.

7. See Penny Lernoux, *People of God: The Struggle for World Catholicism* (New York: Viking, 1989).

8. Max Weber, *Economy and Society,* Vol. 1 (Berkeley: University of California Press, 1968), 591.

9. Bruce Lincoln, "Notes Toward a Theory of Religion and Revolution," in Bruce Lincoln, ed., *Religion, Rebellion, Revolution: An Interdisciplinary and Cross-Cultural Collection of Essays* (New York: St. Martin's Press, 1985), 266–292.

10. See, for example, Brackette Williams, *Stains on My Name, War in My Veins* (Durham: Duke University Press, 1991); Diane Austin-Broos, "Pentecostals and Rastafarians," *Social and Economic Studies* (1991); Leith Mullings, *Therapy, Ideology and Social Change: Mental Healing in Urban Ghana* (Berkeley: University of California Press, 1984); Richard Werbner, "The Argument of Images: From Zion to the Wilderness in African Churches," in Wim van Binsbergen and Matthew Schoffeleers, eds., *Theoretical Explorations in African Religion* (London: KPI, 1985), 253–286.

11. See, for example, Alberto Melucci, *Nomads of the Present* (Philadelphia: Temple University Press, 1989), 52–53; Susan Eckstein, ed., *Power and Popular Protest: Latin American Social Movements* (Berkeley: University of California Press, 1989); David Slater, ed., *New Social Movements and the State in Latin America* (Amsterdam: CEDLA, 1985); Ann Bookman and Sandra Morgen, eds., *Women and the Politics of Empowerment* (Philadelphia: Temple University Press, 1988); Arturo Escobar and Sonia Alvarez, eds., *The Making of Social Movements in Latin America: Identity, Strategy and Democracy* (Boulder: Westview Press, 1992).

12. JoAnn Martin, "Motherhood and Power: The Production of a Women's Culture of Politics in a Mexican Community," *America Ethnologist* 17/3 (1991): 480.

13. Maria Lorena Cook, "Organizing Opposition in the Teacher's Movement in Oaxaca," in Joe Foweraker and Ann L. Craig, eds., *Popular Movements and Political Change in Mexico* (Boulder: Lynne Rienner, 1990), 200.

14. Manuel Castells, *The City and the Grassroots* (Berkeley: University of California Press, 1983), 226.

15. Alain Touraine, *The Voice and the Eye: An Analysis of Social Movements* (Cambridge: Cambridge University Press, 1981), 142.

16. Luiz Alberto Gomez de Souza, "Crise é vida," *Vermelho e branco* 23/24 (December/January 1992): 22–23.

17. Luiz A. G. de Souza, "É bom que haja crise," *Vermelho e branco* 26 (March 1992): 8–9.

18. Ibid.

19. Clodovis Boff, "É preciso trabalhar com as massas," *Vemelho e branco* (March 1992): 10.

20. See the weekly alerts on "sects" in the Sunday church publication *Domingo* (São Paulo), and the periodic dire warnings in the liberationist newspaper *Vermelho e Branco* (Rio de Janeiro).

Glossary

Assembléia	the Assembly of God Church
benzedeira	traditional Catholic prayer specialist
biscateiro	odd-jobber
bom de vida	economically well off
cachaça	sugar-cane brandy
carioca	resident of Rio de Janeiro
celebração	celebrations of the Eucharist in the Catholic Church in which the priest is not present
centro	an *umbanda* ritual center
chefe	chief of the *umbanda* center
churrasco	barbeque
comunidade	community, as in Christian base community
conscientizado	one whose consciousness has been raised
crente	evangelical or pentecostal
criança	in *umbanda,* the spirit of a child
espada	sword-shaped plant believed to ward off evil eye
está comedo	"is able to eat": someone who claims to be at the edge of subsistence
guia	any spirit of *umbanda,* but especially individual guardian spirits
intenções	requests for prayers, especially for the dead, during Catholic Mass
luxo	luxury
macumba	pejorative term for *umbanda*

mãe de santo	"mother of the saint": ritual leader of *umbanda*
malandro	a marginal, dangerous man, usually a trickster
melhor de vida	economically better off
mineiro	inhabitant of Minas Gerais
miserável	extremely poor
miséria	dire poverty
moreno	euphemism for mulatto
mulato	mulatto
negro	black
novenas	in the Catholic Church, holiday prayers that generally last nine days
operador	assembly-line worker
pedidos	requests made to any spiritual being for counsel, protection, blessings, or rewards
os pobres	the poor
povo	the People
ponto	the ritual song that calls down the spirits of *umbanda*
preto	black
preto velho	the old black slave, one of the most popular spirits in the *umbanda* pantheon
profissional	licensed mechanic or tradesman
razoável	getting along reasonably well in economic terms
sala	living room
salgados	salty snacks, often deep-fried meat and potato
servente	manual laborer
terreiro	the compound in which *umbanda* rites take place
umbanda	the fastest-growing Afro-Brazilian religion

Bibliography

Abu-Lughod, Lila. 1991. "Writing Against Culture." In *Recapturing Anthropology*, edited by Richard Fox. Santa Fe: School of American Research Press.

———. 1990. "The Romance of Resistance." *American Ethnologist* 17(1): 41–55.

Adriance, Madeleine. 1986. *Opting for the Poor*. Kansas City: Sheed and Ward.

Alencastro, Luize Felipe de. 1985. "Geopolítica da mestiçagem." *Novos estudos CEBRAP* 11: 49–63.

Alvarez, Sonia. 1990a. "Women's Participation in the Brazilian 'People's Church': A Critical Reappraisal." *Feminist Studies* 16(2): 381–408.

———. 1990b. *Engendering Democracy in Brazil*. Princeton: Princeton University Press.

Alves, Márcio Moreira. 1979. *A igreja e a politica no Brasil*. São Paulo: Brasiliense.

———. 1973. *A Grain of Mustard Seed: The Awakening of the Brazilian Revolution*. Garden City, N. Y.: Doubleday.

Alves, Maria Helena Moreira. 1984. *Estado e oposição no Brasil*. Petrópolis: Vozes.

Alves, Rubem. 1980. *Protestantismo e repressão*. São Paulo: Atica.

Andrews, George Reid. 1991. *Blacks and Whites in São Paulo, Brasil, 1888–1988*. Madison: University of Wisconsin Press.

Antoniazzi, Alberto. 1986. "O catolicismo no Brasil." Paper presented at the Meeting on Religious Diversity of ISER.

Araújo, Frederico G. B. 1982. "As lutas pela terra na Baixada da Guanabara." Ph.D. diss., Universidade Federal de Rio de Janeiro.

Asad, Talal. 1983. "Anthropological Conceptions of Religion: Reflections on Geertz." *Man* 18(2): 237–259.

Association of Black Religious and Seminarians. 1988. "Encontro de Franciscans Negros do Brasil." Rio de Janeiro: Author.

Azevedo, Marcello. 1987. *Basic Ecclesial Communities in Brazil.* Washington: Georgetown University Press.

Azevedo, Thales de. 1975. *Democracia racial: ideologia e realidade.* Petrópolis: Vozes.

Bakhtin, Mikhail. 1986. *Speech Genres and Other Late Essays.* Austin: University of Texas Press.

————. 1981. *The Dialectical Imagination.* Edited by Michael Holquist, translated by C. Emerson and M. Holquist. Austin: University of Texas Press.

Barbosa, Irene Maria F. 1983. *Socialização e relações raciais.* São Paulo.

Barreiro, Alvaro. 1977. *Comunidades eclesiais de base e evangelização dos pobres.* São Paulo: Loyola.

Barros, Neimar de. 1979. *Os Fantoches.* 7th ed. São Paulo: O Recado.

Basso, Keith. 1979. *Portraits of the "Whiteman": Linguistic Play and Cultural Symbols among the Western Apache.* Cambridge: Cambridge University Press.

Bastide, Roger. 1978. *The African Religions of Brazil.* Baltimore: Johns Hopkins University Press.

Batista, Mauro. 1984. "Abordagem pastoral da religiosidade do povo." In *A religiosidade do povo,* edited by José Queiroz. São Paulo: Paulinas.

Beals, A. 1976. "Strategies of Resort to Curers in South India." In *Asian Medical Systems,* edited by Charles Leslie. Berkeley: University of California Press.

Beidelman, T. O. 1982. *Colonial Evangelism: A Socio-Historical Study of an East African Mission at the Grassroots.* Bloomington: University of Indiana Press.

Beloch, Israel. 1986. *Capa preta e lurdinha: Tenório Cavalcanti e o povo da Baixada.* Rio de Janeiro: Record.

Benería, Lourdes, and Martha Roldán. 1987. *The Crossroads of Class and Gender: Industrial Housework, Subcontracting, and Household Dynamics in Mexico City.* Chicago: University of Chicago Press.

Bennett, T., et al. 1984. "Discourse, Consciousness and Literacy in a Puerto Rican Neighborhood." In *Language and Power,* edited by R. Kramarae et al. Beverly Hills: Sage.

Beozzo, José Oscar. 1984. *Cristãos na universidade e na política.* Petrópolis: Vozes.

Berryman, Philip. 1984. *The Religious Roots of Rebellion.* Maryknoll: Orbis.

————. 1976. "Latin American Liberation Theology." In *Theology in the Americas,* edited by John Eagleson and Sérgio Torres. Maryknoll: Orbis.

Betto, Frei. 1981. *O que é comunidade eclesial de base?* São Paulo: Brasiliense.

Bingemer, Maria Clara, and Pierre Sanchis. 1985. "O caso boff: o sentido da obediência." *Religião e sociedade* 12(3): 110–136.

Birman, Patricia. 1988. "Fazendo estilo criando gêneros." Ph.D. diss., Universidade Federal de Rio de Janeiro.

————. 1983. *O que é umbanda.* São Paulo: Brasiliense.

————. 1980. "Feitiço, carrego e olho grande: os males do Brasil são." Master's thesis, Federal University of Rio de Janeiro.

Bloch, Maurice. 1986. *From Blessing to Violence.* Cambridge: Cambridge University Press.

Bobsin, Oneide. 1984. "Produção religiosa e significação social do pentecostalismo a partir de sua prática e representação." Ph.D. diss., Pontífica Universidade Católica de São Paulo.

Boff, Clodovis. 1992. "É preciso trabalhar com as massas." *Vermelho e branco* 26: 6–10.

———. 1982. "'E uma pedrinha soltou-se': as bases do povo de Deus." *REB* 42/168 (December): 661–687.

———. 1979. *Comunidade eclesial, comunidade política*. Petrópolis: Vozes.

Boff, Clodovis, *et al*. 1987. *Cristãos: como fazer política*. Petrópolis: Vozes.

Boff, Leonardo. 1986. *E a igreja se fez povo*. Petrópolis: Vozes.

———. 1981. *Igreja: carisma e poder*. Petrópolis: Vozes.

———. 1980. *O caminhar da igreja com os oprimidos*. Rio de Janeiro: CODECRI.

———. 1978. *A fé na periferia do mundo*. Petrópolis: Vozes.

———. 1977. *Eclesiogênese: as comunidades eclesiais de base reinventam a igreja*. Petrópolis: Vozes.

Bookman, Ann, and Sandra Morgen, eds. 1988. *Women and the Politics of Empowerment*. Philadelphia: Temple University Press.

Boschi, Caio César. 1986. *Os leigos e o poder: irmandades leigas e política colonizadora em Minas Gerais*. São Paulo: Editora Ática.

Bourdieu, Pierre. 1977. *Outline of a Theory of Practice*. Cambridge: Cambridge University Press.

Brandão, Carlos Rodrigues. 1988a. "A partilha da vida." 7th. Caderno de *Condições de vida e situação de trabalho do povo de Goiás: as pessoas e as famílias*. Goiânia: Universidade de Goiás.

———. 1988b. "Catolicismo popular: ética, ethos e sentido de vida." Mimeo for the Encyclopedia of Liberation Theology.

———. 1988c. "Crença e identidade: campo religioso e mudança cultural." Unpublished MS.

———. 1985. *A memória do sagrado*. São Paulo: Paulinas.

———. 1981. *Os sacerdotes de viola*. Petrópolis: Vozes.

———. 1980. *Os deuses do povo*. São Paulo: Brasiliense.

———. 1977a. "Religião, campo religioso e relação entre religião erudita e religião do povo." In *Religião e catolicismo do povo*, edited by Riolando Azzi *et al*. Curitíba: Cadernos da Universidade Católica do Paraná.

———. 1977b. "O número dos eleitos." *Religião e sociedade* 3.

Brettell, Caroline. 1990. "The Priest and his People: The Contractual Basis for Religious Practice in Rural Portugal." In *Religious Orthodoxy and Popular Faith in European Society*, edited by Ellen Badone. Princeton: Princeton University Press.

Brown, Diana. 1986. *Umbanda: Religion and Politics in Urban Brazil*. Ann Arbor: University of Michigan Press.

———. 1985. "Uma história da umbanda no Rio." In *Umbanda e política*, edited by Diana Brown *et al*. Rio de Janeiro: ISER.

———. 1977. "Umbanda e classes sociais," *Religião e sociedade* 1: 31–42.

Bruneau, Thomas C. 1982. *The Church in Brazil*. Austin: University of Texas Press.

———. 1980. "The Catholic Church and Development in Latin America: The Role of the Basic Christian Communities." *World Development* 8: 535–544.

──────. 1974. *The Political Transformation of the Brazilian Catholic Church.* New York: Cambridge University Press.

Brusco, Elizabeth. 1986. "The Household Basis of Evangelical Religion and the Reformation of Machismo in Colombia." Ph.D. diss., Department of Anthropology, City University of New York.

Burdick, John. 1991. "Observações sobre a campanha da fraternidade de 1988 na Baixada Fluminense." *Comunicações do ISER* 40: 42–47.

Caccia Bava, Silvio. 1981. "O movimento de onibus: a articulação de um movimento reivindicatório de periferia." *Revista e debates* 1.

Caldeira, Teresa Pires do Rio. 1984. *A política dos outros.* São Paulo: Brasiliense.

Carvalho Soares, Mariza de. 1983. "É permitido distribuir 'santinho' na porta da igreja?" *Comunicações do ISER* 4.

Castanho, Dom Amaury. 1986. "Caminhos das CEBs no Brasil." *Revista eclesiastica Brasileira* 46: 663–665.

Castells, Manuel. 1983. *The City and the Grassroots.* Berkeley: University of California Press.

CELAM. 1969. *A igreja na atual transformação da América Latina á luz do concílio: conclusões de Medellín.* Petrópolis: Vozes.

Centro de Estudos Migratórios. 1986. *Desperta-2.* 12th ed. São Paulo: Paulinas.

Christian, William. 1972. *Person and God in a Spanish Valley.* New York: Seminar.

Cintra, Raimundo. 1984. *Candomblé e umbanda.* São Paulo: Paulinas.

──────. 1978. "Algumas pistas para a pastoral dos cultos afro-brasileiros." In *A religião do povo,* edited by B. Beni dos Santos. São Paulo: Paulinas.

Cleary, Edward. 1985. *Crisis and Change: The Church in Latin America Today.* Maryknoll: Orbis.

Coleman, Kenneth. In press. "Protestantism in El Salvador: The Political Implications of Religious Belief." In *Rethinking Pentecostalism in Latin America,* edited by David Stoll and Virginia Burnett. Philadelphia: Temple University Press.

Comaroff, Jean. 1985. *Body of Power, Spirit of Resistance.* Chicago: University of Chicago Press.

Comblin, José. 1987. "Os leigos." *Comunicações do ISER* 26: 26–37.

Combs-Schilling, M. E. 1989. *Sacred Performances: Islam, Sexuality and Sacrifice.* New York: Columbia University Press.

Conferência Nacional de Bispos do Brasil (CNBB). 1988. *Caderno da campanha da fraternidade.* São Paulo: Paulinas.

──────. 1979. *Comunidades eclesiais de base no Brasil: experiências e perspectivas.* São Paulo: Paulinas.

Cook, Maria Lorena. 1990. "Organizing Opposition in the Teacher's Movement in Oaxaca." In *Popular Movements and Political Change in Mexico,* edited by Joe Foweraker and Ann L. Craig. Boulder: Lynne Rienner.

Costa, Haroldo. 1982. *Fala, crioulo.* Rio de Janeiro: Record.

Crapanzano, Vincent, and Vivian Garrison, eds. 1977. *Case Studies in Spirit Possession.* New York: Wiley.

Cucchiari, Salvatore. 1990. "Between Shame and Sanctification: Patriarchy and its Transformation in Sicilian Pentecostalism." *American Ethnologist* 17: 687–707.

Dabul, Lygia. 1987. "Um tanto da história de Xerém: análise social e eclesial." In CEDI, *Unidade e prática da fé: pastoral ecumênica da terra em Xerém.* Rio de Janeiro: CEDI.

———. 1984. "Missão de conscientização: agentes e camponeses em experiências comunitárias." In *Cooperativismo e coletivização no campo: questões sobre a prática da igreja popular no Brasil,* edited by Neide Esterci. Rio de Janeiro: Marco Zero.

Damaceno, Caetana. 1990. "Cantando para subir: orixá no altar, santo no peji." Master's thesis, Universidade Federal de Rio de Janeiro.

Daneel, M. L. 1971. *Old and New in Southern Shona Independent Churches.* The Hague: Mouton.

De Kadt, Emanuel. 1970. *Catholic Radicals in Brazil.* London: Oxford University Press.

Della Cava, Ralph. 1989. "The 'People's Church,' the Vatican, and the *Abertura.*" In *Democratizing Brazil,* edited by Alfred Stepan. New York: Oxford University Press.

———. 1986. "A igreja e a abertura, 1974–1985." In *A igreja nas bases em tempo de transição,* edited by Paulo Krischke and Scott Mainwaring. Porto Alegre: LPM.

———. 1985. "A ofensiva vaticana." *Religião e sociedade* 12(3): 34–53.

———. 1978. "Política a curto prazo e religião a longo prazo." *Encontros com a civilização brasileira* 1: 242–258.

———. 1976. "Catholicism and Society in Twentieth-Century Brazil." *Latin American Research Review* 11(2): 7–50.

De Theije, Marjo. 1990. "'Brotherhoods Throw More Weight Around Than the Pope': Catholic Traditionalism and the Lay Brotherhoods of Brazil." *Sociological Analysis* 51(2): 189–204.

Dodson, Michael. 1979. "Liberation Theology and Christian Radicalism in Contemporary Latin America." *Journal of Latin American Studies* 2(1): 203–222.

Doimo, Ana Maria. 1989. "Social Movements and the Catholic Church in Vitória, Brazil." In *The Progressive Church in Latin America,* edited by Scott Mainwaring and Alexander Wilde. Notre Dame: University of Notre Dame Press.

———. 1986. "Os rumos dos movimentos sociais nos caminhos da religiosidade." In *A igreja nas bases no tempo de transição,* edited by Paulo Krischke and Scott Mainwaring. Porto Alegre: LPM.

———. 1984. *Movimento social urbano: igreja e participação popular.* Petrópolis: Vozes.

Duarte, Laura Maria. 1983. *Isto não se aprende na escola.* Petrópolis: Vozes.

Duarte, Luiz Fernando Dias. 1986. *Da vida nervosa nas classes trabalhadoras urbanas.* Rio de Janeiro: Zahar.

———. 1983. "Pluridade religiosa nas sociedades complexas e religiosidade das classes trabalhadoras." *Boletim do museu nacional* 41.

Dzidzienyo, Anani. 1971. *The Position of Blacks in Brazilian Society.* London: Minority Rights Group.

Eckstein, Susan, ed. 1989. *Power and Popular Protest: Latin American Social Movements.* Berkeley: University of California Press.

Escobar, Arturo. 1992. "Culture, Practice, and Politics: Anthropology and the Study of Social Movements." *Critique of Anthropology.*

Escobar, Arturo, and Sonia Alvarez, eds. 1992. *The Making of Social Movements in Latin America: Identity, Strategy and Democracy.* Boulder: Westview Press.

Evans-Pritchard, Edward. 1956. *Nuer Religion.* Oxford: Clarendon Press.

Fardon, Robert. 1990. *Between God, the Dead, and the Wild.* Washington: Smithsonian Institution Press.

Fauset, Arthur Huff. 1971. *Black Gods of the Metropolis: Negro Religious Cults of the Urban North.* Philadelphia: University of Pennsylvania Press.

Fernandes, Florestan. 1969. *The Negro in Brazilian Society.* New York: Columbia University Press.

Fernandes, Rubem Cesar. 1984. " 'Religiões populares': uma visao parcial da literatura recente." *Boletim informativo e bibliográfico de ciências sociais* 18: 3–26.

———. 1983. "Conservador ou progressista: uma questão de conjuntura." *Religião e sociedade* 9.

———. 1982. *Os cavaleiros do bom Jesus.* São Paulo: Brasiliense.

———. 1977. "O debate entre sociólogos a propósito dos pentecostais." *Cadernos do ISER* 6.

Ferreira de Camargo, Candido Procópio. 1973. *Católicos, protestantes, espíritas.* Petrópolis: Vozes.

———. 1971. *Igreja e desenvolvimento.* São Paulo.

Ferreira de Camargo, Candido Procópio, Beatriz de Souza, and Antônio Pierucci. 1980. "Comunidades eclesiais de base." In *São Paulo: povo em movimento,* edited by Paul Singer and Vinicius Brant. Petrópolis: Vozes.

Ferreira dos Santos, Anizio. 1988. *Eu negro: discriminação racial no Brasil, existe?* São Paulo: Loyola.

Figge, Horst H. 1983. *Umbanda: religião, magia e possessão.* Teresópolis: Jaguary.

Firth, Raymond. 1967. *Tikopia Ritual and Belief.* London: Allen and Unwin.

Fiske, John. 1992. "Cultural Studies and the Culture of Everyday Life." In *Cultural Studies,* edited by Lawrence Grossberg *et al.* New York: Routledge.

Follman, José Ivo. 1987. "O 'ser católico': diferentes identidades religiosas." *Comunicações do ISER* 26: 17–25.

Fontaine, Pierre-Michel, ed. 1985. *Race, Class and Power in Brazil.* Los Angeles: University of California Press.

———. 1980. "Research in the Political Economy of Afro-Latin America." *Latin American Research Review* 15.

Fornaro, Robert J. 1985. "Supernatural Power, Sexuality, and the Paradigm of 'Women's Space' in Religion and Culture." *Sex Roles* 12(3, 4): 295–302.

Fowler, Loretta. 1987. *Shared Symbols, Contested Meanings: Gros Ventre Culture and History, 1778–1984.* Ithaca: Cornell University Press.

Frade, Maria de Cáscia Nascimento. 1987. "Santa de casa: a devoção á Odetinha no cemitério São João Batista." Ph.D. diss., Universidade Federal de Rio de Janeiro.

Frederico, Celso. 1979. *Consciência operária no Brasil.* São Paulo: Ática.

Freire, Paulo. 1970. *A Pedagogy of the Oppressed.* Translated by Myra Bergman Ramos. New York: Seabury Press.

Freston, Paul. In press. "Protestants and Brazilian Politics since Redemocratization." In *Rethinking Pentecostalism in Latin America,* edited by David Stoll and Virginia Burnett. Philadelphia: Temple University Press.

Freyre, Gilberto. 1959. *New World in the Tropics: The Culture of Modern Brazil.* New York: Knopf.

———. 1945. *Brazil: An Interpretation.* New York: Knopf.

Fry, Peter, and Gary Howe. 1975. "Duas respostas á aflição: umbanda e pentecostalismo." *Debate e crítica* 6: 75–95.

FUNDREM. 1982. *Plano de desenvolvimento metropolitano: caracterização da região metropolitana do Rio de Janeiro.* Rio de Janeiro: SECPLAN.

———. 1979. *Unidades urbanas integradas do oeste: plano diretor.* Vol. II. Rio de Janeiro: SECPLAN.

Gaiger, Luís Inácio. 1987. *Agentes religiosos e camponeses sem terra no sul do Brasil.* Petrópolis: Vozes.

Geertz, Clifford. 1960. *The Religion of Java.* New York: The Free Press.

Genovese, Eugene. 1974. *Roll, Jordan, Roll: The World the Slaves Made.* New York: Vintage.

Gilkes, Cheryl Townsend. 1987. "Some Mother's Son and Some Father's Daughter: Gender and Biblical Language in Afro-Christian Worship Tradition." In *Shaping New Vision: Gender and Values in American Culture,* edited by Clarissa Atkinson *et al.* Ann Arbor: UMI Research Press.

Gill, Lesley. 1990. "'Like a Veil to Cover Them': Women and the Pentecostal Movement in La Paz." *American Ethnologist* 17: 708–721.

Gluck, Sherna, and Daphne Patai, eds. 1991. *Women's Words: The Feminist Practice of Oral History.* New York: Routledge.

Gomes, José. 1985. "Religião e política: os pentecostais no Recife." Ph.D. diss., Federal University of Pernambuco.

Gomez de Souza, Luiz Alberto. 1992a. "Crise é vida." *Vemelho e branco* 23/24: 22–23.

———. 1992b. "É bom que haja crise." *Vermelho e branco* 26: 8–9.

———. 1984. *A JUC: os estudantes católicos e a política.* Petrópolis: Vozes.

———. 1981. *Classes populares e igreja nos caminhos da história.* Petrópolis: Vozes.

Gordon, Edward. 1991. "Anthropology and Liberation." In *Decolonizing Anthropology,* edited by Faye V. Harrison. Washington: Society for Black Anthropologists.

Gregory, Affonso. 1973. *CEBs: utopia ou realidade?* Petrópolis: Vozes.

Guimarães, Almir. 1978. *Comunidade eclesial de base no Brasil: uma nova maneira de ser igreja.* Petrópolis: Vozes.

Gutierrez, Gustavo. 1980. "A irrupção do pobre na América Latina e as comunidades cristãs populares." In *A igreja que surge da base: eclesiologia das comunidades cristãs de base,* edited by Sérgio Torres. São Paulo: Paulinas.

———. 1973. *A Theology of Liberation.* Maryknoll: Orbis.

Harris, Marvin. 1964. *Patterns of Race in the Americas.* New York: Walker and Company.

Harrison, Faye V. 1991a. "Anthropology as an Agent of Transformation." In *Decolonizing Anthropology,* edited by Faye V. Harrison. Washington: Society for Black Anthropologists.

————. 1991b. "Ethnography as Politics." In *Decolonizing Anthropology,* edited by Faye V. Harrison. Washington: Society for Black Anthropologists.

Hasenbalg, Carlos A. 1979. *Discriminação e desigualdades raciais no Brasil.* Rio de Janeiro: Graal.

Hauck, Joao Fagundes, *et al.* 1985. *História da igreja no Brasil: ensaio de interpretação a partir do povo.* Vol. II, part 2. Petrópolis: Vozes.

Heath, Deborah. 1992. "Fashion, Anti-Fashion and Heteroglossia in Urban Senegal." *American Ethnologist* 19(1): 19–33.

Hebdige, Dick. 1979. *Subculture: The Elements of Style.* New York: Routledge.

Hewitt, Ted. 1991. *Base Christian Communities and Social Change in Brazil.* Lincoln: University of Nebraska Press.

————. 1990. "Religion and the Consolidation of Democracy in Brazil: The Role of the Comunidades Eclesiais de Base." *Sociological Analysis* 51(2): 139–153.

Hock-Smith, Judith, and Anita Spring, eds. 1978. *Women in Ritual and Symbolic Roles.* New York: Plenum.

Hodge, Robert, and Gunther Kress. 1988. *Social Semiotics.* Ithaca: Cornell University Press.

Hoffnagel, Judith. 1978. "The Believers: Pentecostalism in a Brazilian City." Ph.D. diss., Indiana University.

Holquist, Michael. 1990. *Dialogism.* New York: Routledge.

hooks, bell. 1990. *Yearning: Race, Gender, and Cultural Politics.* Boston: South End Press.

Hoornaert, Eduardo. 1986. "Os três fatores da nova hegemonia dentro da igreja católica no Brasil." *REB* 26: 371–384.

————. 1978. "Comunidades eclesiais de base: dez anos de experiência." *REB* 38: 474–502.

Horton, Robin. 1971. "African Conversion." *Africa* 41: 85–108.

Houtart, François. 1979. "Religion et lutte des classes en Amérique Latine." *Social Compass* 26: 195–236.

————. 1977. "Religion et champs politique: cadre théorique pour l'étude des sociétés capitalistes péripheriques." *Social Compass* 24: 265–272.

Howe, Gary N. 1977. "Representações religiosas e capitalismo: uma 'leitura' estruturalista do pentecostalismo no Brasil." *Cadernos do ISER* 6: 39–48.

Humphrey, John. 1987. *Gender and Work in the Third World: Sexual Divisions in Brazilian Industry.* London: Tavistock.

————. 1984. "The Growth of Female Employment in Brazilian Manufacturing Industry in the 1970s." *Journal of Development Studies* 20: 224–247.

Ianni, Octávio. 1972. *Raças e classes no Brasil.* 2nd ed. Rio de Janeiro: Editora Civilização Brasileira.

IBGE (Instituto Brasileiro de Geografia e Estatisticos). 1982. *Sumário de dados dos censos, 1940–1980.* Rio de Janeiro: IBGE.

————. 1940–1980. *Recenseamento demográfico*. Brasília: IBGE.

Idígoras, J. L. 1983. *Vocabulário teológico*. São Paulo: Paulinas.

Ireland, Rowan. In press. "The Politics of Brazilian Pentecostals." In *Rethinking Pentecostalism in Latin America*, edited by David Stoll and Virginia Burnett. Philadelphia: Temple University Press.

————. 1992. *Kingdoms Come: Religion and Politics in Brazil*. Pittsburgh: Pittsburgh University Press.

————. 1981. "The Prophecy that Failed." *Listening: Journal of Religion and Culture* 16: 253–264.

Janzen, J. 1978. *The Quest for Therapy in Lower Zaire*. Berkeley: University of California Press.

Johnson, Richard, *et al.*, eds. *Making Histories: Studies in History-Writing and Politics*. Minneapolis: University of Minnesota Press.

Jules-Rosette, Bennetta. 1975. *African Apostles*. Ithaca: Cornell University Press.

Kanagy, Conrad L. 1990. "The Formation and Development of a Protestant Conversion Movement among the Highland Quichua of Ecuador." *Sociological Analysis* 51: 205–217.

Kardec, Allan. 1987. *O livro dos espíritos*. 67th ed. Rio de Janeiro: Federação Espírita Brasileira.

Keck, Margaret. 1989. "The New Unionism in the Brazilian Transition." In *Democratizing Brazil*, edited by Alfred Stepan. New York: Oxford University Press.

Keesing, Roger. 1985. "Kwaio Women Speak: The Micropolitics of Autobiography in a Solomon Island Society." *American Anthropologist* 87: 27–39.

————. 1982. *Kwaio Religion*. New York: Columbia.

Kent, R. K. 1978. "Palmares: An African State in Brazil." In *Maroon Societies*, edited by Richard Price. Baltimore: Johns Hopkins University Press.

Kleinman, Arthur. 1980. *Patients and Healers in the Context of Culture*. Berkeley: University of California Press.

Kliewer, G. U. 1982. "Assembléia de Deus e eleições num município do interior de Matto Grosso." *Comunicações do ISER* 3.

Kornis, Monica, and Dora Flaksman. 1984. "Fábrica Nacional de Motores." In Alzir Alves de Abreu and Israel Beloch, coords., *Dicionário histórico-biográfico brasileiro*, Vol. 2. Rio de Janeiro: Forense-Universitária/Finep.

Lalive d'Epinay, Christian. 1977. "Religião, espiritualidade, e sociedade." *Cadernos do ISER* 6: 5–10.

————. 1969. *Haven of the Masses: A Study of the Pentecostal Movement in Chile*. London: Lutterworth Press.

Lambek, Michael. 1982. *Human Spirits*. Cambridge: Cambridge University Press.

Lancaster, Roger, 1987. *Thanks to God and the Revolution*. New York: Columbia University Press.

Landes, Ruth. 1947. *A City of Women*. New York: Macmillan.

Landim, Leilah. 1989. *Sinais dos tempos: igrejas e seitas no Brasil*. Rio de Janeiro: ISER.

Lasker, Judith. 1981. "Choosing Among Therapies: Illness Behavior in the Ivory Coast." *Social Science and Medicine* 15A: 157–168.

Lawless, Elaine J. 1988. *Handmaidens of the Lord.* Philadelphia: University of Pennsylvania Press.

Leers, Bernardo, 1963. "A estrutura do culto dominical na zona rural." *Revista da conferencia dos religiosos do Brasil* 99: 521–534.

Lenz, Flávio. 1988. "Três versoes da fraternidade." *Comunicações do ISER* 28: 84–89.

Lerch, Patricia. 1982. "An Explanation for the Predominance of Women in the Umbanda Cults of Porto Alegre, Brazil." *Urban Anthropology* 11(2): 237–261.

Lernoux, Penny. 1989. *People of God: The Struggle for World Catholicism.* New York: Viking.

———. 1980. "The Latin American Church." *Latin American Research Review* 15(2): 201–211.

———. 1979. "The Long Path to Puebla." In *Puebla and Beyond: Documentation and Commentary,* edited by John Eagleson and Philip Scharper. Maryknoll: Orbis.

Levine, Daniel H. 1992. *Popular Voices in Latin American Catholicism.* Princeton: Princeton University Press.

———. 1990. "Popular Groups, Popular Culture, and Popular Religion." *Comparative Studies in Society and History* 32(4): 718–764.

———. 1986. "Introduction." In *Religion and Political Conflict in Latin America,* edited by Daniel Levine. Chapel Hill: University of North Carolina Press.

Levine, Daniel H., and Scott Mainwaring. 1989. "Religion and Popular Protest in Latin America: Contrasting Experiences." In *Power and Popular Protest,* edited by Susan Eckstein. Berkeley: University of California Press.

Lewis, J. Lowell. 1992. *Ring of Liberation: Deceptive Discourse in Brazilian Capoeira.* Chicago: University of Chicago Press.

Lienhardt, Godfrey. 1961. *Divinity and Experience.* Oxford: Clarendon.

Lima, Delcio Monteiro de. 1987. *Os demônios descem do norte.* Rio de Janeiro: Francisco Alves.

Lincoln, Bruce. 1985. "Notes Toward a Theory of Religion and Revolution." In *Religion, Rebellion, Revolution: An Interdisciplinary and Cross-Cultural Collection of Essays,* edited by Bruce Lincoln. New York: St. Martin's Press.

Low, Setha, and Dora Lee Davis, eds. 1989. *Gender, Health, and Illness: The Case of Nerves.* New York: Hemisphere.

Loyola, M. A. 1982. "Cure des corps et cure des âmes: les rapports entre les medicines et les religions dans la banlieue de Rio." *Actes de la recherche em sciences sociales* 43.

Lustosa, José. 1958. *Cidade de Duque de Caxias: desenvolvimento histórico do município.* Rio de Janeiro: IBGE.

Macêdo, Carmen Cinira. 1986a. *Tempo de gênesis: o povo das comunidades eclesiais de base.* São Paulo: Brasiliense.

———. 1986b. *A reprodução da desigualdade.* 2nd ed. São Paulo: Vertice.

MacGaffey, Wyatt. 1983. *Modern Kongo Prophets: Religion in a Plural Society.* Bloomington: Indiana University Press.

Mainwaring, Scott. 1989. "Grassroots Popular Movements and the Struggle for Democracy: Nova Iguacu." In *Democratizing Brazil,* edited by Alfred Stepan. New York: Oxford University Press.

———. 1986a. *The Catholic Church and Politics in Brazil, 1916–1985.* Stanford: Stanford University Press.

———. 1986b. "A igreja católica e o movimento popular: Nova Iguaçu, 1974–1985." In *A igreja nas bases no tempo de transição,* edited by Paulo Krischke and Scott Mainwaring. Porto Alegre: LPM.

———. 1986c. "Brazil: The Catholic Church and the Popular Movement in Nova Iguacu, 1974–1985." In *Religion and Political Conflict in Latin America,* edited by Daniel Levine. Chapel Hill: University of North Carolina Press.

Marcondes de Moura, Carlos Eugênio, orgs. 1987. *Candomblé: desvendando identidades.* São Paulo: EMW Editores.

Mariz, Cecilia. 1989. "Religion and Coping with Poverty in Brazil," Ph.D. diss., Boston University.

Martin, David. 1990. *Tongues of Fire.* Oxford: Basil Blackwell.

Martin, JoAnn. 1990. "Motherhood and Power: The Production of a Women's Culture of Politics in a Mexican Community." *American Ethnologist* 17(3): 470–490.

Maués, Raimundo. 1987. "A tensão constitutiva do catolicismo: catolicismo popular e contrôle eclesiástico." Ph.D. diss., Universidade Federal do Rio de Janeiro.

Medeiros, Leonilda Sêrvolo. 1983. "Lutas sociais no campo no Rio de Janeiro." Ph.D. diss., Universidade Federal de Rio de Janeiro.

Melucci, Alberto. 1989. *Nomads of the Present.* Philadelphia: Temple University Press.

Mesters, Carlos. 1986a. *Círculos bíblicos: guia do dirigente.* 8th ed. Petrópolis: Vozes.

———. 1986b. *O profeta Elias.* São Paulo: Paulinas.

———. 1984. *A sabedoria do povo.* 8th ed. Petrópolis: Vozes.

———. 1971. *Palavra de Deus na história do homem.* Petrópolis: Vozes.

Minha-Ha, Trinh. 1989. *Woman, Native, Other.* Bloomington: Indiana University Press.

Minocha, A. 1980. "Medical Pluralism and Health Services." *Social Science and Medicine* 14B: 217–223.

Monteiro, Duglas Teixeira. 1979. "Igrejas, seitas, e agências: aspectos de um ecumenismo popular." In *A cultura do povo,* edited by Carmen Macêdo *et al.* São Paulo: Cortez e Moraes.

Montero, Paula. 1985. *Da doença á desordem: a magia na umbanda.* Rio de Janeiro: Graal.

Morais, J. F. Regis de. 1982. *Os bispos e a política no Brasil.* São Paulo: Cortez.

Mullings, Leith. 1984. *Therapy, Ideology and Social Change: Mental Healing in Urban Ghana.* Berkeley: University of California Press.

Munoz, Ronaldo. 1982. "Sobre a eclêsiologia na America Latina." In *A igreja que surge da base,* edited by Sergio Torres *et al.* São Paulo: Paulinas.

Nash, June. 1979. *We Eat the Mines and the Mines Eat Us.* New York: Columbia University Press.

Novaes, Regina. 1985a. *Os escolhidos de Deus.* Rio de Janeiro: Marco Zero.

———. 1985b. "Os negros entre os episcopais: cor e lugar social." In *O negro evangélico,* edited by Regina Novaes and Maria da Graça Floriano. Rio de Janeiro: Marco Zero.

———. 1982. "Os crentes e as eleições: uma experiência de campo." *Comunicações do ISER* 3.

Oliveira, Isabel Ribeiro de. 1988. *Trabalho e política: as origens do partido dos trabalhadores.* Petrópolis: Vozes.

Oliveira, Pedro A. Ribeiro. 1986. "Comunidade, igreja e poder: em busca de um conceito sociológico de 'igreja'." *Religião e sociedade* 13(3): 43–60.

———. 1984. "Comunidade e massa: desafio da pastoral popular." *Revista eclesiástica Brasileira* 44.

———. 1983. "Oprimidos: a opção pela igreja." *Revista eclesiástica Brasileira* 41(164): 643–653.

Ong, Aihwa. 1987. *Spirits of Resistance and Capitalist Discipline: Factory Women in Malaysia.* Albany: State University of New York Press.

Oro, Pedro. 1988. "Negros e brancos nas religiões afro-brasileiras no Rio Grande do Sul." *Comunicações do ISER* 28: 33–44.

Ortiz, Renato. 1983. "O mercado religioso." *Comunicações do ISER* 5.

———. 1978. *A morte branca do feiticeiro negro.* Petrópolis: Vozes.

Otto, Dana. 1974. "A conversão no contexto dos cursilhos de cristandade." *Cadernos do ISER* 1: 3–20.

Paiva, Vanilda. 1985. "A igreja moderna no Brasil." In *Igreja e questão agrária,* edited by Vanilda Paiva. São Paulo: Loyola.

———. 1984. "Anotações para um estudo sobre populismo católico e educação popular." In *Perspectivas e dilemmas de educação popular,* edited by Vanilda Paiva. Rio de Janeiro: Graal.

Passo Castro, Gustavo do. 1987. *As comunidades do dom: um estudo de CEBs no Recife.* Recife: Fundação Joaquim Nabuco.

Patterson, Orlando. 1967. *The Sociology of Slavery.* Cranbury, N.J.: Fairleigh Dickinson University Press.

Perani, Claudio. 1984. "Igreja de nordeste: breves notas histórica-críticas." *Cadernos do centro de estudos e ação social* 94: 53–73.

———. 1982. "Pastoral Popular: serviço ou poder?" *CEAS* 82: 7–19.

———. 1981. "Comunidade eclesial de base e movimento popular." *CEAS,* 75: 25–33.

Perelberg, Rosine. 1980. "Umbanda and Psychoanalysis as Different Ways of Interpreting Mental Illness." *British Journal of Medical Psychiatry* 53: 323–332.

Petrini, João Carlos. 1984. *CEBs: um novo sujeito popular.* Rio de Janeiro: Paz e Terra.

Pierson, Donald. 1967. *Negros in Brazil: A Study of Race Contact in Bahia.* Carbondale: University of Illinois Press.

Poblete, Renato. 1979. "From Medellín to Puebla." *Journal of Interamerican Studies* 21(1): 31–44.

Poewe, Karla. 1978. "Matriliny in the Throes of Change." *Africa* 48: 335–365.

Pressel, Esther. 1980. "Spirit Magic in the Social Relations Between Men and Women (São Paulo)." In *A World of Men*, edited by Erika Bourguignon. New York: Praeger.

———. 1977. "Negative Spiritism in Experienced Brazilian Umbanda Mediums." In *Case Studies in Spirit Possession*, edited by Vincent Crapanzano and Vivian Garrison. New York: Wiley.

———. 1974. "Umbanda Trance and Possession in São Paulo, Brazil." In *Trance, Healing and Hallucination*, edited by Felicitas Goodman *et al.* New York: Wiley.

———. 1973. "Umbanda in São Paulo: Religious Innovation in a Developing Society." In *Religion, Altered States of Consciousness, and Social Change*, edited by Erika Bourguignon. Columbus: Ohio University Press.

Pureza, José. 1982. *Memória camponesa.* Rio de Janeiro: Zahar.

Queiroz, Suely Robles Reis de. 1982. *A abolição da escravidão.* São Paulo: Brasiliense.

Quimby, Lucy. 1979. "Islam, Sex Roles and Modernization in Bobo-Dioulasso." In *The New Religions of Africa*, edited by Bennetta Jules-Rosette. Norwood: Ablex.

Raboteau, Albert. 1978. *Slave Religion.* New York: Oxford University Press.

Ramalho, Jether P. 1977. "Algumas notas sobre duas perspectivas de pastoral popular." *Cadernos do ISER* 6: 30–39.

Rebel, Hermann. 1989. "Cultural Hegemony and Class Experience: A Critical Reading of Recent Ethnological; Historical Approaches." *American Ethnologist* 16(2): 350–368.

Reichel-Dolmatoff, Gerardo. 1971. *Amazonian Cosmos.* Chicago: University of Chicago Press.

Ribeiro, Helcion. 1985. *Religiosidade popular na teología latino-americana.* São Paulo: Paulinas.

Robins, Catherine. 1979. "Conversion, Life Crises and Stability in the East Africa Revival." In *The New Religions of Africa*, edited by Bennetta Jules-Rosette. Norwood: Ablex.

Rodrigues Santos, Solange. 1986. "Rumo á nova sociedade?" Master's thesis, State University of Rio de Janeiro.

Rolim, Francisco Cartaxo. 1987. "Afinal, o que estaria levando as pessoas ao pentecostalismo?" Paper presented at ANPOCS seminar on Religious Diversity.

———. 1985. *Pentecostais no Brasil: uma interpretação sócio-religiosa.* Petrópolis: Vozes.

———. 1980. *Religião e classes populares.* Petrópolis: Vozes.

Romano, Roberto. 1979. *Brasil: igreja contra estado.* São Paulo: Kairos.

Romanucci-Schwartz, Lola. 1969. "The Hierarchy of Resort in Curative Practices: The Admiralty Islands, Melanesia." *Journal of Health and Social Behavior* 10: 201–209.

Rose, Susan. 1987. "Women Warriors: The Negotiation of Gender in a Charismatic Community." *Sociological Analysis* 48(3): 245–258.

Saffiotti, Heleieth. 1984. *Mulher brasileira: opresão e exploração*. Rio de Janeiro: Achiame.

Saldanha, Rilza Ferreira. 1969. "Duque de Caxias, espectos históricos." *Coleções de monografias*, No. 446. Rio de Janeiro: Fundaçao IBGE.

Salem, Helena, ed. 1981. *A igreja dos oprimidos*. São Paulo: Editora Debates.

Sallnow, Michael, and John Eade, eds. *Contesting the Sacred*. New York: Routledge.

Santos, Joel Rufino de. 1985. *Zumbi*. São Paulo: Moderna.

Santos, Micênio. 1988. "O treize de maio." *Comunicações do ISER* 28: 72–78.

Schieffelin, Edward L. 1976. *The Sorrow of the Lonely and the Burning of the Dancers*. New York: St. Martin's Press.

Schmink, Marianne. 1986. "Women and Urban Industrial Development in Brazil." In *Women and Change in Latin America*, edited by June Nash and Helen Safa. South Hadley, Mass.: Bergin and Garvey.

Scott, James. 1990. *Domination and the Arts of Resistance*. New Haven: Yale University Press.

Sharma, Ursula. 1992. *Complementary Medicine Today*. New York: Routledge.

———. 1973. "Theodicy and the Doctrine of Karma." *Man* 8: 347–364.

Silva, Nelson do Valle. 1978. "Black-White Income Differentials: Brazil, 1960." Ph.D. disser., University of Michigan.

Skidmore, Thomas. 1974. *Black into White: Race and Nationality in Brazilian Thought*. New York: Oxford.

Slater, Candace. 1990. *City Steeple, City Streets*. Berkeley: University of California Press.

———. 1986. *Trail of Miracles*. Berkeley: University of California Press.

Slater, David, ed. 1985. *New Social Movements and the State in Latin America*. Amsterdam: CEDLA.

Smith, Brian H. 1982. *The Church and Politics in Chile: Challenges to Modern Catholicism*. Princeton: Princeton University Press.

———. 1975. "Religious and Social Change: Classical Theories and New Formulations in the Context of Recent Developments in Latin America." *Latin American Research Review* 10(2): 3–34.

Smith, Brian H., and Sanks Howlands. 1977. "Liberation Ecclesiology: Praxis, Theory, Praxis." *Theological Studies* 38(1): 3–38.

Souza, Beatriz de. 1969. *A experiência da salvação*. São Paulo: Duas Cidades.

Souza, Neusa Santos. 1983. *Tornar-se negro*. Rio de Janeiro: Graal.

Souza Lima, Luiz Gonzaga de. 1980. "Comunidades eclesiais de base." *Revista de cultura vozes* 74(5): 61–82.

———. 1979. *Evolução política dos católicos e da igreja no Brasil*. Petrópolis: Vozes.

Spencer, Paul. 1990. "The Riddled Course: Theories of Age and its Transformation." In *Anthropology and the Riddle of the Sphinx*, edited by Paul Spencer. New York: Routledge.

Starn, Orin. 1991. "*Con los llanques todo barro*": *reflexiones sobre rondas campesinas, protesta rural y nuevos movimentos sociales.* Lima: Instituto de Estudios Peruanos.

Stepan, Alfred. 1988. *Rethinking Military Politics.* Princeton: Princeton University Press.

Stevens, Evelyn. 1973. "Machismo and Marianismo." *Society* 10: 57–63.

Stoll, David. 1990. *Is Latin America Turning Protestant?* Berkeley: University of California Press.

Stoll, David, and Virginia Burnett, eds. 1993. *Pentecostal Politics in Latin America.* Philadelphia: Temple University Press.

Stoll, Sandra. 1986. "Púlpito e palanque: religião e política nas eleições de 1982 num município da grande São Paulo." Ph.D. diss., Universidade Estadual de Campinas.

———. 1982. "Embú, eleições de 1982: a mobilização política de CEBs e pentecostais." *Comunicações do ISER* 3.

Straubhaar, Joseph. 1989. "Television and Video in the Transition from Military to Civilian Rule in Brazil." *Latin American Research Review* 24(1): 140–154.

Sutton, David. 1991. "Is Anybody Out There? Anthropology and the Question of Audience." *Critique of Anthropology* 11(1): 91–104.

Tamez, Elsa, ed. 1987. *Against Machismo.* Oak Park: Meyer Stone Books.

Taussig, Michael. 1992. "Violence and Resistance in the Americas: The Legacy of Conquest." In *The Nervous System*, by Michael Taussig. New York: Routledge.

———. 1987. *Shamanism, Colonialism, and the Wild Man.* Chicago: University of Chicago Press.

———. 1980. *The Devil and Commodity Fetishism in South America.* Chapel Hill: University of North Carolina Press.

Teixeira, Faustino Luiz Couto. 1988. *Comunidades eclesias de base: bases teológicas.* Petrópolis: Vozes.

Thompson, Catherine. 1985. "The Power to Pollute and the Power to Preserve: Perceptions of Female Power in a Hindu Village." *Social Science and Medicine* 21(6): 701–711.

Touraine, Alain. 1983. *Anti-Nuclear Protest: The Opposition to Nuclear Energy in France.* Cambridge: Cambridge University Press.

———. 1981. *The Voice and the Eye: An Analysis of Social Movements.* Cambridge: Cambridge University Press.

Trawick, M. 1988. "Spirits and Voices in Tamil Songs." *American Ethnologist* 15: 193–215.

Trindade, Liana. 1982. "Exú: reinterpretações individualizadas de um mito." *Religião e sociedade* 8.

Turner, Victor. 1974. *Dramas, Fields and Metaphors.* Ithaca: Cornell University Press.

———. 1968. *The Drums of Affliction.* Oxford: Clarendon Press.

———. 1967. *The Forest of Symbols.* Ithaca: Cornell University Press.

Valente, Ana Lucia. 1987. *Ser negro no Brasil hoje.* São Paulo: Editora Moderna.

Van Den Hoogen, Lisette. 1990. "The Romanization of the Brazilian Church: Women's Participation in a Religious Association in Prados, Minas Gerais." *Sociological Analysis* 51(2): 171–188.

Velho, Yvonne. 1975. *A guerra do orixá*. Rio de Janeiro: Zahar.

Wagley, Charles, ed. 1952. *Race and Class in Rural Brazil*. New York: Columbia University Press.

Wallace, Anthony F. C. 1970. *The Death and Rebirth of the Seneca*. New York: Vintage.

Watson, Lawrence C., and Maria-Barbara Watson-Franke. 1985. *Interpreting Life Histories*. New Brunswick: Rutgers University Press.

Weber, Max. 1968. *Economy and Society*, edited by Guenther Roth and Claus Wittich. New York: Bedminster.

———. 1963. *The Sociology of Religion*. Boston: Beacon.

Webster, Peggy Lovell, and Jeffrey Dwyer. 1988. "The Cost of Being Non-White in Brazil." *Sociology and Social Research* 72 (January): 136–142.

Weller, Robert. 1987. "The Politics of Ritual Disguise: Repression and Response in Taiwanese Popular Religion." *Modern China* 13(1): 17–39.

Werbner, Richard. 1989. *Ritual Passage, Sacred Journey*. Washington: Smithsonian Institution Press.

———. 1985. "The Argument of Images: From Zion to the Wilderness in African Churches." In *Theoretical Explorations in Africa Religion,* edited by Wim van Binsbergen and Matthew Schoffeleers. London: KPI.

Willems, Emilio. 1967. *Followers of a New Faith*. Nashville: Vanderbilt University Press.

Williams, Brackette. 1991. *Stains on My Name, War in My Veins*. Durham: Duke University Press.

Woolard, K. 1985. "Language Variation and Cultural Hegemony: Toward an Integration of Sociolinguistic and Social Theory." *American Ethnologist* 12: 738–748.

Worsley, Peter. 1957. *The Trumpet Shall Sound*. London: MacGibbon.

Wyatt-Brown, Bertram. 1988. "The Mask of Obedience: Male Slave Psychology in the Old South." *American Historical Review* 93: 1228–1252.

Zaluar, Alba. 1985. *A máquina e a revolta*. São Paulo: Brasiliense.

———. 1983. *Os homens de Deus*. Rio de Janeiro: Zahar.

Zikmund, Barbara Brown. 1979. "The Feminist Thrust of Sectarian Christianity." In *Women of Spirit,* edited by Rosemary Ruether. New York: Simon and Schuster.

Index

Activists, 196–203; Catholic Church, 200–203, 225; women, 197–200
Adultery, 89
Adventists, 13
Africa, 49; influence in *umbanda*, 163; religion, 158–159, 163
Alagoas, 167
Amigadas, 89–90
Anastasia, 157
Angélico, Dom, 6
Aniceto, Father, 37–39, 40
Apostolate of Prayer, 35–37, 46, 71, 185, 188; domestic conflict, 96; literacy, 78; neighborhood associations, 190–191; women, 35–37
Assembléia, 40
Assembly of God, 4, 13, 56–66, 70, 101, 223; class distinctions, 73; conversion, 131, 133; courtship, 132, 137–138; economic standing of members, 70, 86; leadership, 70; literacy, 78–79; marriage, 137–138; membership, 70, 83–84, 86; men, 131; *mulatos,* 178; *negros,* 146, 172–181; occupations, 70; participation, 14, 83–84; political activity, 206–220, 229–230; seating arrangement, 62; view of sickness, 75; women, 84, 87, 108, 110, 130; youth, 119, 130–137, 142–145. See also *Crentes*; Pentecostals

Association of Black Religious and Seminarians, 156, 158

Baptism: *crentes,* 60, 62, 64; of the Holy Spirit, 64, 83
Baptists, 13, 62–63, 143
Benzedeiras, 34, 37, 242n.8
Bible circles, 2, 3, 12, 38, 73, 81, 185; consciousness-raising, 44, 194–196; domestic conflict, 95; literacy, 76, 77, 78, 79; *negros,* 152, 154, 157; recruiting members, 46, 96; women, 88, 92, 93, 94. See also Catholic Church
Biscateiros, 70, 80, 85, 91
Black Consciousness Movement, 250n.5
Boff, Leonardo, 189
Bom de vida, 22
Brazil: bishops, 2, 222; CEBs, 2, 3–4; economy, 213; military, 11, 218; pentecostals, 4; politics, 234n.9; religious migration, 7; social security, 214, 216; *umbandas,* 4; youth, 118, 119
Brotherhood Campaign of 1988, 156–160

Caboclos, 48, 49, 53, 54, 160, 163, 164, 165; domestic conflict, 99; food, 243n.25

275

Caminhada, 46
Candomblé, 47, 48, 243n.25, 251n.12
Carlos, Roberto, 144
Catholic Church, 68, 70, 163, 165–166,
221–230; activists, 200–203, 225;
conversion from, 139–142; economic
standing of members, 70; evangelism,
127; leadership, 70–71, 76, 211,
225; liturgical changes, 204, 205;
marriage, 123–124; men, 84; mulatos, 156–157, 158, 225; negros, 152–
160, 172, 176, 225; neighborhood
associations, 43, 129, 190–194, 198,
199, 200, 204, 222; noninstitutional,
33–35; occupations, 70; organization,
40; participation, 14, 15, 42, 81; political activity, 182–205, 206, 211;
and the poor, 68–69, 86; post-
Conciliar, 37–39; pre-Conciliar, 35–
37, 38, 39, 46; racism, 151–160,
225; salvation, 45, 225; in São Jorge,
33–47; sin, 43, 45, 242n.15; social
movements, 2, 200, 211; view of
sickness, 74–75; view of suffering,
46–47, 54, 67; women, 15, 84, 87,
91–98, 101, 102–103, 224; and the
world, 45, 72, 101, 102, 124, 147,
151, 156; youth, 119, 123–130, 134,
137. See also Bible circles; CEBs;
Comunidades
Catholic League, 35, 197
CEBs, 2, 3, 5, 12–16, 221–230,
234n.12; membership, 3–4, 7, 15,
85; political activity, 5–7, 222; racism, 15; social movements, 5, 6, 222;
types, 13; women, 7–8. See also Catholic Church; Comunidades
Centros, 51, 53, 98–101, 104–107, 134;
negros, 147, 161, 163, 165, 166, 167,
168, 171. See also Mediums; Umbanda
Chefes, 47, 51, 99
Christian Base Communities. See CEBs
Class distinctions, 6, 70–71, 73, 198,
213, 229. See also Economic
standing
CNBB. See Conferência Nacional dos
Bispos do Brasil
Coisas feitas, 55–56, 58, 59
Comendo. See Está comendo
Comunidade eclesial de base.
See CEBs; Comunidades

Comunidades, 12–16, 40–47, 66, 68–74,
223, 228; domestic conflict, 116;
dress, 71–72; economic standing of
members, 72–73, 85; leadership, 70–
71, 86, 94, 155, 157; liberation theology, 185–186; literacy, 76, 77–78,
224; membership, 42, 69, 70, 82, 85,
86; mulatos, 155, 156; negros, 146,
152, 155–156, 157, 176; participation, 42, 47, 81–83, 185–186, 224;
political activity, 182–205; racism,
155–156; small groups, 71–74, 224;
social movements, 13, 183, 186–
194, 222–223, 225; women, 82, 83,
84, 87, 94, 126; worker's schedules,
82–83, 84–85, 224; youth, 119,
123–130, 136, 224. See also Catholic
Church; CEBs
Conferência Nacional dos Bispos do Brasil, 39
Consciência, 40–44, 46–47, 95, 196,
245n.6
Conversion, 6, 45, 66, 75; to Assembly
of God, 83, 86, 102, 110; from
Catholic Church, 139–142; crentes,
132, 139–142; literacy, 79; men,
114–115, 135, 138; negros, 173; to
pentecostalism, 7, 103, 107–108,
206; women, 112, 113, 133
Cosme, Father, 39–46, 77, 127, 189,
204, 205, 226, 229; Bible circles,
92; domestic conflict, 97; lay associations, 70–71; liberation theology, 222; negros, 155; view of sickness, 74; women, 94; youth, 129,
248n.7
Crentes, 52–53, 58, 59–66, 126, 175,
176, 223; baptism, 60, 62, 64; conversion, 132, 139–142; courtship,
132, 137; economic standing, 70,
73–74, 213–214; Holy Spirit, 64–65,
66, 78, 84, 85, 112, 131, 138; labor
movement, 212–216; leadership, 70;
literacy, 78–79; marriage, 132, 137–
139; membership, 60, 62, 83–84, 85;
men, 84, 109, 111; negros, 172, 173,
175, 176, 177; occupations, 70; participation, 83–84; political activity,
206–220; prayer, 64; prayer healers,
51; premarital sex, 131, 133; racism,
174; salvation, 59, 207; social move-

ments, 226; view of suffering, 59, 67; visions, 63–64; women, 84, 88, 108–115, 138; worker's schedules, 83–85; youth, 119, 131–145. *See also* Assembly of God; Pentecostals
Cults of affliction, 67, 99, 101, 115, 224
Cults of continuity, 151, 224
Cults of transformation, 115, 177, 224
Curandeiros, 34
Cursilho de cristandade, 38, 155
Cursinhos, 12, 76–77

Daughters of Maria, 35
Demonic possession, 59. *See also* Spirit possession
Despachos, 98, 100, 101
Deus é Amor. *See* God is Love Church
Devil: Assembly of God, 58, 102, 131, 132, 133, 134, 137, 175, 212; Catholic Church, 38, 137, 251n.12; *macumba*, 159; music, 143; pentecostals, 67, 114, 218–219; *umbanda*, 67. *See also* Evil; Evil eye
Domestic conflict, 9, 15, 87–116, 223; Apostolate of Prayer, 96; *comunidades*, 116; mediums, 102–107; pentecostals, 101–102, 107–108, 224; *umbanda*, 98–101, 102–107, 224
Duque de Caxais, 11, 39, 183, 208; head church, 56–57; Worker's Party, 199, 200–203, 217

Economic standing, 21–24, 26, 29, 68–71, 80, 85–86, 122, 213; Assembly of God, 70, 86; Catholic Church, 70; *comunidades*, 72–73, 85; *crentes*, 70, 73–74, 213–214; pentecostals, 85, 213
Ecumenism, 230
Está comendo, 26, 69, 70, 82, 86
Ethnographic models of religion, 7, 8, 10
Evil, 56, 58, 101, 102. *See also* Devil
Evil eye, 34, 37, 38, 55, 56, 58, 93, 98, 100. *See also* Devil
Evil spirits. *See* Spirits, evil
Exús, 48, 54, 55, 56, 100, 104–105, 243n.25; *negros*, 49, 160, 164; Zumbi, 169, 170

Filho-de-santo, 106, 169
FNM. *See* National Motor Factory

Gender roles, 107, 110. *See also* Women
God is Love Church, 13, 145
Goiás, 3, 4–5
Guias, 48, 49, 51–52, 54, 56, 100, 105, 167, 243n.25; women, 107

Holy Spirit, 52, 115, 180; baptism of, 64, 83; *crentes*, 64–65, 66, 78, 84, 85, 112, 131, 138; healing by, 75; possession by, 92, 174–175
House of Blessing Church, 13

Illiteracy. *See* Literacy
Incantation, 195–196
Indians, 147, 148, 160, 163
INPS. *See* Instituto Nacional de Previdência Social
Instituto Nacional de Previdência Social, 214, 216
Intereclesial Conference of CEBs, 229
Isabel, Princess, 168, 169, 250n.6
Itapira, 85

Kardec, Allen, 242n.17
Kardecism, 47, 212

Labor market, 11–12
Labor movement, 201, 202; *crentes*, 212–216; Mexico, 227. *See also* Worker's Party
Labor Pastoral, 202
Labor unions, 5, 43, 212, 215, 253n.7; leadership, 183; Mexico, 227. *See also* Strikes
Land Pastoral. *See* Pastoral of Land
Land reform movements, 5
Lay associations, 13, 35, 70–71, 75–76
Liberation theology, 1–2, 39, 67, 86, 202–203, 205, 222, 228, 229, 242n.10; Catholic Church and the world, 45, 66; *comunidades*, 185–186; small groups, 44, 92; social movements, 6, 183–194; women, 94
Libôrio, 217
Life stories, 10
Linz, Father, 204
Literacy, 75–80, 111, 195, 224, 244n.30

Macumba, 34, 59, 121, 218; Catholic Church, 159, 251n.12; *negros*, 163, 166, 167, 172, 176–177, 178; youth, 136
Mãe de santo, 47, 51, 53, 88, 105–107, 161, 168; *negros*, 163, 165, 166–167, 169, 171
Malandro, 49
Marian Congregation, 35, 71, 75–76, 80, 154
Marriage, 123–124, 132, 137–139; arranged, 248n.6; interracial, 150
Mauro, Dom. *See* Morelli, Dom Mauro
Medellín, 2
Medical anthropology models, 8, 9
Mediums, 14, 42, 47–56, 64, 88, 91, 98–101, 160, 163–164, 165; cause of evil, 58; domestic conflict, 102–107; female, 105–107; male, 107; *mulatos*, 162, 163–164, 168, 169, 178–179; *negros*, 147, 159, 161–171, 178–179; photograph of, 50; unconsciousness, 65; white, 168
Melhor de vida, 21–22, 69
Mesters, Carlos, 194
Methodists, 63
Mexico, 227
Minas Gerais, 11, 33, 35, 70, 88
Ministries of the Eucharist, 40, 77, 188
Miserável, 69, 70, 73, 86
Mistura de raça, 150
Morelli, Dom Mauro, 39, 68, 156, 183–184, 186
Moreno, 150
Mulatos, 150; Assembly of God, 178; Catholic Church, 156–157, 158, 225; *comunidades*, 155, 156; mediums, 162, 163–164, 168, 169, 178–179; race and spirituality, 178–179; racism, 151; *umbanda*, 161

National Conference of Brazilian Bishops, 156
National Motor Factory, 11, 12, 71, 91
Negros, 9, 15, 49, 146–181, 223; ancestry, 151; Brotherhood Campaign of 1988, 156–160; Catholic Church, 152–160, 172, 176, 225; *comunidades*, 146, 152, 155–156, 157, 176; *crentes*, 172, 173, 175, 176, 177; mediums, 147, 159, 161–171,

178–179; pentecostals, 172–181; prayer healers, 175–176; spiritual gifts, 160, 162, 173–174, 177, 178, 179; spirituality, 165, 171, 172, 175–176, 177, 180; *umbanda*, 146–147, 159, 160–161, 162, 165, 167, 168, 170, 171, 176, 177
Neighborhood associations, 5, 227; Catholic Church, 43, 129, 190–194, 198, 199, 200, 204, 222; leadership, 183, 208; pentecostals, 206–212, 217

Obatalá, 242n.17
Obra, 64
Ogas, 47, 53
Ogun, 48, 52, 242n.17
Orixás, 48, 52, 99, 100, 169
Orlando, Father, 197, 198–199, 211
Our Lady of Aparecida, 35, 37, 156, 183
Oxossí, 48
Oxum, 242n.17

Pais-de-santo, 105, 106
Palmares, 167–168, 170
Pastoral of Baptism, 12, 40, 81, 188
Pastoral of Land, 43, 200, 202, 203
Patriarchy, 108, 238n.45, 247n.15
Pentecostals, 3, 4, 5, 56–66, 67, 224; conversion, 7, 103, 107–108, 206; domestic conflict, 101–102, 107–108, 224; economic standing, 85, 213; labor movement, 212–216; literacy, 78–79, 111; material benefits, 206, 207, 212; membership, 7, 13–14, 15, 60, 62, 70, 85; *negros*, 172–181; neighborhood associations, 206–212, 217; political activity, 6–7, 206–220, 226; prayer healers, 75, 91, 101–102; racial democracy, 173–174; racism, 15, 225; social movements, 6, 206; spirit possession, 15; women, 7–8, 61–62, 65, 103, 107–115, 224; worker's schedules, 83–85, 224; youth, 142–145, 224. *See also* Assembly of God; *Crentes*
People's Church, 3, 4, 5, 7, 228, 229
Pernambuco, 3
Personal transformation, 66, 67, 160, 176, 181
Petrobrás, 11

Pilar, 183, 198–199, 210–211, 212
Political activity, 5–7, 13, 182–220; Assembly of God, 206–220, 229–230; Catholic Church, 182–205, 206, 211; *comunidades*, 182–205; *crentes*, 206–220; pentecostals, 6–7, 206–220, 226
Political parties, 5, 43, 222; *crentes*, 216–220
Pombagiras, 54, 104
Pontos, 51
Popular Church. *See* People's Church
Popular Pastoral. *See* People's Church
Prayer healers, 42, 57–59, 64–65; *crentes*, 51; *negros*, 175–176; pentecostals, 75, 91, 101–102; view of suffering, 58
Pretos velhos, 48–49, 54, 55, 100, 104–105, 157, 161, 168, 169, 243n.25; domestic conflict, 99; humility, 165; *macumba*, 156; racism, 150; *umbanda*, 160, 163, 164; Zumbi, 167, 170
Progressive discourse. *See* Religious discourse, progressive
Promessas, 37, 39
Prophecy, 65
Protestants, 13
PT. *See* Worker's Party

Racial democracy, 147–151, 161, 162, 181; pentecostals, 173–174
Racism, 147, 150, 160, 172, 177; Catholic Church, 151–160, 225; *comunidades*, 155–156; *crentes*, 174; *mulatos*, 151; pentecostals, 15, 225. *See also Negros*
Razoável, 24, 26, 29, 69, 70, 86
Recife, 85
Religious discourse, 9, 182, 183, 194; progressive, 187, 188, 189, 191, 195, 204, 222
Religious mobility, 7, 8
Religious practices, 9–10
Rezadeiros, 34, 98
Rio de Janeiro, 47
Rural Democratic Union, 234n.9

Saints, 39, 41, 52, 53; Catholic Church, 160, 243n.20
Salvation: Catholic Church, 45, 225; *crentes*, 59, 207

São Jorge, 10–12; Catholic Church, 33–47; photographs of, 18, 20, 21, 22, 36; public health, 19; religions, 12–16; schools, 19; television, 120; youth, 118, 120
São Judas, 190, 191
São Paulo, 3, 6, 85
Sarapuí, 209–210
Self-valorization, 40–43
Serventes, 70, 80
Shango, 48, 242n.17
Sickness, 74–75
Sin, 43, 45, 242n.15
Slaves, 48, 165, 168, 169, 170, 177; abolition of slavery, 156, 168, 169; *umbanda*, 163, 164, 168. See also *Negros*
Socialism, 220, 228
Social justice, 1, 2, 5, 225
Social movements, 226–228; Catholic Church, 2, 200, 211; CEBs, 5, 6, 222; *comunidades*, 13, 183, 186–194, 222–223, 225; *crentes*, 226; liberation theology, 6, 183–194; pentecostals, 6, 206; youth, 128–129, 130
Spirit possession, 9, 45, 66, 99, 159; mediums, 51, 53–54; pentecostals, 15; *umbanda*, 15, 66. *See also* Demonic possession
Spirits, 251n.12; evil, 58, 59, 121; possessing, 48; *umbanda*, 47–48, 49, 53–56, 65, 99, 101, 105, 134, 161, 163. *See also* Mediums; Zumbi
Spiritual gifts, 143, 178; *negros*, 160, 162, 173–174, 177, 178, 179
Spirituality, 229; liberationist, 222; *negros*, 165, 171, 172, 175–176, 177, 180
Spiritual transformation, 147
Strikes, 212, 214–216, 241n.9. *See also* Labor unions
Suffering, 67, 92, 101, 224; Catholic Church, 46–47, 54, 67; *crentes*, 59, 67; *umbanda*, 54, 67; women, 107

Terreiros, 49, 51, 53, 105, 161, 163, 168, 169, 242n.16
Testifying, 108–115
Trabalhos, 244n.32

Tshidi Zionists, 10
Turner, Victor, 45–46

UDR. *See* Rural Democratic Union
Umbanda, 3, 4, 5, 9, 46, 47–56, 98–
101, 134, 210, 224, 251n.12; African influence, 163; domestic conflict, 98–101, 102–107, 224; *mulatos*, 161; *negros*, 146–147, 159,
160–161, 162, 165, 167, 168, 170,
171, 176, 177; participation, 14, 15;
racism, 15, 225; slaves, 163, 164,
168; spirit possession, 15, 66;
view of suffering, 54, 67; women,
87, 98–101, 105–107, 224; youth,
136, 138
Unemployment, 94, 213
Universal Church of the Reign of God,
143, 144

Vatican Council, 38
Velha. See *Pretos velhos*
Veloso, Caetano, 144
Via crucis, 36, 37, 38, 94, 96
Vitória, 3, 5

Wesleyans, 63
Whitening, 160, 161, 162, 163, 168
Women, 7, 9, 87–116, 223; activists,
197–200; Apostolate of Prayer, 35–
37; Assembly of God, 84, 87, 108,
110, 130; Catholic Church, 15, 84,
87, 91–98, 101, 102–103, 224;

comunidades, 82, 83, 84, 87, 94,
126; *crentes*, 84, 88, 108–115, 138;
in labor market, 12, 89, 90; literacy,
79; marriage, 89; mediums, 105–107;
Mexico, 227; pentecostals, 7–8, 61–
62, 65, 103, 107–115, 224; subordination, 88–90, 94, 110, 111, 112;
suffering, 107; *umbanda*, 87, 98–
101, 105–107, 224
Worker's Party, 189, 197, 199–203,
222, 234n.9; Catholic Church, 218;
leadership, 183; pentecostals, 217
Worker's Pastoral, 201

Yemenjá, 243n.17
Yoruba gods, 242n.17
Youth, 9, 15, 117–145, 223; alcoholism,
120, 126, 137; Assembly of God,
119, 130–137, 142–145; Catholic
Church, 119, 123–130, 134, 137;
church participation, 118–119; *comunidades*, 119, 123–130, 136, 224;
courtship, 121–122, 131, 132, 137;
crentes, 119, 131–145; drugs, 121,
137; employment, 122; girls, 121;
mass media, 119–120; music, 143–
144; pentecostals, 142–145, 224; sexuality, 120, 135–136; social movements, 128–129, 130; *umbanda*,
136, 138

Zionists. *See* Tshidi Zionists
Zumbi, 167–170

Designer:	U.C. Press Staff
Compositor:	Braun-Brumfield, Inc.
Text:	10/13 Galliard
Display:	Galliard